MW01010534

NORTH AFRICA

NORTH AFRICA

A History from Antiquity to the Present

Phillip C. Naylor

UNIVERSITY OF TEXAS PRESS ⤳ AUSTIN

Copyright © 2009 by the University of Texas Press
All rights reserved
Printed in the United States of America
First edition, 2009

Requests for permission to reproduce material from this
work should be sent to:

    Permissions
    University of Texas Press
    P.O. Box 7819
    Austin, TX 78713-7819
    www.utexas.edu/utpress/about/bpermission.html

♾ The paper used in this book meets the minimum
requirements of ANSI/NISO Z39.48-1992 (R1997)
(Permanence of Paper).

Library of Congress Cataloging-in-Publication Data
Naylor, Phillip Chiviges.
    North Africa : a history from antiquity to the present /
Phillip C. Naylor. — 1st ed.
    p. cm.
Includes bibliographical references and index.
ISBN 13: 978-0-292-72291-0; ISBN 10: 0-292-72291-5
    1. Africa, North—History. I. Title.
DT167.N39 2009
961—dc22
                                   2008053138

To my family
and
for my students

CONTENTS

LIST OF MAPS

A NOTE TO THE READER

Given the targeted audience for this book, I tried to keep my Arabic transliterations consistent and practical. Thus it is Malik Bennabi rather than Mālik bn Nabī. I used ' for the Arabic 'ayn when that letter appears in the middle of a word or name, such as Ya'qub, but not when it introduces or ends a word or name. Thus, it is Uqba bn Nafi rather than 'Uqba bn Nafi'. Hamzas appear as ' as in Qur'an, *ra'y, qa'id,* Salah Ra'is, and *al-mu'minin.* Introductory and final hamzas are omitted. I have also occasionally kept French transliterations since they frequently appear in English narratives—for example, Abd al-Hamid Ben Badis rather than Abd al-Hamid bn (or ibn) Badis. Although technically *prince* or *commander* should translate or transliterate as *'amir* ("prince, commander"), I use the more common word *emir.* Some Arabic words are not italicized since they appear in English dictionaries or are commonly seen in the press, such as madrasa, sharif, hajj, and ulama. The glossary should help with the terms.

North Africa is understudied, and this must change. In his presidential address on 18 November 2007 at the Middle East Studies Association meeting in Montréal, Canada, Professor Zachary Lockman emphasized the need to devote greater attention to North Africa. Having researched in Algeria and having directed the Western civilization program at Marquette University, I became acutely aware of North Africa's historical significance. Nevertheless, its formative influence on the development of European, Mediterranean, and African civilizations is usually understated or neglected in textbooks. North Africa's contributory significance needs to be asserted or at the least considered.

I wrote this book since no introductory survey of North Africa meets my pedagogical needs. For example, Jamil M. Abun-Nasr's *A History of the Maghrib* (1971) and *A History of the Maghrib in the Islamic Period* (1987) are outstanding, but challenging books for most beginning students. In addition, in spite of Egypt's cultural and historical difference, if not autonomy, I chose to include it along with the Maghrib for reasons mentioned in the Introduction. My book is an interpretive narrative and meant to be a concise rather than a comprehensive historical survey of North Africa for students and general readers—a *sahib* or companion rather than a formal textbook. I hope it will also be useful to scholars, especially those in the field whose indispensable collective work and engagement I have benefited from and admired for decades.

Although I wrote most of this book primarily at home and at Marquette, I wish to acknowledge my cousin, Professor Constance Cryer Ecklund, who provided hospitality and space at her home in Connecticut resulting in several drafted chapters. I reviewed and revised pages at Professor Alex D. Naylor's home in Illinois between fraternal discussions on foreign policy (the need to understand history and culture) and the White Sox (the status of the pitching staff). Colleagues accorded exceptional time and support at Marquette's

Raynor Memorial Libraries and at the American Geographical Society Library at the University of Wisconsin–Milwaukee. I especially appreciate the interest of Marquette professors Richard Taylor, Irfan Omar, David E. Gardinier, F. Paul Prucha, S.J., Roland J. Teske, S.J., Terrence Crowe, and Julian Hills. Abd al-Hamid Alwan, the brother of my *ustadh* (professor) Muhammad Bakr Alwan, kindly checked Arabic translations. Others who provided direct or indirect assistance included Enaya Othman, Adam Reed, Reverend Jon Boukis, Dan Johnson, G. Jon Pray, Nick Schroeder, Greg Shutters, Laura J. Lindemann, and professors Rudolph A. Helling, William A. Hoisington, John Entelis, James Miller, and Robert and Mildred Mortimer. In April 2008, Professor Julia Clancy-Smith delivered the annual Reverend Henry W. Casper, S.J., Lecture at Marquette University. She graciously permitted me to refer to her presentation derived from a chapter from her forthcoming *Mediterranean Passages: Migrants and Mobilities in Nineteenth-Century North Africa* (see Bibliography). I especially want to thank the reviewers of the manuscript.

I wish to acknowledge Robert Sharwood of City Light Books for the reproduction of Ibn Hazm's "My Beloved Comes" in *Poems of Arab Andalusia,* translated by Cola Franzen from the Spanish of Emilio García Gómez, 1989.

Professor Andrew Tallon, editor of Marquette University Press and a professor in the Department of Philosophy, expedited the rapid production of a quickly drafted "brief" edition (2005) custom-published for use only in my North Africa course. The present volume amplifies and expands that book's narrative and corrects its errors. I enjoyed conversations on Andy's front porch. Jim Burr and Wendy Moore of the University of Texas Press enthusiastically embraced the project. In-house copyeditor Lynne Chapman was especially understanding regarding deadlines and provided astonishingly quick responses to my queries. I also appreciate Salena Krug's close reading of the manuscript as well as her questions and comments. As the dedication affirms, my Marquette University students motivated and inspired me, especially those from the History of North Africa course. My wife and children furnish constant encouragement.

While writing this book, my principal *sahib,* especially during late nights and early mornings, was Montague François Naylor, my family's Standard Poodle. Monty's company is especially appreciated. *Huwa sadiqan azizan wa mukhlisan!*

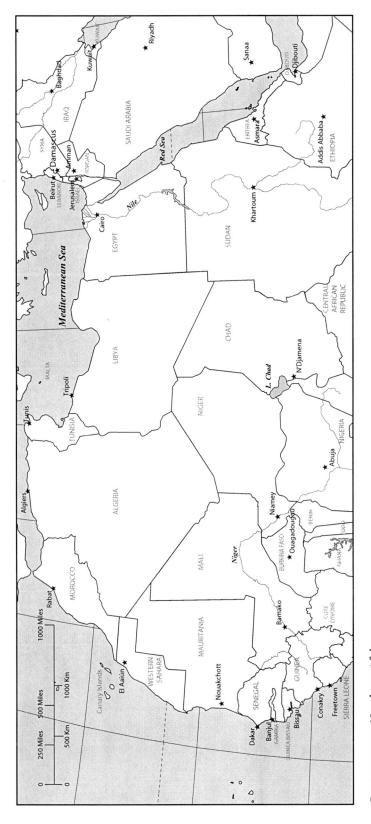

Contemporary Northern Africa

NORTH AFRICA

Introduction

I slip a compact disc into my laptop; it is Cheb Mami's *Meli Meli* (1999). Cheb Mami is an Algerian singer who is world renowned as the "Prince of Rai." Rai is a distinctly North African musical genre, which arose in western Algeria.[1] It blends regional rhythms with those of European pop and American blues and rap. Rai instrumentation is varied. It can include the traditional *derbouka* (drum), *bendir* (frame drum), *karkaba* (large finger cymbals), and *qanun* (three-octave string instrument) as well as the modern electric guitar and bass, synthesizer, violin, and accordion. *Meli Meli* features Mami's Arabic compositions and singing, but it also includes K-mel, an Algerian-French techno-rap star. He adds French lyrics. In addition, Idir, a Berber-speaking Algerian, shares a track with Mami. Rai exemplifies North Africa's "transcultural" character and history.

Studying North Africa offers students and scholars an exceptional opportunity to appreciate the formative and transformative role of historical transcultural relations.[2] *Transcultural history studies and emphasizes the significance of encounters and interactions within and among societies and civilizations.* The consequential conjunctures of cultures, meaning here peoples' values, institutions, religions, materials, technologies, histories, and identities, and the ways cultures are transmitted and transacted (accepted/rejected), are crucially significant when considering transcultural history. There is also an epistemological and existential dimension to this history since transcultural experiences and environments evoke the imagination, identification, and interpretation of others—the construction and representation of others as historical subjects. Transcultural history widens and deepens historical study and immediately makes us conscious of the role of the wider world upon a specific civilization or geographical area.

North Africa is one of those rare regions of the world that serves as an axis of cultures and civilizations. To understand its significance, consider the

Arabic term *jazirat al-maghrib.* It means the island of the west, implying the lands west of Egypt.[3] North Africa is like an island located between two seas, the Mediterranean and the Sahara. Waves of human encounters and interactions have swept ashore and shaped the "island's" rich cultural and historical morphology. Accordingly, extraordinary peoples and histories have fashioned an impressive transcultural legacy.

Where Is Historical North Africa?

Periodization usually daunts historians when organizing their narratives. It is a bit easier in this introductory survey where eras can be distinguished and delineated, e.g., ancient, Roman, Islamic, Ottoman, colonial, post-colonial, and contemporary. Locating North Africa is the perplexing problem since there is no scholarly consensus. Most agree that North Africa generally includes the Sahara and the land north of it bordering the Mediterranean. But should Egypt be included? Its history is vast, illustrious, and, to many scholars, autonomous or more closely linked to West Asia (or the "Middle East"). Egypt's position in northeast Africa, however, has historically hinged Africa to Asia serving as a transcultural conduit, although it has received from the Maghrib as well as relayed to it. Thus, its importance necessitates its inclusion, especially given this book's purpose and thematic perspective.

Nonetheless, there are other demarcating quandaries when circumscribing North Africa. How far south into the Sahara does North Africa extend? This book principally presents North Africa as stretching from Western Sahara along the Atlantic Ocean, north to Morocco and then east to Algeria, Tunisia, Libya, and Egypt; it also tangentially includes the Sahara and the Sahel.[4] Since scholars often identify North Africa with the Maghrib,[5] given my historical consideration and wider geographic context, "Northern Africa" would seem to be a more accurate and appropriate term. I concluded, however, that substituting "Northern" for "North" would confuse my audience (correspondingly Western Africa for West Africa and Eastern Africa for East Africa). To reiterate, readers should simply understand that in this book North Africa also embraces Egypt and the Sahara. This is a history of North (Northern) Africa, not only of the Maghrib, in transcultural context.

North Africa's Land and Natural Life

North Africa's physical topography, the shape and contour of its land, has profoundly affected its history. Environmental and geological diversity have resulted in disparate development and interaction. Fertile coastal plains stretch along the Mediterranean littoral, especially in Morocco, Algeria, Tunisia, and to a lesser degree Libya. For centuries, North Africa's fecund fields served as a Mediterranean granary sustaining states and empires. Moving into the interior, parallel mountain chains descend from west to east where Berbers traditionally found refuge and redoubts in their history of resistance to invaders. The most notable range is the Atlas of Morocco and Algeria. The Sahara features the Ahaggar (Hoggar) Mountains in Algeria and the Ennedi and Tibesti mountains in Chad. Plateaus are also common from Morocco to Libya (notably, the Jabal Akhdar in the latter). North Africa is predominantly desert. Overexploitation and overgrazing compounded by irregular rainfall have expedited erosion and desertification, especially along "coastal" (and Sahelian) lands bordering the Saharan sea of sand and stone. Supplying populations with their alimentary needs is a major consideration faced by contemporary governments. The Nile is the only navigable river. In addition, there are few natural harbors. Across the region, the semi-tropical Mediterranean climate becomes increasingly arid from north to south. Hydrocarbons (oil and natural gas and their byproducts), phosphates, and iron ore elevate the strategic significance of the region. Nevertheless, these are non-renewable resources, posing important challenges to contemporary governments regarding sustainable economic growth.

The Mediterranean and the Sahara have insulated and isolated peoples but have also channeled transcultural currents. In particular, North Africa's trans-Mediterranean and trans-Saharan commerce has expedited the transmission and transaction of ideas as well as cargoes. The Mediterranean's sea lanes have linked North Africa to West Asian and European civilizations (and colonizations). The Sahara's trade routes and the Nile River have connected North Africa to other continental civilizations and cultures in the south. In addition, Egypt's Red Sea historically tied North Africa to the great Indian Ocean trade network and South Asian markets.

Wildlife in North Africa includes the jackal, Barbary ape, gazelle, jerboa, boar, fennec fox, serval, caracal, monk seals, wild dog, ibex, and a variety of lizards and snakes. The Nile River features its fearsome crocodiles and hippo-potami as well as a variety of fish. Although severely affected by deforestation and population growth, mountainous regions in the north contain pine, juni-per, cedar, olive, and cork oak. In southern regions acacia, dwarf palm, jujube trees, and xerophytic vegetation grow in arid zones. Date palm groves (phreato-phytes) are renowned in Saharan oases, especially those of Algeria's Mizab.

North Africa's Peoples

The anthropology of North Africa features the Berbers, regarded as the in-digenous population.[6] They settled primarily west of the Nile Delta and con-tinue to have significant populations in Tunisia, Algeria, Morocco, and the Sahara. Calling themselves *Imazighen,* meaning "freeborn,"[7] the Berbers get their name from the term *barbaroi,* appropriated from the Greeks by the Ro-mans, to differentiate peoples who spoke neither Greek nor Latin. The Arabs adopted this name and derived from it an adjective *barbariyya,* which means primitive and foreign. The population of ancient Egypt blended peoples from Palestine and Syria from the east and north, Nubians (Kushites) from the South, and Libyans from the west.[8] Ancient Greek writers used "Libyan" to refer to the indigenous population of North Africa west of Egypt.[9] By the third century BCE, the Greeks differentiated "Libyans," now identified with Berbers living within the Carthaginian state or its sphere of influence, from "Numidians" or "nomads," a name associated with pastoralism or herding.[10] The Berbers prided themselves on their independence and when confronted by crisis or conflict, often organized confederations led by kings or *aguellids.* Furthermore, Berbers evinced an ability to adapt to and to absorb other cul-tures. Their transcultural receptivity has distinguished their history.

Although Berber beginnings remain a mystery, scholars contend that they originated from migrating populations from northeast and sub-Saharan Af-rica and Western Europe—an ethnic and transcultural fusion. Berbers divid-ed over kinship, not language. Linguistically, dialects (possibly derived from a Hamitic past) are difficult to delineate because of a lack of a universal alpha-bet and a common literature, although there is a strong oral tradition.[11] Ber-bers jealously guard and protect their culture and especially their language, Tamazight.

Besides the Berbers, the other principal ethnic group is the Arabs. They began arriving in the seventh century CE. Over centuries, waves of tribes, notably the Banu Hilal and Banu Sulaym of the eleventh century, and later the Banu Ma'qil, led to the Arabization of North African culture. Arabs brought along with them their religion, Islam, which appealed to Berbers and led to their conversion. Islam and the Arabic language subsequently created a North African cultural unity.

Throughout North Africa over the centuries, transcultural interaction and integration occurred with conquests—namely by the Hyksos (Asiatics/Canaanites), Phoenicians, Kushites, Carthaginians, Greeks, Macedonians, Romans, Vandals, Byzantines, Arabs, Ottomans (Turks), Spanish, French, British, and Italians. In addition, important and sizeable Jewish communities influenced North Africa's development in manifold ways. Furthermore, contact and conquest melded North Africans with Sub-Saharan Africans. Consequently, this remarkable social diversity enriches North Africa's history.

Prehistoric North Africa

Archaeological excavations suggest that North Africa served as a staging point for the hominid colonization of West Asia and Europe. For example, hominid (human-like) remains (*Homo erectus*) dating back to 200,000 BCE have been found near Saïda, Algeria. Paleolithic North Africa featured the Aterian culture that flourished about 30,000 BCE. The name *Aterian* is derived from an archaeological site, Bi'r al-'Atir, south of Annaba, Algeria. The Aterians, a Neanderthaloid group, attained remarkable flake-tool abilities. The Ibero-Maurusians, Mesolithic (15,000 to 10,000 BCE) *Homo sapiens sapiens,* succeeded the Aterians and also produced sophisticated tools. Ibero-Maurusian culture, ranging from Iberia to Libya, is also known as Oranian, since an impressive archaeological site is near Oran, Algeria.

The Capsians achieved the revolutionary transition from Mesolithic to Neolithic culture in about 6000 BCE. Illustrating the importance of transcultural interaction in North Africa's history, the Neolithic revolution featured the introduction of agricultural domestication and animal husbandry, techniques transacted from West Asia (see Diamond 1999, 101–102). Capsian sites are widespread across North Africa, especially in Tunisia. In general, the pre-desiccated Sahara experienced Neolithic changes before the northern littoral, an illustration of the importance of climate and human development (see below).[12] Egypt's "Early Neolithic" period, featuring cattle herding, appeared at Nabta Plaza and Bir Kiseiba in its Western Desert in c. 8800–6800 BCE, attesting to the availability of water. Extant archaeological evidence indicates that the Neolithic period began in Lower Egypt, i.e., the northern Nile Valley, in c. 5300 BCE, which featured agriculture.[13]

There are remarkable stone sculptures in the Tibesti (Chad) and Ahaggar (Algeria) Saharan mountain ranges. In addition, the extraordinary rock illustrations at Tassili N'Ajjer in the Algerian Sahara, which date from approximately 6000 BCE to 100 CE, graphically describe a different Sahara. Before its desiccation, the Sahara was "wet" and featured elephants, giraffes, rhinoceros, horses, and other animals.[14] The Tassili paintings also depict hunters and herders and collectively are one of the greatest displays of prehistoric art in the world. Archaeologists, anthropologists, and historians esteem these paintings and those in Libya's Fezzan as extraordinary aesthetic historical documents, especially illustrating the revolutionary change from Paleolithic to Neolithic culture and society.[15] In addition, Jan Vansina observed that "ancient Egyptian graphic art owes something to the great Saharan tradition that both preceded it and ran parallel to it for most of its history" (Vansina 1984, 6). The Egyptian attraction and assimilation of Saharan artistic expressions affirm the primordial significance of transcultural contact and communication with the development of civilization.

Civilization in North Africa: A Historical Overview

Egypt is immediately recognized as one of the greatest civilizations in Western and world history.[16] It hinged North Africa to West Asia, profoundly influencing Sudan (ancient Kush or Nubia) and, to a lesser degree, Somalia (Punt). During the Hellenistic era, Egypt regularly traded with South Asia and the western Mediterranean. Phoenicia's enterprising maritime city-states, located in today's Lebanon, collectively constituted a major West Asian influence upon North Africa. The Phoenicians established trading posts along the littoral of North Africa and Iberia. Libya featured some of the greatest Greek (and later Roman) colonies. Furthermore, the Saharan Garamantes of ancient Fezzan applied remarkable hydrology and agronomy. Carthage, a former Phoenician colony in Tunisia, emerged as a great power in the western Mediterranean. It rivaled the *poleis* or city-states of Greater Greece (Sicily and southern Italy) and then fought the epic Punic Wars with Rome. After Carthage's defeat, Rome dominated, eventually taking over independent Berber kingdoms

(Numidia and Mauretania) and Hellenistic Egypt. Establishing hundreds of cities, Roman ruins in North Africa are among the most astonishing antiquities extant. North Africa also played a significant role regarding the expansion and evolution of Christianity. For example, Augustine, one of the great "Church Fathers (Doctors)," was born in eastern Algeria.

German invasions are inevitably cited in textbooks as an important cause in the fall of the Western Roman Empire. Germans also arrived in North Africa, namely the notorious Vandals, who established a kingdom stretching from Tripolitania (western Libya) to Morocco that lasted for about a century. Launching a task force from North Africa, the Vandals plundered Rome—hence the association of their name with pillage and destruction. The Eastern Roman or Byzantine Empire mounted campaigns in 533 and 534, ending the Vandal kingdom. The restoration of an imperial "Roman" presence in North Africa east of Egypt (under continual Byzantine administration) varied along the coastline and hinterland. The Byzantines typically exercised power from strongholds along the littoral and from cities, principally Carthage.

The invasion of the Arabs, beginning in the seventh century, confronted and eventually overwhelmed the redoubtable resistance of the Berbers. The Arabs, infused with their new faith, Islam, indelibly influenced the region. North Africa featured remarkable Muslim states headed by dynasties that promoted commerce and culture, including the Rustamids, the Idrisids, the Aghlabids, the Tulunids, the Fatimids, the Zirids, the Hammadids, the Ayyubids, and the Mamluks. The Berber Almoravids of the eleventh and the Almohads of the twelfth centuries were two of the most powerful states in the history of Western civilization's Middle Ages. The great philosopher Ibn Rushd (Averroës), usually mentioned in Western civilization textbooks, served the Almohad court. The Hafsids, Zayyanids, and Marinids succeeded the Almohads in the Maghrib.

Egypt and the Maghrib, except for Morocco, fell under the Ottoman Empire during the course of the sixteenth century. Morocco's Sa'di and Alawi dynasties protected Moroccan independence from the predations of the Ottomans, Portuguese, and Spanish. Although nominally under the suzerainty of the sultan in Constantinople, the Ottoman Regency of Algiers exercised virtual independence as one of the most powerful states in the western Mediterranean. The Ottoman regencies in Tunis and Tripoli also asserted their autonomy.

After the *Reconquista*,[17] Spain systematically seized outposts on the North African littoral and still controls the presidios of Ceuta and Melilla along the Moroccan coast and offshore islets. In addition, the Habsburgs waged war against the Ottomans, which involved significant North African campaigning. Beginning in 1798 with Napoleon's expedition to Egypt, Europe took a greater invasive and imperial interest in North Africa. France captured Algiers in 1830 and in 1848 organized northern Algeria into three departments. Tunisia and central and southern Morocco became French protectorates in 1881 and 1912, respectively. Spain acquired Ifni (along the Moroccan Atlantic coast) in 1860, Western (Spanish) Sahara in 1884, and northern Morocco and the Tarfaya zone in the south in 1912. Italy seized Libya (at that time called "Tripolitania") in 1911–1912. Great Britain purchased control of the Suez Canal in 1875 and occupied Egypt in 1882. European colonialism had a manifold effect upon North African peoples. Nevertheless, by the time Algeria acquired its independence in 1962, North Africa had decolonized, except for Spain's territories—the Spanish Sahara, Ifni, the presidios, and islets. North Africa's post-colonial history is also significant as its countries have confronted the controversial consequences of colonialism, especially regarding political, economic, and social development. In contemporary North Africa, cultural questions concerning the roles of Westernization, modernization, globalization, and Islamism are particularly provocative.

Approaching North African History: Ibn Khaldun, Malik Bennabi, and Jacques Berque

Having located North Africa geographically, surveyed its prehistory, and recognized its historical significance, how has its complex recorded history been recounted, explained, and appreciated? There are important historical surveys of North Africa that cover the period from the seventh-century Arab conquest to the modern period. Charles-André Julien, *Histoire de l'Afrique du Nord,* was originally published in 1931. Julien's book is not only an important academic contribution, but also a heroic work. It dispelled the French colonial myth regarding the vacuity of pre-colonial North African (Maghribi) history. Roger Le Tourneau revised Julien's work in 1952 and it was translated into English in 1970. Jamil M. Abun-Nasr's *A History of the Maghrib* (1971) and *A History of the Maghrib in the Islamic Period* (1987) are more detailed than

Julien's book. (Three chapters are devoted to the pre-Islamic period in *A History of the Maghrib* [1971]). Julien and Abun-Nasr provide excellent coverage from the Arab conquest of the seventh century. Abdallah Laroui's *The History of the Maghrib: An Interpretive Essay* (1970; translated into English 1977) critically assesses the historiography of North Africa from prehistory to his contemporary era.

For the ancient period, Stéphane Gsell's *Histoire ancienne de l'Afrique du Nord* remains a monumental survey. Herodotus, Polybius, Julius Caesar, and Livy include valuable but passing information on North Africa. Sallust is an exception given his *The Jugurthine War*. Nevertheless, his work is short and limited. The encyclopedist Pliny the Elder and the geographer Strabo also provide fragmented information within their "global" perspectives. Augustine's *Confessions* illustrates the diverse intellectual and spiritual currents circulating between North Africa and Europe. Procopius, while serving as secretary to the military commander Belisarius, recounts a history of the Byzantine campaign against the Vandals.

Writing during the ninth century, Ibn abd al-Hakam examines the history of Egypt and the Muslim conquest of the Maghrib and al-Andalus (Muslim Iberia). In the eleventh century, Abu Ubayd al-Bakri furnishes a fascinating geographical and sociological itinerary. Ibn Idhari al-Marrakushi (fl. late thirteenth–early fourteenth centuries) chronicles the history of North Africa from the Arab conquest to the Almohads (Muwahhidun). Leo Africanus's (Hasan bn Muhammad al-Wazzani) sixteenth-century reflections recall those of al-Bakri. Abd al-Rahman al-Jabarti renders an invaluable account of Napoleon's invasion of Egypt and its political and cultural confrontations and consequences. Algeria's Mahfoud Kaddache, Ahmad Tawfiq al-Madani, and Mubarak bn Muhammad al-Mili exemplify impressive "national" historiography. Collectively, these contributions and others listed in the bibliography are all valuable. Nevertheless, there are three intellectuals who especially exemplify North African scholarly breadth and depth.

Ibn Khaldun (1332–1406)

Ibn Khaldun was born in Tunis, the capital of today's Tunisia. During his colorful and capricious career as a statesman and scholar he lived throughout the Maghrib and in al-Andalus. He eventually attained the position of *mufti* or principal judge of the Maliki school of jurisprudence in Egypt. In his *Muqad-*

dima (Introduction),[18] he distinguishes between "surface" and "inner meaning" histories: "Surface history is no more than information about political
events, dynasties, and occurrences of the remote past.... It ... brings to us an
understanding of human affairs. (It shows) how changing conditions affected
(human affairs), how certain dynasties came to occupy an ever wider space in
the world, and how they settled the earth until they heard the call and their
time was up." This is the history of names and dates. He continues: "The inner
meaning of history, on the other hand, involves speculation and an attempt
to get at the truth, subtle explanation of the causes and origins of existing
things, and deep knowledge of the how and why of events" (Ibn Khaldun 1967,
1:6). This latter history especially interested this erudite scholar.

In addition, Ibn Khaldun presented a pluralist interpretation of history:
"It should be known that history is a discipline that has a great number of
(different) approaches.... The (writing of history) requires numerous sources
and greatly varied knowledge" (Ibn Khaldun 1967, 1:15). He underscored his
methodological approach with a warning:

> If [the historian] trusts historical information in its plain transmitted form and
> has no clear knowledge of the principles resulting from custom, the funda-
> mental facts of politics, the nature of civilization, or the conditions governing
> human social organization, and if, furthermore, he does not evaluate remote or
> ancient material through comparison with near or contemporary material, he
> often cannot avoid stumbling and slipping and deviating from the highroad of
> truth. (Ibn Khaldun 1967, 1:15–16)

Ibn Khaldun recognized the significance of economics, sociology, psychology, religion, geography, climate, and what we call today political science toward the development and explanation of history. According to Philip Hitti:
"No Arab writer, indeed no European, had ever taken a view of history at once
so comprehensive and philosophic" (Hitti 1970, 568).

He attributed the repeated rise and fall of North African states and their exercise of power and influence to a historical agent, known as *asabiyya,* which
can be translated as a "group feeling."[19] When a dynasty's social and political
cohesion weakened, it inevitably declined. Ibn Khaldun's historiography and
methodology remain very valuable toward understanding North Africa's past
(and present). His interdisciplinary approach evinces an exceptional intellectual sophistication.

Malik Bennabi (1905–1973)

Malik Bennabi, our second influential figure, imparts keen insight into the history of North African and Muslim civilizations. Born in Constantine, Algeria, Bennabi also lived in France and Egypt. He insisted on the need for Muslims, especially Maghribis (peoples of the Islamic West) and Mashriqis (peoples of the East) to become historically conscious, which he viewed as an active and affirming praxis. A prolific writer in French and Arabic, he argued that the failure of Muslims to appreciate and engage the history of their Islamic culture made them "colonizable." He wrote that "one does not cease to be colonized until one ceases to be colonizable: it is an immutable law" (Bennabi 1949, 22).[20] To Bennabi, the "colonizability" of North Africa and the wider Muslim world or "Islamdom" (Marshall G. S. Hodgson's term) occurred after the disintegration of the Almohad empire in the thirteenth century and not solely as a consequence of European imperialism. General intellectual and moral lassitude within an exhausted Muslim civilization characterized this "Post-Almohadean" period. Jamil M. Abun-Nasr interpreted "'colonizability' as a sort of moral paralysis which leads a community to accept that its life becomes determined by the thought and values of others. Consequently it ceases to be able to contribute to world civilization" (Abun-Nasr 1987, 325). Bennabi's critique is incisive and meant to be instructive.

Influenced by Arnold Toynbee and Oswald Spengler as well as by Ibn Khaldun, Bennabi was fascinated by the development and decline of civilization. He perceived the history of Muslim civilization as proceeding through spiritual, rational, and instinctual "psycho-temporal" stages while catalyzed by the synergy of three agents: man, land (soil), and time. In that he regarded religion as foundational in a civilization (Bennabi 1949, 33), the spiritual stage acquired special influence and importance for him. Bennabi contended that the Muslim civilization's spiritual stage ended with the divisive battle of Siffin in 657, leading to the establishment of the Umayyad Caliphate.[21] The rational stage followed as the civilization's "soul" or "spirit" leveled, albeit at a sophisticated plane. After centuries, ending with the life and times of Ibn Khaldun, Muslim civilization stagnated and declined toward an "instinctual primitive stage," an ancestral, regressive condition marked by torpor and superstition.[22] Bennabi believed that the *Nahda* (Renaissance) or Islamic modernist movement of the late nineteenth and early twentieth centuries signaled a reviving and recovering Muslim civilization. Nevertheless, he also criticized the modernists for failing to "transform the Muslim soul" and realize Islam's "social function" (Bennabi 1954, 56). Bennabi viewed Islamism as a means to regain not only a spiritual reawakening but also an appreciation for the secular contributions of Muslim civilization.[23] He was not existentially torn between Muslim and Western European/American civilizations. Furthermore, he considered spirituality and faith compatible with rationality and secularism (see Naylor 2006a; Christelow 1992). Subscribing to Friedrich Nietzsche's idea of an "eternal return," Bennabi anticipated an eventual restoration of a dynamic Muslim civilization.

Jacques Berque (1910–1995)

Jacques Berque is our third North African scholar-exemplar. Like Ibn Khaldun's, Berque's life and research, especially in anthropology, sociology, and history, spanned North Africa from Morocco to Egypt. Born in Frenda in the Oranie (western Algeria), Berque was significantly influenced by his father, Augustin, a colonial official and perceptive observer of Arab and Berber social relations. The son acquired the father's appreciable acumen. Berque served in the French army in North Africa and befriended Moroccan soldiers, with whom he savored "the other side of things" (Berque 1989, 43). The Moroccans allowed him, for example, to accompany them into native neighborhoods.[24] Like his father, Berque eventually joined the colonial administration. His candid, critical, and courageous appraisal of French colonial policy ended, however, the possibility of a government career. Nevertheless, Berque's expertise and erudition distinguished his scholarship whether describing the ethnic customs of the peoples of the High Atlas or the consequences of colonialism and decolonization in Algeria and Egypt.[25] His wider interests included the history of Arabs and Islam. Berque's impressive scholarship led to his appointment as a professor at the prestigious Collège de France. Sharply critical of Orientalists' presumptions, Edward Said found Berque's work exceptional. He admired Berque and his colleague Maxime Rodinson for "their methodological self-consciousness. . . . What one finds in their work is always, first of all, a direct sensitivity to the material before them, and then a continual self-examination of their methodology and practice, a constant attempt to keep their work responsive to the material and not to a doctrinal preconception" (Said 1979, 326–327). Berque challenged atavisms, including his own.

Like Ibn Khaldun and Bennabi, Berque was an independent intellectual.[26] Nevertheless, he also benefited from interdisciplinary interaction with colleagues like Rodinson, Louis Massignon, Maurice Merleau-Ponty, Fernand Braudel,[27] Michel Foucault, Georges Marçais, Vincent Monteil, Robert Montagne, Jacques Lacan, and Claude Lévi-Strauss. Although the philosophical issue of binary "othering" was an intense interest, the description, location, and context of othering, or the condition of alterity, distinguished Berque's writing, such as the consequences of industrialism as well as colonialism in North Africa. To quote Albert Hourani: "Berque has taught us to distinguish the different rhythms of history: that which foreign rulers have tried to impose upon the Arab Muslim countries they have ruled, and that which those peoples have produced within themselves" (Hourani 1991b, 5). His sympathy and identification with North Africans (especially Algerians, Moroccans, and Egyptians) characterized his work. Berque cultivated an intimate as well as intellectual relationship with North Africa. Albert Hourani admiringly wrote: "Berque's writings indeed are full of sights and sounds, smells and tastes. He has absorbed the Arab world through all his senses" (Hourani 1991b, 132). An adept (colloquial and classical) Arabist, he published an acclaimed commentary of the Qur'an in 1991. Berque mirrored Ibn Khaldun's philosophy of history: "One cannot write history without exploring the deeper levels below history" (Berque 1972, 297). He shared with Ibn Khaldun and Bennabi a fascination with the evolution of civilization.

Ibn Khaldun, Malik Bennabi, and Jacques Berque appreciated the historical and didactic significance of North Africa. Ibn Khaldun's multidisciplinary approach mirrors postmodern methodologies. Bennabi's studies of the "Post-Almohadean" period and the role of a genuinely redemptive Islamism are especially important in the contemporary context. Berque's remarkable ability to pass between and among North African cultures, despite his French colonialist background, conveys an inspiring personal and professional engagement.

The space devoted here to Ibn Khaldun, Malik Bennabi, and Jacques Berque is not meant to suggest that they provide the conceptual framework for this book, although they will be referred to occasionally. The objective of this book, an introductory work, is much more modest: to present a primarily political historical survey of North Africa illustrating the importance of transcultural influences. These scholars' inquisitive and acquisitive intellects epitomize the transcultural character of North Africa. Nevertheless, they represent but three notable and inspiring examples of North Africa's intellectual contributions to global civilization.[28]

Conclusion

North Africa offers historic personalities, complex cultures, and sophisticated civilizations. Furthermore, the region's transcultural character and history connect it intimately with three continents, endowing North Africa with a global significance. Recently, I watched a television performance by Robert Plant, the renowned vocalist of the classic rock band Led Zeppelin.[29] Plant performed a song derived from North African rhythms.[30] His inspiring rendition disclosed how the pervasive, even if subtle, influence of North Africa affects our lives. Plant's interest also serves as an invitation to explore the history of a relatively neglected part of the world that deserves careful attention and considerable appreciation.

Ancient North Africa and Its Expansive Civilizations

Ancient North Africa significantly contributed to the development and expansion of Western civilization. As the Introduction reminded, North Africa is a geographic component of Western civilization along with West Asia and Europe. North Africa's importance immediately became apparent during the emergence of Western civilization. Egypt's civilization arose only several hundred years after that of Sumer in Mesopotamia with its sophisticated city-states.[1] Illustrating its transcultural significance, Egypt inspired and influenced the development of Kushite (Nubian) and Greek civilizations. As Egypt declined in the late twelfth century BCE, Phoenicia, a narrow strip of coastline in West Asia's northern Canaan, asserted its importance. Phoenicia's ambitious maritime city-states, such as Tyre, established trading colonies in the western Mediterranean, including along the North African littoral. One of the Phoenician outposts, Carthage, eventually exercised impressive power. Greece's ambitious city-states conflicted with each other as well as with their Phoenician competitors over maritime markets and lands in the western Mediterranean. By the end of the seventh century BCE, Greek colonies dotted Sicily, southern Italy, and France as well as Cyrenaica or eastern Libya. Greek civilization, later mediated by Macedonian culture in the fourth century BCE, produced one of the greatest kingdoms of North Africa and for that matter of Western and world civilization, Hellenistic (meaning Greek-like) or Ptolemaic Egypt.

There are two principal themes in this chapter. First, North Africa played a vital role in shaping Western civilization, thereby affirming its fundamental historical and geographical significance. Second, from its recorded beginning, transcultural influences imprinted North Africa. Indeed, without the infusion and the diffusion of cultures, these illustrious ancient civilizations would never have attained their brilliance.

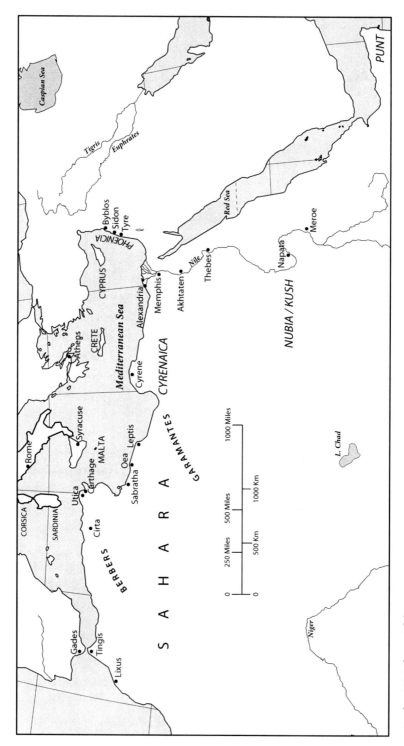

Ancient Northern Africa

Egypt: A Sedimentary Civilization

Dating from antiquity, Egypt has played a pivotal role in the history of North Africa. Hinging Africa to Asia, it has served as a conduit of cultures and commodities. Egypt's historical development is "sedimentary," a silted land layered by civilizations. Lady Duff Gordon observed in February 1863: "This country is a palimpsest, in which the Bible is written over Herodotus, and the Koran over that" (Gordon 1969, 65). Jacques Berque reflected: "[Egypt's] everlasting clay can be cast into any form imposed on her by others or by herself, without ever surrendering her essential character. . . . She incorporates in herself all these relationships; she is the product of them all" (Berque 1972, 39). Egyptians retained and sustained an identity in Egypt's enduring history, despite centuries of foreign rule. In this chapter, we will study two of Egypt's civilizations, that of the pyramids and pharaohs, and later, that of the Hellenistic kings and queens.

Egypt's Timelessness

As in other primordial alluvial global civilizations that generated in Mesopotamia (the Tigris-Euphrates watershed), South Asia (the Indus River valley), and China (along the Yellow River), nature endowed Egypt with a nurturing river, the Nile. As the Greek historian Herodotus (fl. fifth century BCE) recognized, the Nile nourished Egypt; its civilization was "the gift of the river" (Herodotus 1978, 131).

Other geographical reasons accounted for Egypt's emergence. Deserts in the east, south, and west, the Nile's cataracts in Kush (Nubia/Sudan), and the Mediterranean Sea in the north isolated and insulated Egyptian civilization. Its geographical position protected Egypt from enemies and permitted an exceptional development. Uninterrupted political stability lasted for centuries. Over a period of millennia, only the Hyksos of West Asia (specifically Canaan)[2] successfully invaded, or more precisely, infiltrated Egypt. The Nile's annual floods not only deposited nutrients replenishing the soil, but their predictable occurrence also reinforced the idea of Egypt's changelessness. In addition, the permanence of the country's sepulchral architecture, such as the Old Kingdom's pyramids, and, most significantly, the eschatology of its polytheistic religion, emphasizing an eternal afterlife similar to temporal existence, expressed timelessness (thematic in Naylor 2000b, 15–32).

Egyptian civilization was confident, complex, and continuous. Its sophistication necessitated the development of recordkeeping. This resulted in a pictographic writing system known as hieroglyphics, a Greek term meaning holy scripts or carvings. Buried by centuries of historical sedimentation, the ancient hieroglyphics could not be read until French troops unearthed the "Rosetta Stone" in 1798. This document etched on a basalt surface displayed a Ptolemaic proclamation engraved in Greek, demotic Egyptian, and hieroglyphics.[3] Working from the Greek, François Champollion and Thomas Young deciphered the hieroglyphic script in the 1820s. Although scholars recognized ancient Egypt's significance from Greek and Latin accounts, translated hieroglyphics exponentially enhanced Egyptology and our understanding of one of the West's and the world's earliest and greatest civilizations.

Egypt's History to the Hellenistic Period

The Early Dynastic Period (c. 3000–2686 BCE)[4] united the northern Nile's delta region and banks (Lower Egypt) with its southern banks (Upper Egypt). Scholars traditionally attribute this achievement to a semi-legendary leader named Narmer (sometimes called Menes, his Greek name). Narmer reputedly founded Memphis, strategically located before the Nile's delta fanned, and instituted a centralized monarchy that continued for millennia. The Early Dynastic Period also inaugurated a trade network with the eastern Mediterranean and with Nubia (Kush). Thus, Egypt's agency as a transcultural hinge dates at least from the beginning of its civilization (and before that period given the dissemination of Neolithic ideas, such as the domestication of plants and animals from West Asia).

The Old Kingdom (2686–2160 BCE) featured pyramid building. The pyramids served as tombs meant to preserve and protect the bodies of dead kings, who, according to popular belief, experienced an exclusive immortality. Djoser (Zoser), a king of the Third Dynasty (2686–2613 BCE), charged the remarkable Imhotep to design and build his funerary monument.[5] Imhotep dutifully constructed a step pyramid rising nearly 200 feet, which still impresses today. The Fourth Dynasty (c. 2613–2494 BCE) configured and constructed the familiar necropolis at Giza, distinguished by massive pyramids and mastabas. The Great Pyramid of King Khufu rises about 480 feet to its apex. The second tallest pyramid is that of King Khafre, who most scholars believe to be the sculpted "face" of the neighboring Sphinx. King Menkaura's (Mycerinus) (r.

2532–2503 BCE) is the smallest of the three pyramids. The rulers of the Old Kingdom, eventually deified as "sons of Re (Ra)," the sun god, inextricably linked spiritual with political royal authority.

Egyptian civilization suffered a disruptive era of uncertainty and instability, known as the First Intermediate Period, from 2160 to 2055 BCE. Historians attribute its causation to weak kings, rivalries between the priesthood and the nobility, poor harvests (caused by irregular flooding), and climatic changes. The Middle Kingdom (2055–1650 BCE) restored order and ushered in a new age of Egyptian greatness. Its kings governed from Thebes in central Egypt, where they exercised extensive and expansive authority. Senusret I (r. 1956–1911 BCE) constructed a hand-excavated canal linking the Nile Delta with the Red Sea (Russell 2001, xiii; Hitti 1970, 32). Under Senusret III (Sesostris) (r. 1870–1831 BCE), Egyptian power stretched from Syria to Kush (reaching the Second Cataract of the Nile). The Middle Kingdom marked the golden age of Egyptian literature, which emphasized social ethics and moral responsibility. An ethos, a sense of community, bonded Egyptians, underscored by a belief in an inclusive afterlife, a potential reward for all. The domineering Hyksos, "Asiatic" Canaanites, ended the Middle Kingdom and initiated the Second Intermediate Period (1650–1550 BCE).

The Hyksos infiltrated rather than invaded Egypt. Their rising numbers eventually led to their control of northern Egypt. Concurrently, the kingdom of Kush pressed from the south, squeezing the Egyptians in a geostrategic and political vise. The Hyksos embraced Egyptian culture and ritually ruled as kings, but they also kept close relations with their compatriots in West Asia. Transculturally, the Hyksos introduced new technology, especially regarding warfare (the composite bow and the horse and chariot), which native Egyptians adopted and deployed against them.

Thebes revolted against these intolerable political, social, and cultural conditions. The relentless and successful campaigns of Kamose and his brother Ahmose (r. 1550–1525 BCE), inaugurating the dynamic Eighteenth Dynasty (1550–1295 BCE), generated a surging patriotism that drove out the "Asiatics" (Hyksos) and the Kushites. Consequently, Egypt's martial momentum produced a powerful empire that extended Egypt's borders northward along the eastern Mediterranean littoral into northern Syria and southward to the Fourth Cataract in Kush. The New Kingdom kings featured extraordinary rulers who called themselves "pharaohs."

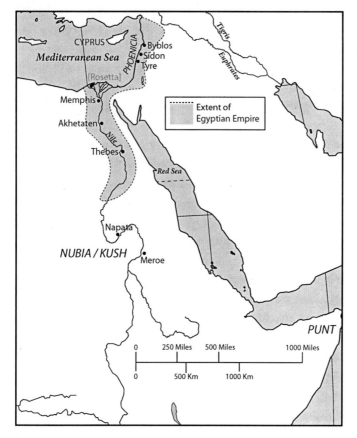

The Egyptian New Kingdom

While serving as regent, Queen Hatshepsut (r. 1473–1458 BCE) usurped the throne from her stepson Tuthmosis III and fashioned herself a pharaoh (complete with false beard). Hatshepsut deservedly earned the reputation of being the first great woman ruler of Western and world civilization. She commissioned many construction projects, especially her funerary temple in the Valley of the Kings. A portico of the temple displays a sculpted interpretation of one of the great achievements of her reign, a commercial expedition to Punt, a country located at the horn of Africa (today's Somalia). Although her enterprise was not the first Egyptian venture to Punt,[6] the sculptures graphically detail Egyptian ships, imported commodities, such as plants and animals, and Egyptian perceptions of the Puntites—an invaluable document depicting natural, economic, and transcultural history. Egyptian expeditions to Punt illustrated an Egyptian maritime orientation toward the south and the east, which eventually resulted in a flourishing Indian Ocean trade during the Hellenistic era.

Tuthmosis III (r. 1479–1425 BCE), renowned for his many military campaigns in Asia, expanded the Egyptian empire to its greatest extent. Furthermore, the Egyptian navy dominated the eastern Mediterranean. The pharaoh also cultivated his interests in botany and literature. Amenhotep IV's (r. 1352–1336 BCE) spirituality became an important and controversial issue. Changing his name to Akhenaten, the pharaoh practiced a new religion and worshipped Aten, graphically portrayed as a sun disk. Akhenaten's monotheistic faith confused and convulsed Egyptian polytheistic society.[7] Furthermore, the pharaoh disrupted and dislocated his administration and ordered the construction of a new capital called Akhetaten (Amarna). His reign also marked an aesthetic shift to naturalism rather than idealized static depictions and portraits. After his death, religious and cultural tradition revived and reasserted itself and portrayed Akhenaten as an apostate. The teenage pharaoh Tutankhamun (r. 1336–1327 BCE) restored the time-honored faith, abandoned Akhetaten, and returned to Thebes. Building programs distinguished the long reign of Ramesses (Ramses) II (r. 1279–1213 BCE), notably the massive statues of the pharaoh at Abu Simbel. He also concluded a peace treaty with the Hittites, ending centuries of conflict between the two empires. Ramesses III (r. 1184–1153 BCE) reasserted Egyptian power in Canaan and successfully repelled the Libyans from the west and the mysterious "Sea Peoples" from the north.[8] Egypt was on the defensive and in decline after Ramesses III's rule; its weakness expedited foreign conquests.

The disintegration of the New Kingdom's central authority resulted in the Third Intermediate Period, lasting from 1069 to 664 BCE. Beginning in the Twenty-first Dynasty (1069 to 945), Libyans exercised principal roles in governing Egypt. Their presence recalled that of the Hyksos. They infiltrated and settled in Lower Egypt, often serving as mercenaries in the Egyptian army. Their growing population allowed them to dominate politically and militarily fragmented Egypt, especially in the Twenty-second Dynasty (945 to 715 BCE).[9] The Kushites invaded and established the Twenty-fifth Dynasty (747–656 BCE), but the fierce Mesopotamian Assyrians drove them back to Nubia. Egyptians exercised an intermittent independence between conquests. For example, the Twenty-sixth Dynasty briefly restored Egypt's prominence and prestige. Nevertheless, King Cambyses II of the Persian Empire overwhelmed Egypt in 525 BCE, inaugurating a period of alien rule, despite temporary flashes of freedom, which lasted over two millennia, approximately the length of time when ancient Egypt's kings, queens, and pharaohs ruled with dignity and divinity.

Egypt's Religious, Social, and Cultural Values

Egypt's polytheistic and ethical religion secured state and society. The principal eschatological belief was immortality. Egyptians believed that life after death was a continuation of their relatively pleasant temporal existence. They conceived the human self as composed with five parts, the name, the shadow, the *ba,* the *ka,* and the *akh.*[10] Released at death, the *ba,* portrayed as a bird with a human head, equated with the personality of the person, while the *ka,* illustrated as the (invisible) twin of the person, represented the life force of the individual. Migrating back and forth from the body, the *ka* needed nutrition, which accounts for food found in tombs. It rested in the body (or in life-like statues of the deceased); therefore, the corpse needed to be inviting, which necessitated a meticulous cleansing and preserving, the ritual and science of mummification.

Attaining a pleasant afterlife subjected the individual to a demanding rather than a routine ritual. The believer had to live a righteous life and faithfully adhere to the principles of *maat,* the moral order, as well as pass tests as revealed by the *Book of the Dead.* At the supreme moment after death, the jackal-headed god Anubis weighed the deceased's heart alongside the feather of truth. If that heart was pure (thereby "light"), the deceased, with the *ka* and *ba* united as a spiritual *akh,* would be led to a welcoming Osiris, the god of the underworld and symbol of resurrected life.

Egyptian religion was transculturally attractive. The conquering Hyksos and Libyans adopted it. Centuries of exposure to Egyptian culture profoundly affected the Kushites. Sandstone pyramids near Napata, north of the Fourth Cataract of the Nile, illustrate Egypt's religious and architectural influence.[11] Furthermore, local values and beliefs also influenced the captive Israelites, who probably first arrived in Egypt during the Hyksos era. The aphorisms associated with *maat* approximate those of Proverbs in the Hebrew Bible (see Ben-Jochannan 1991, 24). Akhenaten's moving prayer to Aten resembles

Psalm 104 (Wilson 1958, 226–230; see also Ben-Jochannan 1991, 24). The evidence of transcultural spiritual transaction remains circumstantial rather than conclusive. Nevertheless, Egyptians and Hebrews experienced centuries of interaction, as illustrated by the story of Joseph and the Book of Exodus. Indeed, the Hebrew Bible is an important source of Egyptian history.

Egyptian society mirrored the pyramids. The king or pharaoh ruled from the apex, with priests and nobles, free peasants, merchants, peasants, and slaves layered below. This hierarchical stratification was not impervious and permitted social fluidity. Virtue and merit, exemplified by the pursuit of *maat*'s precepts, procured social promotion. On the other hand, corruption and decadence incurred demotion. Funerary art suggests that women experienced an elevated social position unlike that of their Mesopotamian counterparts. Women operated their own businesses and inheritance was matrilineal. Hatshepsut was an exceptional example of an assertive political woman, but Egyptian queens traditionally exercised significant power and influence in court. Most Egyptians farmed and fulfilled state and religious tax duties by laboring on public works during the flood season. Egyptian homes were usually comfortable, and some even extravagant with bathing or swimming pools.

Egypt's culture usually overwhelmed conquerors such as the Hyksos, Kushites, Libyans, and later Hellenistic Greeks. According to Michael Rice and Sally MacDonald, Egypt's cultural power projected appealing and easily adaptable archetypal representations and forms (such as architecture) (MacDonald and Rice 2003, 4–5). Martin Bernal's controversial book *Black Athena: The Afroasiatic Roots of Classical Civilization* (1987) claimed that Greek civilization derived from Egyptian culture. Although his argument that Egyptians colonized Greece especially incited debates and refutations, Bernal reoriented historiographical interest toward Egypt's transcultural significance.[12] Indeed, Homer and Herodotus spoke respectfully of Egypt despite its decline. For example, in the *Odyssey,* Homer admired the Egyptians for their pharmacopeia (see below). Herodotus devoted Book II in his *Histories* to Egypt.

It is also important to remember that Egypt not only gave but also gained from transcultural interactions, especially during the expansive Middle and New kingdoms. Acquisitions ranged from the aforementioned military technology to musical instruments and clothing. Technologically, Egyptian agriculture benefited from the ancient water-hoist (known from the New

Kingdom), augmented by the saqia, an ox-driven water wheel believed to be of Persian invention, and later by the Archimedes screw from the Hellenistic period (Ritner 1998, 2–3). Furthermore, Asiatics and Kushites also served as soldiers, workers, servants, and slaves. Egyptian art and material culture provide various representations of Kushites, Puntites, and Libyans, who are often prejudicially posed in subjugated postures (see O'Connor and Reid 2003, 13–16).

Egypt's Independent and Interdependent Economy

The state steered Egypt's economy and exploited the country's mineral resources and commercial networks. Because of the Nile, Egypt was agriculturally self-sufficient, with surplus food providing valuable export commodities. Other important exports included papyrus, linens, jewelry, and glass. The state also mined and traded gold and turquoise. Notwithstanding these valuable products and assets, Egypt suffered from a scarcity of natural resources. It relied on foreign markets, which necessitated the development of an interdependent commercial network. Byblos, located in northern Canaan, furnished cedar (since at least the Second Dynasty [2890–2686 BCE]) that the expansive Egyptian state eventually absorbed. Egypt also imported timber from Crete and copper from Cyprus. Fabrics found in Egyptian tombs imply the existence of trading routes with Central and East Asia. Lapis lazuli, a favorite Egyptian semiprecious stone, arrived from Afghanistan.

Within Africa, Punt provided flora and fauna as depicted on Hatshepsut's funerary temple. In addition, Punt exported myrrh and frankincense for Egyptian religious rituals. Kush's wealth in resources included gold, ebony wood, ivory, gum resins (used for perfumes), and wildlife. In addition, merchants traversed the length of the Sahara and delivered West African gold. Of course, cultural interaction complemented commercial activity. Historical circumstances limited the extent of Egypt's cultural influence beyond its borders. Nevertheless, Egypt enjoyed a particular prestige in the eyes of others and still does.

Over time, conquerors deposited their layers of legacies over Egypt's founding civilization. Yet the immense ancient heritage and physical presence of mysterious monuments remained a constant reminder of an earlier grandeur. The decoding of hieroglyphics and the development of Egyptology revived the ancient past in an Osirisian way. In the twentieth century, native elites and nationalists identified with the glorious ancient kingdoms (see Chapter 7). Today, exhibitions of ancient Egyptian material culture are among the most popular in museums. Appropriately, I. M. Pei's glass pyramid at the entrance of Paris's Louvre is a testament to ancient Egypt's timelessness.

Carthage: Power of the Western Mediterranean

The story of Carthage begins with the Phoenicians, an enterprising mercantile people. The Phoenicians, a mixed Semitic and Indo-European speaking people, lived in northern Canaan, today's Lebanon and southern Syria. Their written language eventually influenced that of the Greeks. At first, the Phoenicians farmed in the Canaanite hinterland before being forced to the coastline, where they fortified city-states, such as Byblos, Sidon, and Tyre, and developed maritime economies. The Phoenicians also founded outposts and colonies along the Mediterranean and even the Atlantic coastline of Iberia and Morocco. They enjoyed a prosperous independence from about 1200 to 850 BCE. Even when submitting to powerful West Asian neighbors, their cities maintained a certain autonomy. Renowned for their trading talents, the Phoenicians served as Mediterranean middlemen for West Asia, North Africa, and Europe. Commercial clients especially esteemed Phoenician purple textiles, colored from a dye extracted from the secretions of the murex, a small mollusk. Canaan's cedars furnished another important export. Merchants also profited from trans-shipments of wine, weapons, glassware, jewelry, papyrus, ivory, and other commodities.

The Phoenicians especially valued their North African colonies. They reputedly founded Utica, in today's Tunisia, and Gades, Cadiz of contemporary Spain, in approximately 1100 BCE.[13] Historians now contend that colonization occurred later, flourishing in the eighth century BCE. Phoenician colonies dotted Algeria, including Ikosim and Hippo, respectively, today's Algiers and Annaba. Lixus was an important colony in Morocco near the Atlantic Ocean coast. Phoenicians also ventured into the Atlantic, reputedly reaching Britain and Ireland.[14] Herodotus, who deeply admired their seafaring, claimed that they also circumnavigated Africa. The inhabitants of its most famous colony, Carthage, inherited their seamanship and enterprise.

Carthage's History to the Punic Wars

Located near today's Tunis in Tunisia, Carthage was reputedly established by a renegade Phoenician queen named Elissa (also known as Dido) during the late ninth century BCE.[15] Historians now place its actual founding by the city-state Tyre in the mid- to late eighth century. As the centuries passed, Carthage eventually became independent and absorbed old Phoenician commercial colonies, controlling territory along the Mediterranean littoral from Tripolitania in western Libya to Iberia and along the Atlantic coastline. Carthage also ruled Malta, the Balearic Islands, Corsica, and Sardinia. As B. H. Warmington noted: "Carthage was the first city state to attempt to rule an empire, and was able to maintain her rule for centuries" (Warmington 1969, 47–48). Carthaginian territorial ambitions in Sicily clashed with those of the Greeks and later the Romans.

Respecting the strength of the Berbers, the Carthaginians initially made little effort to conquer tribes in the interior. Instead, they exacted tribute from nearby potentially hostile tribes; above all, the Carthaginians sought trade, especially metals—gold, silver, copper, and tin. The Carthaginians accumulated great wealth while serving as middlemen between the Berbers and Mediterranean clients. In turn, the Berbers also participated in trans-Saharan trade, thus offering the Carthaginians additional commodities (including soldiers and slaves). The Carthaginians perceived the political strategic importance of maintaining cordial relations with the Berbers. Not only were the Berbers important commercial partners, but also exceptional horsemen, providing the Carthaginians with auxiliary cavalry.[16] Carthage influenced the development of proximate Berbers, principally the Massyli and Masaesyli of western Tunisia and eastern Algeria and the Mauri of western Algeria and Morocco.[17] These tribes found Carthaginian culture appealing and adapted it—an outstanding example of transcultural transmission.

Beginning in the sixth century BCE, the Carthaginians became more assertive under the Magonid dynasty (most likely an elective monarchy). In part, this policy responded to the growing threat posed by the equally enterprising Greeks. Their competition in Sicily bred war in 580 BCE, when the Greeks attempted to establish a town in Carthaginian-controlled territory. The Carthaginians repelled the Greek incursion, but the conflict continued elsewhere. Greeks threatened Leptis (Lepcis in Tripolitania) and Gades (Cadiz in Iberia).

They also pressed the Carthaginian position in Sicily. In 480, King Hamilcar mounted an invasion, but a savage storm crippled the task force. At the battle of Himera, Gelo, the tyrant of the Sicilian city-state Syracuse, and the Greeks overwhelmed the outnumbered Carthaginians.[18] According to Herodotus, citing a traditional Carthaginian account, the catastrophe caused King Hamilcar's self-immolation while sacrificing to the gods (Herodotus 1978, 499). On the other hand, Warmington contended that Hamilcar "was cut down as he was carrying out a sacrifice" (Warmington 1969, 53).

After this disaster, Hamilcar's son Hanno redirected Carthaginian policy. He campaigned against the Berbers, extending Carthaginian power into the hinterland from Tripolitania to Morocco.[19] This reorientation was not only political but also economic. The economy diversified from a principally commercial, maritime economy to one that increasingly included agriculture. Always enterprising, the shrewd Carthaginian overlords usually collaborated with rather than oppressed Berbers.[20] Amicable relations strategically procured political and military cooperation as well as profitable economic compensation. Hanno also implemented austere financial policies in order to replenish Carthaginian coffers. The Greek danger, spearheaded by Syracuse, remained a constant concern, but by the end of the fifth century BCE, Carthage dominated the western Mediterranean and regained a powerful presence in Sicily.

Endemic warfare existed between Carthage and Syracuse throughout the fourth century BCE. In 311, the Carthaginians launched another major campaign to reduce their rival. Yet the Carthaginians faced a wily adversary, the tyrant Agathocles. While the Carthaginians besieged his city, Agathocles mustered his own force, secretly left Syracuse, and invaded North Africa, forcing the Carthaginians to break off their assault. He battled against the Carthaginians and their Berber allies from 310 to 307 and in turn besieged Carthage. Although Agathocles achieved military successes, he failed to rally enough Berbers to his side to give him a strategic advantage, a testament to the Carthaginians' foresighted cultivation of cordial relations with them.[21] Defeated outside the walls of Carthage, Agathocles withdrew and returned to Syracuse. An uneasy peace ensued between the exhausted Carthaginians and Syracusans. Carthage would not face another direct threat until Regulus's invasion in 258 BCE during the First Punic War (see Chapter 2).[22]

Carthaginian Society, Economy, and Culture

There are few detailed descriptions of Carthage, but its population possibly reached 400,000 at its height. It retained its West Asian character and legacy in many ways, such as the use of the Punic language and alphabet and the fervid worship of Canaanite gods such as Baal(-Hammon), Astarte, Melqart, and, especially, Tanit. Carthaginian religious ritual included child sacrifice.[23] Originally a monarchy, by the fourth century power passed to an assembly (also known as a Tribunal or "Senate") of wealthy citizens who annually elected two executives or magistrates known as "sufets" (suffetes).[24] The "Council of Thirty," drawn from the Senate, also played an important role in governance. Carthage's commercial and agricultural magnates controlled the state. Aristotle praised Carthage's "constitution," actually an aristocratic oligarchy. Mercenaries augmented by Berber and Iberian auxiliaries composed the aristocratic government's armed forces.[25] During wartime, the Assembly also elected generals to lead the state (see Chapter 2). Their indefinite term in office allowed effective generals, such as Hamilcar Barca, to exercise power and influence for years.

Carthage's principal commodities consisted of manufactured textiles, precious metals (especially silver and gold), and produce (grain, olives, and wine). Its commercial interests encompassed Western civilization and beyond. Hanno, who astutely governed Carthage after the catastrophic battle of Himera, sailed westward into the Atlantic with a fleet of sixty ships. He turned back after possibly reaching as far south as Guinea-Bissau or possibly Gabon.[26] Himilco, a Carthaginian believed to be Hanno's contemporary, sailed north into the Atlantic.[27] He may have reached Brittany; geographers and historians speculate if he sailed as far as Britain and Ireland. Given the lack of archaeological evidence, Warmington considers Himilco's voyage to Britain as "highly problematical" (Warmington 1969, 77). Nonetheless, Carthaginian outposts also appeared along the Atlantic coastline of today's Portugal. In addition, the Carthaginians engaged the Garamantes, who controlled the Saharan trade. The Garamantes used horses as their pack animals.[28] (Dromedary camels were introduced in the Maghrib between the first and fourth [possibly the fifth] century CE.)[29] The Carthaginian Mago Barca reputedly undertook several trans-Saharan trade expeditions in the late fifth century BCE.

Herodotus explained what would be a regular method of trade between

North Africans and sub-Saharan Africans. He reported that Carthaginians trading with peoples "beyond the Pillars of Heracles" (Gibraltar) would come ashore and display their wares. Natives would then bring gold to match their value. He explained: "If they think it represents a fair price . . . they collect it and go away; if, on the other hand, it seems too little, they go back aboard and wait, and the natives come and add to the gold until they are satisfied. There is perfect honesty on both sides" (Herodotus 1978, 336). Carthage also sustained strong and sentimental ties with its ancestral West Asian homeland. Thus, Carthage, like Phoenicia, diffused commodities and culture throughout the Mediterranean world and beyond.[30] Furthermore, conflict with the Sicilian Greeks and commercial rivalry with Hellenistic Egypt significantly Hellenized the Carthaginians.[31] Over the years, a Greek quarter appeared in Carthage. Interestingly, despite their commercialism, the Carthaginians circulated foreign money and only began minting their own coinage at the end of the fifth century BCE (Gsell 1920–1928, 2:324).[32] In addition, the Carthaginians valued their strong commercial and political relations with the Italian Etruscans. Like Hellenistic Alexandria (see below), Carthage's transcultural character made it a cosmopolis, a city of the world.

Greater Greece and Hellenistic North Africa

Greater Greece, the territories beyond the Greek mainland, played a crucial role in the development of Western civilization. Consider these celebrated names: Homer, Thales, Heraclitus (from Ionia, southwestern Anatolia, Turkey), and Empedocles and Archimedes (from Sicily). Furthermore, Greek civilization profoundly influenced the Macedonians, who lived in northern Greece. They became Greek-like or Hellenistic. Under kings Philip II (r. 359–336 BCE) and especially Alexander III (the Great) (r. 336–323 BCE), Hellenistic culture spread to Western, Central, and South Asian civilizations and to Egypt (see below).

The Greeks emerged as the Phoenicians' main maritime and commercial rivals. During the fourteenth and thirteenth centuries, the "Mycenaean Greeks," celebrated in the Homeric epics, probably confederated with the "Sea Peoples" who threatened Egypt. Storms drove King Menelaus to Egypt in *The Odyssey*. After returning to Sparta, characters admiringly spoke about Egypt's fertility and medicines. Homer described Egypt as a "land where the teeming soil bears the richest yield of herbs in all the world. . . . Every man is a healer there, more skilled than any other men on earth" (Homer 1996, 131). These portrayals illustrate a long-standing Egyptian relationship. Beginning with the Mycenaean period, the Greeks traded extensively with Egypt. In addition, *The Odyssey*'s island of the Lotus Eaters "has been confidently identified with . . . Jerba (Djerba), in the Gulf of Gabès [offshore Tunisia]" (Raven 1993, 8). Phoenicians are also mentioned in the epic.

Beginning about 1000 BCE, the Dorian invasion of Greece led to centuries of social and cultural "fusion" known as the "Dark Age." Writing disappeared then later reappeared with an alphabet adapted from that of the Phoenicians, a profound transcultural transmission. (The Greeks added vowels to the alphabet.) Vibrant Greek city-states developed on the Aeolian and Ionian coasts of Asia Minor (Turkey) and then flourished on mainland Greece. Nevertheless, severe economic and social problems emerged. A lack of resources compounded by population growth incited internecine conflict among city-states and also impelled colonization, which began in the early eighth century BCE. Densely populated Greek settlements arose in the Black Sea region as well as in southern Italy and Sicily.

The Greeks in North Africa

According to Herodotus, "transcultural" encounters between "Libyans" (Africans) and Greeks had occurred for centuries: "It is evident, I think, that the Greek took the 'aegis' with which they adorn statues of Athene from the dress of the Libyan women. . . . Another thing the Greeks learnt from Libya was to harness four horses to a chariot [suggesting interaction with the Garamantes]" (Herodotus 1978, 334). The Greeks also targeted North Africa sites for colonization. Clearly, the Phoenicians had already staked strategic locations, most notably Carthage. Nevertheless, the small island of Thera (Santorini), suffering from economic distress and drought, dispatched colonists to the coastline of eastern Libya. They founded the city of Cyrene in 631 BCE and eastern Libya became known as Cyrenaica. Eventually, the Greeks built four other cities nearby Cyrene, establishing a regional "Pentapolis."[33]

Although having Greeks on their eastern border concerned the Carthaginians, Carthage and Cyrene established cordial relations and peacefully demarcated borders.[34] Cyrene's vulnerability also influenced an accommodating, passive policy. Ruled by its own monarchs, Cyrene prospered. It eventually came under the control of Hellenistic Egypt.

Hellenistic North Africa

After routing the Persians twice, Alexander the Great arrived and claimed Egypt in 332 BCE.[35] Recognized as a "pharaoh" by priests at Siwah, a sacred oasis located in the western Egyptian desert, Alexander embodied the transcultural fusion of Greek secularism and Egyptian spirituality. He founded Alexandria, which became one of the greatest cities of the ancient world, before leaving in 331 BCE to continue his extraordinary Asian conquests. Following Alexander's untimely death in 323 BCE, his generals divided his vast empire. Ptolemy, one of the generals, craftily sought and secured Egypt as well as Cyrene and Cyprus.[36] He and his descendants styled themselves politically (and artistically) as traditional pharaohs and queens. Nevertheless, the court spoke Greek and moved the capital from Memphis to Alexandria, an emerging cosmopolis, a global city.

The founding of the Museum and Library of Alexandria occurred during Ptolemy I Soter's rule (323–285 BCE).[37] The Museum housed laboratories and the Library reportedly held 600,000 to 700,000 scrolls. The state patronized these institutions, which served as "think tanks" that attracted intellectuals from the wider Greek world. Consequently, Alexandria inaugurated Western civilization's first "scientific revolution." Aristarchus (310?–?230 BCE) arrived from Samos (a large island in the Aegean Sea), studied in Alexandria, and theorized the solar system. The physician Herophilus (335?–?280 BCE) came to Alexandria from Chalcedon in northwest Anatolia and performed anatomical research including dissections. He also perceived the brain's importance regarding the nervous system and intelligence. Erasistratus (fl. 250 BCE) established a school of anatomy and earned the title of "father of anatomy." Euclid (fl. 300 BCE) taught in Alexandria and composed *Elements,* the classic text of geometry. The aforementioned Archimedes (287?–212 BCE) emerged as one of the greatest physicists of world civilization. Although a citizen of Syracuse, he also studied in Alexandria. He propounded the principles of the lever, pulley, and screw and proved their applicability with ingenious inventions. His later work in hydrostatics led to "Archimedes' Law" regarding buoyancy and weight (i.e., specific gravity). Archimedes calculated pi (π) as approximately equal to 3.14159, the ratio of the circumference of a circle divided by its diameter. Eratosthenes (c. 285–194 BCE), from Cyrene, exemplified the Alexandrian scientific revolution. Appointed the director or curator of the Museum and Library, Eratosthenes disclosed formidable knowledge in many disciplines, a polymath. His interests included astronomy, literary criticism, and history. He especially excelled in geography where he applied lines of latitude and longitude and also calculated the approximate circumference of the earth. Other important Hellenistic geographers include Posidonius (135?–?51 BCE) and Strabo (63BCE?–?25 CE). In addition, Aristarchus of Samothrace (c. 217–145 BCE) served as a librarian and a grammarian and excelled in literary criticism and research.[38] The poets Theocritus, believed to be a native of Syracuse, Callimachus of Cyrene (both from the third century BCE), and Apollonius of Rhodes (late third–early second centuries BCE) composed verse in Alexandria.

Egypt enjoyed one of its most glorious and prosperous periods during the Hellenistic era. Immigrants arrived from the Greek world, especially Asia Minor and the Greek islands. A large Jewish community also settled in Egypt. The population of the kingdom grew impressively and may have attained 8,000,000 by the end of the first century BCE (not be reached again until the modern period). The Ptolemies actively participated in the Hellenistic "commercial revolution." Egyptian ships regularly plied the waters of the Red Sea to India, inaugurating the cosmopolitan Indian Ocean trade. Alexandria's famous lighthouse, known as the *Pharos,* towered four hundred feet and could be seen twenty-five miles away. The city featured wide streets and brisk business. Its diverse population grew to about 500,000. It became the Hellenistic world's greatest megalopolis until the rise of imperial Rome. Nonetheless, Peter Green reminds: "Alexandria, that humming center of mercantile activity, was also, looked at in another way, a monument to consumerism. A top-heavy, luxury-loving, exploitative court and bureaucracy sucked in the produce of the countryside" (Green 1990, 158). Certainly, economic manipulation and mistreatment resulted in an uneven distribution of wealth. On the other hand, Hellenistic rule offered stability and the Egyptians regarded the Ptolemies as pharaohs, who, in turn, demonstrated remarkable sensitivity toward their subjects.

Hellenistic Egypt exemplified North Africa's historical transculturalism. Macedonian religious beliefs merged with those of Egypt. For example, the attributes of the Macedonian deity Serapis evolved, becoming more Egyptian. The cult symbolized the syncretism of Hellenistic Egypt. Subtle Greek influences appeared in Egyptian story cycles. As the Rosetta Stone indicated, Greek, hieroglyphics, and demotic Egyptian (introduced at this time) illustrated the cosmopolitan, even collaborative, character of Egypt at this time. Ptolemy III Euergetes (246–221 BCE) earned the esteem of native Egyptians by defeating the Seleucids in battle and retrieving statues taken by the Persians and restoring them to their temples. Although the Hellenistic Greeks composed the elite, there were opportunities for social mobility. Egyptians and Jews sought to be Hellenized and learned Greek as a means to acquire status. Scholars in Alexandria translated the Torah, the first five books of the Hebrew Bible, into Greek—the Pentateuch.

Politically, Egypt fought with its Hellenistic neighbors, notably the aforementioned Seleucids of West Asia. Hellenistic queens especially distinguished themselves. Arsinoë II (d. 270 BCE) was a redoubtable, honored military leader, as illustrated by her image engraved on coinage along with her brother and husband Ptolemy II Philadelphus (r. 285–246). Cleopatra (69–30 BCE) embodied Hellenistic Egypt's transcultural character. She could speak several languages and her intellect charmed two of Rome's most powerful figures, Julius Caesar and Mark Antony. Her story must wait for the next chapter. By Cleopatra's time, the disintegrating dynasty became reliant upon Roman intervention. Indeed, Ptolemy Apion, who ruled Cyrene, bequeathed the city to Rome in 96 BCE.

Conclusion

The brilliant civilizations presented in this chapter underscore the importance of North Africa regarding the direction and destiny of Western civilization. Egypt's manifold contributions such as mathematics, architecture, and agronomy remain impressive. Its history, ethics, and spirituality influenced Western civilization's three universal religions: Judaism, Christianity, and Islam. Although Malik Bennabi's ideas focused on Muslim civilization, ancient Egypt, where religion was also foundational, exemplified as well the creative and collaborative synergy of man, land, and time. The deep interest in Egypt, renewed by passing generations, reaffirms ancient Egypt's timelessness. From a regional context, ancient Egypt had little direct influence in the

Maghrib, except for its contacts and conflicts with the Libyans. Nevertheless, Egypt's position as a hinge between Asia and Africa increased in strategic significance as the Maghrib developed its civilizations.

Carthage emerged as the first great Maghribi civilization. Its power acquired and exercised in the Mediterranean illustrated the importance of North Africa in the development and expansion of Western civilization. Transcultural sensibility underlay Carthage's surface history and significance. The Carthaginians possessed an appreciation and ability to understand and relate to peoples of different cultures, ranging from Saharan Berber traders to ethnically diverse mercenaries. Furthermore, Carthage's sophisticated culture, expressed by its religious pantheon and language, impressed the acutely receptive Berbers.

The modest but important Greek presence in Cyrenaica also fastened North Africa to Europe, as did the Sicilian wars between the Carthaginians and the Greeks. In particular, Hellenistic Egypt's "globalization," featuring the Indian Ocean trade and South Asian markets, linked North Africa with the wider world. Hellenistic syncretism, a salient example of transculturalism, also strengthened the Ptolemaic state. Alexandria became the hub for the Hellenistic commercial revolution and the center of Western civilization's first scientific revolution. Rome greatly gained by appropriating and exploiting these North African legacies.

CHAPTER 2

Rome and North Africa

Rome unified North Africa by defeating Carthage and Hellenistic Egypt and by subduing Berber tribes. North Africa's littoral and, in varying degrees, its hinterland became Romanized—an urban and urbane civilization. Remarkably designed cities still awe urban planners. Rome especially valued North Africa's economic importance. The Maghrib principally provided grain and olive oil. Egypt exported grain, glass, and an array of commodities, which Hellenistic middlemen diffused, including those plying the Erythraean Sea (Red Sea–Indian Ocean) trade network. Many North Africans contributed to Roman culture and to the development and dissemination of Christianity. Indeed, North Africa's provinces converted to Christianity well before those in Western Europe.

Germanic invaders, such as the Visigoths and Ostrogoths, hastened Rome's decline and the end of the Western Empire. In turn, the Vandals invaded North Africa and ended Roman rule in eastern Algeria and Tunisia. In the sixth century, the inheritors of the Eastern Roman Empire, the Byzantines, conquered the Vandals and reinstalled imperial government, but not the stability, wealth, and cosmopolitanism that had prospered in North Africa during the Pax Romana (27 BCE–180 CE). North Africa fragmented politically and fractured culturally, leaving the Byzantines in a dangerously tenuous position.

Rome versus Carthage: The Punic Wars

In 509 BCE, Carthage concluded a treaty with Rome recognizing the latter's independence from Etruscan rule. Subsequent accords cemented relations between the two states. Carthage left Rome with a free hand in Italy in return for its non-interference in Carthage's Mediterranean trade. They also formed an alliance against the audacious Agathocles of Syracuse in the fourth cen-

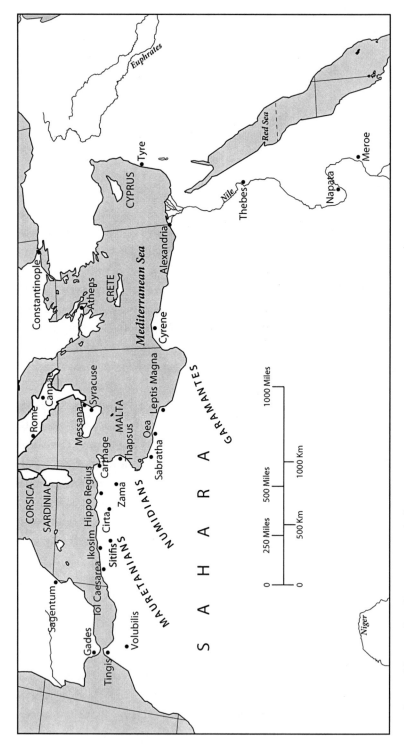

Northern Africa During the Roman Period

tury. The intervention of King Pyrrhus of Illyria in southern Italy and Sicily on behalf of the Greeks in the early third century BCE threatened Roman and Carthaginian interests. Once again, Rome and Carthage allied in opposition. When the Illyrian king withdrew, Rome took over the last independent Greek city-states in Italy. Consequently, the Greek city-states in Sicily faced surging Roman power as well as traditional Carthaginian hostility. Rome and Carthage viewed each other with veiled suspicion.

Rome provoked the first of the three Punic Wars when it defended, despite Carthaginian and Greek protests, pirates who had seized Messana, a strategic city sited on the Straits of Messina (between Italy and Sicily). The first two of the three Punic Wars between Carthage and Rome determined which state would dominate the western Mediterranean. The final war illustrated outright Roman aggression. The struggles featured remarkable personalities, such as Hannibal, Scipio, and Masinissa. As a result of these epic conflicts, Rome established itself in the Maghrib.

The First Punic War (264–241 BCE)

While Rome waged a successful campaign against Carthage's Sicilian Greek allies, the Carthaginian navy raided the Italian coastline. In a daring operation, the consul Regulus disembarked near Carthage in 256 BCE with a large army, but the Spartan Xanthippus and his Carthaginian mercenaries destroyed the invaders during the following year. During the course of the conflict, Rome launched a navy modeled after Carthaginian warships. The inventive Romans widened the boarding plank, known as the "crow," in order to permit their superior army to fight at sea. Despite repeated disasters at sea, Rome persistently pursued its naval campaign and won the decisive battle of the Aegates Islands in 241 BCE. The combatants concluded a peace treaty by which Carthage gave up its Sicilian territories and agreed to an indemnity.

Carthage then confronted a "Mercenary War" (241–237 BCE) over its soldiers' unpaid wages. Furthermore, over-exploited and insurgent peasants identified with rebellious mercenaries, compounding the conflict. With Carthage's survival at stake, the government reorganized and increased the power of generals.[1] In particular, General Hamilcar Barca with the help of Massyli Berber allies suppressed the mercenaries and peasants; but Rome took advantage of Carthaginian weakness and repudiated its recently concluded treaty, seizing Corsica and Sardinia, and demanding a greater indemnity. Rome's aggression piqued Carthaginian sensitivities and contributed to the outbreak of the Second Punic War.

The Second Punic War (218–201 BCE)

Carthage spectacularly rebounded from its defeat by Rome and its harrowing Mercenary War. It extended its power to southern Iberia (Spain) and secured copper and silver resources. Hamilcar Barca and his son-in-law, Hasdrubal, conceived and implemented this brilliant geopolitical and economic strategy. The reinvigoration of Carthage worried Rome to the point of making Sagentum, a remote Iberian (and Greek) city, a client under its protection. An inevitable conflict arose between Carthage and Sagentum, Rome's new ally, and the Second Punic War commenced.

Hannibal, Hamilcar's son and a sworn enemy of Rome, dominated the war. Tapping his family's wealth in Spain, thus not solely relying upon the Carthaginian treasury, Hannibal mustered an army of 59,000 but lost over half of it along the way.[2] He allied with Celtic tribes in southern Gaul (France) and then passed through the Alps in 218 BCE. He invaded Italy with 26,000 soldiers. His superb Berber cavalry gave Hannibal "superiority" (Livy 2006, 47). A brilliant tactician, he trapped Roman legions in a lethal double envelopment at Cannae in 216 BCE. Livy assessed that the Romans suffered 45,500 infantry and 2,700 cavalry deaths (Livy 2006, 118), but military historians calculate approximately 62,000 Roman and 6,000 Carthaginian losses (Dupuy and Dupuy 1977, 66). This stunning setback encouraged Greeks in Sicily to revolt against Rome and convinced Macedonia to ally with Carthage. Ever resilient, Rome recovered from these multiple reverses and methodically defeated its enemies. The Romans prevented the Macedonians from uniting their forces with Hannibal's, a strategic political as well as military success. Furthermore, they suppressed or neutralized the Sicilian Greeks. Scipio (236?–183 BCE), an outstanding general, successfully campaigned against the Carthaginians and their Iberian allies in Spain from 209 to 206 BCE. From there he invaded North Africa in 204, forcing Hannibal to withdraw from Italy to defend Carthage. In 202 BCE, Scipio defeated Hannibal at Zama. The peace agreement stipulated that Carthage pay another large indemnity, surrender Spain to Rome, and hand over a considerable tract of its territory to Rome's ally Masinissa, the king of "Numidia" (western Tunisia and eastern and central Algeria).

Hannibal remained the leading figure of Carthage (also holding the office of sufet), and the city soon prospered despite its reduced political status. Fearful once again, Roman agents plotted against Hannibal. He fled Carthage and attempted to rally the Hellenistic east (namely Antiochus III) against Rome. Meanwhile, Romans relentlessly stalked the Carthaginian; surrounded by his Roman enemies, Hannibal committed suicide to avoid capture.

Transcultural sensibility, as well as tactical acuity and audacity, characterized Hannibal's military greatness. He knew how to communicate with his soldiers and understood the value of understanding and appreciating the particular and peculiar. In evaluating Hannibal's career, the Greek historian Polybius, who served the house of Scipio, noted the Carthaginian's leadership qualities:

> An admirable feature in Hannibal's character, and the strongest proof of his having been born ruler of men, and having possessed statesmanlike qualities of an unusual kind, is that, though he was for seventeen years engaged in actual warfare, and though he had to make his way through numerous barbaric tribes, and to employ innumerable men of different nationalities in what appeared desperate and hazardous enterprises, he was never made the object of a conspiracy by any of them, nor deserted by any of those who had joined him and put themselves under his command. (Polybius 1962, 2:331)

Livy complemented Polybius's generous assessment as he described Hannibal's exceptional transcultural consciousness, which the Carthaginian exploited:

> Hannibal's army was composed of so many men who had nothing in common in terms of language, culture, law, weaponry, dress, physical appearance, and their reasons for fighting, and he varied his exhortations accordingly. . . . The Gauls could be aroused by their own particular and instinctive hatred for the Romans. The Ligurians, who had been brought down from their rugged mountain homes, were inspired to hopes of victory by the prospect of the rich plains of Italy. The Moors and Numidians Hannibal frightened by telling them how brutal Masinissa's rule would be. He worked on the various races by inspiring different hopes and different fears. (Livy 2006, 602)

Although Polybius and Livy admired Hannibal's transculturalism, Carthaginians characteristically evinced these sensitivities for centuries given their commercialism and their need to enlist mercenaries.[3] They realized that

Carthage's survival depended on positive and patient interaction with diverse societies. Carthaginian transculturalism was not casual but crucial and compulsory.

The Third Punic War (149–146 BCE)

Carthage remained independent, but hardly a threat to Rome. Instead, Numidia loomed as Carthage's greatest menace, whose dynamic King Masinissa aspired to unite the Maghrib. The growth of Numidian power, coupled with the pathological fear of a potentially resurgent Carthage, led to another Roman expedition against its archrival.[4] Aided by their Numidian allies, the belligerent Romans, commanded by the adopted grandson of Scipio, Scipio Aemilianus, finally breached Carthage's walls after a determined and desperate defense. The Romans enslaved the survivors and destroyed the city, reputedly plowing its debris underground and then symbolically salting the land to prevent its regeneration. Establishing a new province, Africa Proconsularis, Romans settled permanently in North Africa.

Rome Takes Over North Africa

Significant Berber kingdoms exercised considerable power and influence by the time the Romans defeated Carthage, notably Numidia. In addition, Mauretania (the country of the Mauri) bordered Numidia on the west and included Morocco. Although the Romans had allied with Berbers, specifically the Massyli, against Carthage, relations between them declined and ultimately led to the Jugurthine War. In the first century BCE, rivalries among Roman commanders contesting for power embroiled North Africa, ending the Berber kingdoms and also Hellenistic Egypt. For the first time, an imperial state, the Roman Empire, ruled North Africa's Mediterranean littoral and, in varying degrees, its hinterland from Egypt to the Atlantic.

Masinissa and the Kingdom of Numidia

Masinissa (240?–148 BCE), a prince of the Massyli tribe, had ably served with Carthaginian forces in Spain.[5] After his father died, a rival named Syphax of the Masaesyli overthrew him with Carthaginian support, forcing Masinissa to flee for his life.[6] In turn, Rome supported Masinissa, who regrouped and defeated Syphax. At the battle of Zama in 202 BCE, Masinissa allied with

Scipio against Hannibal. The Roman victory ensured Masinissa's accession to greater prominence. Rome recognized Masinissa as king of "Numidia" and rewarded him with a sizable slice of Carthaginian territory.

Polybius met Masinissa and described him as "the best man of all the kings of our time.... He was, besides, the most powerful man physically of all his contemporaries" (Polybius 1962, 2:511). Writing approximately two centuries after these events, Livy repeatedly lauded Masinissa for his personal qualities as a natural leader. During his long reign, Masinissa built a strong kingdom stretching from western Tunisia to central Algeria. He established his capital at Cirta (Constantine, Algeria), enlarged the army and navy, and promoted economic development, especially agriculture, the latter being to Polybius "his greatest and most divine achievement" (Polybius 1962, 2:512). He styled himself as a Hellenistic ruler and his reputation rose in the Greek world. Statues of Masinissa adorned Delos, the sacred island of Apollo and Artemis in the Aegean.

For most of his reign, Masinissa conducted cordial relations with Carthage, despite his territorial ambitions. When the Carthaginians attempted to support Numidian rebels, however, Masinissa responded by seizing more Carthaginian territory in 154. Fearing more predations, Carthage sought an alliance with Mauretania, bordering Numidia in the west. This strategic initiative caused further conflict between Numidia and Carthage. A Numidian victory in 150 BCE brought Masinissa closer toward realizing his dream, the takeover of Carthage. Numidian aggression also persuaded Rome to launch the Third Punic War. The prospect of another dynamic North African state troubled the apprehensive and anxious Roman Senate.

Once again, Masinissa provided Rome with Numidian military support. The destruction of Carthage brought more Romans to North Africa and Africa Proconsularis. The unbridled Roman profiteering and exploitation of former Carthaginian territory perturbed the Numidians. Furthermore, enterprising Romans also operated within Numidia. Rome succeeded in weakening Numidia, which declined into client status.

Jugurtha versus Rome and Numidian Consequences

Controversies regarding Numidian royal succession compounded changing geopolitical matters. After the death of the extraordinary Masinissa, his sons jointly governed until one of them, Micipsa, asserted sole authority. Micipsa had two sons, Adherbal and Hiempsal, but one of his brothers also sired a son, Jugurtha. Sallust described the Numidian prince as "endowed . . . with great strength and handsome looks, but above all with a powerful intellect" (Sallust 1967, 39). Perhaps out of malicious jealousy (as Sallust suggests), Micipsa sent Jugurtha with the Numidian cavalry to Spain to assist the Romans against fierce Iberian tribes. His outstanding service during this dangerous mission as a Roman auxiliary forced Micipsa to accept Jugurtha as a co-heir along with his two sons. After Micipsa's death in 118 BCE, a struggle for power ensued. Jugurtha ordered Hiempsal's execution and defeated Adherbal, who sailed for Rome to lobby for support. In turn, Jugurtha followed and bribed his own constituents. The Senate then decided to divide the client kingdom between the two aspirants, but hostilities inevitably renewed between the cousins. Jugurtha besieged Cirta for giving Adherbal refuge. His forces overpowered the defenders, destroyed Adherbal, and massacred the citizenry. Among the dead were Roman citizens. Jugurtha reunited Numidia, but at a fateful cost.

The Senate responded and dispatched an army against Jugurtha, which the Numidian king defeated. Subsequently, the Romans and Jugurtha concluded a conciliatory peace, which infuriated the Senate. It dispatched another army. Although the Romans successfully seized Numidian cities, Jugurtha remained at large in the countryside. The Romans defeated Jugurtha in 106 BCE and subsequently, in collusion with his traitorous father-in-law, King Bocchus of Mauretania, seized him in an ambush. Jugurtha died imprisoned in Rome. His resistance against Roman imperialism along with his grandfather's illustrious reign resonated in Algerian memories and inspired twentieth-century nationalists opposing French colonialism.[7] Jugurtha's capture marked the beginning of the end of an independent Numidian monarchy.

Rome allotted a large portion of Numidia to Bocchus in return for his collaboration. Meanwhile, Jugurtha's half-brother, Gauda, ruled as a malleable client king. After his death in 88 BCE, his two feuding sons became entangled in the Roman rivalry between Marius and Sulla and supported opposite sides. Sulla's victory left the winning brother, Hiempsal, in charge of Numidia.[8] Hiempsal and his son and successor, Juba I, subsequently supported Pompey against Julius Caesar. In 46 BCE, Caesar arrived with an army to end the Pompeian-Numidian threat.[9] While supporting anti-Caesar legions, Juba also faced internal revolts against his authority. At the battle of Thapsus, Caesar achieved one of the greatest victories of his career. He vanquished his enemies while his forces suffered very low casualties.[10] King Juba ordered his own death and a friend slew him. Caesar established Africa Nova, composed of most of Numidia, as Rome's second North African province. Africa Proconsularis was renamed Africa Vetus. Caesar displayed typical kindness toward Juba's son, Juba II, who subsequently grew up in his household and became a close friend of Octavian, Caesar's nephew and the future Augustus.

Rome Conquers Cleopatra and Hellenistic Egypt

In pursuit of Pompey, Caesar arrived in Egypt and regretfully discovered that his rival had been slain there in 48 BCE. Subsequently, Caesar became embroiled in a succession struggle among the Ptolemies. Caesar supported Cleopatra and her brother. Sadly, during this strife the Museum and Library sustained serious damage—a grievous cultural loss to Western and world civilization.[11]

Intrigued by Cleopatra, now queen of Egypt, Caesar brought her (and the son he sired) with him to Rome. Her arrival in the capital created a sensation. Senators assassinated Caesar in 44 BCE, which forced Cleopatra to return to Egypt. In the subsequent civil war, she supported the forces of Caesar's avengers against the conspiring senators. Enamored with Cleopatra, Mark Antony, one of Caesar's lieutenants, divorced his wife and married the Egyptian queen.

Legend and Hollywood fabricated Cleopatra's image as a ravishing, sultry temptress. As Plutarch remarked, she possessed neither stunning nor incomparable beauty. Instead, her intelligence and her transcultural nature accounted for her appeal:

> [She] had an irresistible charm, and her presence, combined with the persuasiveness of her discourse and the character which was somehow diffused about her behaviour towards others, had something stimulating about it. There was sweetness also in the tones of her voice; and her tongue, like an instrument of many strings, she could readily turn to whatever language she pleased, so that in her interviews with Barbarians she very seldom had need of an interpreter, but made her replies to most of them herself and unassisted, whether they were Ethiopians, Troglodytes, Hebrews, Arabians, Syrians, Medes or Parthians. Nay, it is said that she knew the speech of many other peoples also. (Plutarch 1988, 9:197)

Simply, Cleopatra matched any man. She knew how to wield power and did so effectively. Her relentless ambition, which Antony shared, proved to be her fatal political flaw.

The success of the Second Triumvirate, composed of Octavian, Mark Antony, and Marcus Lepidus, against the senators' forces set the stage for an ultimate confrontation for control of Rome. Lepidus retired, leaving Octavian dominant in the west and Mark Antony and Cleopatra in the east. Octavian shrewdly portrayed Antony as an incompetent leader who had abandoned Roman virtues, a man that the wily Cleopatra orientalized.[12] In turn, Antony and Cleopatra dreamed of uniting the Mediterranean from Alexandria, creating a vast Hellenistic empire. The rivalry incited yet another civil war, which decisively impacted North Africa.

At the momentous naval battle of Actium in 31 BCE, Octavian's forces defeated those of Antony and Cleopatra. The famous couple committed suicide and Egypt became part of the expansive Roman Republic. Recognizing Egypt's great wealth, Octavian placed the new province under his personal rule and integrated Cyrenaica into the administration of Crete and the Aegean.

Juba II and the End of the Last Client Berber Kingdom

The astute Octavian accepted the title of *Princeps* or first citizen of the state, artfully masked his accumulation of uncontested power, and subtly reorganized the Republic into the Empire. The Senate acclaimed Octavian as Augustus in 27 BCE. His plans for North Africa involved Juba II, who grew up in his household. Augustus arranged Juba's marriage to the daughter of Antony and Cleopatra, Cleopatra Selene. Given the end of the Mauretanian dynasty, Augustus chose Juba and Cleopatra to rule as client monarchs in North Africa. They governed from Iol Caesarea (Cherchell, Algeria) in a reorganized Mauretania encompassing central Algeria and Morocco.[13] The royal couple established a splendid capital and court.[14]

A polymath of the Greco-Roman world, Juba (r. 25 BCE–?19 CE) wrote histories, geographies, and discourses on literature, art, and theater in Greek; unfortunately, none of this remarkable corpus is extant. (He also had an interest in science, especially botany.) Juba created an outstanding library, which reputedly included works by Pythagoras, the sixth century BCE philosopher and mathematician (Roller 2003, 158). Plutarch highly admired Juba and referred to him as "the most accomplished of kings" (Plutarch 1988, 9:31) and "among the most accomplished historians of Hellas [Greece]" (Plutarch 1986, 7:571). Pliny the Elder especially relied on his scholarship in his *Natural History*. As a "cultural geographer," Juba served as a consultant and assisted in the preparation of a Roman military campaign in northern Arabia.

Juba's rule inaugurated a period of prosperity in the Maghrib until Tacfarinas, a former Roman auxiliary, mounted a serious Berber revolt that lasted from 17 to 24 CE; Mazippa, another Berber leader, allied with Tacfarinas. With great difficulty, the Romans suppressed the revolt and Tacfarinas fell in battle.

By that time, Ptolemy had succeeded his father as king of Mauretania. His popularity in Rome provoked the unstable Emperor Caligula (r. 37–41), who ordered his execution. Was this cruel act purely out of jealousy, given the emperor's notorious character? Perhaps. On the other hand, why sustain a client king? Indeed, after the death of Ptolemy in 40 CE and another Berber revolt (led by Aedemon), Rome disestablished the kingdom and divided it between two provinces: Mauretania Tingitana and Mauretania Caesariensis. Tripolitania's coastline was also renamed as Africa Proconsularis.

Although Romans subdued the Numidians and the Mauretanians, the remarkable Garamantes of Fezzan in Libya remained independent and often hostile. Credited with introducing writing to the Sahara as well as the horse and wheeled transport, the Garamantes provided extraordinary transcultural service. In addition, they conceived a remarkable agronomy, which featured *foggaras,* underground irrigation channels tapped from Saharan aquifers (see Keys 2004, Introduction).[15] Nevertheless, the Romans considered them a menace to their North African possessions. Under the command of Cornelius Balbus, a Roman expeditionary force marched 400 miles into the Sahara and captured Garama (Germa), the Garamantes capital, in 19 BCE, an extraordinary logistical as well as military achievement.[16] Although the Romans penetrated the northern Sahara in today's Libya, Algeria, and Morocco, often during punitive operations, they never subjugated it.[17]

Clashes also flared between the Romans and the Kushites along the southern Egyptian-Nubian border. In 25 BCE, Roman troops under Publius Petronius destroyed the Kushite capital of Napata in an ongoing conflict against Queen "Candace" (r. 41–12 BCE).[18] As a result of Emperor Augustus's personal diplomatic intervention, the Romans and Kushites fixed a frontier at Hiera Sykaminos (Maharaqqa), the old Ptolemaic border, approximately 80 kilometers south of Aswan (Jackson 2002, 149). The demarcation lasted for 300 years. With peace established, trade flourished. A kiosk at Meroe, deep within the kingdom of Kush, indicated Rome's mercantile presence and its interest in trans-African as well as trans-Saharan trade (see Elleh 1997, 54–55). Furthermore, the Romans mined quarries in Egypt's Eastern Desert and also settled in oases in the Western Desert (see Jackson 2002). Pliny pointed out that the Romans also explored along the Atlantic. Scipio Aemilianus, who commanded Roman forces during the Third Punic War, commissioned an exploratory expedition along the Atlantic Coast "at the service of the historian Polybius." While the Romans did not venture as far southward as Hanno, Pliny later compiled considerable information regarding the littoral (Pliny 1942, Book V, 225).

Life in Roman North Africa

North Africa was crucially important to the Roman Empire. As North African agriculture expanded, Rome deepened its dependence on its grain.[19] Furthermore, hundreds of new cities arose. Roman North Africa also offered social opportunities for Berbers. Many of them assimilated and excelled in the use of Latin. On the other hand, restive Berber tribes on the frontier occasionally rebelled. In turn, Augustus deployed the Third Augustan Legion, a formidable force. The legion historically garrisoned a transcultural mélange initially composed of Gauls and Italians and later manned by Anatolians, Syrians, and Egyptians as well as Numidians and Mauretanians (including children born to legionnaires).[20] Backed by Iberian, Thracian, Dalmatian, and local auxiliaries, the Roman military served as a daunting deterrent for three hundred years. Furthermore, a string of frontier outposts, known as the *limes,* also secured Roman North Africa from marauders.

An Urban and Urbane North Africa

Older established cities flourished under Roman rule, such as Egypt's Alexandria, Libya's Cyrene, Leptis (Lepcis) Magna, Oea, and Sabratha (Sabrata). Octavian refounded Carthage in 29 BCE, overcoming a century of Roman apprehension. Carthage again became one of the most populous cities in the Mediterranean.[21] In addition, it developed into a renowned intellectual and academic center.[22] The Romans brilliantly designed new cities such as Timgad and Djemila in Algeria. Other important Roman cities in Algeria included Tipasa, Icosium, Sitifis (Sétif), Iol Caesarea (Cherchell), Hippo Regius (Annaba), and Theveste (Tébessa), one of several posts of the Third Augustan.[23] Volubilis continued to thrive in the Moroccan hinterland. Roman cities featured amphitheaters,[24] business districts, sporting venues, and baths.[25] Legionnaires constructed roads to connect these cities. Sophisticated hydrology and hydrodynamics, notably aqueducts (such as those in the Tunisian countryside) and *qanats* (like *foggaras*), underground channels from upslope aquifers (notably engineered in Algeria), provided water (Reebs 2006, 14). It is estimated that the Maghrib, excluding Egypt, had 500 to 600 cities.

Exquisite mosaics decorated upper-class homes. The common urban home featured an outer windowless wall facing the street and an inner court surrounded by rooms. This spatial configuration would be transculturally transmitted to the Arabs. Given the public facilities available to inhabitants, urban designers also accommodated the poor with baths and other amenities. City dwellers were the most Romanized; they spoke Latin and served the imperial administration. Berber tribes on the periphery or beyond perpetuated Punic and its alphabet, as well as native languages and dialects.

Expansive agriculture supported the cities. The Romans encouraged the production of grain; consequently, North Africa became a granary for the empire, exporting an estimated half million tons annually beginning in the first century CE (Raven 1993, 81). Its olive oil production and viticulture (production of wine) were also economically significant. Berber pastoralists provided livestock and wool while Saharan tribes traded leather goods and sub-Saharan slaves.[26] Furthermore, North Africa shipped wildlife for Roman gladiatorial events and circuses.[27]

Egypt, the richest imperial province, featured glass production as well as grain exportation. In addition, the Erythraean Sea trade (Red Sea and Indian Ocean) flourished. Products of South Asia such as silk arrived in Rome.[28] Strabo observed:

> At the present time . . . large fleets are dispatched as far as India and the extremities of Aethiopia [Ethiopia], from which the most valuable cargoes are brought to Aegypt [Egypt], and thence sent forth again to the other regions; so that double duties are collected, on both imports and exports; and on goods that cost heavily the duty is also heavy. And in Alexandria alone is not only the receptacle of goods of this kind, for the most part, but also the source of supply to the outside world. (Strabo 1949, 53–55)

Cosmopolitan Alexandria, the empire's second largest city after Rome, retained its reputation as a transcultural cosmopolis of Hellenistic civilization.[29]

Plotinus (205?–270) embodied the importance of Egypt as a transcultural conduit. Born in Egypt, he had a strong interest in Persian and Indian philosophy that influenced his reworking of Plato's ideas. He became a principal advocate of Neoplatonism, teaching in Alexandria and later Rome. He replaced the traditional Platonic idea or form of the Good with that of the One. According to Plotinus, by galvanizing rational and spiritual energies, thereby merging with the One, absolute forms (truths) could be experienced. This blending of philosophy with religion exemplified a changing discourse and mentality in Western civilization (Naylor 2000b, 127–128). Plotinus's ideas especially influenced prominent North African Christians (see below) (see Brown 1967, 88–100, 425–426).

Famous Romanized North Africans

North Africans distinguished themselves throughout Roman history, but especially during the Pax Romana (27 BCE to 180 CE). Terence (185–159 BCE), a Berber slave brought to Rome, charmed his owner, who subsequently freed him, allowing Terence to receive an education. Consequently, Terence became a renowned playwright and friend of Scipio Aemilianus. Lucius Quietus, a Berber from Morocco, served with great distinction as a military commander and senator under the Emperor Trajan (r. 98–117 CE). Considered a candidate for emperor, he was executed by rival supporters of Hadrian.[30] Marcus Cornelius Fronto (100–160 CE), a consul born in Cirta, became one of the most famous Stoic rhetoricians produced by the empire. He also tutored Emperor Marcus Aurelius (r. 166–80 CE). Lucius Apuleis (fl. second century CE), also from today's Algeria, authored *The Golden Ass,* a "novel" that displayed a highly polished Latin style and provided a rare description of rites associated with the cult of Isis. During the Pax Romana, North Africans composed a third of the Senate, affirming the importance of their region.

After the death of Marcus Aurelius, the last "good emperor" of the Pax Romana, the empire slowly declined, marked by successive crises and conflicts. A dynasty, known as the Severi, emerged in North Africa, specifically from Tripolitania's Leptis Magnus. Septimius Severus (r. 193–211) briefly stemmed the empire's erosion but at the expense of militarizing the empire. Aided ably by his remarkable wife Julia Domna (from West Asia), Severus secured the succession of his son, the unfortunately incompetent Caracalla. After Caracalla's murder in 217, Macrinus, a Berber, briefly became emperor until his deposition in 218. In 222, Alexander Severus, a cousin of Caracalla's, became emperor, but his murder in 235 ended the Severi. Rome then suffered a turbulent period of unstable succession known as the "barracks emperors" (including the North African Gordian I and Gordian II) from 235 to 284, when twenty-five of the twenty-six emperors suffered violent deaths. During this exacting era, Queen Zenobia of Palmyra (Syria) revolted against Rome and seized Egypt in 271 before being repulsed. Emperor Aurelian (r. 270–275) and the future Emperor Probus (r. 276–282) played important roles in defeating Palmyra and reestablishing authority in Egypt. Nevertheless, Roman control in Upper Egypt diminished as raiding Blemmye tribesmen repeatedly assaulted southern borders.

Furthermore, recurrent Berber revolts, such as those of Faraxen (253–262), Firmus (372–375), and Gildo (397–398), weakened Roman authority. The Saharan Austuriani tribe repeatedly devastated Leptis Magna (and its surrounding fertile lands) from 363 to 367; the irreversible damage desolated that once great city.

Christianity in North Africa

Christianity appealed to North Africans as well as other citizens and subjects of the Roman Empire for many reasons. The universal, egalitarian message of Christianity attracted adherents. The Incarnation of Jesus Christ as an immediate historical figure differed from traditional religions and cults with their remote, inscrutable, and capricious deities. Christianity's transcultural character reflected the monotheism of the Hebrews, the immortality of the Egyptians, and the philosophy of the Greeks.[31] In many ways, Christianity synthesized the belief systems of Western civilization and received, in particular, a rich yet controversial expression in North Africa.

North African Christians

Christianity's "otherworldliness," especially its emphasis on the afterlife, conflicted with the temporal realities of the Roman Empire. Furthermore, Christian detachment and refusal to respect imperial dictums, such as emperor worship and military service, aroused suspicion. The fervor of North

African Christians, perceived as subversive, provoked persecutions. Among the most famous North African martyrs were Perpetua in 203 and Bishop Cyprian of Carthage in 258.

North Africa featured a number of early Christian advocates and theologians.[32] Tertullian (160?–?230 CE), a trained lawyer and famous Christian polemicist, presented his exhortative *Apologia* in 197 CE. Minucius Felix (fl. third century) wrote *Octavius,* which is considered the earliest Christian dialogue written in Latin. The Carthaginian Origen (185?–?254 CE) melded Neoplatonism and Stoicism with his Christian faith. His theological methodology, which applied and synthesized philosophy with scripture, exemplified "scholasticism." Church prelates eventually declared Origen's writings heretical. Marius Victorinus (fl. fourth century), an important grammarian, Neoplatonist, and eventual Christian convert, influenced Augustine. Lactantius (fl. fourth century), another Christian convert, tutored Crispus, Emperor Constantine's son. The Jewish scholastic Philo (20 BCE?–?50 CE) from Alexandria infused Platonic thought in his studies of the Hebrew Bible and Judaism.

Roman Egypt became a Christian fountainhead. According to Christian tradition, Mark the Evangelist preached and proselytized in Alexandria. Anthony (Antony) (250?–?350) rejected materialism and secular life and sought solitude in the desert. His eremitism inspired monasticism. In the early fourth century, Arius questioned the unity of the Trinity, which led to Christianity's most widespread heresy, Arianism. Athanasius, the patriarch of Alexandria, opposed Arian's position. The patriarch's staunch doctrinal defense and prolific writings earned him great esteem within the Church.

Remarkable women played important roles in Egypt's Christianization. Amma Sycletica was born in Alexandria in 380. Attractive, well educated, and wealthy, she chose the life of an ascetic. Her writings anticipated those of the seventh century John Climacus, a monk living in the Sinai, the author of *The Ladder of Divine Ascent,* one of the most important works of the Eastern Orthodox Church. Mary of Egypt, a courtesan of the fifth century, journeyed to Jerusalem and reportedly became temporarily disabled before entering the Church of the Holy Sepulcher. In repentance for her sinful past, she lived in solitude and sanctity, earning her respect, reverence, and sainthood.

Although Christians distinguished themselves through their convictions and sacrifices, they also destroyed pagan temples and sculptures or converted temples to churches.[33] Hostilities between Christians and pagans especially intensified in Alexandria. Patriarch Theophilos of Alexandria ordered the destruction of the Serapeum in 391, one of the most revered Hellenistic temples, which also housed a famous library. In addition, Christian extremists perpetrated an especially heinous crime in 415—the murder of Hypatia of Alexandria, a brilliant pagan philosopher, scientist, and teacher. Usually interpreted as an illustration of barbaric religious fanaticism and intolerance for humanistic inquiry, her murder also related to tempestuous local politics. Hypatia's prominence in Alexandrian society, specifically her perceived support of state over church (governor over patriarch), incited this atrocity. Beyond religious issues, Hypatia's elevated social status also represented a threat to dominant patriarchy. Christian writers later deplored her murder (see Dzielska 1995). A century earlier another gifted intellectual, a Christian rhetorician from Alexandria named Catherine, suffered a torturous death, this time at the hands of pagans. Christians subsequently glorified Catherine's martyrdom and sainthood.

By the middle of the fifth century, North African and Western civilization had shifted socially and culturally. Christians patronized or joined thousands of monasteries, notably beginning with the inaugural and exemplary endeavor of Pachomius, who established his first monastery along the Nile in the early fourth century. He also established communal rules. The monastery of St. Catherine in the Sinai, founded in the sixth century, became the repository of some of the earliest and most brilliant Christian iconography and illuminated manuscripts extant.[34] Churches, such as that of St. Maenas near Alexandria, became important social as well as religious centers.

Besides Arianism, which the Council of Nicaea addressed and rejected in 325, Monophysitism also attracted Egyptian Christians. Monophysitism emphasized Jesus Christ's divine rather than human nature. This spiritual movement also had important secular consequences. It not only remonstrated against the established Church, but also represented Egyptian resentment against the political, economic, cultural, and social privileges enjoyed by the Greeks since Alexander the Great's arrival in 332 BCE. The Council of Chalcedon in 451 condemned the Monophysites as heretics and the Byzantines (see below) carried out punishments. The split between the established Orthodox/Catholic and Monophysite/Coptic churches (the latter being perhaps the first "protestant" church) also led to the gradual replacement of Greek with Coptic as the ecclesiastical language of the Egyptian church.

Concurrently, Donatism appeared in the Maghrib, which scrutinized the sanctity, virtue, and dedication of church leaders. Named after Donatus, a bishop of Numidia, the Donatists insisted on the sinlessness of priests. They denounced clerics who compromised their faith during persecutions (notably that of Diocletian from 303 to 305 [see Frend 2004, 260–261]). The Church's opposition to the Donatists and their most fervent advocates, the Circumcelliones, gave Donatism an anti-establishment character.[35] The aforementioned rebellions of Firmus and Gildo received substantial Donatist support.

Arianism and Donatism arose as the Roman Empire endured yet another civil war, which ended Emperor Diocletian's tetrarchy.[36] Constantine eventually reunited the empire in 324. His Christian proclivities resulted in his sponsoring the Edict of Milan, which provided religious (read Christian) toleration in 313. Constantine's championing of Christianity, his chairing the Council of Nicaea, his founding of a Christian capital at Constantinople, and his deathbed conversion to the religion had momentous consequences. It illustrated how the Roman state identified with Christianity. Constantine's reign marked a decisive point in the history of Western civilization. As Bernard Lewis perceived: "The conversion of Constantine in the early fourth century and the establishment of Christianity as the state religion [by the end of that century] initiated a double change; the Christianization of Rome and—some would add—the Romanization of Christ" (Lewis 2002, 98).

Augustine (354–430 CE), a native of Tagaste (Souk-Ahras) in eastern Algeria, became one of the greatest figures in the history of the Church. He graphically detailed the tortuous existential and spiritual journey resulting in his conversion to Christianity in *Confessions,* one of the most remarkable autobiographies ever written. Augustine takes the reader through the spiritual and religious ferment of the late empire. According to Christine Mohrmann: "The essence of [*Confessions*] as a literary work of art is that [it is] at the same time historical narrative and meditation" (Mohrmann 1961, 381). Peter Brown admired Augustine's syncretism: "*Confessions,* a unique history of the heart, showed the Latin language caught alight in a man whose sensibility could combine, with equal mastery, Vergil, Plotinus and the rhythms of the Psalms" (Brown 1971, 118). After his conversion and baptism in Milan in 387 by Ambrose (340–397 CE), the ardent preacher and prelate, Augustine returned to North Africa and became the bishop of Hippo Regius (Annaba). His prolific writings included *City of God,* which presents a providential, Christian phi-losophy of history.[37] *City of God* responded to the shocking pillage of Rome in 410 by the Visigoths, a Germanic tribe. He claimed that Rome's pagan materi-alism led to the catastrophe. Augustine's writings also challenged the Dona-tists and the Council of Carthage in 411 denounced them as heretics.[38]

The Arrival of the Vandals and the Byzantines' Restoration of "Roman" Power

Augustine died in 430 as the Vandals, a Germanic tribe, laid siege to Hippo. The Vandals numbered among the Germanic invaders of the Western Roman Empire.[39] Instead of following the usual route through Italy to Rome, they by-passed the peninsula and headed southwest, reaching Spain in 409. Under the enterprising King Gaiseric, the Vandals crossed from Spain to North Af-rica with approximately 50,000 to 80,000 followers in 429 (Pohl 2004, 38–39). They captured Hippo Regius one year after Augustine's death. Carthage fell several years later.

The Vandals were adventuresome and audacious. Furthermore, like oth-er foreign invaders, they demonstrated transcultural sensibility regarding the Berbers. Consequently, Berber allies expedited the extension of Vandal authority into the North African hinterland. Once established in North Af-rica, the Vandals built a formidable fleet, manned significantly by Berbers, which dominated the western Mediterranean and led to their occupation of Sardinia, Corsica, Sicily, and the Balearic Islands. Led by Gaiseric, the Van-dals pillaged Rome for two weeks in 455, "a more thorough assault than that of Alaric's Goths" (Pohl 2004, 40). The Eastern Roman or Byzantine Empire repeatedly tried to expel the Vandals from North Africa but failed.[40] From the Byzantine perspective, the Vandals' adherence to Arianism, tolerance of Don-atism, and persecution of the official Church exacerbated the embarrassment of a barbarian presence in "Roman" North Africa.

The Vandals' notorious reputation needs revision. "Vandalism" is a term that dates from the late eighteenth century. Arguably, the Vandals were no more destructive than other barbarian invaders and committed less damage. For example, the plunder of Rome, whereby an enormous amount of loot and treasure was collected and carried off to North Africa, was systematic rather than anarchic. The Vandals also became Romanized like their fellow German tribes across the Mediterranean, and displayed impressive sophistication. According to Judith W. George: "North Africa under the Vandals . . . provided a rich cultural context for poets and poetry. . . . The indirect evidence of the poems . . . suggests that the vigorous cultural life of Roman North Africa continued. It had perhaps been slowed or redirected by the Vandal presence, but there was continuity" (George 2004, 143). Although the sixth century Byzantine historian Procopius portrayed the Vandals as "luxurious" and decadent, a more careful reading illustrates that these "barbarians" possessed refinement and wealth:

> The Vandals, since the time when they gained possession of Libya, used to indulge in baths, all of them, every day, and enjoyed a table abounding in all things, the sweetest and best that the earth and sea produce. And they wore gold very generally, and clothed themselves in the Medic garments, which now they call "serie" [silk], and passed their time, thus dressed, in theatres and hippodromes and in other pleasurable pursuits, and above all else in hunting. And they had dancers and mimes and all other things to hear and see which are of a musical nature or otherwise merit attention among men. (Procopius 1953, 257)

Nevertheless, the Byzantines viewed the Vandals as an affront to their political, cultural, and historical sensibility. As Charles Diehl pointed out: "The emperors never abandoned hope to retake the lost [North African] province" (Diehl 1966, 1:3). Procopius reiterated (and overstated): "The Libyans had been Romans in earlier times and had come under the Vandals by no will of their own and had suffered many outrages at the hands of the barbarians. For this reason the emperor [Justinian] had entered into war with the Vandals" (Procopius 1953, 175). One of the greatest emperors of Byzantium, the relentless Justinian (r. 527–565), aimed to restore Roman power to the Mediterranean.

Dispatching the very capable Belisarius in 533, Byzantine forces overwhelmed the Vandals. Procopius, serving as Belisarius's secretary, accompanied the campaign. While undeniably biased toward Belisarius, he describes a general with transcultural sensitivity reminiscent of Hannibal and Caesar. Belisarius effectively commanded an army composed of diverse nationalities, including fierce "Hunnic" troops.[41] In 534, the Byzantines eliminated remaining Vandal resistance, captured King Gelimer, and dispatched him to a comfortable retirement in Anatolia. The Byzantines established themselves along the littoral and the immediate hinterland, especially under the rule of the governor Solomon, who fell in 543 while battling Berbers in the mountainous Aurès region of Algeria (Procopius 1953, 397–401). Some Byzantine fortifications still stand in North Africa.[42]

Constantly overtaxed and chronically rebellious, the "hardy" (Procopius's description) Berbers challenged the tenuous Byzantine presence. Byzantine diplomacy and military operations struggled to secure the cooperation of tribes. The Byzantines built churches and monasteries, and missionaries proselytized Berber tribes (see Diehl 1966, 2:527–528; Frend 2004, 265). Nevertheless, Donatism persisted, resulting in persecution, which deepened Berber resentment.

Carthage throve under Byzantine rule as a commercial hub linking North Africa with Sicily and Egypt. Along with Alexandria, the city also strategically served as an important naval base. Furthermore, North Africa resumed its role as an important imperial granary supplying Constantinople, as it had Rome. As Charles Diehl underscored, the Byzantines persevered, despite their often corrupt and rapacious administration, and prolonged the Roman achievement (Diehl 1966, 2:594–595).[43]

Emperor Maurice's (Maurikios) murder in 602 provoked Heraclius (Herakleios), the powerful exarch or governor in North Africa. He sent his son, also named Heraclius, to mobilize North Africa against the new Emperor Phocas (Phokas). The Byzantines' North African provinces' revolt succeeded in overthrowing the emperor in Constantinople, in part by preventing shipments of grain from Egypt. The younger Heraclius became emperor in 610. He subsequently led the Byzantines in an arduous number of campaigns against the Sasanid Persians. At one point, as Persians and Avars besieged Constantinople, Heraclius considered relocating the Byzantine capital in Carthage. During the course of this epic struggle, the Sasanids also overran Egypt beginning in 617 and remained until 629. Nevertheless, Heraclius rallied the empire to victory by 630, but the emperor could not savor his hard-fought, exhausting success. In that same year, the Prophet Muhammad entered Mecca in triumph and destroyed the idols of the Ka'aba. Islam galvanized its strength and the source of that power emanated from an extraordinary, transcendent "Message."

Conclusion

Although Rome's political authority and cultural influence did not reach far into the North African hinterland, its achievements, still observed in its ruined cities, remain awe inspiring. North Africa contributed substantially to Rome's greatness, especially its economic wealth, ranging from the commerce of the Erythraean Sea to the granaries of the Maghrib's coastal plains. Furthermore, North African Romanized subjects and citizens distinguished this period, especially during the Pax Romana.

North Africa's conversion to Christianity represented an outstanding example of the transcultural transmission of faith; nonetheless, convictions also became contentious. The emergence of Arianism, Monophysitism, and Donatism fragmented North African Christianity and subsequently weakened the Roman and Byzantine empires. In his studies, Malik Bennabi asserted that religion underpinned civilization. During this period, Christianity's divisions and chronic disputes, however, fractured the social and cultural cohesion (or to apply Ibn Khaldun, *asabiyya*) that had bonded the pagan past and, as we shall see, enhanced and expedited the Islamic future. Islam would have its sects and its "heresies," but it set a strong foundation for a new unified North African civilization, which would be transcultural, tolerant, and transformative.

CHAPTER 3

Medieval North Africa

From the Arrival of Islam to the Berber Empires

During the period of late antiquity, North Africa and Europe underwent similar historical experiences. Europe endured invasions by Germans and Slavs who grafted their identities on a Christian Greco-Roman civilization. As discussed in the last chapter, the Germanic Vandals arrived and settled in North Africa and from there controlled the western Mediterranean's sea lanes for a century. Compared to their tribal kinsmen's significance in the development of Europe, the Vandals' ephemeral presence hardly left an imprint upon the identity and development of North Africa. With the subsequent resumption of Roman or Byzantine rule in North Africa, Spain, and Italy, the traditional currents of Mediterranean and North African politics, society, and economy seemingly returned. This was an illusion, since Byzantine power in North Africa never matched that of the Roman Empire.

The irruptive Arabs then overran North Africa, which resulted in a historic disruption and discontinuity. They also introduced an appealing new religion, Islam. Although the Egyptians and substantial numbers of Berbers were highly cultivated and participated in centuries-old civilizations, the Arabs confronted a different political and social situation in North Africa compared with that of sophisticated West Asia. As observed in Chapter 2, many North Africans, especially in the Maghrib, shunned sedentary living, remained on the periphery of "civilized" life, and retained their tribal and nomadic way of life. The transmission and transaction of Islam among the peoples of North Africa and the melding of Arabs and Berbers mark two of the most profound transcultural events in the history of North Africa and Western civilization.

Islam transformed North Africa. Muslims, meaning those who submit to the will of God and profess Islam, also embarked from North Africa and settled in Spain, southern France, and Sicily. As Europe synthesized Roman and Germanic cultures, developing a new civilization, a powerful syncretic Islam-

ic civilization concurrently emerged with its Umayyad and Abbasid caliphates and corollary emirates. North Africa played an integral role in launching
and widening Islam's temporal and spiritual authority. The autonomous and
independent states that appeared in North Africa added their luster to a collective brilliant Muslim civilization, which is belatedly beginning to receive
greater attention in Western civilization textbooks (see Peters 1972).

Islam: Submission to the Will of God

In 610, a successful businessman named Muhammad was told to "recite."
That "message," believed to have been delivered by the Angel Gabriel, occurred on Mount Hira near Mecca, a cosmopolitan city located in the Hijaz,
the western coast and hinterland of Arabia. Muhammad continued to receive
revelation, which led to the third great monotheistic and Abrahamic religion
to emerge from Western civilization, Islam.[1]

Islam is very similar to Judaism and Christianity. The faith's fundamental
doctrine (*iman*) is the belief in one God (Allah means "The God"), who is the
same as Yahweh of the Jews and God the Father of the Christians, and His An-
gels. Muhammad is a "messenger" (*rasul*), since he provided revelation, and
is the last or "seal" of a line of prophets, who include Moses and Jesus (who are
also regarded as messengers). The Qur'an, meaning the recitation, comprises
Muhammad's revelation of the word (*kalam*) of God. To Muslims, the Qur'an
represents the final revelation of God. About the length of the Christian New
Testament, the Qur'an includes familiar stories, such as that of Noah, Joseph,
Moses, and Jesus (especially parallels with the Book of Matthew; see Hitti 1970,
125–126). The Qur'an, also known as "The Book" (*al-kitab*), does not dismiss
previous revelation but clarifies and corrects it. God is presented as supreme
and merciful. Every chapter or sura (there are 114) begins with the words: "In
the name of God, the Compassionate, the Merciful." Islam is strictly monotheistic and admonishes any partnership or association of another deity or
person with God (the sin of polytheism or *shirk*). For example, to Muslims the
idea of the Holy Trinity is an alien concept, as well as the notion of Jesus as
the "Son of God." Jesus and Mary are, however, profoundly respected. The former is esteemed as a messenger and prophet and the latter is not only deeply
admired, but also mentioned more in the Qur'an than in the New Testament.
The Qur'an also includes the belief in a "Last Day" or "Judgment" as well as

a bodily resurrection. There is no "original sin" in Islam. While the Qur'an prescribes personal and public social behavior and ethical morality as well as diet proscriptions against pork and alcohol, and is renowned for its simplicity and practicality, it is also profoundly mystical, as exemplified by the lyrical beauty of God's mystical light ([Sura]24:[*ayat*/verse] 35–36).[2] Ibn Khaldun reflected: "Our Prophet wrought no greater miracle than the Qur'an and the fact that he united the Arabs in his mission" (Ibn Khaldun 1967, 1:193).

Five principles, duties (*ibadat*), or "pillars" (*arkan*) explicate Muhammad's message:

1. *Shahada*: A Muslim believes that there is no god but God and Muhammad is his messenger. This is the testimony of faith.
2. *Salat*: A Muslim must pray five times a day (sunrise, noon, mid-afternoon, sunset, evening). The prayer is the *fatiha,* the first sura in the Qur'an (the recitation).
3. *Zakat:* A Muslim must be charitable and be generous toward others. This could mean providing for religious foundations and charities or simply offering food and drink to someone.
4. *Sawm*: A Muslim must fast during the daylight hours of Ramadan, the ninth month of the Islamic (lunar) calendar. This holy month should include spiritual reflection and meditation.
5. Hajj: If possible, a Muslim should make a pilgrimage to Mecca and perform rituals relating to Muhammad's life and message. By uniting believers from the Muslim world, the hajj reinforces Islam's universality.

The idea of jihad, or struggle or exertion or "holy war," is occasionally termed a "sixth pillar." There is an obligation for Muslims to defend their religion. The Prophet Muhammad distinguished between the "lesser" and the "greater" jihad. The former being an external defensive struggle against the enemies of Islam and the latter an internal struggle to become a better Muslim or, as Seyyid Hossein Nasr explains, "to battle the negative tendencies within the soul, tendencies that prevent us from living a life of sanctity and reaching the perfection God has meant for us" (Nasr 2003, 34).

Muhammad's preaching failed to appeal to the people of Mecca. Nevertheless, he had important supporters, including his wife, Khadija (d. 619), his cousin and son-in-law Ali bn Abi Talib, and his best friend, Abu Bakr. Two other converts and future caliphs, Umar bn al-Khattab and Uthman bn Affan, joined the believers. Forced to emigrate from Mecca in 622, an event known as the Hijra, Muhammad and his companions were welcomed by the citizenry of Yathrib, a city to the north of Mecca.[3] Yathrib became known as Medina (Madina), the city of the Prophet. The Medinans embraced the Five Pillars as well as other doctrinal beliefs. Indeed, Islam asserted the equality of all believers no matter their ethnic or social background. Muhammad's revelations, which continued in Medina, not only provided a guide for individual salvation, but also a social project for the organization of the *umma,* the community or totality of believers. For example, Islam significantly elevated the status of women and orphans. In particular, Islam gave women property rights, which their European sisters attained only in the nineteenth century (Esposito 2005, 95).[4]

Muhammad had hoped that Arab Jewish tribes would accept his revelation, but they did not. Jews questioned Muhammad as a prophet and Christians objected to the Muslim denial of Jesus Christ's divinity as the "Son of God" and the Trinity. Nevertheless, Muslims recognized Jews and Christians as "People of the book" and thereby *dhimmi*s or protected ones.[5] Eventually, Muslims expelled Jews from Medina, less for their religious beliefs than for their political activities, specifically their collaboration with Mecca. It must be immediately noted that Jews significantly contributed to Muslim society and history and usually lived under much more tolerant conditions compared to their coreligionists in Christian Europe. In addition, Christians under Muslim rule customarily received respectful religious acceptance and accommodation. Although generally protected, *dhimmi*s confronted discriminatory taxation and occasional persecution (see below). Despite their common second-class status, Jews and Christians still had opportunities to acquire high social, economic, and political influence and position.

Seyyid Hossein Nasr wrote that "Islam is both a religion and civilization. . . . It is also a spiritual and metahistorical reality that has transformed the inner and outer life of numerous human beings in very different temporal and spatial circumstances" (Nasr 2003, xi). Ibn Khaldun, Malik Bennabi, and Jacques Berque, among so many others, subscribed to Nasr's statement and especially studied in depth the development, the dynamism, and, for that matter, the degeneration of Islamic civilization. They especially recognized the historical significance of North Africa's contributions to the *Dar al-Islam,* the house or abode of Islam, and to Western civilization. Thus, Islam introduced not only a third Abrahamic religion, but also a vital civilization.

The Rightly Guided Caliphs

By 630, Muslim Medina dominated Mecca. Muhammad entered the city and destroyed the idols in the Ka'aba, but preserved the sacred "black stone" or meteorite, a symbolic illustration of God's ineffable omnipotence.[6] Two years later, the Prophet died, leaving the *umma* leaderless. Abu Bakr, who had taken over as prayer leader for the ailing Muhammad, succeeded the Prophet as *khalifa* or caliph, a word meaning successor or deputy.

During his brief caliphate, Abu Bakr (r. 632–634) quelled revolt and secured the *umma* in Arabia. Umar bn al-Khattab (r. 634–644) succeeded Abu Bakr and ordered Muslim armies, inspired by shared spiritual and secular interests, northward against Byzantine and Sasanid forces exhausted after their latest series of wars. The Arabs acquired Palestine and Syria after defeating the Byzantines in 636.[7] A year later, they overwhelmed the Sasanids, opening Iraq and Iran to Islam. Amr ibn al-'As invaded Byzantine Egypt in 639. According to Walter Kaegi, the Muslim invasion occurred at a "propitious" moment given divisive succession issues within the Byzantine Empire (Kaegi 1998, 54). Weakened also by internal dissent between Orthodox and Monophysite Christians, and, in general, Byzantine exploitation, the Muslims finally took over Egypt in 642—a devastating loss for Constantinople. The Byzantines regained Alexandria in 645 but were repulsed in early 646. The local Egyptians' response to the Muslims varied. Although the Monophysites regarded Islam as heretical, the Muslims' promise of religious freedom appealed to them.[8] Furthermore, Egyptians appreciated Amr's political and social sensibilities, prohibiting, for example, the looting of the country.[9] Serving again in its geographic role of hinging Africa to West Asia, Egypt became the Arabs' base for launching forays westward along the North African littoral. The Arabs occupied Cyrenaica in 642 and entered Tripolitania in 643. During their conquests, the Arabs built separate cities for themselves, such as Fustat in Egypt and later Qayrawan in Tunisia.[10] This shrewd urban strategy kept Arab strength concentrated, but it also allowed judicious adjustment to a wider world. Despite their nomadic tradition, Arabs adapted quickly to sedentary life.

By the time of Umar's death (assassinated by an unbalanced man), the *umma* had become an empire. Under Uthman bn Affan (r. 644–656), a member of the powerful Umayyad family and another of the Prophet's companions, the empire continued to expand and consolidate its holdings. Significantly, a standardized version of the Qur'an emerged at this time. After rebels murdered Uthman, Ali, the first cousin and son-in-law of the Prophet Muhammad, became caliph.

Ali's controversial reign (656–661) remains very consequential. His personality either inspired respect, even reverence, or incited rebellion. The *umma* suffered its first *fitna,* meaning trial or strife, resulting in civil war partly caused by Aisha, the daughter of Abu Bakr and youngest wife of the Prophet, whom Ali had implicitly accused of infidelity. Ali successfully suppressed this rebellion. A greater problem loomed when Mu'awiya, the governor of Syria and an Umayyad, contended that Ali had conspired against Uthman. Mu'awiya mounted a momentous revolt against the caliph. At the battle of Siffin in 657, with his forces weakening, Mu'awiya ordered that pages of the Qur'an be torn and affixed on weapons as a request for arbitration. Ali's acceptance infuriated many of his followers who wanted God to decide the battle. They subsequently seceded from the caliph and viewed him as an apostate. These seceders became known as the Khariji(tes) (*kharaja* means to leave or secede). Although the caliph persecuted and scored military success against them, the Khariji assassinated the caliph. The Khariji would later play a crucial role in the political development of North Africa.

To Malik Bennabi (see Introduction), the divisive battle of Siffin circumscribed the spiritual phase of Muslim civilization's development. The civilization leveled, albeit at a high plane, and entered the rational stage, which lasted until the death of the great polymath, Ibn Khaldun (1332–1406), who will be discussed in further detail in Chapter 4.

The Umayyad Dynasty (661–750) and Arab Expansion into the Maghrib

Mu'awiya succeeded Ali and established a hereditary monarchy known as the Umayyad Caliphate. Arabs dominated the caliphate, although previous administrators, who had served the Byzantines or the Sasanids, often retained their positions. Indeed, impressive toleration toward other religions, although not toward different ethnic groups, distinguished Umayyad conquest and government.[11] An economic consideration also tempered proselytism. Non-Muslims paid the *jizya,* a head tax; conversion cut into revenues. On the other hand, Arabs discriminated against non-Arabs, even if they converted

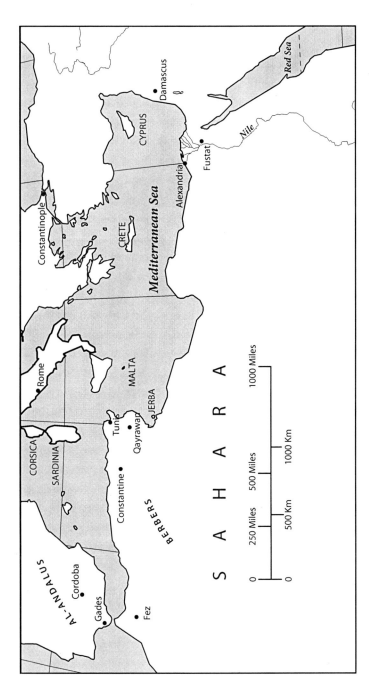

North Africa During the Early Islamic Period

to Islam. Non-Arab converts, known as *mawali,* resented this paradoxical prejudice.

Amr ibn al-'As, the conqueror and governor of Egypt, mounted incursions into Cyrenaica, but his nephew, Uqba bn Nafi, especially distinguished himself in North Africa west of Egypt. Although Arabs had raided the Maghrib beginning in the 640s, Uqba's campaigns aimed to establish a permanent presence. In 669, he took over Tripolitania and founded Qayrawan in Tunisia in 670. This city would serve as the headquarters for Arab westward expansion. He penetrated the interior of Algeria, but he did not possess the resources to secure it. He also entered Fezzan.

According to inconclusive evidence and interpretation, Uqba also led an extraordinary expedition westward, reputedly reaching the Atlantic Ocean. Ibn Idhari's thirteenth century chronicle portrays Uqba as a Muslim hero deeply devoted to the spread of Islam. Apocryphal or not, Ibn Idhari's chronicle provides great drama in its description of the Uqba's intrepid epic: "He rode until he reached the ocean; and he entered it, until the water reached the belly of his horse; and thereupon he lifted his hand to the heavens and said: 'Oh Lord! If it were not for the sea preventing me, I would have advanced [on land] on a path like that of the two-horned [Alexander the Great], defending your faith, fighting those who disbelieve in you!' " (Ibn Idhari 1948–1951, 1:27). Jamil M. Abun-Nasr contended that Uqba attained the Sus in southern Morocco (Abun-Nasr 1987, 30).[12] Charles-André Julien contended that he may have gone as far as central Algeria (Julien 1970, 9–10). What is certain is that Uqba embodied Arab and Muslim conquest and expansion westward and that his ambition alienated Berbers. He displayed a devout but prejudiced personality, especially toward the *mawali,* who believed in the principles of Muslim equality and expected it. Kusayla, a prominent Berber leader and convert, despised Uqba's discrimination. Leading Berbers accompanied by Byzantine allies, Kusayla ambushed Uqba and his small force and killed the Arab commander at Tahuda near Biskra (Algeria) in 680.

Kusayla advanced to Qayrawan and briefly asserted a regional authority, earning him hero status among Berbers. Nonetheless, the Umayyad Caliph Abd al-Malik mobilized an Arab army under the command of Zuhayr bn Qays al-Balawi,[13] which forced Kusayla to withdraw westward. Arab forces subsequently destroyed him in 686. Despite this victory, Berbers and Byzantines continued to assail the Arabs. Hassan bn al-Nu'man received orders to secure the region. He seized and sacked Carthage, forcing the Byzantines to flee to Sicily. He also campaigned against the redoubtable leader of the Jarawa tribe, a woman known as Dihya or al-Kahina (the prophetess), who may have been Jewish. She mobilized Berbers against the Arabs and defeated Hassan, forcing him to evacuate what would be today eastern Algeria and Tunisia. Recuperating from his loss to al-Kahina, Hassan launched a new campaign against her, and she perished in c. 698.[14] Meanwhile, the Byzantines continued to try to recover their lost land. In 697, a Byzantine task force temporarily recaptured Carthage. Nevertheless, the Muslims seized the city a year later.

With the Berbers quelled and the Byzantines expelled, the Arabs organized the territory in what would be today western Libya or Tripolitania, Tunisia, and eastern Algeria.[15] This province would be known as "Ifriqiya." Replacing Hassan bn al-Nu'man, Musa bn Nusayr, ably assisted by Tariq bn Ziyad, his trusted and adventuresome Berber lieutenant, embarked on the conquest of the far west (the *maghrib al-aqsa* or Morocco), eliminating residual Byzantine resistance along the way. Preceding Musa, Tariq embarked for the European peninsula, Iberia (Spain and Portugal) or al-Andalus, the actual land of the Visigoths, although it toponymically refers to the Vandals, "al-Andalish" (possibly "al-Andlish" or "al-Andlis"). He crossed the straits separating North Africa from Europe and reached the promontory massif sited on the European side—commemorated as Gibraltar for "*Jabal* Tariq" (Tariq's mountain). Iberia remained an attractive target for its mineral wealth (namely gold, silver, iron, and copper), which had been exploited since antiquity (see Chapter 1). Politically, internal divisions among the Visigoths had also weakened the increasingly vulnerable Germanic kingdom.

Once in Iberia, Tariq and his troops quickly defeated the Visigoth King Roderic(k) in 711 and amassed a fortune. Mughith al-Rumi, a freedman, captured Cordoba (Cordova). Within a year, Musa, commanding an army of 18,000 soldiers, most of whom were Arabs, joined Tariq and his forces and they jointly continued the conquest by seizing Saragossa. Al-Andalus fell under Muslim control by 713. Musa strategically selected Seville as the capital, which also served as a naval base. Muslims also crossed the Pyrenees and advanced into France. (The Visigothic kingdom included southern France.) In 725, raids reached as far north as Burgundy. Another Muslim foray northward terminated at Tours/Poitiers (Balat al-Shuhada) in 732, when Charles Martel, the mayor (principal minister) of the Frankish kingdom, defeated Abd al-

Rahman al-Ghafiqi.[16] Despite this setback, Muslims remained in France for decades before withdrawing across the Pyrenees.

The extraordinary expansion of the Umayyads also led to problems in North Africa. Animosity intensified between Berbers and Arabs. Berbers, especially those who contributed to Arab success in al-Andalus and elsewhere, demanded the application of Muslim equality. Despite legal prohibitions, Arab administrators imposed taxes and even enslaved Berbers, fellow Muslims, and sent them to the East. The renowned Abbasid historian al-Tabari recounted how Berbers questioned the caliph and Umayyad authority: "They make us give them the most beautiful of our daughters, and we say, 'We have not found this in the Book or in the Sunna [the customs of the Prophet Muhammad (see below)]. We are Muslims and we wish to know: is this with the approval of the Commander of the Faithful or not?'" (Lewis 1974, 2:57–58).[17] The Berbers subsequently revolted and in 741, led by a self-proclaimed "caliph" named Maysara, defeated an Arab force sent from Qayrawan. Although Maysara was eventually killed, the Berber revolt spread into Algeria and al-Andalus. By this time, the caliphate confronted a greater problem in the East.

Rising resistance to the Umayyads rallied around the Abbasids, who claimed kinship to the Prophet Muhammad through an uncle. A growing group of Muslims, known as the *shi'at* Ali (party/partisans of Ali) or Shi'a, supported the Abbasids. The Shi'a revered Ali as a martyr and denounced Mu'awiya and his family as treacherous usurpers. In 680, Ali's son Husayn mistakenly thought that he could take over the caliphate, but the Umayyads destroyed him at Karbala, Iraq. His martyrdom symbolized a defining event in Shi'ism. The Shi'a continued to follow imams, religious leaders related to the family of Ali. From the Shi'i perspective, the imams represented the true leaders of Islam. The Shi'a recognized the hadiths, the written accounts reporting the behavior and customs or Sunna of the Prophet. The recorded actions of the imams, however, also held explicit significance. The vast majority of Muslims, the Sunni, rejected the influence, the authority, and the interpretive privilege exercised by the imams. The Shi'a allied with the Abbasids and the *mawali,* who despised Arab pretentious superiority, such as the proud Persians and the exploited Berbers. In 750, the Abbasids and their allies overwhelmed the Umayyads. One Umayyad prince escaped the carnage, Abd al-Rahman bn Mu'awiya (of the Marwanid branch of the dynasty), who managed to reach al-Andalus and establish his authority there by 756.

The Abbasids (750–1258) Accept a Decentralized Empire

Although the Abbasids assumed the caliphate, their attitude markedly differed from that of the Umayyads. They believed in a Muslim rather than Arab state. Caliph al-Mansur (r. 754–775) transferred the capital to Baghdad, a move that gave the caliphate a more Persian character. The Abbasids' establishing a dynasty, rather than recognizing the spiritual and political legitimacy of imams, embittered the Shi'a. They became determined enemies of the Abbasids. Nevertheless, the *mawali* enjoyed the liberality and opportunity provided by the Abbasids, whose transcultural toleration and patronage resulted in a brilliant constellation of scholars in all fields.[18]

Given the turmoil caused by the Umayyad-Abbasid rivalry, regions of the empire had asserted their independence—for example, the Berbers in Morocco. Abu al-Qasim al-Midrari secured the Saharan entrepôt Sijilmasa and its surrounding area and inaugurated a dynasty that lasted for two hundred years.[19] The empire fragmented, but the Abbasids accepted decentralization as long as they still received tribute and recognition as nominal suzerains. On the other hand, political and communal differences hardly affected commerce. Under the Abbasids, a global commercial network extended from al-Andalus to China. According to a ninth century inventory attributed to al-Jahiz, North Africa especially contributed rare commodities such as "leopards, acacia, felts, and black falcons" (Lewis 1974, 2:154). Nevertheless, during these centuries North Africa developed remarkably diverse and complex economies that supported a variety of states.

The Tulunids (868–905) and Ikhshids (935–969) Rule Egypt

Umayyad and Abbasid caliphal rule in Egypt featured high taxation and restive populations. In 868, the caliph charged a Turkish general, Ahmad ibn (bn) Tulun, with a difficult assignment, governing troublesome Egypt in the name of the Abbasids. Although Ibn Tulun recognized the caliph as his suzerain, he and his descendants, aided by a native Egyptian bureaucracy, ruled autonomously until 905. The Tulunids introverted the economy by exploiting and allocating resources domestically. They encouraged agriculture (especially by irrigation restoration projects) and promoted commerce. Consequently, Egypt reassumed a position of prominence and wealth. Impressive public works arose, such as the Mosque of Ibn Tulun, constructed between 876 and 879, which is one of the most famous in the Islamic world. The mosque covers six and a half acres (Williams 1993, 52). One can easily spot the Iraqi influence (specifically that of Samarra) given the spiraling minaret. In 878 and 879, Ibn Tulun incorporated Syria into his state, which the apprehensive Abbasids regarded technically as an *iqta* or a fief. Ibn Tulun's son Khumarawayh also exercised impressive independent authority. An excellent military commander and astute diplomat, however, Khumarawayh enjoyed extravagance. His recklessness, notably his sumptuous palace,[20] emptied the treasury, leaving his successor powerless, which enabled the Abbasids to reassert direct control.

Once again the Abbasids found it difficult to maintain stability. The caliph ordered another Turk, Muhammad ibn (bn) Tughj(g), eventually known as "the Ikhshid," to govern Egypt.[21] Like Ibn Tulun, Ibn Tughj ruled effectively, reforming the government and eliminating corruption.[22] After securing his position in Egypt, he reestablished control over Syria and also governed the Arabian Holy Sites (Mecca, Medina, and their peripheries). Nevertheless, his sons faced a usurper named Kafur. The subsequent struggles, compounded by low Nile floods and earthquakes, weakened the Ikhshids. In addition, they repulsed repeated attempts by the Shi'i Fatimids to take over Egypt. In 969, Jawhar and his Berber troops finally defeated the Ikhshids, inaugurating a new era and ruling dynasty for Egypt (see below).

The Rustamids (777–909), Idrisids (789–920), and Aghlabids (800–909) in the Maghrib

To understand the importance of the Rustamids, we must return to the seminal battle of Siffin, when Ali agreed to arbitrate with Mu'awiya. The caliph's decision profoundly alienated the Khariji(tes) or seceders (see above). They subsequently assassinated Ali, producing momentous consequences—the inauguration of the Umayyad Caliphate and the rise of Shi'ism. The Kharijis rejected the Umayyads and the Shi'a. Instead, they believed in an elective emirate, meaning that any righteous Muslim could rule the *umma* (and be removed if he did not live up to expectations). Their heterodoxy resulted in persecution as subversives and apostates, but the Kharijis found a home among the independent-minded Berbers of the Maghrib. Robert Hillenbrand observed a historic continuity in that Kharijism "with its ethical intransigence, its concern with authority and legitimacy, and its care to define the respective value of faith and works, has distinct affinities with the Donatist heresy" (Hillenbrand 1976, 43).

Khariji egalitarianism contrasted starkly with Umayyad Arab superiority and offered the Berbers an appealing Islamic alternative. Kharijis elected upright adherents as imams, political and religious leaders. In Algeria, Abd al-Rustam, of Persian ancestry, established an independent Ibadi (a sect of Kharijism) imamate in Tahart, a city that was advantageously located to exploit the Saharan trade.[23] The Rustamids ruled until the tenth century. Tahart became the leading Ibadi/Khariji intellectual and cultural center. Rustamid power extended from central Algeria to Ifriqiya. In the west, another dynasty arose, which would establish a legacy that still lives in Morocco's political culture.

The Abbasids had wide support in the overthrow of the Umayyads, in part because of their prestigious linkage to the family of the Prophet Muhammad. They confronted anyone who claimed similar descent. Idris was a sharif or a descendant of the Prophet Muhammad, but not a Shi'i.[24] His opposition to

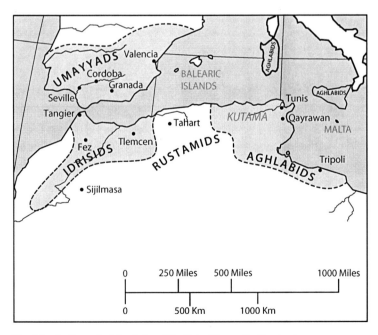

The Maghrib and al-Andalus: Ninth to Eleventh Centuries

the Abbasids forced him to flee to the west. He arrived in Morocco, still reeling from its Berber revolts against the Umayyads. Idris's prestige as a sharif and his engaging personality immediately appealed to the Berbers, especially the Awraba tribe, and a state developed. An Abbasid agent eventually assassinated Idris in 791. Nevertheless, as Ibn Khaldun pointed out, the Abbasids "no longer could . . . aspire to the control of remote regions." The most renowned Abbasid ruler, Caliph Harun al-Rashid (r. 788–814), "had just enough power, and no more, to poison [Idris]" (Ibn Khaldun 1967, 1:49). Idris's Berber concubine, Kanza, gave birth to Idris II (r. 803–828), who is credited with officially founding (or refounding) Fez in 808.[25] The city became an intellectual center and featured the mosque of al-Qarawiyyin, inspired and built by Fatima bint Muhammad al-Fahari, a prominent woman of the mid-ninth century, and political and religious dissidents from Qayrawan (from where the mosque-university received its name). Al-Qarawiyyin claims to be the oldest university extant (Williams 1993, 166). In addition, refugees from strife in Cordoba also settled in Fez and constructed the mosque of al-Andalusiyyin. During the tenth century, Isma'il al-Darras played a prominent role in establishing Malikism in Fez and Morocco.[26] The city's reticulated water supply amazed observers. With Fez strategically poised to take advantage of Saharan, Atlantic, and Mediterranean commerce, Idris and his successors laid the foundation for a sharifian state that continues today.

Restive Ifriqiya forced Caliph Harun al-Rashid to send Ibrahim bn al-Aghlab to restore order and Abbasid rule. Like Ahmad Ibn Tulun, al-Aghlab arranged to have his family rule Ifriqiya as long as the "Aghlabids" recognized Abbasid suzerainty. The Aghlabids faced domestic opposition and revolts. Indeed, Ibrahim fortified an administrative center south of Qayrawan called al-Qasr al-Qadim (also known as al-Abbasiyya). Nevertheless, the Aghlabids also managed to create an extraordinary and expansive state.

The Aghlabids ruled from 800 to 909. In the course of the "Aghlabid century," Ifriqiya prospered and became another renowned cultural center. Qayrawan became the splendid capital including its renowned Aghlabid-built Great Mosque. Not surprisingly, Aghlabid architecture commingled Roman, Byzantine, and Mashriqi (Abbasid) styles (see Hillenbrand 1976, 44). Between 856 and 864, the Aghlabids reconfigured and reconstructed al-Zaytuna in Tunis, one of the most famous mosques in Islamdom.[27] Vast cisterns, veritable lakes, ensured the water supply. The Aghlabids adhered to the Hanafi school of Sunni jurisprudence, but the Maliki school became especially popular in Ifriqiya, through the teachings of Shaykh Abd al-Salam Sahnun (who authored the *Mudawwana,* a digest of Maliki thought) and the prolific writings of Ibn Zayd. The Aghlabids patronized Ibn Rashiq, an important scholar and historian. Bakr bn Hammad al-Tiharti epitomized this transcultural age. A native of Rustamid Tahart, he studied in Qayrawan with Shaykh Sahnun, and then lived in Basra and Baghdad in the Mashriq. He later returned to the Maghrib, earning esteem as a spiritual and secular poet and a religious teacher. Like the Carthaginians, Vandals, and Byzantines before them, the Aghlabids controlled the western Mediterranean. They took over Sardinia, dominated southern Italy, and eventually seized Sicily.

The first raid on Sicily occurred in 652 when Arabs plundered Syracuse. The Aghlabids intervened on the island in 827 as a result of an invitation of a dismissed, vengeful Byzantine governor. Palermo fell in 831 (Messina in 843) and Syracuse in 878. The Aghlabids completed the occupation of the island by 902. Furthermore, they established themselves on the Italian mainland. In 837, they reached Naples, at the request of city's besieged Christian duke, and during the following decade established themselves along the Adriatic at Bari.[28] The Aghlabids reached Rome in 846 and raided its surrounding territory. Pope John VIII (r. 872–882) reportedly paid tribute (Watt 1972, 4). The Fatimids eventually inherited Aghlabid territories (see below).

The resurgent Byzantines invaded southern Italy and drove off the Fatimids, who ruled through a local dynasty known as the Kalbids (948–1040). The end of the Kalbids led to civil strife, which spread through Sicily, consequently weakening the Muslim hold on the island. In the first half of the eleventh century Norman knights under Robert Guiscard seized southern Italy from the Byzantines. His brother Roger invaded Sicily in 1060 and completed the Norman conquest of the island by 1091. The Normans famously admired and adopted Muslim culture. Highly stylized Norman architecture and ornamentation clearly illustrate Mashriqi and Maghribi influences, especially Roger II's Cappella Palatina, an addition to the royal palace in Palermo. Roger II (r. 1127–1154) and his grandson, the Holy Roman Emperor Frederick II (r. 1215–1250), were referred to as "'the two baptized sultans of Sicily'" (Watt 1972, 5; Hitti 1970, 609). Embodying transculturalism, Frederick II also earned the name *stupor mundi* or wonder of the world. He spoke Arabic and his magnificent cosmopolitan court at Palermo astounded Europe and the Mediterranean world.[29] The great geographer al-Idrisi (1100–1166), especially benefited from the patronage of Roger II and his son William I (r. 1154–1166). The Normans later established an ephemeral presence in Ifriqiya by capturing Tripoli in 1146, Mahdiyya, Sousse, and Sfax in 1148, and Annaba, Gabès, and Jerba in 1153, before being weakened by internal revolts and then expelled by the mighty Muwahhidun or Almohads (see Chapter 4). William II (r. 1166–1189) also allied with the Egyptian Fatimids against Saladin.

The Fatimids (909–1171)

The powerful Aghlabid emirate weakened because of poor leadership, Berber restiveness, and especially because of the arrival of a *da'i,* a Shi'i "summoner" or missionary named Abu Abd Allah al-Shi'i. Abu Abd Allah converted the Kutama tribe of eastern Algeria to Shi'ism, in particular, to Isma'ili Shi'ism practiced by the Fatimids.[30] The Fatimids, active in southern Iraq and then Syria, claimed descent from Fatima (Ali's wife), the daughter of the Prophet.

Abu Abd Allah's charge included a complementary political objective—the takeover of the Aghlabid emirate to prepare for the arrival of the Fatimid imam and leader, Ubayd Allah, who dreamed of Shi'i domination of the Maghrib and Mashriq. Abu Abd Allah and the Kutama campaigned relentlessly against the Aghlabids. In 909, Qayrawan fell, terminating the Aghlabid dynasty. This success propagated Isma'ili doctrine throughout the Maghrib, Egypt, and the Mashriq (including the Hijaz). After a series of adventures, reminiscent of Abd al-Rahman and Idris, Ubayd Allah eventually landed in the Maghrib from the Mashriq, but he ended up as a captive of the Midrarids in Sijilmasa.[31] Abu Abd Allah marched westward to free his master. Along the way, his formidable forces confronted and overwhelmed the Rustamids; their emirate/imamate ended in 909.[32] Reaching Sijilmasa, Abu Abd Allah freed Ubayd Allah and the Fatimids took over that city. Ubayd Allah returned to Ifriqiya in triumph. In January 910, he officially proclaimed himself the Mahdi, the rightly guided one or redeemer, and *amir al-mu'minin,* commander of the faithful, a caliphal title.[33] Abu Abd Allah increasingly questioned the Mahdi's prerogatives and pretensions. Along with his brother Abu-l-Abbas and leaders of the Kutama, Abu Abd Allah apparently conspired against Ubayd Allah. The caliph ordered the execution of the faithful Abu Abd Allah and his brother in 911. Paul E. Walker states that Fatimid historiography blamed Abu-l-Abbas for this tragedy: "Such an explanation, while probably the officially approved account of the matter, like the whole incident itself, continues to be puzzling" (Walker 2002, 24).

The Fatimids presented themselves as both imams and caliphs. Their overriding strategy sought to use the Maghrib as a base to take over Egypt and ultimately overthrow the Sunni Abbasid caliphate in Baghdad. Thus, they perceived their political presence in the Maghrib as strategic but provisional. After initial assaults against Egypt failed in 913 and 914, the Fatimids decided to strengthen their position in the Maghrib.[34] They built a more defensible capital called Mahdiyya (in Tunisia), which featured a mosque that served as an architectural model for future Isma'ili designs. Al-Bakri described the new capital as a maritime entrepôt where ships arrived from Alexandria, Sicily, and al-Andalus (al-Bakri 1965, 30/67). They mustered and trained a larger army that impressively campaigned in the west against Berbers, logistically supported by the Umayyads of al-Andalus (see below). Fez fell to Fatimid forces in 921. Thus, the Fatimids created a North African empire that would not be matched until the rise of the Almoravids and Almohads (see Chapter 4). They also secured the Muslim presence in Sicily and launched raids in northern Italy (between Genoa and Pisa) in 934–935 (and resumed from 1004 to 1015) (Walker 2002, 53).[35]

Even with Ibn Hawqal's partiality toward the Fatimids taken into account, the Muslim establishment in Italy impressed observers. Writing in the tenth century, he provided this contemporary description of Fatimid Sicily: "Among the countries in the hands of the Muslims, Sicily, by virtue of its fine situation, may be put in the same class as Spain. . . . In Palermo and [neighboring] Khalisa, together with the quarters outside the walls, there are more than 300 mosques." Regarding the economy in the Palermo-Khalisa region, Ibn Hawqal noted "Persian sugar canes, vegetable gardens, and excellent cucumber fields. Among the fields there are groves full of papyrus, from which scrolls are made. I know of no papyrus in the whole world which can be compared with the papyrus of Egypt, except the papyrus of Sicily. Most of it is plaited into ropes for ships' anchors, and a small part is used to make scrolls" (Lewis 1974, 2:87, 89, 91). Ibn Bassal favorably compared the cotton production of Sicily with that of Spain in the late eleventh century (Lewis 1974, 2:147).

A widespread Khariji revolt in 934, incited and led by Abu Yazid, a rather unimposing but inspiring elderly figure, impeded the Fatimids' Egyptian am-

bitions. Known as "the man on the donkey," Abu Yazid mobilized the Khari-
jis against the despised Fatimids and also received substantial support from
Maliki Sunni, especially their repressed ulama. By 944, the Fatimids' North
African empire had disintegrated. Sheltered by Mahdiyya's fortifications,
Caliph Isma'il al-Mansur rallied his forces and dealt the Kharijis a decisive
defeat in August 947. The Fatimid victory ended Kharijism as a political force.
Subsequently, al-Mansur built a new capital city south of Qayrawan called
Sabra al-Mansuriyya, modeled after Baghdad, which featured impressive cis-
terns. In turn, Sabra al-Mansuriyya later inspired the planning of al-Qahira
or Cairo (see below) (Halm 1997, 13–14). It took decades for the Fatimids to
recover territories in the Maghrib, let alone attempt another assault on Egypt.
Furthermore, the Fatimids also faced another major and constant threat in
al-maghrib al-aqsa, the far west—Umayyad al-Andalus.

Al-Andalus from the Umayyads to the Party Kingdoms

With al-Andalus conquered, Musa bn Nusayr and Tariq were summoned to
Damascus.[36] Musa left the governorship of al-Andalus to his son Abd al-Aziz,
but Caliph Sulayman apparently ordered his assassination (716)—an illustration of the machinating Umayyad court. Al-Andalus then suffered from a lack
of a strong centralized administration. They also suffered setbacks across the
Pyrenees in France. Abd al-Rahman al-Ghafiqi's defeat at Tours/Poitiers in
732 by the Franks did not terminate the Muslim political presence in France.
After returning to Narbonne, the Arabs advanced into Provence. But Martel defeated another Muslim force led by Uqba bn al-Hajjaj in 737. Pepin the
Short, the first Carolingian Frankish monarch, took Narbonne in 751. These
setbacks all but ended the Muslim presence in France, although Muslims
mounted an incursion in the ninth century.

Meanwhile in al-Andalus, ulama secured Malikism by the end of the eighth
century, inaugurating a tradition of exceptional scholarship and jurisprudence.[37] The population readily converted to Islam, in part to take advantage of its civil and economic privileges.[38] Al-Andalus's population became a
unique transcultural amalgam of Muslims, Christians, and Jews, who, in general, peacefully coexisted—an exceptional social situation called *convivencia.*
The Christians, known as "Mozarebs" or "Arabizers," found Muslim secular
culture very appealing. Jews played their familiar prominent roles in expedit-

ing commerce with Europe, North Africa, and West Asia. Their transcultural aptitude also led to important political appointments among Muslims and Christians. Jews also played an important part in al-Andalus's cultural life. Other important populations included Berbers, principally from Morocco, who became Arabized; immigrants from the Mashriq, notably Syrian Arabs; and Sudanic (West African) blacks, originally imported as slaves. Furthermore, campaigns against Europeans resulted in the Muslim capture of Germans and Slavs, adding yet another population to the social diversity of al-Andalus. In the far north in Galicia and Asturias, however, Christians proclaimed at Pelaya their resistance, thus initiating the *Reconquista,* or reconquest of the Iberian Peninsula. The *Reconquista,* an enduring "Crusade," took 750 years to attain its objective. Its success against the Muslims contrasted with the "Crusades" pursued in the Mashriq's "Holy Land," Egypt, and Ifriqiya.

The arrival of Abd al-Rahman bn Mu'awiya inaugurated a glorious period for al-Andalus. His rule as emir necessitated protecting his throne, especially against relatives who arrived in al-Andalus from the Abbasid-controlled Mashriq. He also survived an incursion by Charlemagne (r. 768–814), the powerful Frankish king, whose campaign meant to convince the Muslims of his strength—an exercise of power politics rather than "crusading" (see Buckler 1931). He eventually established a buffer known as the Spanish March south of the Pyrenees.[39] Abd al-Rahman started the construction of a huge mosque in Cordoba, his capital on the Guadalquivir River destined to be Western Europe's greatest city for centuries. Cordoba grew as a cosmopolis, a city of the world that throve on transcultural relations. Fernand Braudel considered Cordoba "the center of learning for all Spain, and the entire Western world" (Braudel 1972–1973, 1:83). Concurrently, Seville developed as a Mediterranean emporium.

After Abd al-Rahman's death in 788, the Umayyad emirate suffered from succession problems, which allowed the Christian states to strengthen in the north. Besides threats from the Spanish Christians and also the Franks, Abd al-Rahman II (r. 822–852) faced marauding Vikings but repelled them. The emir also ordered his army to campaign in the Frankish-held Spanish March and Cerdagne along the Pyrenees. He also suppressed a Mozareb insurrection in Cordoba. Abd al-Rahman II and Emperor Theophilos of the Byzantine Empire cultivated close relations. Theophilos aspired to create an alliance against the Abbasids.

With the emirate stabilized, Abd al-Rahman II no longer feared Abbasid plots. He encouraged cultural infusions from the Mashriq, highlighted by the arrival of the musician Ziryab (Zaryab) from Iraq. As a boy, Ziryab performed in Harun al-Rashid's court. He subsequently lived in Cordoba from 822 to 857. Thus, al-Andalus became inextricably linked to the great syncretic trans-cultural Muslim civilization that fused Greek, Persian, Indian, and Egyptian influences. Indeed, the Umayyads' Great Mosque at Cordoba featured Byzantine glass mosaics (Parker 1981, 14) as well as Roman and Visigothic influences. Abd al-Rahman II enlarged the mosque given Cordoba's growing population.[40] Imported Mashriqi agronomy also aided the development of Andalusian agriculture (Hourani 1991a, 42). After Abd al-Rahman II's death, the Umayyads resumed civil strife, especially over the chronic issue involving the emirate's succession.

Abd al-Rahman III (r. 912–961) was the greatest European ruler of his time and arguably of his century.[41] He asserted Cordoba's authority over the northern Christian states and forced them to pay tribute. He also addressed the Fatimid threat in the Maghrib by occupying Ceuta and by allying with Zanata Berbers, who served as Umayyad political and military proxies. Umayyad intervention in the Maghrib diffused Andalusian ideas and practices, especially in Morocco, an important transcultural interaction. The Umayyad and Fatimid fleets also indecisively engaged in 955 and 956.[42] Abd al-Rahman amassed enough power to proclaim himself commander of the faithful (*amir al-mu'minin*), a caliphal title; thus, the emirate became a caliphate. Signaling his heightened power and influence, Abd al-Rahman III ordered the construction of an administrative capital, actually a palace complex known as the Madinat al-Zahra. Though it was sacked repeatedly in the eleventh century, its ruins still reveal exquisite uses of stone, marble, and brick. Geometric patterns also illustrate Byzantine artistic influence.

Al-Hakim (r. 961–976), the son of Abd al-Rahman III, continued his father's policies. His library reputedly held 400,000 books.[43] The powerful commander Muhammad bn Abi Amar, known as al-Mansur (the victorious), protected and defended Hisham II (r. 976–1009) before the caliph reached maturity. The caliph, with al-Mansur's supervision, extended Cordoba's Great Mosque. He requested and received Byzantine mosaic artists. The additional vaulting also indicated Abbasid as well as Byzantine architectural influences. By 1031, Umayyad power disintegrated and numerous independent Muslim states arose, known as the Party Kingdoms (*Muluk al-Tawa'if* or Party Kings). Internecine rivalries wracked and weakened these states. Christians took advantage of Muslim vulnerability, highlighted by King Alfonso VI of Castile's capture of Toledo in 1085.[44] Despite their turbulent political condition, Muslim party states admirably contributed to Andalusian intellectual achievement.

Medicine, literature, and poetry flourished in al-Andalus. The renowned surgeon from Cordoba, Abu-l-Qasim al-Zahrawi, bridged the ninth and tenth centuries. Muhsin Mahdi compares Sa'id's (?–1040) *Classes of Nations* with al-Biruni's *India*. As for Ibn Hayyan (987?–1076), "one of the greatest political historians of all time," Mahdi claims that "his pensive, melancholy, and apocalyptic account of the fall of Cordova, in his understanding of the psychology of the rulers and the masses, and in his analysis of the causes of the decline of Muslim Spain . . . remains unexcelled among Muslim historians" (Mahdi 1964, 143–144). Ibn Abd Rabbih (860–940), a renowned poet, compiled *al-'Iqd al-Farid* (The Unique Necklace), an encyclopedic compendium of knowledge. Ibn Hazm (994–1064), an Umayyad partisan and a polymath, possessed one of the greatest intellects in Islamdom and Western civilization. Renowned in what we may call psychological, linguistic, and religious studies, Ibn Hazm studied Aristotelian philosophy and logic. His interests included jurisprudence, literature, and historiography. He authored *Tawq al-Hamama* (The Necklace of the Dove) and the *Fisal,* a history of religions.[45] Ibn Hazm's poetry influenced the development of courtly love in France. Consider the imagery in his poem, "My Beloved Comes":

> You came to be just before
> the Christians rang their bells.
> The half-moon was rising
> looking like an old man's eyebrow
> or a delicate instep.
>
> And although it was still night,
> when you came, a rainbow
> gleamed on the horizon,
> showing as many colors
> as a peacock's tail.
> (Franzen 1989, 2)

Ibn Zaydun (1003–1071), a contemporary of Ibn Hazm's, also exemplified Andalusian poetic sensibility.

In the sciences, Maslama al-Majriti, Ibn al-Samh, and Ibn al-Saffar flourished as mathematicians/astronomers in the late tenth and first half of the eleventh centuries. These Muslim Europeans represent a fraction of a plethora of outstanding Andalusian scholars, writers, and poets. The current of this "information flow" accelerated in the twelfth century (see Chapter 4). Furthermore, the commercial network that developed between the Maghrib and the Mashriq expedited the exchange of works. Intellectual exchange regularly occurred.[46] Increased contacts also included technological transfers, such as the manufacture of paper. With Spain and, to a lesser degree, Sicily as conduits, the advanced sophistication of Islamdom diffused throughout Europe. *Convivencia* expedited transcultural transmissions, which valued difference and diversity.

The era of *convivencia* represented one of the greatest transcultural moments in the history of Western civilization; it also cohered the Umayyad state. While Ibn Khaldun reserved *asabiyya* for single tribes or groups, *convivencia* disclosed a "group feeling" shared by diverse groups.[47] A fascinating illustration of *convivencia* occurred during the reign of Abd al-Rahman III. The Christian King Sancho the Fat of Castile (r. 955–967), deposed because of his obesity, sought medicinal help from Cordoba, a medical center. Abd al-Rahman ordered his best doctor, a Jew named Hasdai ben Shaprut, who also served as his foreign affairs minister, to help the king. Nevill Barbour recounted: "Sancho recovered both his figure and his throne; but it also proved expensive, since he had to hand over several frontier fortresses in payment" (Barbour 1959, 21). Gerbert of Aurillac, who became Pope Sylvester II (r. 999–1003), reputedly studied math with Muslims in al-Andalus (ibid., 21–22). The eighteenth century historian Ahmad bn Muhammad al-Maqqari (al-Makkari) quoted Ibn Ghalib's transcultural characterization of the Andalusians:

> Andalusians . . . are Arabs by descent, in pride, in the haughtiness of their
> temper, the elevation of their minds, the goodness of their heart, and the purity
> of their intentions. . . . They are Indians in their love of learning, as well as in
> their assiduous cultivation of science, their firm adherence to its principles,
> and the scrupulous attention with which they transmit down to their posterity
> its invaluable secrets. . . . They are Turks in their aptitude for war, their deep
> acquaintance with every one of its stratagems, and their skilful preparation of

the weapons and machines used in it, as well as their extreme care and fore-sight in all matters concerning it. They have been further compared with the Chinese [by Ibn Hazm], for the delicacy of their work and the subtlety of their manufactures, and their dexterity in imitating all sorts of figures. And, lastly, it is generally asserted that they are of all nations that which most resembles the Greeks in their knowledge of the physical and natural sciences. (al-Makkari 2002, 1:117–118)

Ibn Hawqal visited al-Andalus during the reign of Abd al-Rahman III. Al-though biased toward the Fatimids, Ibn Hawqal noted that

one finds there uncultivated land but the greatest part is cultivated and densely populated. There is running water everywhere, forests and orchards, and rivers with sweet water. Abundance and ease are characteristic of life; the enjoyment of it and the means of acquiring these blessings are even extended to workers and to artisans thanks to low taxes, to the excellent condition of the land, and because the prince does not impose heavy demands in taxes upon his people. (Kish 1978, 205)

Nevill Barbour considered Andalusian civilization "the most advanced in the western world" (Barbour 1959, 138).

The Fatimids Realize a Dream

In 969, the Fatimid general and Christian convert Jawhar (al-Katib) and his Berber army invaded and seized Egypt from the debilitated Ikhshids. Jawhar founded a new city known as al-Qahira (Cairo), meaning "the victorious," which eventually absorbed the old Arab city of Fustat. After Jawhar consoli-dated the Fatimid position, Caliph al-Mu'izz moved to Cairo in 973. The Fati-mids finally realized their dream of taking over Egypt. The caliph assigned Fatimid Maghribi territories to the Zirids, Sanhaja Berbers, who served as loyal emirs. Georges Marçais noted that Louis Massignon, the famous French Orientalist, considered the tenth century as "the Isma'ili century of Islam" (Albertini et al. 1937, 1955, 157).[48]

The Fatimids did not force Shi'ism on Egypt's Sunni population, but quick-ly engaged the Abbasids, then under the military domination of the Shi'i Buyids. Palestine and Syria fell under Fatimids, thereby creating a "greater Egypt" reminiscent of the Tulunids and Ikhshids. Given the Persian Nasir al-

Khusraw's mid-eleventh-century description, the Fatimids' redoubtable army garrisoned a transcultural mélange composed of Berbers (notably the Kutama and Masmuda [from Morocco]), Bedouins, Turks, Persians, and Black Africans. He noted that the infantry had

> soldiers coming from all countries. They have their own separate commander who looks after them. . . . There was also a corps composed of the sons of kings and sovereigns from various part of the world who had come to Egypt. . . . They came from North Africa, the Yemen, Byzantium [Rum], the lands of the Slavs, Nubia, and Ethiopia. The sons of the king of Delhi and their mother had gone there, as had the sons of the kings of Georgia, the princes of Daylam [from the lands south of the Caspian Sea], and the sons of the Khaqan of Turkistan. (Lewis 1974, 1:217–218)[49]

The "ultimate dream" of capturing Baghdad and terminating the Abbasids' caliphate seemed realizable, if not inevitable. Unlike the Tulunids and Ikhshids, under the Fatimids, Egypt became an independent rather than autonomous state. Besides the Zirid-controlled west (and the Kalbids in Sicily), the Fatimid caliphate included Palestine, southern Syria, the Red Sea coast of Africa, Yemen, and the Hijaz in Arabia encompassing Islam's Holy Sites—an Isma'ili empire.

During the first century of Fatimid rule, Egypt enjoyed remarkable political, economic, and social success. A Jewish convert, Ibn Killis, served as the first vizier (Arabic, *wazir*) or principal minister in Egypt and established an exceptionally efficient administrative system.[50] Ibn Killis also promoted education. Illustrating their transcultural sensibility, the Fatimids placed Jews (and Christians) in high positions in government, to the point that al-Suyati recorded a contemporary poet's (Rida ibn Thawb) observation: "O people of Egypt, I advise you, turn Jew, for the/Heavens have turned Jew!"[51]

The Fatimids encouraged Egyptian agriculture, protected commerce, and secured markets (with low tariffs). At the beginning of the eleventh century, al-Muqaddasi described Alexandria as "a distinguished city, with a goodly meed of upright and devout people" where "every conceivable type of product is brought. . . . The countryside round about is splendid, producing excellent fruits and fine grapes" (al-Muqaddasi 2001, 166). Furthermore, the *Pharos* still operated "firmly anchored in a small peninsula." Al-Muqaddasi observed: "A custodian continuously attends to it every day and night, and as soon as a ship

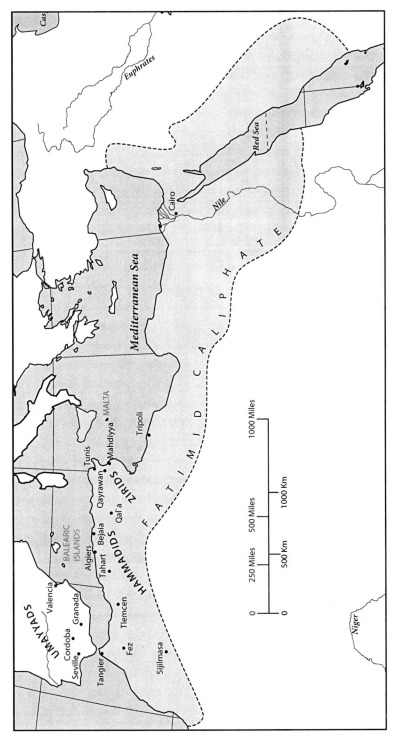

The Fatimid Era

comes into his range of sight he notifies the commander, who dispatches the birds that go to the shore, that those there may be in a state of readiness" (al-Muqaddasi 2001, 178). Christian as well as Muslim merchants participated in the Fatimid economy, trading especially for flax, the principal export. The Fatimids also greatly profited from transit services. Fatimid Egypt not only hinged Africa to West Asia, but also connected Europe with the markets of South Asia as the Red Sea and Indian Ocean trade again flourished.[52] Alexandria had a large Maghribi community, facilitating communication and commerce with the Maghrib and al-Andalus. Furthermore, the Fatimids protected and profited from Italian commercial colonies sited in their territories in West Asia and North Africa (Karsh 2007, 70).[53] Unquestionably, Fatimid transculturalism as well as patronage empowered the caliphate.

In order to promote and propagate Shi'ism, the Fatimid rulers, in their double role as caliphs and imams, built al-Azhar (the resplendent), the famous university-mosque in Cairo, which retains its religious and intellectual prestige today. Indeed, other Egyptian dynasties, namely the Mamluks and in the modern period the Alids, built additions to al-Azhar. The Fatimids sought to train missionaries (such as the exemplary Abu Abd Allah al-Shi'i). The Fatimids also constructed mosques, madrasas (religious secondary or college-level schools), and often highly decorated mausolea. Furthermore, patrons sought Fatimid artists and artisans throughout the Mediterranean.[54] Relating to the decorative arts, Sibylle Mazot noted the importance of Egypt's transcultural location: "Cairo became a major center for the production of valuable artifacts, superseding Baghdad and Constantinople. The Egyptian capital ably exploited the considerable economic and artistic potential of its geographical situation on the Mediterranean coast, where brisk commercial and cultural exchange had been going on for centuries" (Mazot 2004, 154). The Fatimids featured exquisite lusterware, glassware, and ceramics.

Shi'i jurisprudence tempered the justice system, but to a very limited extent. Instead, the Fatimids generally allowed traditional Sunni qadis or judges to adjudicate cases. The Copts continued to dominate financial affairs and also attained high governmental posts. Sunnis, Jews, and Christians endured persecution, including the destruction of synagogues and churches, during the reign of the capricious yet mystical Caliph al-Hakim (r. 996–1021).[55] Paula A. Sanders nonetheless pointed out: "He often repealed those measures as suddenly as he announced them" (Sanders 1998, 152).[56] According to John

Esposito, al-Hakim perceived himself as "the cosmic intellect, linking God with creation" (Esposito 2005, 47).[57] He founded the Dar al-'Ilm (House of Knowledge) in 1005, which had little to do directly with the *da'wa* or Ismai'ili summoning or proselytism. Furthermore, al-Hakim appointed Sunnis to the complementary scholar-teachers staff, "a fact that has puzzled historians" (Walker 2002, 44). Quoting al-Hakim's friend al-Musabbihi, al-Maqrizi wrote in regard to the Dar al-'Ilm that

> the jurists took up residence there, and the books from the palace libraries were moved into it. People could visit it, and whoever wanted to copy something that interested him could do so; the same was true of anyone who wanted to read any of the material kept in it. . . . Lectures were held there by the Qur'an readers, astronomers, grammarians and philologists, as well as physicians. . . . Into this house they brought all the books that the commander of the faithful of al-Hakim . . . ordered to bring there, that is, the manuscripts in all domains of science and culture, to an extent to which they had never been brought together for a prince. He allowed access to all this to people of all walks of life, whether they wanted to read books or dip into them. . . . He granted substantial salaries to all those who were appointed by him there to do service—jurists and others. . . . He also donated what people needed: ink, writing reeds, paper and inkstands. (Halm 1997, 73–74)[58]

Hakim also hired Hasan bn al-Haytham, one of the greatest medieval scientific minds (especially regarding optics), to study the Nile's flooding. Al-Khusraw wrote that "men of letters, poets, and jurists" were state-supported, "receiving regular salaries" (Lewis 1974, 1:218). The caliph also ordered the construction of the Mosque of al-Hakim, modeled after that of Ibn Tulun but also evincing Maghribi influences.

Two disasters in the 1060s profoundly affected Fatimid power and prosperity. A rare low Nile River flood devastated Egypt. In addition, the Fatimid army, once exemplifying transcultural organization and collaboration, fragmented as different ethnic groups competed for rank and allegiance. This competition became conflictive, leading to violence and instability.[59] These crises jeopardized the Fatimids' remarkable achievements and, in particular, Egyptian independence. Furthermore, a series of momentous events also convulsed the Maghrib.

When the Fatimids moved to Egypt, they left their Maghribi possessions in the hands of the aforementioned Zirids (973–1148). Under the dynamic Bulukkin bn Ziri (r. 973–984), the Zirids campaigned westward, seized Fez, and briefly held most of Morocco by 980. The Maghrib continued to flourish at this time. Although he complained about Qayrawan's water (collected in cisterns) as "inferior in quality," and that "culture is scant," al-Muqaddasi described the city under the Zirids as

> a delightful, expansive place, where the bread is very good, the meats excellent; it produces fruits of every diverse kind. . . . It has great prosperity and learning, and remarkable lowness of price. . . . It is the point of departure of travelers going west, and is the center of commerce for the two seas. One will not find an area having more towns, or more agreeable people than its inhabitants. There are none other than Hanafites and Malikites here, and between them remarkable harmony—no discord, no factionalism. . . . This town is the glory of the Maghrib, the seat of power, and one of the pillars of the realm. It is more gracious than Naysabur, longer than Damascus, more splendid than Isfahan. (al-Muqaddasi 2001, 186–187)

The Zirids' capital, Ashir, featured an impressive palace complex. Nevertheless, intra-Zirid conflict coupled with intra-Sanhaja rivalry arose, leading to the establishment of a separate state ruled by their cousins, the Hammadids (1014–1152), who established Qal'a as their capital at the base of the Hodna Mountains in Algeria.[60] Qal'a included palaces and a mosque whose extant minaret illustrates Mashriqi and Maghribi influences.

Zirid-Fatimid relations slowly deteriorated and then disintegrated during Emir al-Mu'izz's reign (1016–1062).[61] Under pressure from Maliki ulama, which reinforced the emir's desire to free himself from the caliph in Cairo, al-Mu'izz declared himself a supporter of the Abbasids in 1048, thereby repudiating the Fatimids. (Concurrently, the Hammadids also severed links with the Fatimids.) In response to this outrage, the Fatimids persuaded troublesome Arab Shi'i tribes that had settled along the Nile valley to head westward. Led by the Banu Hilal and the Banu Sulaym, these nomadic Arabs entered the Maghrib, a veritable "second Arab invasion" (Welch 1972, 278). The consequences were enormous.

The Hilalian Invasion and Its Consequences

The Banu Sulaym stayed in Cyrenaica before later advancing; however, the Banu Hilal reached Ifriqiya and defeated the Zirids in 1052. Their success encouraged other Arab tribes to traverse Egypt and the Maghrib. Ibn Khaldun and others describe the invasions in catastrophic terms: "The Hilal, who were Arab Bedouins, gained power over the country and ruined it" (Ibn Khaldun 1967, 2:289). Later in the *Ibar,* he referred to them as a "swarm of locusts" and elaborated on the "devastation" in Qayrawan, including the destruction of businesses, homes, and public monuments (Ibn Khaldun 1968–1969, 1:34, 37). Although scholars question the degree of the destruction wrought by the Arab tribes, the Maghrib profoundly transformed. The Arab tribes used the hinterland for pasturage and transhumance, thereby replacing cultivated fields. The change in the land's usage had an enormous environmental effect upon the soil and crop production, which had, in turn, momentous historical consequences. Without agriculture to sustain them, cities in the Maghribi interior, notably the Hammadids' Qalʻa, had to be abandoned. The Hammadids moved to Bejaia along the coast, a city that the dynasty founded in an effort to reverse its economic losses. Consequently, the Hammadids shifted toward maritime commerce. The Zirids had withstood the Banu Hilal's onslaught, but the Normans overwhelmed them in 1148.[62] Another important Arab group, the Banu Maʻqil, originally from Yemen, traversed North Africa, reaching southern Morocco and the Atlantic in the early thirteenth century. The Banu or Awlad Hassan of the Banu Maʻqil entered Western Sahara and Mauritania by the end of the century and exercised a profound regional influence.[63]

Culturally, the arrival of so many Arabs increased the use of Arabic. Wilfrid Knapp and others suggest that Arabization "was facilitated by the fact that the people were talking a kindred language at the time of the Arab invasion and were already impregnated with a Semitic culture" (Knapp 1977, 16). Intermarriage between Arabs and Berbers also occurred, such as that between the Banu Maʻqil's Awlad Hassan and Sanhaja Berbers. Indeed, the Sanhaja adopted the colloquial Hassaniyya Arabic dialect. The invasions of the Banu Hilal, the Banu Sulaym, and the Banu Maʻqil rank as among the most important transcultural events in the history of the Maghrib and comparable in long-term impact to the German invasions of the Roman Empire. In both situations, transcultural fusions took place.

The Ayyubids

As the Fatimids tried to recover from the Nile's low floods, the military's debilitating divisions, and multiple Maghribi problems, their prestige suffered an irremediable and grievous blow that affected not only their dynasty but also Islamdom. In 1099, Western European Crusaders captured Jerusalem from the Fatimids. The aggressive Western Europeans continued to attack Fatimid territory, to the point that the caliphate, exhausted by internal factional violence, briefly became a Crusader protectorate. Fatimid weakness made Egypt very vulnerable to a rising Muslim commander, Salah al-Din bn Ayyub, popularly known as Saladin. A Kurd, Saladin loyally served the Abbasids and campaigned successfully against the Crusaders. Invited by Fatimid officials to intervene on their behalf, he took over the office of vizier (*wazir*) and then in 1171, he ended the Fatimid dynasty and established his own, the Ayyubids. Significantly, Egypt resumed its traditional place within Sunni Islam—its Shi'i centuries were over.

Saladin governed Egypt and a larger empire including the Holy Sites of the Hijaz, Yemen, and Syria in the name of the Abbasids. He earned lasting esteem within the Muslim world for recapturing Jerusalem in 1187 and withstanding the powerful Third Crusade principally commanded by Richard I (the Lionhearted) of England.[64] Within Egypt, Saladin reduced taxes, except for those authorized by Islam.[65] Cairo retained its intellectual importance as Al-Azhar changed from a Shi'i to a Sunni institution of higher education. Saladin also patronized the madrasa system of education featuring Islamic schools at the secondary and college level to remove Shi'i influences and propagate Sunnism.[66] He also built the Citadel that dominates Cairo and founded the Maristan (Bimaristan), an outstanding medical facility.[67] Although he embodied opposition to the Christian political presence in West Asia, Saladin generously tolerated the Copts, who maintained their important financial dealings and positions, and traded actively with Italian commercial cities. The Jewish community prospered and its brilliant polymath Maimonides (1135–1204), whose family had left al-Andalus because of growing intolerance, became Saladin's personal physician. Maimonides rates as one of the greatest medieval intellects produced by Western civilization, as evinced by his scholastic *Guide of the Perplexed.*

The Ayyubids provided stability and prosperity. They also benefited by the arrival of Muslim immigrants uprooted by the Crusades. Given Egypt's predominance, Saladin's successors dealt with Crusader attacks from 1218 to 1221 and from 1249 to 1250. Sultan al-Kamil concluded a remarkable agreement, actually an alliance, with Holy Roman Emperor Frederick II in 1229, which returned Jerusalem to the Christians for a pledge of assistance against any threat to the Ayyubids.[68] The Papacy repudiated this remarkable conciliatory rather than combative "Sixth Crusade," since Frederick had earlier been excommunicated. Nevertheless, Muslim-Christian accommodation regularly occurred during this period. The Ayyubids profited from relations with European trading states such as Genoa, Pisa, and Venice, despite a legacy of crusading. Indeed, the Crusades (including the *Reconquista*) must be viewed as part of a complex and contradictory relationship between Christendom and Islamdom. The Ayyubids continued to control the Indian Ocean trade as the "Karimi," a group of merchants specializing in this route, distinguished themselves.[69]

Concurrently, the Ayyubids became increasingly reliant upon imported Turkish slave troops called Mamluks (*mamlukun* or owned ones). Expertly trained to defend the dynasty and highly effective in the battlefield, the Mamluks successively dealt with the crisis of Louis IX's crusade in 1249–1250 and repelled the Mongol invasion of Syria in 1259–1260. The Mamluks ended up overthrowing the dynasty. By 1260, when the last Ayyubid died, power had already gravitated to the Mamluk army.

Conclusion

The arrival of the Arabs and Islam decisively linked North Africa with West Asia and, given Muslim conquests of al-Andalus and Sicily, Europe. The Arab-Berber synthesis resulted in sophisticated caliphates and emirates. Furthermore, this period initiated the geopolitical trilateralism that would become prevalent in the Maghrib, given the appearance of the Aghlabids in Tunisia, the Rustamids in Algeria, and the Idrisids in Morocco.[70] With the Fatimids and Ayyubids, Egypt added new layers to its illustrious sedimentary civilization. Above all, the role of transculturalism disclosed its important role in the health and prosperity of polities and societies. Undoubtedly, *convivencia* represents one of the greatest examples of transcultural consideration and cooperation experienced by any civilization. Indeed, transculturalism enhanced the prosperity of the Andalusian Umayyads and the power of the Fatimid caliphate. Bennabi's historical agents of man, land, and time operated with remarkable synergy, generating exceptional polities and societies. There are important lessons here. In addition, these civilizing centuries initiated the diffusion and dissemination of the Muslims' vast corpus of knowledge and technology through al-Andalus and Sicily to the rest of Europe. These information conduits, especially that coursing via al-Andalus (e.g., paper technology), would continue with the rise of the great Maghribi Berber empires—the Almoravids and the Almohads.

CHAPTER 4

The Almoravid and the Almohad Empires and Their Successor States

The Arab nomads that swept across North Africa, beginning in the eleventh century, decisively transformed the Maghrib. In those unsettling, disruptive times, two great empires appeared, among the most powerful ever produced in Islamdom—the Almoravids and the Almohads. These Berber empires, fired by religious fervor, forged a legacy of unification that continues to inspire contemporary Maghribis.

After the disintegration of the Almohad empire in the thirteenth century, three other Berber dynasties—the Hafsids, Zayyanids, and Marinids—took over and reconfigured another Maghribi trilateralism. According to Malik Bennabi, something else also happened in the "post-Almohadean" period, a gradual loss of sophistication, especially after the death of one of the great figures of this period, Ibn Khaldun.[1] The dynamic intellectual breadth which had characterized the Maghrib and Mashriq narrowed. The post-Almohadean period would be marked by unimaginative centuries of slow decline, leaving Muslims susceptible to "colonizability."

The Almoravids

There is something appealing about the Lamtuna Berbers, a tribe of the Sanhaja confederation. Located in what is today Mauritania and Western Sahara, this pious people examined their Islamic beliefs and wondered if their devotions were correct. With this in mind, a group of Lamtuna pilgrims, returning from Mecca after performing the hajj, sought out a renowned Moroccan Maliki scholar named Abu Imran al-Fasi. In turn, Abu Imran introduced the Lamtuna to a bright young scholar from southern Morocco named Abd Allah ibn Yasin. Impressed with the tribesmen's faith, Ibn Yasin decided to return with the pilgrims to their tribal lands.

Ibn Yasin soon became the spiritual leader of the Lamtuna. He reinforced his authority by performing a hijra of his own. He mobilized his followers in a military *ribat,* a retreat-fortress, where he inculcated Berber (and Black) initiates with a strict Maliki interpretation of Islam. They became known as the al-Murabitun, meaning those of the *ribat,* or the "Almoravids," a Spanish derivative. Their clothing especially distinguished the Almoravids. They wore a *litham* or facial scarf and were synonymously called the *al-mulathamun,* the veiled ones.

The Almoravids seized Sijilmasa in 1055, which provided them with the resources of the lucrative Saharan trade. Almoravid power grew under the commands of Yahya ibn Umar and his brother Abu Bakr ibn Umar (al-Lamtuni). They successfully fought against the Barghawata Berbers of central Morocco, a tribe regarded as heretical.[2] Although Ibn Yasin probably died in battle in 1058 or 1059 fighting the Barghawata, his teachings continued to motivate the Almoravids profoundly. They especially practiced a puritanical Malikism based on a literal interpretation of the Qur'an, the Sunna, and the theological exegeses of the Maliki ulama and *fuqaha,* jurisconsults (Abun-Nasr 1993, 84). Abu Bakr founded Marrakesh (Marrakish) in 1062, which became the Almoravid capital.[3] Fez fell in 1069.[4] Yusuf ibn Tashfin (Tashufin) (1006–?1106), Abu Bakr's cousin, became the supreme commander known as the commander of the Muslims (*amir al-muslimin*) and the Almoravids' greatest leader.[5] He expanded Almoravid authority into central Algeria, capturing Tlemcen, Oran, and Tenès; Algiers fell in 1082. Resolute Hammadid defense defined the limits of Almoravid power.[6] Nevertheless, the Almoravid presence also acted as a counterpoise against the invasive Banu Hilal.

Besides expanding to the east, the Almoravids also campaigned in the Sahara/Sahel and in al-Andalus. They targeted the Soninke kingdom of Ghana, renowned for its gold, and Awdaghust fell in 1076. Although Ghana continued to exist as a state, the Almoravid assault considerably weakened the kingdom. The Almoravid incursion sought to control Saharan trade.[7] The Andalusian Party Kingdoms then invited Almoravid intervention against the advancing Christian Castilians. Ibn Tashfin, now an octogenarian, successfully drove back Alfonso VI's Castilians at Zallaqa in 1086. Tired of the Muslim states' bickering and betrayals, Ibn Tashfin methodically annexed them. The Almoravids continued their campaigns against the Christians. They reached Toledo, where the Christians resisted fiercely and successfully, notably, Rodrigo Díaz de Vivar (1043?–1099), popularly renowned as "El Cid."[8] Neverthe-less, the Almoravids took Toledo and then Valencia in 1102, which El Cid had captured and defended. Their domination of al-Andalus lasted from 1090 to 1145. In addition, the Almoravids adapted from the Sahara to the sea. Their formidable fleet patrolled the shorelines of al-Andalus and the Maghrib, en-suring, for example, Almoravid control of the Balearic Islands.

According to Ibn Khaldun and others, the Almoravids softened after im-mersing in Andalusian culture, which led to their decline, if not decadence—a loss of *asabiyya*. As Robert Mantran assessed: "These magnificently wild 'veiled ones' were soon transformed into propagators of the Andalusian civi-lization unlike the Hilalis [Banu Hilal] who remained shepherds, both physi-cally and spiritually" (Mantran 1970, 223). Ronald A. Messier offered a differ-ent assessment of the Almoravids' decline. They had to fight a "two-front war" against the Almohads in the Maghrib and the Christians in al-Andalus, which severely taxed their resources. Messier contended that the Almoravids were not prepared to rule "a distant, urban-based empire" (see Messier 2001). Al-moravid disintegration resulted in the roiling resumption of the discordant Party Kingdoms and emboldened the relentless Spanish Christians to renew their campaigning.[9] According to Nevill Barbour: "It is to the credit of the Almoravids as Muslim rulers that without their intervention Muslim Spain would almost certainly have succumbed to the Christians 200 years sooner than it did" (Barbour 1966, 60).

Their invasion of al-Andalus weakened or overextended these Saharan war-riors. Nevertheless, aesthetically, the Almoravids also diffused Andalusian culture and beautified the Maghrib. Numerous architectural works attest to Almoravid artistic interest and initiative, such as the Qubbat al-Barudiyyin at Marrakesh and the ornamentation and enlargement of the mosque of al-Qarawiyyin at Fez, evincing stylistic nuances from Iraq and Persia as well as Cordoba.[10] "Great Mosques" arose in Tlemcen and Algiers, reflecting a pre-Andalusian austerity. Subsequently, the Almoravids revisited and embel-lished the Great Mosque in Tlemcen.

Historians agree that the Almoravids' puritanical religious beliefs con-solidated Malikism in the Maghrib, an enduring contribution. On the other hand, contradiction also conflicted the Almoravids. Their ambivalent Anda-lusian cultural sensibilities uneasily coexisted with their religious rigidity. Their dogmatism often led to persecutions threatening the precarious ves-

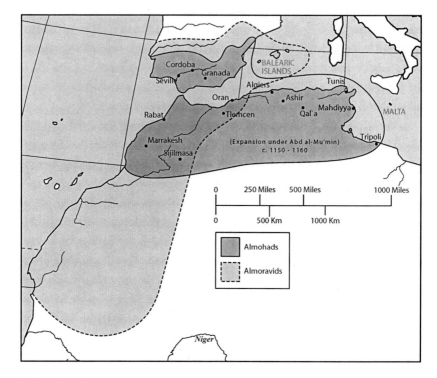

Berber Empires

tiges of Andalusian *convivencia*; yet they valued Christian troops and especially deployed them against the Almohads. The Almoravids also denounced
the works of the Mashriq's Abu Hamid al-Ghazali, Islam's most renowned
theologian, as heretical and burned them in public. They never conclusively
reconciled their sedentary lifestyle with their nomadic desert tradition or resolved their identity—arguably another cause of their decline. The Almoravid
experience represented a historical and cultural liminality, which had profound consequences.

The Almohads

The Almoravids' paradox, characterized by critics as spiritual inflexibility and
secular "immorality," highly affected Muhammad bn Abd Allah ibn Tumart,
a native of mountainous southern Morocco. After studying in al-Andalus,

Ifriqiya, Egypt, and the Mashriq, he began to preach religious reform, emphasizing the transcendental "oneness" and unity of God.[11] He directly challenged Almoravid scriptural literalism, which seemed to ascribe human attributes to God. Rejecting what he viewed to be sinful anthropomorphism, he called for a return to the Qur'an and a renunciation of personal opinion (*ra'y*) and community consensus (*ijma*) in legal matters. Ibn Tumart's followers, specifically, the Masmuda Berbers of the High Atlas, identified themselves as the Muwahhidun, meaning those of oneness or unitarians, or, as derived from the Spanish, the "Almohads." Ibn Tumart eventually perceived himself not only as a reformer, but also as the Mahdi, the guiding redeemer with a mission to renew and restore Islam.[12] His compelling ideas and charismatic personality also appealed to the Zanata, the archrivals of the Sanhaja. Reminiscent of Ibn Yasin's strategy, Ibn Tumart established a redoubt in the Atlas where the Almohads prepared to challenge the Almoravids' spiritual authority and temporal power. Abu Hafs Umar, whose descendants established the Hafsid dynasty in Ifriqiya, protected the Almohad leader.

Ibn Tumart discovered among his followers a remarkable young man, a Zanata Berber named Abd al-Mu'min (1094?–1163). A native of southern Morocco, Abd al-Mu'min became Ibn Tumart's principal assistant or *khalifa* (deputy). Ibn Tumart died in battle in approximately 1130. His death was kept a secret until Abd al-Mu'min consolidated his power as the commander of the faithful (*amir al-mu'minin*), the traditional caliphal title, which also signaled symbolic independence from the Abbasids' claim of pan-Islamic leadership. Although the Mahdi had established an administrative hierarchy, Abd al-Mu'min inaugurated a dynasty. Charles-André Julien wrote: "The original formula set out by Ibn Tumart, that sort of federative and aristocratic republic which appeared to be acceptable to the Berbers, gave way to a family monarchy for which those same Berbers had strong distaste" (Julien 1970, 108–109).[13] Nevertheless, Abd al-Mu'min and his immediate successors, the "Muminids," were capable and, when needed, coercive.

Abd al-Mu'min became one of the greatest conquerors in the history of North Africa. Securing and strengthening his army in the Atlas and the Rif Mountains, he marched against the hard-pressed Almoravid leader Tashfin ibn Ali and defeated him near Tlemcen.[14] Tashfin later accidentally perished. Fez fell to the Almohads, then Marrakesh in 1147, virtually ending Almoravid power in Morocco. Abd al-Mu'min then campaigned in the east, capturing Bejaia in 1151 and terminating the Hammadids, who had successfully resisted the Almoravids.[15] The Almohad caliph defeated the troublesome Banu Hilal near Sétif, which ended their immediate threat. Nevertheless, the Banu Hilal inspired the westward migration of other nomadic Arab tribes, which later created regional instability. Abd al-Mu'min campaigned in Ifriqiya from 1159 to 1160 and expelled the Normans from coastal strongholds. His conquests united North Africa from Morocco to Tripolitania.

Almohad authority also expanded into al-Andalus. Although Abd al-Mu'min had established a protectorate there, his successors took it over.[16] Abu Ya'qub Yusuf (r. 1163–1184) directed his considerable energies in Ifriqiya and especially al-Andalus. Abu Yusuf Ya'qub al-Mansur (r. 1184–1199) secured the Almohad position in al-Andalus by overwhelming Alfonso VIII of Castile (r. 1158–1214) at Alarcos in 1196.

The adventuresome and ambitious Almoravid Banu Ghaniya clan of the Balearic Islands invaded Ifriqiya, but al-Mansur drove them away. Ever resilient, this last group of Almoravids resumed their Ifriqiyan adventure, necessitating another Almohad campaign, this time by al-Mansur's successor, the Caliph Muhammad al-Nasir (r. 1199–1214). In order to maintain a stronger Almohad presence, al-Nasir appointed Abu Muhammad bn Abi Hafs as governor. Nevertheless, Yahya Ibn Ghaniya remained active in Ifriqiya with his Banu Hilal and Banu Sulaym allies. Eventually forced out of Ifriqiya, he campaigned against the Almohads and the Hafsids in neighboring Algeria before his death in 1237.

Like the Almoravids, the Almohads left an impressive architectural and cultural legacy. They felt no contradiction between their religious asceticism and architectural grandeur as indicated by their mosques. Power equated with architecture. They built the mosque of al-Kutubiyya, and a fortress, al-Qasba, in Marrakesh and the Great Mosque in Tinmal. Abd al-Mu'min founded Rabat (Ribat al-Fath), which became the Almohad capital. His grandson Abu Yusuf Ya'qub al-Mansur expanded the city. The "Hassan Tower," a massive minaret, testifies to al-Mansur's intention (never realized) to build the largest mosque after that of Mecca, a symbol of Almohad strength. Abu Ya'qub Yusuf constructed the Great Mosque of Seville with its soaring minaret.

The Caliphs Abu Ya'qub and al-Mansur patronized Ibn Tufayl (1110–1185), a rationalist and official court physician, as well as the greatest Aristotelian philosopher produced by Islamdom, Ibn Rushd (Averröes) (1126–1198). Abu

Ya'qub especially enjoyed his philosophical discourses with both men. Abu Madyan (1126?–1197), the great scholar and Sufi, earned esteem and a reputation as the Maghrib's al-Ghazali. He died near Tlemcen on his way to the Almohad court (probably to discuss and defend his beliefs before the caliph). Ibn Idhari al-Marrakushi (fl. second half of the thirteenth century), a qa'id of Fez, surveyed the history of North Africa and al-Andalus from the Muslim conquest of Egypt to his contemporary period (see Ibn Idhari 1948). His work is especially valuable since he cites chronicles that are no longer extant. Significant Sufi leaders, namely Sidi Bel Abbès and Mawlay Abd al-Salam bn Mashish, attracted adherents. One of Abd al-Salam bn Mashish's students, Abu-l-Hasan Ali al-Shadhili, founded one of the most popular Maghribi Sufi orders, the Shadhiliyya.

With the establishment of the Almohad Empire, the Maghrib reached the apogee of its power and influence. According to Charles-André Julien: "The power of the Almohad empire, its wealth[17] and the reputation of its army and fleet[18] conferred great prestige on the caliphs. An Arab writer goes so far as to declare that the Muslims of Cairo and Alexandria hoped that Abu Ya'qub would conquer Egypt" (Julien 1970, 128). Anxious over the strength of the Almohads, England's King John (r. 1199–1216) dispatched an apprehensive investigative delegation to determine possible Almohad designs concerning English Aquitaine across the Pyrenees (Barbour 1966, 7). Pisa and Genoa concluded commercial treaties.[19] Nevertheless, the Almohads lacked available human and material resources to administer and defend their far-flung empire that stretched from al-Andalus to Tripolitania. Despite the Muminids' determined efforts to preserve its integrity, the empire fragmented and the Maghrib experienced a geopolitical reconfiguration.

A New Trilateralism

The Almohad victory against the Christians at Alarcos in 1195 was impressive but not conclusive. King Alfonso VIII rebounded and organized a coalition including the kingdoms of Castile, León, Navarre, and Aragon and inflicted a crushing defeat upon the Almohads at Las Navas de Tolosa in 1212. This decisive victory catalyzed the irreversible disintegration of Almohad and Muslim power. Cordoba fell to the Spanish Christians in 1236, Valencia in 1238, and Seville in 1248, leaving the small vestigial kingdom of Granada ruled by the Nasrids. The Nasrids managed to survive for almost 250 years, principally by paying tribute to the Christians and by concluding timely alliances with the Marinids of Morocco (see below). The fabulous palace, the Alhambra (*Al-Hamra,* meaning "the red," for the red brick used in its construction), represents Granada's greatest cultural contribution, a fitting and final architectural testament to the glory of al-Andalus.

Reeling from its defeats in al-Andalus and from internal rivalries, the Almohads' power also crumbled in the Maghrib. They suffered a grievous blow when rebels destroyed the ambitious Caliph al-Sa'id near Tlemcen in 1248. Al-Sa'id hoped to reunite and revivify the empire. Instead, new regional dynasties appeared—the Hafsids of Ifriqiya, the Zayyanids of the Central Maghrib, and the Marinids of Morocco. The Marinids took Marrakesh in 1269 and annihilated the last of the Almohads in 1275 in Tinmal, the founding site of Ibn Tumart's movement. The new dynasties reintroduced Maghribi trilateralism. For the next two hundred years these three states vied with each other for geopolitical strategic advantage and predominance. They often enlisted Europeans for statecraft and soldiering. In their chronic bilateral conflicts, the

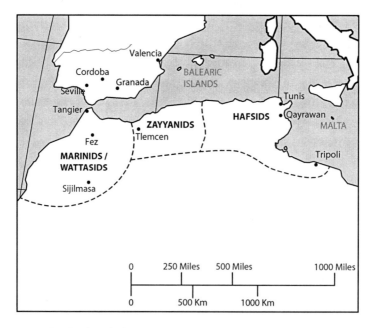

Post–Almohad Period

Zayyanids and especially the Marinids deployed Banu Maʿqil levies. Initially, the Hafsids scored extraordinary political and military success.

The Hafsids (1227–1574)

The Hafsids rightfully claimed that they were closest to the Almohads and deserved to be their legitimate successors. Abu Hafs Umar distinguished himself as one of Ibn Tumart's most faithful Masmuda followers. To the Muminids, the Hafsids remained a latent threat, however, to the caliphate and their dynasty. Nevertheless, the Hafsids remained steadfast supporters. As mentioned, Caliph al-Nasir assigned Abu Muhammad bn Abi Hafs to administer Ifriqiya. Abu Zakariyya Yahya (1236–1249) and al-Mustansir (1249–1277) extended Hafsid power into Zayyanid and Marinid territories.[20] After the Mongols destroyed the Abbasids and sacked Baghdad in 1258, Muslims briefly regarded the Hafsids as the paramount state in western Islamdom. Before the Mamluks invited an Abbasid to Cairo (see Chapter 5), the sharif of Mecca recognized al-Mustansir as the caliph. Furthermore, as Almohad power eroded in al-Andalus, Muslims fled to flourishing Ifriqiya.

Tunis, rather than Qayrawan and Mahdiyya, became the principal city of Ifriqiya under the Hafsids. It featured the great mosque-university of al-Zaytuna, founded in the late eighth century and completely refashioned and refurbished by the Aghlabids. Transcultural interaction with Egypt also contributed to Tunis's sophistication. Illustrating the extent of its political and economic influence, the Hafsid court entertained delegations from Africa south of the Sahara to Scandinavia.

Understandably, Louis IX of France targeted Tunis (at the request of Charles of Anjou) during the Eighth Crusade in 1270. Although the French king died there from disease and the crusade disintegrated, the deployment of Europeans to Tunis undermined Hafsid prestige and power. Soon afterward, the Aragonese began to dominate the Hafsid state economically and to threaten it politically. The Hafsids finally expelled the Spaniards in 1313 and from Jerba in 1335.[21]

After the death of al-Mustansir, dynastic rivalries weakened the Hafsids. The Zayyanids took advantage of the situation and seized territory. The Marinids captured Tunis in 1347, were expelled the next year, and returned in 1357. Fortunately for the Hafsids, the fifteenth century brought stability under effective rulers such as Abu'l Abbas (r. 1357–1394), Abu Faris (r. 1394–1414), and

Abu Amr Uthman (r. 1435–1488). Tunis regained its prestige and influence. The Hafsids also patronized the building of madrasas and oversaw the restoration of al-Zaytuna. Nevertheless, the sixteenth century brought renewed turmoil and with it, susceptibility to Spanish and Ottoman Turkish ambitions and incursions.

The Zayyanids (1236–1550)

The Zayyanids are often referred to as the Abd al-Wadids. They were Zanata Berbers who selected Tlemcen as their capital, a strategic choice since the city also served as an important trans-Saharan terminus. In addition, Tlemcen's proximity near the Mediterranean provided an ideal location for transit and commerce. The dynasty began with the rule of Yaghmurasan bn Zayyan (1236–1283), described by Ibn Khaldun as "the most brave, most redoubtable, most honorable man of the Abd al-Wad family" (Ibn Khaldun 1968–1969, 3:340). Although occasionally dynamic and successful, their more powerful rivals, the Hafsids and Marinids, limited the Zayyanids' ambitions. The Marinids often occupied Tlemcen during the fourteenth century. The Hafsids also seized the Zayyanid capital in the fifteenth century. Furthermore, the Zayyanids were notoriously treacherous toward each other, often with the contrivance of the Marinids.[22]

Nevertheless, all who ruled from Tlemcen appreciated the capital's intellectual and religious heritage. Under the Zayyanids (as well as the Marinids) Tlemcen became one of the greatest cultural centers of the Maghrib. Among significant Zayyanid rulers were Abu Hammu Musa I (r. 1308–1318), who asserted strong central authority and fortified the capital, and Abu Tashfin I (r. 1318–1337), who notably had a Christian named Hilal serve as his principal minister. Of the three post-Almohadean Maghribi dynasties that emerged in this new geopolitical trilateralism, the Zayyanids were the most vulnerable.

The Marinids (1244–1465)

The Marinids played a very important role in developing a "Moroccan" identity. Unlike the Idrisids, the Zanata Marinids were not a sharifian dynasty. Under the leadership of Abu Yahya, the Marinids seized Fez in 1248. Subsequently, Abu Yusuf Ya'qub (not to be confused with the famous Almohad caliph) captured Marrakesh in 1269 and Almohad authority collapsed. The Marinids controlled Morocco and bolstered Granada in al-Andalus against mounting

Christian pressures. Although the Marinids failed to regain Andalusian territories, their efforts secured Granada. Ibn Khaldun describes an impressive Marinid caravan dispatched to the East, in part to protect pilgrims performing the hajj but also to project Marinid power. Embassies were sent between the Marinids and Mashriq, notably Mamluk Egypt (Ibn Khaldun 1969, 4: 153–155).

During the rule of Abu'l-Hasan Ali (1317–1351) and his son Abu Inan (1348–1358), the Marinid state flourished and expanded into Ifriqiya. Tlemcen and Tunis fell before Abu'l-Hasan Ali, the most dynamic Marinid.[23] Abu'l-Hasan sent the Mamluks 500 horses, 500 bundles of Maghribi manufacture merchandise (such as arms and shields, furniture, robes, and wool and silk textiles), and reputedly a copy of the Qur'an written in his own hand for delivery to Mecca) (Ibn Khaldun 1968–1969, 4:240–241). He built the city of Mansura, with its celebrated mosque, adjacent to Tlemcen. Its towering minaret illustrates a continuing Almohad influence. Mansura arose as an armed camp constructed during the enduring siege of the Zayyanid capital. The Marinids declared Fez their capital city and also created a new administrative center, which served as a second city ("New Fez" or Fas al-Jadid) (see Le Tourneau 1961). Abu'l-Hasan ordered the construction of the Sharabliyyin (Slippermakers') and Abu'l-Hasan mosques in Fez as well as the Misbahiyya and Sahrij madrasas. He also established the Abu'l-Hasan madrasa in Rabat (completed in 1342). Completed in 1339, the al-Ubbad Mosque located outside of Tlemcen at the site of the tomb of (Sidi) Abu Madyan is one of the most famous mosques in the Maghrib. Abu Inan deposed his father but continued to exercise impressive Marinid authority. He contributed madrasas in Fez and Meknès.

Unlike their Maghribi rivals, the Marinids also allocated substantial resources to stem the relentless momentum of the *Reconquista*. Abu'l-Hasan suffered a major defeat at Rio Salado in 1340, but the Nasrids managed to preserve their precarious independence by providing tribute to Christians.

European pressures exerted against the Muslim states resulted in the acquisition of positions in the Maghrib, some of which became permanent. Sicilians and Genoese took over the island of Jerba off the Ifriqiyan coast in 1383. Most significantly, Christians crossed the Straits of Gibraltar. The Spanish captured Tetuan in 1401. The Portuguese seized Ceuta in 1415 and secured enclaves from Tangier to Agadir. Their success led to a shift in power within the Marinids. Beginning in 1420, their relatives, the Wattasids (Banu

Wattas), began to exercise greater power as chief ministers or *wazirs* (viziers). Although the Marinids reigned, the Wattasids actually ruled. This political fiction ended when the Wattasid Muhammad al-Shaykh assumed the sultanate. Later in that century, Ferdinand of Aragon and Isabella of Castile mounted a final assault against the Muslim presence in al-Andalus. In January 1492, Granada surrendered, marking the end of a Muslim political presence in al-Andalus that had lasted for almost eight hundred years.[24] The Spanish then seized Melilla along the Moroccan coast in 1497, establishing a presidio (fortress enclave), which Madrid still possesses today. The Portuguese and Spanish invasions significantly affected the political, economic, and cultural development of the Maghrib.

The Transcultural Maghrib during the Age of Berber Empires and Their Successor States

The age of the Berber empires and their successor states featured extensive transcultural interactions. Robert Mantran appreciated the fusion of Andalusia and the Maghrib: "The poets, historians and theologians were numerous and often notable. This can certainly be called the golden age of Maghribi civilization. . . . Spain added its delicate charm, and Berber austerity gave the whole an original note of proud reserve and of indisputable grandeur" (Mantran 1970, 225). As indicated above, Maghribi architecture experienced an illustrious age. Richard Parker recognized that "a happy concurrence of Visigothic, Hellenistic, Roman, Syrian and North African influences produced an architectural style which set the pattern for succeeding centuries in both Spain and Morocco. Tunisia played an important role in the development of this Hispano-Moorish style, but the mechanics of that role are uncertain." Parker suggests that although there is no certain evidence if "Tunisian artisans were imported into Spain[,] . . . it seems quite likely that the Great Mosque at Qayrawan (Kairouan), for instance, influenced Spanish and Moroccan architectural development" (Parker 1981, 14). The Almoravids' desert past hardly determined their aesthetic potential. Their public monuments remain impressive. The Almohads' "towers" continue to awe observers. Furthermore, the Hafsids, the Zayyanids in Tlemcen, and the Marinids in Fez also patronized architecture as a means of illustrating their piety and power. The Marinids and the Zayyanids especially melded Almoravid and Almohad forms and styles. Furthermore, the Nasrids of Granada, while maintaining a fragile independence, undertook what is considered the masterpiece of Andalusian architecture, the Alhambra.

The Almoravids and Almohads developed monetary economies. Their commercial networks stretched from sub-Saharan Africa to Scandinavia while maintaining the traditional connections with the Mashriq (see Bovill 1995). Relatively rapid communication linked the Maghrib with the Mashriq. Furthermore, there was intellectual interaction. Ibn Rushd responded to al-Ghazali's *The Incoherence of the Philosophers* with *The Incoherence of the Incoherence.* Ibn Rushd's translated *Commentaries* on Aristotle's thought eventually reached and illuminated the great Christian scholastic, Thomas Aquinas (1225?–1274). Furthermore, cities along the coast, especially in the post-Almohadean period, such as Bejaia and Algiers, gained autonomy and developed their own maritime networks. The Hafsids maintained strong commercial relations with the Italian maritime states, which were "far from hostile, being marked on the contrary by an appreciation of mutual interests and by a spirit of genuine collaboration and cordiality" (Barbour 1959, 286). Privateering, common on both sides of the Mediterranean, however, became an increasing concern among Muslim, Jewish, and Christian merchants.

The period contributed great intellectual achievement. Ibn Zuhr (Avenzoar) (1091–1161), a physician and clinician, served the Almoravids and Almohads (specifically, Abd al-Mu'min) and is regarded as the greatest medical mind in Western civilization since al-Razi (Rhazes) of ninth century Baghdad. Ibn Rushd, a student of Ibn Zuhr, was also a renowned physician and jurist as well as a philosopher. Ibn Bajja (Avempace) (d. 1138), another polymath, excelled in philosophy and especially musicology. Ibn Arabi (1165–1240) was born in al-Andalus, studied there and in the Maghrib, and met Ibn Rushd before journeying to the Mashriq, where he earned his renown in theosophy (see Hourani 1991a, 176–179). Ibn Quzman's poetry, like Ibn Hazm's earlier verse, continued an Andalusian heritage that influenced courtly love and troubadours' lyricism in France. This period (twelfth–thirteenth centuries) also produced two significant astronomers from Seville, Jabir bn Aflah (Geber) and al-Bitruji (Alpetragius). In addition, Jabir was an important mathematician who studied spherical trigonometry, while al-Bitruji was an Aristotelian philosopher. Andalusian Jews added their cultural contributions. Judah Halevi, a renowned poet, departed al-Andalus for the Mashriq (and especially the Holy

Land) to escape growing intolerance. During the twelfth century, Abraham bar Hiyya ha Nas (Savasorda) translated Arabic scientific works into Hebrew, which in turn scholars rendered into Latin and disseminated throughout Europe. Indeed, King Alfonso X of Castile and León (r. 1252–1284) established a translating institute in Toledo.

Andalusians and Maghribis considered themselves highly sophisticated and cultured. We have already noted the Aristotelian presence at the Almohad court embodied by Ibn Tufayl and Ibn Rushd. The aforementioned Abu Madyan, like al-Ghazali in the Mashriq, synthesized and reconciled Sufism with Sunni Orthodoxy. The Maliki *faqih* Ibn Battuta (1304–1377) left Morocco in 1325 and traveled throughout Islamdom and beyond to China. He returned to Morocco in 1349 and then visited the Mali empire in 1353. According to Ross Dunn, Ibn Battuta "visited territories equivalent to about 44 modern countries, and put behind him a total distance of approximately 73,000 miles" (Dunn 1989, 3). Ibn Battuta served the Delhi Sultanate for years. His recorded travels, the *Rihla,* also showed the vitality of North Africa as well as its "connectedness." Ibn Battuta traveled from Tangier to Tlemcen, Bejaia, and Constantine, offering some information about these cities.[25] Hafsid Tunis, at that time a city of about 100,000 inhabitants, impressed him. He compared Alexandria, "a beautiful city . . . and a magnificent port," with others such as Calicut in India and Zaytun in China (Ibn Battuta 1929, 46). In Alexandria, he met Burhan al-Din the Lame, a Sufi ascetic. He intuited Ibn Battuta's love of travel and said that he should visit three Sufi companions, two of whom were in India and the other in China. Ibn Battuta wrote: "My journeys never ceased until I had met these three that he named and conveyed his greeting to them" (ibid., 47). The Moroccan jurist highly admired Mamluk Cairo, a city with a population of 500,000 inhabitants, which enjoyed its reputation as the intellectual center of the Arab world. He described the Maristan, the great hospital in Cairo, as having "an innumerable quantity of appliances and medicaments" (ibid., 51).[26] Decades later while returning to Morocco, he observed the catastrophic effects of the Black Death in West Asia and North Africa. He recounted that in Cairo, he "was told that the number of deaths during the epidemic rose to twenty-one thousand a day" (ibid., 306). Ibn Battuta's travels and descriptions illustrated that Fernand Braudel's concept of a "Greater Mediterranean" with its global links, which characterized the sixteenth century, existed during this earlier period as well.

Ibn Khaldun (1332–1406) was an exceptional intellectual who distinguished this period. He was born in Hafsid Tunis to a family displaced from al-Andalus as a consequence of the Almohad empire's disintegration. He studied Sufism and Aristotle and had broad interests in history, geography, religion, literature, philosophy, and in what we may call anthropology and sociology. Above all, Ibn Khaldun possessed a critical and perspicacious mind. He served the Marinids, the Zayyanids, and the Hafsids before being appointed by the Mamluks as Grand Qadi of Malikism in Cairo.[27] The Mamluks dispatched him on a difficult diplomatic mission to temper Tamerlane's devastating conquests. Nevertheless, he failed to prevent Tamerlane's ravaging of Syria.

Ibn Khaldun's greatest work was the *Muqaddima,* which he composed at Qal'a bn Sala'ma (Ibn Salamah), near Oran in 1377. (The *Muqaddima* introduced the *Kitab al-Ibar* [the Book of Exemplary Information], Ibn Khaldun's universal history.) The Introduction to this book presented some of the *Muqaddima*'s principal ideas—a pluralist approach to history; distinction between "surface" and "inner meaning" history; and the historical agent *asabiyya* (see Introduction). Ibn Khaldun insisted that the historian

> needs to know the principles of politics, the (true) nature of existent things, and the differences among nations, places, and periods with regard to ways of life, character qualities, customs, sects, schools, and everything else. He further needs a comprehensive knowledge of present conditions in all these respects. He must compare similarities or differences between the present and the past. . . . He must know the causes of the similarities in certain cases and of the differences in others. . . . His goal must be to have complete knowledge of the reasons for every happening, and to be acquainted with the origins of every event. Then, he must check transmitted information with the basic principles he knows. If it fulfills their requirements, then it is sound. (Ibn Khaldun 1967, 1:56)

To Ibn Khaldun, "history . . . is information about human social organization, which itself is identical with world civilization" (Ibn Khaldun 1967, 1:71). Thus, he presented a global North African perspective. Jacques Berque viewed Ibn Khaldun as most interested in how the world became acculturated (*la culturation du monde*) (Berque 1974, 61). Erwin I. J. Rosenthal wrote: "His is a novel, perhaps the first theory of human culture and civilisation as a humanist concept, and at the same time the first independent political theory of a

Muslim who as such looked at humanity and the world at large" (Rosenthal 1979, 1). Above all, Ibn Khaldun sought *mubtada,* the causative evidential antecedents or catalytic variables (like *asabiyya*) activating social and political formation and civilization (see Berque 1974, 59, and Khatibi 1983, 65–75).

According to Malik Bennabi, Islamic civilization's rational stage culminated with Ibn Khaldun's life and achievement. Ibn Khaldun's historical and theoretical work and critical methodology collectively represented an exceptional accomplishment, given the milieu of an increasing inflexibility among jurists in the Maghrib. The publication of Khalil ibn Ishaq's (d. 1378) *Mukhtasar,* a highly influential work of Maliki jurisprudence, signaled an intolerant attitude toward new interpretations and methodologies.[28] Fernand Braudel wrote: "Islam . . . became the prisoner of its own success, of the comfortable conviction of being at the centre of the world, of having found all the right answers and not needing to look for others" (Braudel 1972–1973, 1:187–188). Robert Mantran perceived: "There were many worthy chroniclers, poets, geographers or writers of travel accounts, as well as jurists, theologians and hagiographers; but among all their works there was nothing which had the feeling of novelty and discovery which characterized the preceding period. . . . It was, in short, a period when artists and intellectuals lived on the attainments which they had inherited, but showed no sign of any creativity" (Mantran 1970, 235). Indeed, Ibn Khaldun condemned contemporary intellectual decadence and even described North Africa's environmental deterioration.

In particular, disease devastated the region. Ibn Khaldun provides one of the few extant descriptions of the effect of the Black Death in North Africa. The pandemic "devastated nations and caused populations to vanish. It swallowed up many of the good things of civilization and wiped them out. . . . Civilization decreased with the decrease of mankind. Cities and buildings were laid waste, roads and way signs were obliterated, settlements and mansions became empty, dynasties and tribes grew weak. The entire inhabited world changed" (Ibn Khaldun 1967, 1:64). Ibn Khaldun observed:

> Al-Qayrawan and Cordoba were centers of sedentary culture in the Maghrib and in Spain, respectively. Their civilization was highly developed, and the sciences and crafts were greatly cultivated and very much in demand in them. Since these two cities lasted a long time and possessed a sedentary culture, scientific instruction became firmly rooted in them. But when they fell into ruins, scien-

tific instruction ceased (to be cultivated) in the [Muslim] West. Only a little of it, derived from (al-Qayrawan and Cordoba), continued to exist during the Almohad dynasty and because of the shortness of time between its beginning and its destruction. Sedentary culture enjoyed only a very minor continuity there. (Ibn Khaldun 1967, 2:427)

For Bennabi, the decline was marked by a general lack of intellectual curiosity and a lack of historical consciousness.[29] "Post-Almohadean man," to use Bennabi's term, reverted to pre-Islamic habits. The recurrent arrivals of migrating, unsophisticated Arab tribes to the Maghrib also played important roles. Like the earlier Banu Hilal, they were nomadic and pastoral, transforming the once urban, or to use Ibn Khaldun's terminology, "sedentary," hinterland of the Maghrib. Transhumance replaced agriculture, trading networks, and urbanization. Furthermore, political instability and fragmentation left North Africa from Egypt to Morocco demoralized, vulnerable, and "colonizable." Referring to Bennabi's thought, Jacques Berque termed this period of multiple disintegration a "dispersion" (Berque 1978, 539).

There were other important changes. Although the Almohads protested Malikism's rigidity, that school's *madhab* or doctrine remained the principal juridical source. The Almohad period also witnessed the rise of Sufism in the Maghrib, which was interpreted as a new expression of spirituality for many, like Abu Madyan, or to Maliki jursiconsults (*fuqaha*), a subversive superstition. Almohad doctrine, like that of the Almoravids, became increasingly intolerant, resulting in the persecution of Maliki ulama and Jews (Julien 1970, 119). Indeed, an enlightened ruler like Caliph Yusuf Ya'qub al-Mansur rigidified his religious outlook and subsequently destroyed the works of philosophers.

Writing in the twelfth century, Ibn Abdun explained Seville's commercial regulations, which illustrated a flourishing economic life, but the rules included certain prohibitions: "A Muslim must not massage a Jew or a Christian nor throw away his refuse nor clean his latrines. The Jew and Christian are better fitted for such trades, since they are the trade of those who are vile. A Muslim should not attend to the animal of a Jew or of a Christian, nor serve him as a muleteer, nor hold his stirrup. If any Muslim is known to do this, he should be denounced" (Lewis 1974, 2:162–163). The proscriptive tone signaled the end of *convivencia*.[30] Positive transculturalism marked by social coexistence and co-respect precipitously declined, which weakened Muslim al-Andalus. Furthermore, the conquests of the Almoravids and the Almohads intensified the Christian crusader spirit as illustrated by the militant *Song of the Cid* and the *Song of Roland*. Politicized Islam and Christianity narrowed perspectives and produced "misreceptions" and misperceptions of others.[31]

The conquest of Granada, ending the Muslim present in al-Andalus, resulted in the immigration/expulsion of Muslim families to North Africa, including that of Hasan bn Muhammad al-Wazzani (1485?–?1554). Hasan's family settled in Fez, where he received an excellent education, including studies at al-Qarawiyyin. The Marinids appointed Hasan's uncle to perform diplomatic missions and Hasan accompanied him. Hasan traveled in West Africa, where he observed the Songhay empire, and traversed North Africa. He may have journeyed to the Mashriq and to Constantinople. Captured by Spanish corsairs in 1518, he ended up as a slave in Rome and was gifted to Pope Leo X (r. 1513–1521). Hasan converted to Christianity and was renamed Giovanni Leone.[32] The pope patronized Giovanni's scholarship, and his Arabic manuscripts recounting his travels resulted in *The History and Description of Africa*, which was published in Italian in 1526. Giovanni became renowned as the author "Leo Africanus."

In many respects, Leo's work continued the tradition of al-Bakri and of Ibn Battuta. He provides a valuable description of North Africa derived from his travels. Yet his narrative is especially important since it was composed during a period of significant transformation. The Ottoman and Habsburg empires contested the control of the Mediterranean. Furthermore, the Berber successor states of the Almohad empire neared the end of their political viability. Leo's perspective is exceptionally transcultural. He embodied each side of the Mediterranean. His narrative often refers to Muslim markets, commodities, and buildings in comparison to European counterparts.

Despite the political crises and military conflicts, North Africa remained vital and sophisticated. Leo glowingly described Fez: "A world it is to see, how large, how populous, how well-fortified and walled this city is" (Leo Africanus 1970, 2:419). He admired the city's remarkable hydraulic system, the size of al-Qarawiyyin, and the beauty of the madrasas. Leo also appreciated Tlemcen, although he stated that "the buildings of Fez are somewhat more stately" (ibid., 668). As for Tlemcen's surrounding region, "besides the beautiful pastures and clear fountains, there is such abundance of all kind of fruits to delight both the eyes and the taste, that to my remembrance I never saw a more pleasant place" (ibid., 669). He added that "the citizens and merchants of this city are so neat and curious in their apparel, that sometimes they excel the citizens of Fez" (ibid., 670). Bejaia's "houses, temples [mosques], and colleges . . . are most sumptuously built. Professors of liberal sciences here are great store, whereof some teach matters pertaining to the law and others profess natural philosophy" (ibid., 3:700). Throughout the *Description,* Leo detailed North Africa's cosmopolitanism. Regarding a suburb of Fez, Leo recounted: "I never saw neither in Asia, Africa, nor Italy, a market either more populous, or better furnished with wares" (ibid., 2:473). Tunis had a quarter where Venetians, Genoese, and other Christian merchants lived and prospered. English, Dutch, and Portuguese ships anchored in Alexandria. Cairo's international market included commodities from Italy and Flanders as well as India.

Conclusion

The Maghrib was at its height during these centuries and achieved an exceptional cultural unity. The Almoravids and the Almohads collectively evoked a reimagination of the Maghrib—a Maghrib united. Concerning the Almohads, Abun-Nasr wrote: "Through unifying the Maghrib under their rule, the Almohads gave for the first and only time a concrete historical existence to the conception of the Maghrib as a distinct religio-cultural entity. This conception crystallized in the context of the role which Islam played in transforming the political consciousness of Maghribi society" (Abun-Nasr 1987, 101). Maghribis kept the memory of an integrated Maghrib alive. The establishment of the Union du Maghreb Arabe (Arab Maghrib Union [UMA/AMU]) in 1989, despite its disappointing efforts so far to promote unity (see Chapters 8 and 9), is still inherently inspired by the legacy of the Almoravids and Almohads. Furthermore, Malikism, infused with the insistent legality of the Almoravids and the exacting morality of the Almohads, remains intrinsic to Maghribi societies. In regards to the Maghrib's "post-Almohadean" political and cultural geography, despite the fluidity of its frontiers, the trilateralism of the Hafsids, Zayyanids, and Marinids significantly mapped the modern identities of contemporary individual states.

The sixteenth century inaugurated important geopolitical changes in North Africa. The growing intervention of Europeans in Morocco incited wars of resistance if not independence. The emergence of a new Muslim power, the Ottoman Empire, resulted in new North African conquests, which politically linked North Africa once again, with the exception of Morocco, to the Mashriq.

CHAPTER 5

Turkish Ascendance
and Moroccan Independence

From the thirteenth to the nineteenth centuries North Africa experienced the ascent and descent of Turkish power. In the mid-thirteenth century the Turkish Mamluks replaced the Ayyubids in Egypt. In turn, the Ottoman Turks defeated the Mamluks in the sixteenth century but allowed them to exercise considerable local administrative and economic influence. Concurrently, combative Ottoman adventurers campaigned along the North African coastline and in its hinterland and founded "regencies" centered in Algiers, Tunis, and Tripoli. Turkish expansion embroiled North Africa in imperial rivalries between the ambitious Ottomans and the equally aggressive Habsburgs. Meanwhile, two sharifian dynasties, the Sa'dis and the Alawis, resolutely preserved Moroccan independence from the predations of Europeans and the encroachments of Turks. This was an age of dynamic empire and state builders and dauntless corsair captains. In particular, the portentous power and ambitions of European states, namely Portugal, Spain, France, and Great Britain, characterized this era. Although Morocco defended its independence and exercised impressive authority, by the beginning of the nineteenth century the sultanate, as well as the Ottoman regencies, were in decline. As for Egypt, France's shocking invasion and occupation in the late eighteenth century jolted it politically, socially, and culturally. The ease of the French conquest delivered a greater psychological blow, signaling the infirmity of the once invincible Ottoman Empire.

The Ottoman Turks and North Africa

The Ottoman Turks' relentless conquests reinstalled a commanding authority in the East. Although the sultan personally conducted the conquest of Egypt, enterprising individuals achieved Ottoman expansion in the Maghrib.

The result was the establishment of an Ottoman political presence that persisted in North Africa until the eve of World War I.

An Overview of the Ottoman Empire

The Ottomans emerged from the Seljuk Turkish conquest and occupation of Anatolia (Asia Minor) during the eleventh and twelfth centuries at the expense of the Byzantine Empire. Serving their Seljuk overlords, the Ottomans administered a principality in western Anatolia. As Seljuk power waned and the Abbasid caliphate collapsed before the Mongol onslaught during the thirteenth century, the Ottomans asserted their independence. Ruled by a succession of gifted leaders beginning with Osman (r. 1280–1324), the Ottomans methodically dominated Anatolia and then crossed into Europe. Murad I's (r. 1359–1389) victory at the battle of Kosovo in 1389 secured the Ottoman takeover of the Balkans. In 1453, Sultan Mehmed II's (r. 1444–1446, 1451–1481) army, backed by European-forged artillery, ended Byzantium's millennium by blasting and breaching Constantinople's walls. The great imperial city became the Ottoman capital.

It is important to understand the nature and significance of the Ottoman state. It exemplified transculturalism, especially in its first three hundred years, before nationalism fomented and fractured the empire. The Ottomans recognized and rewarded talent, no matter the ethnic background, as learned by the "Barbarossa" brothers and their corsair cohorts. The Turkish sultan was often of mixed ethnic parentage. Furthermore, it was not unusual for Christians to attain high administrative positions. The sultanate also selected, adopted, and converted male Christian children (known as the *devshirme* system), who subsequently dedicated their lives in service to the sultan and the empire.

After Mehmed II's success and consolidation of the empire in eastern Europe and Anatolia, Selim I (1512–1520) expanded to the east and south, defeating the powerful Persian Safavids at the battle of Chaldiran in 1514. (The Persian-Ottoman rivalry continued for centuries.) Selim next aimed his powerful army against the Mamluks.

The Mamluks

The Mamluk usurpation of the Ayyubids resulted from chronic external threats, namely Louis IX's crusade of 1249–1250 (Seventh Crusade) and the Mongol invasion of Syria ten years later. These former slave soldiers proved to be effective rulers and great patrons of the arts. Nevertheless, like the Fatimids, the Mamluks also faced natural disaster, not only the irregular flooding of the Nile, but also the Black Death. Intense internal dissension and rivalries within their ranks followed, weakening the Mamluks and thereby expediting their demise at the hands of the dynamic Ottomans.

Unlike previous dynasties, the Mamluks must be considered as a "group" of leaders. Emirs assisted (or contested with) the Mamluk sultan. At first, the Bahri Mamluks ruled from 1250 to 1383. They received their name from their barracks located on Rawda Island in the Nile. One of the Bahris, Sultan Qalawun (r. 1279–1290), succeeded in establishing a dynasty that lasted until 1382. (His was the only dynasty in the history of Mamluk Egypt.) The Bahri Mamluks were primarily Kipchak (Qipchaq) Turks, originating from the steppes along the banks of the Volga River near the Caspian Sea. The second ruling group was the Burgi Mamluks, who dominated from 1382 to 1517. They were Circassian Turks from the Caucasus Mountains. In general, the strongest Mamluk commander ruled an independent Egypt.

Baybars I (r. 1260–1277) was principally responsible for installing the Mamluks in power in Egypt and securing West Asia, including Palestine and Syria (see also Chapter 3). He also played an important role in repelling Louis IX's crusade in 1250. (Louis was captured and ransomed.) Along with Sultan Sayf al-Din Qutuz, Baybars defeated the Mongols at Ayn Jalut in Palestine in 1260 and stemmed their extraordinary conquests, which included the aforementioned devastation of Baghdad in 1258 and the termination of the Abbasid caliphate. The resounding Mamluk victory at Ayn Jalut "had tremendous psychological impact"; according to Linda S. Northrup, "it demonstrated that the Mongols were not invincible" (Northrup 1998, 274). Abd al-Rahman al-Jabarti (see below), the renowned Egyptian historian of the late eighteenth and early nineteenth century, stated that the Mamluk success "emboldened" people who "went on harassing [the Mongols]" (al-Jabarti 1994, 1:25). The Mamluks invited a descendent of the Abbasids to Cairo and symbolically restored the caliphate in 1261. Thus, after being situated for centuries in the Mashriq, the caliphate arrived in North Africa, signaling a shift in Muslim power as well as location. The Mongols and their successors, the Il-Khanids of Persia, threatened and rivaled the Mamluks for decades.[1] Nevertheless, the Mamluks still secured much of the Mashriq and held on to it until the Ottoman conquest three centuries later. Baybars also systematically reduced residual Crusader strongholds.

A figurehead caliph's presence did not change the power realities in Egypt. The Mamluks governed and did so successfully until the middle of the four- teenth century. The most able and ambitious commanders competed for power, often ruthlessly. Indeed, after the battle of Ayn Jalut, Baybars killed Qutuz and seized the sultanate. Sultan al-Nasir Muhammad (r. 1293–1294; 1299–1309; 1310–1341) marked the apogee of Mamluk power. He placed im- portant emirs or "magnates" in important governmental positions rather than his personal Mamluks. Soon after al-Nasir's death, the Circassian Mam- luks pressed to assert their dominance.

Mamluk sultans sought to legitimize their rule in different ways. Patronage played an important part in Mamluk power relations and ploys. Sultans espe-

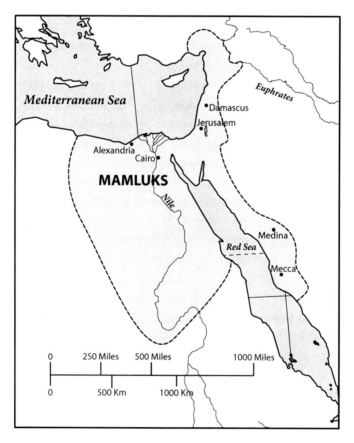

The Mamluk Sultanate

cially sponsored public works. The beneficence of Sultan Qalawun resulted in the Mansuri (al-Maristan al-Mansuri) hospital, one of the greatest medical facilities of Western civilization's medieval period, which arose in Mamluk Cairo. With Baghdad plundered and Persia devastated by the Mongols, Cairo became the greatest city of the Muslim world, its intellectual center, and one of the most prominent in Western civilization, with a population estimated at 500,000 (see Chapter 3). Sultans al-Nasir Muhammad and al-Ghuri (r. 1501–1516) sponsored the construction of an aqueduct. Sultan al-Nasir also ordered a canal (al-Khalij [al-Nasiri]) built between the Nile and Khanqah to supply the city with water. The Mamluks lavished money upon educational facilities and supported ulama representing the four schools of Sunni jurisprudence (Maliki, Shafi'i, Hanafi, and Hanbali), thus illustrating a remarkable juridical toleration (see Berkey 1998b, 163–173). The madrasa of Sultan Hasan (r. 1347–1351; 1354–1361), a son of al-Nasir Muhammad, is "unquestionably one of the masterpieces of Mamluk architecture in Cairo" (Williams 1993, 66). Sultans Baybars I, al-Nasir Muhammad, and Qatbay also charged the building of impressive mosques.

The Mamluks were proud of their Turkish heritage. They dressed differently and flaunted their privileges. They also segregated themselves from the Egyptians. Nevertheless, as Jonathan P. Berkey pointed out: "It would be misleading, however, to overstress the Mamluks' alienation from native Egyptian society, or to underestimate the links which bound them to broader, international patterns of Islamic culture. The Mamluks were, in fact, deeply embedded in the society over which they ruled, and were bound to their subjects by complex ties of patronage, as well as more intimate human relations" (Berkey 1998a, 1:392). They welcomed and benefited from Arab immigration as a consequence of the Mongol invasion of the Mashriq.[2] The arrival of the dislocated immigrants as well as migratory tribes from Arabia contributed to the growing Arabization and Islamization of Egypt.[3] Persecution rather than proselytism also played a role in the increase of converts to Islam. The ulama assailed Christians since their co-religionists rode with the Mongols.[4] There was also Muslim jealousy regarding the Copts' wealth and their influence as financiers. Despite these social tensions, traditional commercial networks linking Egypt to the Maghrib and Mashriq, to the cosmopolitan cities of the East African coast, and to South Asia remained intact. Nevertheless, there was deep concern about Mongol-controlled land routes, which diverted commerce from

Egypt. The Mongols generally provided security for merchants.[5] Mamluk-controlled Aleppo served, nonetheless, as a terminus of the Silk Road with its wondrous commodities, including textiles, spices, and precious stones. Politically, the Mongols and other rivals, such as the Seljuk Turks, threatened to sever Mamluk recruiting grounds in the Turkish homelands of Central Asia (see Northrup 1998, 1:277–279). Mamluk deft diplomacy involving a constellation of relations backed by impressive military force proved to be persuasive, ensuring the vital flow of Kipchak and later Circassian slave soldiers.

A series of catastrophes enormously impacted the Mamluks during the Circassian era. Egypt suffered like the rest of North Africa from the Black Death, which mercilessly swept through Western civilization. Historians estimate that 25 percent of Europe's population was lost. This equated with the fatalities in Egypt, where the bubonic plague arrived in 1347–1348, followed by the pneumonic plague (see Chapter 4). The pandemic severely affected agriculture. Irrigation canals silted and the loss of labor left fields uncultivated. The Mamluks' growing corruption and rapacity compounded the disastrous Black Death. They ruthlessly exploited the surviving peasantry. Mamluk state control of the lucrative transit trade marginalized merchants and restricted their enterprises. Internecine crises over power and succession provoked conflicts among the Mamluk elites. In the early fifteenth century, Timur or Tamerlane and his Tartars (Turco-Mongols) overran Mamluk-controlled Syria, devastating Damascus and Aleppo, and also "carried off the best artisans to his capital Samarqand" (Gladiss 2004, 171). (As mentioned in Chapter 4, Ibn Khaldun participated in a failed diplomatic mission sent to negotiate with Tamerlane.) Fortunately for the Mamluks, who failed to score a military success like Ayn Jalut 150 years before, Tamerlane's empire lasted only during his lifetime and its menace to Egypt evaporated. Although several Mamluks governed effectively in the fifteenth century, the dynasty suffered irreversible decline. By the end of that century, the Safavid Persians and the Ottoman Turks sought their Syrian territory (resulting in war from 1485 to 1491 with the Ottomans) and the Portuguese endangered their Indian Ocean trade.

The Ottomans Take Over Egypt

After defeating the Safavid Persians at Chaldiran in 1514, which secured his empire's eastern border, the Sultan Selim I turned toward his southern border and resumed the Ottomans' conflict with the Mamluks. The proud Mamluks scoffed at the firearms wielded by Selim's army, although Sultan al-Ghawri futilely attempted to modernize his forces (Winter 1998, 1:494). In 1516, the Ottomans cut down the Mamluks and their sultan at the battle of Marj Dabiq in Syria. Selim eliminated other Mamluk forces led by the new Sultan Tumanbay. He arrived in Cairo in 1517 and established Ottoman control over Egypt. Tumanbay continued to resist until he was seized and executed. The Ottomans deported Mamluks to Constantinople and also the last figurehead Abbasid caliph, al-Mutawakkil, who was captured at Marj Dabiq. Thus, Egypt once again lost its independence and became a province in a larger empire. Leo Africanus described Sultan Selim's conquest of Egypt as a "wonderful alteration" (Leo Africanus 1970, 3:888). To al-Jabarti, Selim's son Sulayman al-Kanuni (Suleyman the Lawgiver, the Magnificent [r. 1520–1566]) "shone in darkness, lifted up the shining light of religion, and extinguished the fire of the infidels." He respected the early Ottomans as "among the best to rule the (Islamic) community since the Rightly-Guided Caliphs" (al-Jabarti 1994, 1:33). Al-Jabarti's opinion of his contemporary Ottomans was not so complimentary (see below and Chapter 6).

The Ottomans appointed a governor or pasha, but allowed the Mamluks considerable administrative authority, in part to limit the pasha's power (and autonomous ambitions) (see Hourani 1991a, 227–228). The Ottomans also integrated Mamluks into their Ottoman army. The inclusion of Egypt (as well as Syria and Palestine) facilitated the acquisition of commodities such as sugar, grain, textiles, and fruits and resulted in important new revenues for the Ottoman treasury, such as custom duties and land and urban taxes. At first, the Ottomans administered a system of direct taxation, but they eventually replaced it with odious tax farming. Thus, with the imposition of Ottoman rule as well as the continuation of Mamluk exploitation, the Egyptian peasantry's suffering deepened. Factional strife among Ottomans and Mamluks provided opportunities for the ulama to mediate and exert important influence. Christians (Copts) and Jews also benefited from liberal Ottoman toleration.

Unlike Egypt under the Mamluks, Ottoman rule did not equate with great architecture and aesthetics. According to Michael Winter: "The explanation for this is simple. Mamluk sultans and high-ranking amirs saw Egypt as their only home. . . . The Ottoman viceroys' term of office in Egypt was temporary. . . . The pashas did not have the time, motivation, or the funds to undertake construction of monuments. Besides, the Ottoman sultan would not have allowed his viceroy to build an 'imperial' mosque for himself" (Winter 1998, 2:6). On the other hand, there was a great increase in literacy as "much oral history passed into writing" (Hanna 1998, 2:106–107). Furthermore, the exponential growth of coffee houses provided venues for the performing arts such as puppet shows and musical entertainment. From hundreds of coffee houses in the seventeenth century, there were approximately 1,200 by the end of the eighteenth century in Cairo alone (see Hanna 1998, 107–109). Indeed, the coffee transit trade from Arabian and East African markets enriched the Egyptian economy.

Although the Ottomans ruled, local power substantially remained in the hands of competing Mamluk beys and families who manipulated complicated patronage networks. The Mamluk Ridwan Bey al-Fiqari exercised real power for twenty-five years in the first half of the seventeenth century. In the late 1760s and early 1770s, Ali Bey (al-Kabir, the Great) ruled Egypt and attempted to centralize authority and initiate technological modernization. Although he did not retain power long, his initiatives, including territorial expansion in the Hijaz and Syria, foreshadowed the ambitions of Muhammad Ali (Mehmed Ali) in the nineteenth century. By that time, the Ottoman Empire had weakened as a result of its grueling European and Persian wars. Egypt managed to exercise a semblance of autonomy, but it was also vulnerable. Its commercial economy remained strong into the eighteenth century, but commodities from European colonies in the Western Hemisphere such as coffee, sugar, and rice successfully competed with what had been traditional Egyptian export staples (Crecelius 1998, 2:68).

The Brothers Barbarossa and the Maghrib

The sixteenth and seventeenth centuries marked the height of Muslim (and European) corsair or privateer activity in the Mediterranean.[6] As the Hafsids' power diminished, cities along the Maghribi coast such as Tripoli, Bejaia, Annaba, and Algiers became independent. Their economies featured agricultural products, locally manufactured goods, and privateering. Muslim corsairs supported the revolt of their co-religionists in Spanish Granada in 1502. Their interference and activity in the western Mediterranean provoked Spain, still infused with the relentless crusading spirit of the *Reconquista*. In addition, the vulnerability of the politically fragmented Maghrib also appealed to the opportunistic Spanish court. Consequently, a privateer named Pedro Navarro, fervently supported by Cardinal Ximenes de Cisneros, embarked on a campaign along the Maghribi littoral that resulted in the acquisition of cities and the construction of presidios along the coast or the immediate hinterland, including Oran in 1509 and Algiers, Tlemcen, Bejaia, and Tripoli in 1510. Cities not under Spanish rule or influence still felt pressured to pay tribute.

Finding the Spanish presidio on the rocky islet of Peñon intolerable, the leaders of Algiers called for help. The Barbarossa brothers—Aruj, Khayr al-Din (Hayreddin), and Ishaq—answered their appeal.[7] They embodied the ethnic transculturalism of the Ottomans by having Greek as well as Turkish ancestry.[8] The brothers earned a reputation of being effective corsairs to the point that the Hafsids allowed Aruj to use the island of Jerba as a base. Aruj tried to free Bejaia twice and failed; he captured Jijel (another city in Algeria) in 1514. This success convinced the inhabitants of Algiers to invite his intervention on their behalf. Aruj arrived in Algiers but resisted repeated pleas to attack Peñon. Instead, he eliminated the city's leadership and took over the city in 1516. Later that year, the brothers rallied their forces and soundly defeated Spanish invaders. Nonetheless, Peñon remained in Spanish hands.

Khayr al-Din Establishes the Algiers Regency

Aruj's territorial ambitions brought him to Tlemcen, which the Spanish promptly besieged. (By that time, Ishaq had perished campaigning against the Spanish.) Aruj broke free from Tlemcen, but the Spanish tracked him down and killed him. It appeared as if momentum had decisively shifted from the Ottomans. Nevertheless, the resourceful Khayr al-Din, left in charge of Algiers, keenly perceived his tenuous situation. He contacted Sultan Selim, offered his allegiance, and obtained Ottoman assistance in 1519. Selim dispatched 2,000 Turkish troops with artillery and allowed Khayr al-Din to recruit more soldiers from the Ottoman east.

Before he could take advantage of the sultan's generous support, Khayr al-Din's enemies forced him from Algiers. An excellent commander, Khayr al-Din mustered his forces and methodically seized cities in eastern Algeria, notably Annaba and Constantine, before vengefully retaking Algiers in 1525 and executing his enemies. Nevertheless, he endeared himself to the citizenry in 1529 by attacking and destroying the Peñon presidio, thereby freeing the city from the Spanish presence. In a major public works project, he removed the rocky islets and created a causeway substantially enlarging the harbor into a

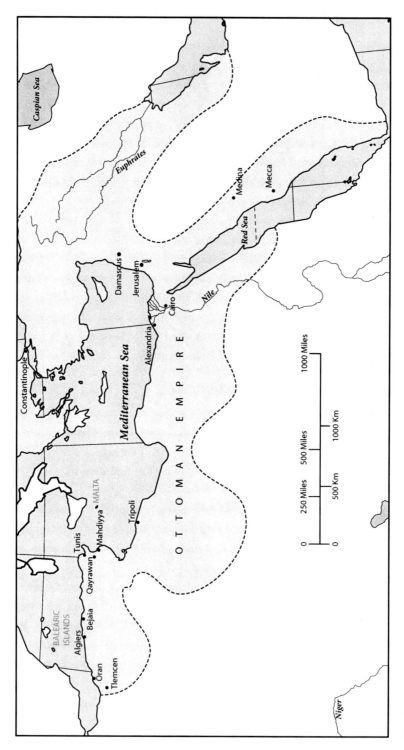

The Ottoman Empire

major port, which headquartered his growing corsair fleet. Khayr al-Din also asserted his authority in the interior with notable success.

The Ottoman Empire's greatest ruler, Sultan Suleyman the Magnificent (r. 1520–1566), appointed Khayr al-Din *kapudan pasha* (admiral) of the Ottoman fleet in 1533. In the following year, Khayr al-Din invaded Ifriqiya, captured its major cities (Tunis, Bizerte, and Qayrawan), and overthrew the Hafsids. A year later, Emperor Charles V (r. 1519–1555) amassed a fleet of approximately 250 vessels, forced Khayr al-Din to withdraw from Tunis, and reinstalled the Hafsids, who then served as clients of the powerful Habsburg emperor.

Khayr al-Din waged continuous war against the Habsburg-led Christian Holy League. In response, Charles V sought to eliminate Khayr al-Din's corsair capital and ordered Admiral Andrea Doria to launch an assault against Algiers in 1541. Doria assembled a fleet, reportedly numbering five hundred ships, for the invasion. Hassan Agha, whom Khayr al-Din appointed to govern in his absence, resolutely defended the city and, with the help of a fortuitous gale, defeated the Habsburg task force.

The Three Regencies: Algiers, Tunis, and Tripoli

The three regencies of Algiers, Tunis, and Tripoli had similar political histories. Real power devolved from appointed governors to local soldiers or corsairs, who received administrative recognition by Constantinople. The regencies also enjoyed various degrees of autonomy, as long as they acknowledged and honored the sultan's authority.[9] With its predominant power, the Algiers Regency exercised a de facto independence. Its aggressive policies and adventuresome corsairs influenced the establishment of the regencies of Tunis and Tripoli.

The Algiers Regency featured a number of outstanding *beylerbeys* (commanders of commanders) in the sixteenth century. They included the son of Khayr al-Din, Hassan bn Khayr al-Din, Salah Ra'is, and Uluj (Eulj [Uluç]/Kilij [Kiliç]) Ali. Collectively, they extended the power of the regency into the interior. Salah Ra'is (?–1556), an Egyptian, supported the Moroccan Wattasids (see below) and seized Fez in 1554 before withdrawing. He especially expanded Ottoman authority in the Algerian hinterland and ended the Zayyanids' rule in Tlemcen, who by that time were dependents of the regency. Salah Ra'is died from the plague while on a campaign against Spanish-held Oran.

Corsairs captured Uluj Ali off the coast of Calabria (southern Italy). He converted to Islam, rose through the corsair ranks, and commanded the Algerian forces with distinction at the Battle of Lepanto in 1571.[10] The Ottoman Empire continued to rely upon its Algerian province for naval expertise and leadership, resulting in Uluj Ali's appointment as *kapudan pasha*.[11] Along with Grand Vizier Sinan Pasha, Uluj Ali secured Tunis for the empire in 1574, established a regency there, and ended the Hafsid dynasty (and Habsburg strategic influence).

Algerian corsairs were spectacularly successful privateers, bringing in prizes and captives to be enslaved or ransomed. One of the most famous corsairs was Turghut (Dragut) (?–1565), who was of Greek ancestry and a protégé of Khayr al-Din. He participated in the successful Ottoman assault on Tripoli in 1551 against the Knights of St. John of Malta. Consequently, the Ottomans inaugurated a regency and in 1553, Turghut became Tripoli's pasha. Turghut also secured the Tripolitanian hinterland and the island of Jerba. While pasha, he built up Tripoli and adorned it, making it one of the most impressive cities along the North African littoral. He died while campaigning on Malta.

The Algiers Regency exercised its greatest influence and independence during the seventeenth century. Its corsairs roved the Atlantic, even reaching Iceland, to prey upon shipping. The nationalist historian Ahmad Tawfiq al-Madani referred to the regency as an "Algerian Ottoman Republic" (see al-Madani 1968, 5–11). Aghas (commanders) and then deys (governors) selected from the *ojaq,* the military corps or caste of Janissaries, governed at this time.[12] The regency benefited most from agricultural wealth and a strong manufacturing sector rather than the popularly perceived impression of a piratical economy. Nonetheless, corsair-related activities may have involved "25 percent of the economically active population of Algiers at certain periods" (Bookin-Weiner 1993, 26). This included the ransoming of captives.[13]

Algiers changed dramatically under the Ottomans. The port was modernized, defenses fortified, and new neighborhoods, such as the renowned Casbah, constructed. Mosques based on Anatolian models also arose, such as the Mosque of Fisherman's Wharf (seventeenth century) and the Katshawa (late eighteenth century). Algiers became an important entrepôt of the Mediterranean.[14] Consider Jacques Heers's description:

> More than any other Mediterranean port, Algiers surprised and astonished. It was crowded with all manner of people and with social and ethnic groups

distinguishable from each other through dress, language, physical characteristics, and even hairstyle. . . . The population was often swamped and enlarged
by waves of new arrivals. . . . Authors and witnesses couldn't help being dazzled
and confused by the diversity which pervaded every street, alley, or stairway;
they emerged charmed but a little breathless. (Heers 2003, 146)

During the seventeenth century, Algiers held 100,000 to 125,000 inhabitants (Wolf 1972, 97). The regency was sovereign in all but in name. Punishing
bombardments from French, English, and Dutch squadrons hardly diminished the regency's defenses, policies, or maritime operations. The Spanish
launched an expedition against Algiers in 1775 under the leadership of Alexander O'Reilly, a soldier of fortune. Nevertheless, the Ottomans and their
Arab and Berber allies mounted a harassing defense that repulsed O'Reilly's
invasion. This was the last major military operation in the centuries-old conflict between the regency and Spain (see al-Madani 1968).

Khayr al-Din Barbarossa enjoyed ephemeral success in Ifriqiya taking
Tunis in 1534 before the Habsburgs expelled the Ottomans and restored the
Hafsids (see above). After the battle of Lepanto, the Ottomans displayed their
resilience and military strength when Grand Vizier Sinan Pasha and Uluj Ali,
the *kapudan pasha,* overwhelmed the Hafsids and took Tunis in 1574. The
new Ottoman administration was modeled after the Algiers Regency. Deys
initially led the Tunis Regency. Uthman Dey (r. 1598–1610) supported local
manufacturing and Moriscos, expelled from Spain in 1609, found Tunis especially inviting. His successor Yusuf Dey (1610–1637) continued strong and
effective governance. Then two dynasties dominated the Tunis Regency ruling as beys—the Muradids from 1628 to 1705 and the Husaynids from 1705 to
1957.[15] The beys offered many commercial opportunities to European merchants, while still promoting relatively moderate privateering operations.[16]
Silk and woolen commodities highlighted Tunisian production. According
to Abdelhamid Largueche: "Tunis played the role of a pivotal commercial
exchange centre between Europe, Africa and the Levant"[17] (Largueche 2001,
121). Furthermore, the beys were usually capable and autonomous, such as
Murad Bey (r. 1659–1679), Ali Bey II (r. 1759–1782), and Hammuda Bey (r. 1782–
1814), and kept the hinterland under control through local leaders known as
qa'ids. Furthermore, the Ottoman pashas and beys or their representatives
(heirs) traditionally reinforced their authority by touring their territory with
troops to ensure the collection of taxes. This practice, known as the *mahalla,*

demonstrated the power of the ruler. L. Carl Brown explained: "The mahalla was more than an inspection tour. It was the government itself going out to meet the tribes, establish order and make decisions on the spot" (Brown 1974, 128). Through the *mahalla,* the Muradids and the Husaynids asserted a "Tunisian" independence while consolidating their authority with tribes in the hinterland.

In regards to the Tripoli Regency, the Porte (the Ottoman government in Constantinople) appointed pashas; nonetheless, autonomous beys, who commanded the Janissaries, ruled from 1609 to 1711. The Tripolitanian Ottomans avidly pursued privateering. They also penetrated Fezzan in 1576–1577 to secure trans-Saharan trade and threatened the Sudanic empire of Kanem-Bornu or Bornu.[18] Bornu's renowned *mai* (ruler) Idris Alawma (Alooma) (r. 1569–1609) dispatched a delegation to Constantinople to protest the Tripoli Regency's aggressive policies. Amicable relations had previously existed and Turkish arms sent to Bornu had supported its military campaigns against non-Muslims. Sultan Murad III was sympathetic, and although it is difficult to assess how much restraint his government advised, the Ottomans failed to take over Fezzan and monopolize Saharan trade. On the other hand, they managed to force the resident Banu Muhammad to pay tribute.[19] Concurrently, Idris adroitly communicated with Morocco's Sultan Ahmad al-Mansur as a diplomatic counterpoise (see below). In 1711, Ahmad Qaramanli (Karamanli), a popular local military leader, overthrew the Ottoman government in Tripoli.[20] He created what Jamil M. Abun-Nasr has called a "quasi-national dynasty similar to that of the Husaynids" and, save for a brief usurpation from 1793 to 1795 by the Algerian corsair Ali Burghul, the Qaramanlis lasted to 1835. (Abun-Nasr 1987, 192–193). Ahmad eventually received Constantinople's recognition and legitimation as pasha in 1722. Yusuf Qaramanli, who seized power in 1796, was notable for his conflict with the United States (a chapter in the "Barbary Wars").[21] In 1805, William Eaton, the American consul to Tunis, unsuccessfully attempted a "regime change." Supported by American troops (who were considered to be "Marines") and soldiers of fortune, Eaton hoped to replace Yusuf with his brother Ahmad. Eaton reached Derna (not the "shores of Tripoli"), where he learned that Tripoli had come to terms with the United States (see Parker 2004, 145–147). With the American conflict resolved, Yusuf turned his attention toward Bornu and the Sahara. His efforts to expand his authority and acquire new revenues in the south were impeded by the growing European presence and influence in Tunis. Yusuf failed to contain or control the competition for influence between the French and British consuls, thereby eroding the pasha's authority. In 1830, a French fleet forced Yusuf to come to terms with a humiliating treaty that ended tribute, demanded indemnity, and limited Tripoli's navy. The British then pressured the pasha, hoping to attain similar results. Yusuf Qaramanli abdicated in 1832.

European (and American) historiography has vilified the three regencies. For example, the regencies profited from the heinous trans-Saharan slave trade, which transported sub-Saharan Blacks to North African markets.[22] Nevertheless, Christian states also captured and enslaved Muslims, a pursuit approved by the papacy. The Knights of St. John of Malta were notoriously involved in this odious practice until Napoleon took over the island in 1798 on his way to Egypt. Consequently, with the knights eliminated, North African trade revived in the Mediterranean (Morsy 1984, 67).

By the end of the seventeenth century, aggravated European powers had bombarded corsair bases, including Algiers and Tripoli. Nevertheless, Europeans (and later Americans) also supplied the regencies, which helped outfit corsairs. Furthermore, Europeans countenanced the Barbary privateers or "pirates" for other reasons. Merchant vessels of major European naval powers rarely confronted corsairs. On the other hand, the regencies targeted weaker countries, like the United States, with negligible means to protect its commerce. European maritime powers refrained from safeguarding American merchants. Lord Sheffield, speaking before the House of Commons in 1783, viewed the regencies' predations as economically advantageous: "The Americans cannot pretend to a navy and therefore the great nations should suffer the Barbary pirates as a check on the activities of the smaller Italian states and America" (Morsy 1984, 73). The development of the United States Navy related directly to the corsairs' threats and operations (see Parker 2004).

During the eighteenth century and into the nineteenth the North African and "Barbary" coast shared a slow decline.[23] Furthermore, regarding the Algiers Regency, the Islamic brotherhoods of the Darqawiyya, Qadiriyya, and Tijaniyya also stirred resentment in the hinterland against the Ottomans.[24] The Darqawiyya also threatened the Moroccan sultanate, which had determinedly defended itself against Ottoman and European incursions and invasions.

Morocco Secures Its Independence

Morocco seemed to be on the verge of disintegration twice during this period. Each time a new dynasty arose to save the sultanate. This period in Morocco's long history was of tumult and triumph. Morocco not only secured its independence, but also earned respect and recognition from its aggressive neighbors. This period also significantly shaped Morocco's identity.

The Rise of the Sa'dis (1549–1654)

The Portuguese exploited the Wattasid-Marinid rivalry and seized Ceuta, al-Qasr al-Saghir, Tangier, and Arzila during the fifteenth century. Spain completed the *Reconquista* but continued crusading in collaboration with Portugal by taking Melilla in 1497. Under Dom Manuel, the Portuguese occupied cities along the Atlantic seaboard. Al-Jadida (Magazan) was taken in 1502, Agadir in 1504, Safi in 1508, and Azemmour in 1513.[25] Indeed, with its outlets to the Mediterranean and the Atlantic closed, Marrakesh found itself under siege in 1515. Morocco's political dissolution seemed imminent.

Nevertheless, restless and resistant sharifs (*shurafa*) in southern Morocco opposed Portuguese operations and ambitions. They, along with marabouts and Sufis, rallied around the Banu Sa'd or the Sa'dis of southern Morocco, who claimed descent from a grandson of Ali and Fatima. Jacques Berque argues that historians have underestimated religious resentment and resistance. As mirrored in the colonial and decolonizing periods, religio-political leaders and fraternal orders, for example Muhammad bn Sulayman al-Jazuli, founder of the Jazuliyya, raised popular consciousness and mobilized the people (see Berque 1978).[26] The Sa'dis viewed the Wattasids as ineffective; they also despised the Christian intruders who dismembered the sultanate.

The dynasty began with Muhammad al-Qa'im (d. 1518). The Sa'dis strengthened and expanded at the expense of the Wattasids and the Europeans. Marrakesh fell in 1524 and Fez was captured in 1549. The Sa'dis expelled the Portuguese from Agadir in 1541 and forced their abandonment of Safi and Azemmour, thereby reopening the Atlantic coasts to Moroccan commerce, as well as sugar and gold from West Africa.

Successes against the Portuguese enabled the Sa'dis to turn their undivided attention toward the Wattasids, who sought and secured help from the Algiers Regency. The intervention of Salah Ra'is, the powerful *beylerbey* of Algiers, led to the brief occupation of Fez by the Wattasids and Ottomans in 1554. In a battle fought later that year, however, the Wattasid leader Abu Hassun was killed, ending that Berber dynasty. With the reestablishment of a sharifian dynasty, the Sa'dis subdued or suppressed Sufis and marabouts.

Sultan Muhammad al-Shaykh (r. 1542–1544 [co-ruler]; 1544–1557) aimed to end Ottoman interference and intervention in Moroccan affairs. To deal with the Turks, he pursued a conciliatory policy with Spain, at that time engaged against the Ottoman Empire in an epic struggle for control of the Mediterranean. The sultan ignored the Spanish settlements at Melilla, Oran, and Mers el-Kébir, which affronted Moroccan and Ottoman political sensibilities. Instead, he marched against Turkish-controlled Tlemcen, which barely held out against the Sa'dis. The Ottomans later took their revenge on Muhammad al-Shaykh; their agents assassinated the sultan in 1557. By the time of his death, Muhammad al-Shaykh perceived himself as the Mahdi or rightly or divinely guided one who had successfully secured Moroccan independence.

Sultan al-Ghalib (r. 1557–1574) adopted al-Shaykh's policies. To secure Sa'di rule, he mounted campaigns against Sufis, marabouts, and brotherhoods (such as the Yusufiyya). The sultan viewed these groups as threats to Sa'di power and legitimacy. Al-Ghalib ordered the construction of several notable public works, notably a madrasa (the Ibn Yusuf) and mosque in Marrakesh. He also displayed an exceptional interest in urban design and planning. Under al-Ghalib, the Sa'dis sustained their strategic relationship with Spain and refrained from interfering in the suppression of the Morisco rebellion (1568 to 1570). Sa'di rule seemed secure until the Portuguese revived their Moroccan territorial ambitions.

Portugal had experienced extraordinary success and wealth, given its new commercial networks with India and the East Indies and settlement of Brazil. Nevertheless, factions in court persuaded the monarchy to resume an aggressive Maghribi policy as a matter of faith, an illustration of the *Reconquista*'s impelling crusading influence. Thus, King Sebastian (r. 1557–1578) reoriented Portugal's policy from John III's (r. 1521–1557) global perspective to a more immediate regional one.

The quixotic Sebastian filled with mystical zeal found an opportunity to pursue his Maghribi ambitions. There was a succession controversy after the

death of al-Ghalib. The enthroned al-Mutawakkil confronted the opposition
of his uncle, Abd al-Malik, who garnered the support of the Ottomans and
Spanish. Subsequently, Abd al-Malik engaged and routed al-Mutawakkil, who
fled to Portugal, where he allied with King Sebastian. Sebastian decided to
lead an expedition into Morocco, against the advice of his uncle, Philip II of
Spain. By this time, the Sa'dis fielded an army with modern equipment including disciplined arquebusiers and formidable Andalusian and renegade
(Christian converts to Islam) units.

Sultan Ahmad al-Mansur

On 12 July 1578, the battle of Wadi al-Makhazin (also known as the battle of
the Three Kings) near al-Qasr al-Kabir resulted in the deaths of Sebastian,
who had poorly deployed his overmatched and tired troops, al-Mutawakkil,
who drowned, and Abd al-Malik, who probably suffered a fatal heart attack
as the battle began (Mantran 1970, 244; Smith 2006, 35–36).[27] Abd al-Malik's
brother Ahmad became sultan. The great victory that he and his late brother scored earned Ahmad the name of al-Mansur, the victorious. Al-Mansur
went on to become one of the most dynamic sultans in Morocco's history. His
strong rule protected Morocco from the predations and ambitions of Spain
and the Ottoman Empire. He also cultivated close relations with England.
The Sa'di sultanate was at its height during his reign.

Al-Mansur's greatest achievement was administrative. He created the *makh-
zan,* a nebulous term connoting the central organization of government, including the territory under the direct control of the sultanate. The unsubdued
or imagined part of Morocco, called the *bilad al-siba,* represented territory
beyond the sultan's direct authority and was referred to as a "dissident" land.
He ruled from the fabulous al-Badi'a (the splendid) Palace (completed in 1593)
in Marrakesh, the dynasty's capital.

His court was one of the most splendid in Moroccan history. He imported
technicians and artisans and encouraged commercial enterprise. A veritable
transcultural panoply of merchants from Muslim and Christian lands, especially the English, took advantage of Moroccan commodities ranging from
leather and brass works to sugar and saltpeter. Furthermore, the sultan brilliantly staged sumptuous public spectacles projecting his power and majesty.
Shakespeare reputedly modeled the Prince of Morocco in *The Merchant of
Venice* and Othello after al-Mansur.

The sultan also played power politics very well. Learning that the Algiers Regency's Uluj Ali planned an attack, al-Mansur sent extravagant gifts to Constantinople in 1581. Impressed with the Moroccan monarch's generosity, the Ottoman sultan prohibited the *beylerbey*'s invasion. Concerning Iberian politics, the sultan pursued a coy policy. Dom Antonio, the pretender to the Portuguese throne, who had the backing of England, expected Moroccan assistance. It never appeared, however, and his attempted takeover of Portugal in 1590 ended disastrously. Curiously, King Philip II, who inherited Portugal after the death of Sebastian, evacuated Arzila (Asila, Argila) a year before allowing al-Mansur to occupy the important Atlantic coastline port. In regards to Spain, al-Mansur continued a policy of détente, but suspicion pervaded both sides. Relations cooled with England after the Dom Antonio fiasco; nonetheless, Queen Elizabeth and al-Mansur exchanged correspondence where the monarchs fancied the conquest of Spain and its New World possessions.[28] As mentioned above, Idris Alawma of Bornu requested assistance from al-Mansur. It is not known if Morocco and Bornu concluded a formal agreement. The *mai*'s appeal to the sultan, however, demonstrated the extent of al-Mansur's reputation and prestige.

In a manner reminiscent of the Almoravids, al-Mansur struck into the *bilad al-sudan* (land of the Blacks) in 1591. Although the Almoravids had enjoyed ephemeral success against the kingdom of Ghana, the strength of the Sudanic empires such as Mali and Songhay prevented further strikes from Morocco. The Almoravids' incursion disrupted the traditional salt-for-gold trade, but it later resumed. Al-Mansur aimed to establish a permanent presence to control the entire commercial enterprise, including the salt and gold mines.[29] By now al-Mansur perceived himself as a caliph whose mission was to unite the Muslim *umma*.

Nevertheless, ulama protested the sultan's war plans and campaigns, claiming that it was morally unjust to attack another Muslim state. Al-Mansur retorted that he intended to reestablish a Muslim presence in al-Andalus, but that he had to garner greater resources in order to achieve this ultimate objective. The sultan pursued his expansive policy despite the ulama's religious and moral objections. A Moroccan expedition, commanded by a renegade named Jawdhar, defeated the Songhay (Songhai) Empire's forces at the battle of Tondibi.[30] Jawdhar seized Gao in March 1591 and Timbuktu a month later. Adopting the Turkish term, Jawdhar served as a pasha or governor. Dissatisfied with Jawdhar's willingness to compromise with Songhay, al-Mansur dispatched the callous and brutal Mahmud bn Zarqun to replace the pasha. Subsequently, Songhay suffered irreparable losses. Soon after al-Mansur's death in 1603, the Moroccans pulled out of the *bilad al-sudan,* leaving a legacy of political disintegration and destruction.[31] Indeed, the gold trade that had flowed for centuries dried up for three principal reasons: (1) war dislocated commerce; (2) centuries of exploitation exhausted mines; and (3) accessible gold arrived from the New World.

The Sa'di legacy is difficult to assess given its contradictions. The dynasty arose because of its sharifian status and its indomitable opposition to hostile Europeans exploiting Morocco. Notwithstanding the Sa'dis' efforts to assert their sharifian political privilege, Muslims resisted their power and pretension—especially the Ottomans and ulama. Furthermore, once in power, the Sa'dis pursued conciliatory policies with Christian powers, despite Sebastian's foolhardy adventure, in part to contain the belligerent Ottomans. The Sa'dis unequivocally patronized architectural and aesthetic splendor. They built impressive monuments in Marrakesh, such as the mosques of Bab Dukkala and Mu'assim. A hospital for Christian captives and a new Jewish quarter arose. The densely decorated Sa'di royal tombs suggest a Mamluk influence (see Smith 2006, 44). Palaces also indicate Sa'di grandeur, even the vestiges of the great al-Badi'a that the Alawis later demolished. The Yusuf Madrasa became the largest in Morocco. It was during the time of al-Mansur when the renowned scholarly family known as the al-Fasiyyun (Fasiyyin) or al-Fasi settled in Fez. They founded *zawaya* and wrote numerous religious treatises and literary works for the next 250 years. As a consequence of the Sudanic campaign, renowned West African ulama were forcibly exiled to Marrakesh. They included Qadi Umar and his cousin Ahmad Baba. The latter especially earned a reputation as an honored teacher and scholar. Sultan Zaydan (r. 1603–1628) allowed Ahmad Baba to return to Timbuktu.

Al-Mansur ruled with absolute authority. After his death, the Sa'dis confronted fratricidal rivalries, civil wars, and fierce marabouts.[32] Rabat and Salé asserted their autonomy and launched corsairs against Spain, England, and Ireland. Notorious European "renegades"/"converts" (such as the Dutchman Jan Jansz, also known as Murat Ra'is) and expatriate Moriscos often commanded crews.[33] Pandemics also repeatedly afflicted the tormented sultan-

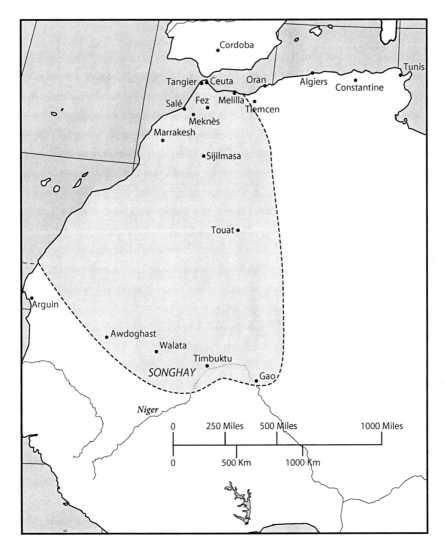

Sa'di Expansion

ate. The plague may have been the cause of al-Mansur's death. Nevertheless, another sharifian dynasty arose to rescue Morocco, the Alawis, who claimed (like the Idrisids) descent from Hasan, the son of Ali and Fatima and brother of the slain Husayn (martyred at the battle of Karbala in 680).

The Alawis (1664–) Regenerate Morocco

The Alawi Mawlay (Mulay) Rashid (r. 1664–1672) restored order by conquering Morocco and deposing the Sa'dis. In 1666, he captured Fez and seized Marrakesh in 1669. Respecting scholarship, Rashid founded the Cherratine madrasa in Fez in 1670. After Rashid's accidental death while hunting, his brother, Mawlay Isma'il (r. 1672–1727), succeeded him and secured the monarchy by overwhelming rebellious tribes. He mustered special regiments known as the *abid*.[34] His powerful armies drove into the *bilad al-siba* to reassert or reaffirm Banu Ma'qil tribal allegiance to the sultanate (reminiscent of the Tunisian *mahalla*). Morocco forces reached the southern Sahel and occupied for a short time today's Mauritania.

The Alawis recovered European enclaves, including al-Ma'mura in 1681, al-Ara'ish in 1689, and Asila in 1691, from the Spanish. They also besieged their Mediterranean presidios and threatened the French presence in Senegal. As a result of Moroccan pressure, the English evacuated Tangier in 1684, which they had received from the Portuguese in 1662. The sultan also promoted privateering and greatly profited from corsairs' booty and captives' ransoms. He was also active diplomatically and desired an alliance with France (proposing a marriage with the princesse de Conti, an illegitimate daughter of Louis XIV). Mawlay Isma'il also advised King Louis XIV to convert to Islam or at least become a Protestant (see Abun-Nasr 1987, 233)![35] The neighboring Ottomans remained a constant threat, fomenting Berber revolts and intrigues. Moroccan punitive incursions in Algerian territory in 1679, 1682, and 1695–1696 reminded the Ottomans of the consequence of incurring the sultan's displeasure.

Mawlay Isma'il favored Meknès (Miknasa) as the dynasty's capital. His construction of palaces there rivaled those of Louis XIV. As Richard Parker points out: "In one sense at least [Mawlay Isma'il] was well ahead of Louis. He had inside plumbing" (Parker 1981, 106). In part, his rivalry with Fez's ulama, who questioned the legal and moral legitimacy of the *abid* and implicitly, his absolutism, caused the relocation to Meknès. The sultan regarded the *abid* as his slaves, although among the *abid* were free Muslims. To the ulama, the "slave army" contradicted the Shari'a. The increasingly oppressive sultan regarded the ulama as subversives. Instead of co-opting the influential scholars, he persecuted them; the result was a stagnation in exegeses and general learning. To Abun-Nasr: "His reign marked the high point of a transformation in Morocco's religio-political culture, . . . the most important aspect of which being the reduction of the influence of the *'ulama* in the society" (Abun-Nasr 1987, 236).

Economically, Morocco actively traded with Europe, especially England. Jews served as intermediaries, although the sultan profited from his personal commercial monopolies, selling specific commodities to collaborating merchants. His invasion of the *bilad al-siba* and the Sahel aimed to assert Moroccan political authority and to appropriate trans-Saharan trade for the sultanate.

Undoubtedly a dynamic sultan, Mawlay Isma'il was also capricious, rapacious, and cruel. Furthermore, he failed to prepare his succession. After his death, there was no one who could exert a comparable absolutism. The *abid,* in particular, destabilized the sultanate. Moroccan authority in the Sahel and the Sahara also evaporated. Political and civil strife continued until Sultan Muhammad bn Abdallah (r. 1757–1790) reestablished order, in part by disestablishing the *abid.* After the short reign of Yazid (1790–1792), Mawlay Sulayman (Sliman) (r. 1792–1822) took over. Influenced by the Islamist Wahhabi movement exported from the Mashriq, the Sultan denounced Sufis, marabouts, and, in particular, the Darqawiyya brotherhood. He also isolated Morocco from Europe. That isolation would end with the creeping yet unremitting intrusion of European imperialism.

Napoleon's Invasion and Occupation of Egypt

Napoleon Bonaparte's invasion of Egypt, considered as a turning point in the history of North Africa and West Asia, was significant for political, economic, cultural, and psychological reasons. Its significance as a watershed event in Egyptian and European history may be historiographically overstated, but this is certain, the French irruption expedited the Alids' rise to power.

The French Revolution and Napoleon

The French Revolution and especially the ideologies it engendered eventually pervaded and profoundly affected North Africa, West Asia, and the world. Napoleon Bonaparte emerged from the Revolution's tumult, which commenced in 1789. The opportunities presented by the Revolution enhanced Napoleon's brilliant military career. He served with distinction at Toulon in 1793 against the British. He took full advantage of his political appointment to the French "Army of Italy" and led it to victory against the Austrians, culminating in his negotiation of the Treaty of Campo Formio in 1797 that awarded northern Italy to France. His success and popularity skyrocketed. The French Directory, the revolutionary government ruling at that time, charged Napoleon with preparing a plan for the invasion of England. Understanding that traversing the English Channel was impossible without control of the sea, Napoleon's gaze turned toward the East, which, in his opinion, needed a "man." He decided to attack England indirectly by threatening its trade routes to the eastern Mediterranean and India.

Napoleon perceived Egypt as the most strategic country in the world whose resources and commercial opportunities promised to profit France at the expense of England. He informed the government of his intentions to invade Egypt.[36] The Directory, pleased to have a popular general and a political threat distracted by an adventure, accepted the plan and outfitted Napoleon with a fleet and an army. Darrell Dykstra concluded: "The sheer size of the expeditionary force, the size of the war fleet sent to accompany it, and the inclusion of civilian savants all suggest that the French . . . intended to reap benefit from *keeping* Egypt" (Dykstra 1998, 119).

Egypt was in a desultory state. As mentioned earlier in this chapter, in the early 1770s, the Mamluk pasha Ali Bey al-Kabir provided exceptionally dynamic leadership, intimating the political, military, and territorial ambitions as well as modernization policies that Muhammad Ali implemented in the first half of the nineteenth century. Economically, new coffee supplies coming from the New World, notably Antigua, undercut Egypt's lucrative coffee transit trade between the Hijaz and Europe. A low Nile flood in 1783 resulted in famine in 1784, which the plague exacerbated in 1791. Domestic Egyptian textile production also poorly competed with cheaper European products (Hanna 2003, 10–11). The incipient European industrial revolution menaced Egypt as well as Napoleon's grandiose ambitions.

Bonaparte's instructions and objectives were paradoxical and problematic. The French government ordered Napoleon to conquer Egypt in order to secure it as a base (specifically Suez) for the future destabilization of British India. Another objective called for the dissemination of the ideology of the

Revolution.[37] Geoffrey Symcox identified a contradiction: the attainment of these objectives "was somehow to be achieved without offending the Ottoman government" (Symcox 2003, 20–21).

Napoleon in Egypt and the Levant

After taking over Malta, the French then slipped by the British fleet commanded by Lord Horatio Nelson. Napoleon landed with 36,000 troops, seized Alexandria on 2 July 1798, and routed the Ottomans and Mamluks at the battle of the Pyramids on 21 July, clearing the way to Cairo. In an attempt to win over the population, Napoleon crafted an extraordinary document claiming that the French were not only friends of Islam but were also "faithful Muslims." He trumpeted his victory over the Papacy, "which was always exhorting the Christians to make war with Islam." Napoleon assured that the French were staunch enemies of the exploitative, avaricious Mamluks (al-Jabarti 1975, 41). The Egyptian ulama, such as the erudite Abd al-Rahman al-Jabarti, rendered a blistering critique of the proclamation (including its orthography and grammar). A member of the Khalwatiyya Sufi order that aimed to revive (and modernize) Islam, al-Jabarti criticized the notion of "equality" on scriptural grounds and questioned how the French republic governed given the execution of its "sultan" (Louis XVI) (ibid., 42–43). Taking an early "Occidentalist" position, Jabarti perceived the French as faithless and blatant "materialists" (ibid., 47).[38] Nevertheless, the relatively easy defeat of the Muslim forces and occupation of Egypt stunningly signaled the weakness of the Ottoman Empire. Napoleon's invasion was a psychological as well as a political blow to the astonished Muslim world. Locally, the Mamluks' defeat "had broken the ties" between the Egyptians and their overlords (Marsot 2007, 61).

Meanwhile, Admiral Horatio Nelson discovered Napoleon's fleet and destroyed it in Aboukir Bay (the battle of the Nile) on 1 August. The loss of the fleet isolated Napoleon and his army in Egypt and changed the entire nature of the operation. This was a decisive moment not only militarily but also culturally, if not epistemologically. Geoffrey Symcox explained:

> After Aboukir, what had thus far been a superficial clash between cultures became an infinitely more profound transformative encounter. The consolidation of the French occupation and the foundation of the Institut d'Egypte mark a formative moment in the emerging discourse of Orientalism [see below]. The

Enlightenment now came face to face with Islam, and deployed the forces of science and reason to measure, to understand and ultimately to dominate this alien reality. (Symcox 2003, 26)[39]

After securing his position and harshly quelling native resistance, such as the uprising in Cairo in October 1798,[40] Napoleon campaigned in the Levant, seeing it as a strategic threat to his position in Egypt. He reached Syria in January 1799 before fierce resistance and an outbreak of the plague forced his retreat in May and return to Cairo in June.

According to Napoleon's private secretary, Louis-Antoine Fauvelet de Bourrienne, Napoleon "earnestly wished to preserve his conquest, and to make it a French colony" (Bourrienne 1993, 145). He also discussed an Alexandrine-like campaign to India (ibid., 161). General Alexander Berthier also noted that Napoleon explored the possibility of a Suez canal and ordered preliminary planning (*Military Journal* 1800, 91). Nevertheless, the destruction of his fleet at Aboukir and the failure of his Levantine campaign curbed the colonial project and the pursuit of further conquests. Napoleon collaborated in a plot to overthrow the Directory and secretly left Egypt, abandoning his army, which surrendered to British and Turkish forces in August 1801.[41]

The manifold significance of the French occupation has produced a lively historiography (see Gelvin 2003). While building ramparts, French soldiers unearthed the Rosetta Stone, a basalt slab with etched Greek, demotic Egyptian, and hieroglyphics. Although it involved over two decades of intense study, the artifact served as the cipher revealing the meaning of hieroglyphics (see Chapter 1). Furthermore, the scholars and engineers who accompanied Bonaparte meticulously studied the Egyptian antiquities.[42] They eventually produced the monumental, multi-volume *Description de l'Egypte* (1809–1828), which inspired a wide range of academic interests.[43] The *Description*'s artistic depictions of the inventoried ancient architecture contributed significantly to Orientalism, a European intellectual and aesthetic construction of the "East" (meaning the Mashriq and Maghrib), which exoticized and inferiorized these regions and their peoples. Jean-Baptiste Joseph Fourier, a mathematician, wrote the "Historical Preface" to the *Description* and articulated French imperial ambitions:

> Egypt, which unites the riches of agriculture with those of commerce, has other advantages that only a distant colony would offer. It is separated from France

by only a small extent of ocean, the navigation of which is the prerogative of
this power and her natural allies. The proposal [for a canal] engages with the
common defence of the neighbours of Italy, those of the Adriatic and the Ar-
chipelago. . . . This country offers to France [the] very remarkable advantage of
an intermediate situation: placed at the doors of Asia, it is possible to continually menace the rich possession of an enemy state [England] and to threaten
or make war by incursions on the source of her opulence [India]. . . . A French
colony, so favourably situated, will exercise its influence on the state of the
neighbouring countries. Arabia and Syria will participate in the first advantages. . . . We will contract durable and beneficial alliances with Persia and the
monarchies of Asia. We will penetrate all parts of the vast continent of Africa.
(Russell 2001, 17)

Fourier regretted that those ambitions were unfulfilled, given the restoration
of "ancient oppressors" (ibid., 26).[44] Nevertheless, he, Napoleon, and others
posited an imperial discourse regarding North Africa. Europeans also perceived the weakness of Egypt, the Ottoman Empire, and the Maghrib, which
inspired imperialist imaginations. Darrell Dykstra reminds that "the French
occupation, particularly through the subsequent publication of the memoirs
and engravings of the savants, had an immense impact on what Europeans
knew about Egypt—but that impact was upon Europe, not Egypt. . . . The ideas
and images of an Egypt so thoroughly and authoritatively 'described' would
shape European thinking . . . for generations" (Dykstra 1998, 2:137). European
representations of Egypt shaped discourse and scholarship and manufactured knowledge that unfortunately presented and perpetuated convenient
and expedient stereotypes and binary relationships. Juan R. I. Cole perceived
that

The French attempted to construct the Egyptian in many ways, both as Other
and as Self. . . . The French occupation of Egypt was perhaps the first in a long
line of liberal colonial adventures. . . . The rhetoric of liberal colonialism, pioneered by Napoleon Bonaparte and his officers, was constituted by several sets
of contradictions, between Self and Other, civilization and barbarism, liberty
and dominance, public and private, male and female, Great Powers diplomacy
and local politics. (Cole 2003, 48)

France's Egyptian adventure disclosed the manifold complexity of European
imperialism and later colonialism in North Africa (and elsewhere). Deeper
discursive and epistemological consequences lay beneath apparent surface

political and economic considerations. The ramifications of this transcultural experience were enormous.

Although he assailed the French, al-Jabarti grudgingly admitted an appreciation for some of their intentions which benefited Egypt: "The French nation . . . longed to deliver Egypt from its sad state and to relieve its people from the Ottomans who dominated it in ignorance and stupidity." He noted that the French "did not interfere in anyone's affairs nor did they deal cruelly with the population. Indeed, their purpose was to set Egypt's affairs in order" (al-Jabarti 1975, 86).[45] Furthermore, al-Jabarti valued the books the French brought with them:

> When some Muslims would come to look around they would not prevent them
> from entering. Indeed they would bring them all kinds of printed books in
> which there were all sorts of illustrations and *cartes* (*karat*) of the countries
> and regions, animals, birds, plants, histories of the ancients, campaigns of the
> nations, tales of the prophets including pictures of them, of their miracles and
> wondrous deeds, the events of their respective peoples and such things which
> baffle the mind. (ibid., 116)

He observed that the French

> have a great interest in the sciences, mainly in mathematics and the knowledge
> of languages, and make great efforts to learn the Arabic language and the collo-
> quial. In this they strive day and night. And they have books especially devoted
> to all types of languages, their declensions and conjugations as well as their
> etymologies. They possess extraordinary astronomical instruments of perfect
> construction and instruments for measuring altitudes of wondrous amazing
> and precious construction. And they have telescopes for looking at the stars and
> measuring their scopes, sizes, heights, conjunctions, and oppositions, and the
> clepsydras [water clocks] and clocks with gradings and minutes and seconds, all
> of wondrous form. (ibid., 117)

A display of chemical reactions presented by the French also astonished al-Jabarti. He concluded: "They had strange things . . . and devices and appara-tus achieving results which minds like ours cannot comprehend" (al-Jabarti 1994, 3:57). Nevertheless, ideas were exchanged. Al-Jabarti recounts that "the French head physician sent gift copies of his study on the treatment of small-pox to the members of the *diwan,* in order that the study might be disseminated. . . . The members accepted the gift, and sent a letter of thanks to the author. It is not a bad study on the subject" (ibid., 3:224).

Al-Jabarti's writings are some of the most important in the history of modern North Africa. They describe in detail the interaction between the French and the Muslims. His *Tarikh muddat al-Faransi bi Misr* (History of the French Period in Egypt) was probably written concurrent to the first ten months of the French occupation. Al-Jabarti's narrative captures the immediacy of this emotional event. His perspective is conflicted. Appalled by the invasion and occupation, he yet finds French technology and scholarship intriguing. His more detached narrative, a running chronicle of Egyptian history during this time, known as the *Tarikh 'Aja'ib al-Athar fi-l-Tarajim wa-l-Akhbar* (History of Remarkable Remnants of Lives and Events), densely chronicles the period. He reiterates his criticisms, but the perspective widens. Indeed, he despises the Ottomans' backwardness since it impedes Egypt's potential. Al-Jabarti recognizes the importance of European advancements, but he still has difficulties reconciling them with his religious beliefs and culture. His significance is thus doubled. First, he provides us with a first-hand account of a Muslim's critical perspective of incipient modern European imperialism. Second, his narrative illustrates a troubling realization—the ossification of Muslim society and culture. Al-Jabarti appreciated the need to appropriate French and European knowledge, but he also struggled with the inevitable consequences of that interaction.[46] His scholarship offers an existential dimension to this exceptional example of transcultural history.

The ephemeral French occupation remains a seminal event in North African history. The conquest and occupation shocked Egypt, the Ottoman Empire, and Islamdom. It created new sets of power relations ranging from political affairs to scientific experiments. Modernity became identified with imperial conquest and colonialism. It also made Europeans aware of their growing power in contrast to that of non-Europeans, what Edward Said called a "positional superiority" (Said 1979, 7). That realization fueled political ambitions and fashioned academic and popular discourse. Yet, in the short term, the potential of European technology and science especially inspired an ambitious Ottoman officer, who eventually became the de facto ruler of Egypt. His name was Muhammad (Mehmed) Ali.

Conclusion

From the arrival of the Ottomans to the departure of Napoleon's troops, several important changes occurred in the transcultural relations between North Africa and its wider world. Fernand Braudel believed in "the unity and coherence of the Mediterranean region" and held "the firm conviction that the Turkish Mediterranean lived and breathed with the same rhythms as the Christian, that the whole sea shared a common destiny... with identical problems and general trends if not identical consequences" (Braudel 1972–1973, 1:14). Nevertheless, he also acknowledged that the Ottomans and Habsburgs occupied two "maritime worlds," although there were "trading links and cultural exchanges." Each was autonomous with "their spheres of influence. Genuine intermingling of populations was to be found only inside each region, and within these limits it defied all barriers of race, culture, or religion" (ibid., 1:134–135). Andrew C. Hess questioned Braudel's "unitary vision of the Mediterranean world." In his interpretation, he posited that "the separation of the Mediterranean world into different, well-defined cultural spheres is the main theme of its sixteenth-century history" (Hess 1978, 2–3). As the competition and conflict between the two empires roiled the Mediterranean and especially North Africa, frontiers became sharply delineated. To Hess, "The attendant disappearance of cultural ambivalence along the Ibero-African frontier was the border manifestation of a much larger, unique divergence of Latin Christian and Turko-Muslim civilizations" (ibid., 207). He pointed out that "each imperial center contributed to the formalization of a border structure that inhibited cultural diffusion" (ibid., 211). Actually, the interpretations of Braudel and Hess were not that far apart. Braudel stated that "each [empire] was a separate historical zone" and recognized that "the economic and cultural differences between the two zones became increasingly marked in the sixteenth century" (Braudel 1972–1973, 1:137).[47] Furthermore, the Mediterranean began to lose its strategic significance. The Habsburgs and Ottomans shifted their energies to other fronts and enemies—Protestants and Persians—and campaigned against each other in central Europe (failed Turkish sieges of Vienna in 1529 and 1683). Nevertheless, despite the widening power gap favoring Western Europe over the Ottoman Empire, caused in part by Europeans bypassing North African corsairs and Levantine middlemen regarding South and East Asian trade, Braudel contended that "for the easterners, it was essential to be associated with the superiority of the West, to share in its wealth whatever the price: from the West they wanted precious metals . . . and they were obliged to follow the progress of European technical advance. In return, developing western industry had to find markets for its surplus production" (Braudel 1972–1973, 1:138). The emerging modern world economy (or world-system) featured the dynamic and diverse yet specialized "core" economies of Western Europe and the increasingly marginalized ("monoculture") "peripheral" economies of Eastern Europe, Africa, and Asia (see Wallerstein 1974, 1:102). Consequently, European capitalism convergent with political centralization harnessed extraordinary resources and energies, allowing for venture investment that eventually led to the industrial revolution. Furthermore, European power and ambition, fueled by capital accumulation and technological superiority, stirred an incipient and subtle imperialism that also aimed to incorporate peripheral economies into the growing world (European-dominated) economy. These changing economic and political realities transformed transcultural relations, affecting the decline of interactions on an equal level between Europeans and Muslims.[48] Thus, another result of these changes was epistemological, an altering of the reception and perception of others.

   "Uncritical and unrevised" eighteenth century geographical and historical compilations stereotyped North Africa and its peoples. By the end of the century the academic tone became more judgmental and dangerously aggressive. In *Encyclopédie des voyages* (1796), Jacques Grasset de Saint-Sauveur wrote: "The Turks and Algerians, not anxious for large families, behave as true pirates on the marital bed. They ravage the fields of sensual delight without making any effort to have them bear fruit." He added: "Nature fertilizes their lands in vain; the slothful citizens turn deaf ears to the imprecations of nature." He queried: "When will those nations concerned about the freedom of the seas unite in a political crusade against this African rabble whose brigandage is encouraged only by our patience?" (Valensi 1977, xx–xxi).[49]

   The decline of Turkish energy and enterprise in the Mediterranean in the late sixteenth century compounded by the continental defeats in Europe at the end of the seventeenth century steepened the decline of Ottoman power. Although Napoleon's invasion illustrated Ottoman weakness, France's Royal Company of Africa already dominated the commerce in the western Mediterranean. In addition, French merchants enjoyed "capitulations" or economic, cultural, and legal extraterritorial privileges within the empire. The tone of transcultural encounter represented the final major change. Reinforced by their belief in their political, social, economic, technological, and economic superiority, Napoleon, in spite of his intellectual sensibilities toward Islamic civilization, and the French imposed upon rather than interacted with Egyptians. They regarded the Egyptians as inferior, which inhibited positive transcultural relations except during occasional individual or private encounters. Long after Napoleon and his troops departed Egypt, this attitudinal superiority perpetuated through diverse Orientalist expressions and discourses.

The history of the Ottoman Empire's regencies and Morocco's sharifian dynasties during this period illustrated that North Africa remained politically impressive. Yet there was also fragmentation. Jacques Berque perceived that the Ottoman arrival represented a discontinuity that led Algeria and Tunisia (as well as Libya and Egypt) "to take different paths than that of Morocco" (Berque 1978, 543). European imperialism eventually intersected those paths, including Morocco's.

Notably, the Algiers Regency and the Saʿdi sultanate repelled European incursions and invasions. The Ottomans, Saʿdis, and Alawis succeeded in retaking several European coastal enclaves. Nevertheless, European powers remained aggressively ambitious, as illustrated by Napoleon's startling adventure. Even the fledgling United States asserted itself in North Africa, negotiating the release of captives in Algiers and, from 1801 to 1805, engaging militarily the Tripoli Regency. In 1815, after a brief conflict, the United States dictated terms to the dey of Algiers, demanding an indemnity and the termination of tribute, thereby ending its "Barbary Wars" (see Parker 2004).[50] By the early nineteenth century Morocco had entered a self-imposed isolation. The Ottoman regencies disclosed dangerous vulnerabilities and Ottoman Egypt had experienced a brief but consequential European conquest and occupation. Lacking countervailing power, North Africa from Cairo to Western Sahara's Cape Bojador faced a foreboding future.

European Colonialism in North Africa

In 1816, Edward Pellew (Lord Exmouth), commanding a formidable Anglo-Dutch fleet, sailed into Algiers's harbor under a white flag and then ordered a ferocious bombardment of its ramparts at point blank range. The salvoes delivered a message to the regency and to other corsair states that with the wars of the French Revolution over, Europe would no longer tolerate predatory privateering.[1] Indeed, France seized Algiers, ending the Ottoman regency in 1830. Subsequent campaigns resulted in the demarcation of three North African departments that assimilated "Algeria" as an integral part of France.

There were other historic forces at work that inevitably transformed North Africa and the world. During the course of the nineteenth century, industrialization revolutionized European capitalism and politics as financial institutions backed by national governments insidiously intruded upon fragile, vulnerable polities, such as Tunisia and Egypt. Furthermore, European mass-produced commodities overwhelmed those produced by North African manufacturers and artisans. Despite varying degrees of resourceful and recalcitrant resistance, by the beginning of World War I, North Africa and the Sahara were under European control.

Each North African colonial experience had its individual character. In Egypt, a new dynasty asserting independence ironically paved the way for British intervention. The initial French presence in Algeria was incidental, but it eventually resulted in the implantation of European settlements and the institutionalization of an oppressive colonialism. Tunisia and Morocco became French protectorates primarily because of European continental as well as overseas rivalries. Italy's takeover of Ottoman Tripolitania exploited a debilitated, anachronistic empire. Even Spain, a marginal second-rate power, resumed its historical aggression in North Africa and claimed territory, notably Western Sahara. The multiple consequences of European colonialism in North Africa were and are enormous.

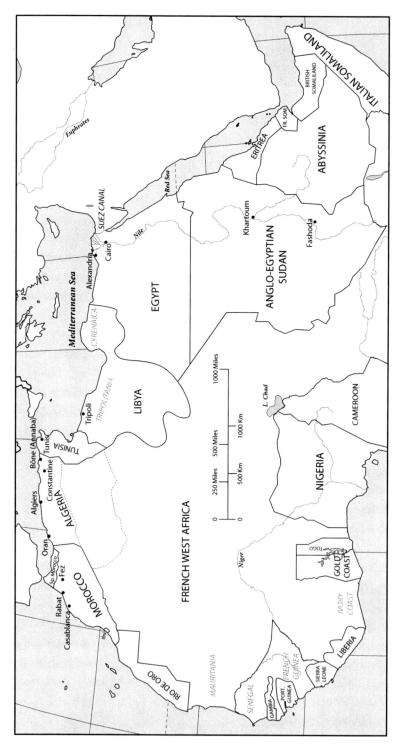

Colonial Northern Africa (1914)

The Alids in Egypt

The Alids' legacy in Egyptian history is considerable and controversial. Like other foreign dynasties in Egypt's sedimentary history, the Alids began with an impressive leader, Muhammad Ali. His achievements in modernizing Egypt worried Great Britain to such a degree that it mounted efforts to stem his ambitions. His grandson, Isma'il, accelerated modernization, but he fell deep into debt, which eventually led to European intrusive interference and, in 1882, British intervention and occupation.

Muhammad Ali: Modernizer

After overthrowing the Directory and replacing it with the Consulate, Napoleon emerged as First Consul and began one of the most productive periods in his storied career. The failure of his Egyptian and Levantine adventure was overlooked and refashioned to manufacture an image of military success and French largesse, an example of the French *mission civilisatrice* or civilizing mission.[2] On the other hand, Egypt had not forgotten Napoleon. The political morass left by the French general provided an opportunity for the enterprising Ottoman, Muhammad Ali. He was among the Ottoman troops who landed in Egypt allied with the British to expel the French. After the British, in turn, left Egypt in 1803, the Ottomans, perceiving the weakness of the Mamluks, took advantage of the situation to reassert their rule and end Mamluk autonomy. Nevertheless, Albanian troops rebelled from Ottoman command and elevated their leader to power. After he was assassinated, Muhammad Ali assumed control. Appointed pasha or governor of Egypt in 1805, he methodically amassed power despite the growing apprehension of Constantinople. In addition, Muhammad Ali thwarted British designs regarding Egypt. The British had captured Alexandria, but the pasha repelled them when they attempted to seize Rosetta in 1807. The British subsequently withdrew from Alexandria.

Muhammad Ali's plans for the transformation of Egypt could not be attained until he neutralized or eliminated the influence of the ulama and Mamluks. In 1809, he moved against the ulama by confiscating their properties. The loss of their economic base ensured their dependence upon his government. Then he ruthlessly plotted the decisive destruction of the Mamluks. In 1811, he invited Mamluk leaders to a banquet and massacred them. The pasha was now unrivaled.

In a tradition dating from the Tulunids, Muhammad Ali imported Turko-Circassian soldiers to help him dominate Egypt. Ironically, this practice revived "mamlukization" and eventually resulted in the creation of an Alid Turko-Circassian elite. Coptic and especially European financial advisers also assisted in designing Muhammad Ali's modernization reforms. One of the most notable Europeans was a Frenchman, Antoine-Barthélemy Clot. "Clot Bey" played a decisive role in introducing European medicinal practices (see Sonbol 2003). Furthermore, enterprising Europeans (especially Greeks), in collaboration with the state, played an important role in multiplying import/export mercantile links in the Mediterranean. Foreign merchants competed with Egyptian businessmen, reducing the latter's political potential and economic power (see Lawson 1992, 69–70).

Muhammad Ali also mobilized a large army, which included Egyptian conscripts,[3] and outfitted an impressive navy to serve his suzerain, the Ottoman sultan, as well as his own ambitions.[4] Commanded by his son Ibrahim Pasha, Alid armed forces by 1813 recovered the Holy Sites and most of the Hijaz (Mecca and Medina) from the Wahhabis, a late eighteenth-century Islamist movement fervently opposed to Sufism. The Egyptian troops captured their capital, Dar'iyya, in 1818. Muhammad Ali's army also fought against Greek rebels in Crete and in the Morea (southern Greece). Nevertheless, the pasha feared the intervention of European powers.[5] His apprehension was well founded. After his navy joined with that of Sultan Mahmud II (r. 1808–1839), an allied European fleet (British, French, and Russian) annihilated the Egyptian-Turkish fleet at the battle of Navarino in 1827. This victory ensured Greek independence. Egyptian sacrifices and losses also alienated Muhammad Ali from Constantinople. Muhammad Ali had provided costly assistance with little or no gain. From his perspective, serving the sultan impeded his own imperial dreams. Beginning in 1820, Isma'il, another son of Muhammad Ali's, campaigned in the south (Upper Egypt) and eventually secured northern Sudan (ancient Nubia or Kush). The principal reasons for the Egyptian empire-building in Sudan was to obtain gold, slaves, soldiers, and laborers.

Muhammad Ali concurrently accelerated the modernization of Egypt. He created a European-styled government with officials, who served like ministers, heading divans or departments. The pasha organized a centralized, command economy that monopolized trade and promoted cotton, grain, flax, safflower, sugar cane, and rice production. Consequently, the government appropriated crops and controlled prices from the overworked and overexploit-ed peasantry. It also abolished tax farming and replaced it with more efficient direct taxation. Muhammad Ali also eliminated middlemen and imposed the state in their stead. To al-Jabarti: "The pasha . . . began fiendishly acquiring money by any means possible, he invented taxes and had them entered in the registers kept by the clerks and accountants . . . so that these became a part of the state funds insofar as collection, expenditure, and remittance were con-cerned" (al-Jabarti 1994, 4:236). With the direct revenues and monies earned from cash crops, Muhammad Ali invested in a manufacturing (second) sec-tor featuring textiles and munitions. A lack of natural resources to produce energy dashed his hopes for widespread industrialization. Nevertheless, he prudently monitored his finances and expenditures, emplaced high tariffs to protect his incipient industries, and stayed out of debt.[6] To Afaf Lutfi al-Sayyid Marsot, Muhammad Ali's mercantilist mentality fueled his autarkic ambitions (see Marsot 2007, 65–66).

He recognized the need to support and extend education. He inaugurated technical schools, which translated European textbooks. According to al-Jabarti, "the pasha became convinced . . . that Egyptians have a superior apti-tude for the sciences" (al-Jabarti 1994, 4:359). A printing press began distrib-uting literature in 1815. Furthermore, he encouraged overseas studies. Rifa'a al-Tahtawi embodied the modernizing Egyptian. A perceptive young religious scholar, al-Tahtawi lived in France from 1826 to 1831. He contrasted Europe's knowledge and power (especially its technology) with those of Muslim states and societies and reported:

> The pre-eminence of these Christians in the sciences will become clear to you. At the same time, you will recognize that many of these sciences are absent from our countries, despite the fact that the venerable al-Azhar mosque in Cairo, the Umayyad mosque in Damascus, the Zaytuna mosque in Tunis, the Qarawiyyin mosque in Fez, the religious schools of Bukhara, etc., all radiate through the traditional sciences as well as certain rational sciences such as Arabic philology, logic and other auxiliary sciences. (al-Tahtawi 2004, 256)

Although al-Tahtawi witnessed upheaval, notably the Revolution of 1830, he admired the French political system: "Their wonderful government system can serve as an example to those wishing to learn from it" (ibid., 189). Enthu-siastically advocating extensive reform, al-Tahtawi also pioneered Islamic modernism (see below).

Inevitably, Muhammad Ali moved against Sultan Mahmud II, who was also a modernizer. Indeed, Mahmud's destruction of the corrupt Janissaries and development of a modern army threatened Muhammad Ali's cherished autonomy. Conflict broke out and Ibrahim Pasha drove into Syria in 1831. After he defeated an Ottoman army, Mahmud surrendered Syria to Egypt in 1833. The sultan viewed the loss of Syria as provisional and plotted his revenge. Ottoman forces attacked Syria in 1839, but Ibrahim Pasha repulsed them. Mahmud died soon afterward and it appeared that Muhammad Ali would take over the Ottoman Empire. European powers, led by Lord Palmerston of Great Britain, quickly intervened and forced Ibrahim to leave the Levant.[7] Furthermore, Great Britain imposed economic conditions, including free trade, which deprived Egypt (and the Ottoman Empire) of tariff protection.[8] Without protection Egypt's second sector could not compete with Europe's and especially Great Britain's industrial production. Subsequently, European commodities flooded Egypt, inundating Muhammad Ali's industrial aspirations—a telling example illustrating how global economics influenced policy and power. In the context of Wallerstein's world-system ideas, Britain prevented Egypt from attaining its "core" economic ambitions and assigned it to a subordinate "peripheral status" (Wallerstein 1974, 3:151). On the other hand, the Ottomans recognized the establishment of Muhammad Ali's hereditary line, the Alids, as Egypt's rulers. With his most coveted ambitions unfulfilled, the pasha died in 1849.[9] Nevertheless, as Marsot explained: "Muhammad Ali Egyptianized Egypt, although he himself did not plan to do that and never knew that he had done it" (Marsot 2007, 77). He left a legacy as not only the father of modern Egypt, but also, on an existential level, he contributed to the formation of the modern Egyptian's identity and character.[10] Furthermore, Muhammad Ali was a transcultural agent, insisting upon interaction with and integration of European techniques and technologies. Once again, Egypt served as a transcultural conduit, this time mediating modernity from the West to the East.

Khedive Isma'il

After the death of Muhammad Ali, his eldest grandson Abbas I Hilmi (r. 1849–1854) ruled Egypt. A reactionary, Abbas slowed most of the modernization projects, including the translations of European books. He allowed the British to build, however, a railroad from Alexandria to Cairo and then to

Suez. The increasing British presence was intended to impede the expanding French influence in Egypt.[11] Nevertheless, Sa'id (r. 1854–1863) resumed rapid modernization and assigned a concession in 1854 to his French friend, Ferdinand de Lesseps, to build the Suez Canal.[12] The pasha also ended the state monopoly over the land and opened it up to private owners. On the surface, peasants seemed to benefit, but they were vulnerable to the vagaries of the agricultural market, often fell into debt, and sold their holdings. Consequently, large, wealthy landowners and large estates dominated the agricultural sector. Landless peasants, lacking economic opportunity or evading forced labor and military conscription, headed toward Egypt's swelling cities.

Isma'il (r. 1863–1879) came to power during a lucrative period in the Egyptian economy. With southern ports blockaded during the American Civil War, European ("core") industries, starved for cotton, devoured Egypt's long staple crop. In turn, Isma'il lavishly spent the influx of income from cotton sales to modernize, if not Europeanize, Egypt. He built railroads, installed telegraphs, and initiated urban renewal. Like Muhammad Ali, Isma'il considered Egypt's development and modernization as crucially important. Furthermore, he asserted Egyptian independence by minting coins in 1866 and by officially acquiring from Constantinople (through bribes) the title of "khedive" or viceroy. The khedive created ministries of state and even a Chamber (or Assembly) of Notables, apparent steps toward a constitutional monarchy, although it is doubtful that he would have relinquished decisive power. Unlike Muhammad Ali, he overspent and fell dangerously into debt. After the American Civil War ended, Egyptian cotton prices plunged, collapsing the economy.

By that time he was committed toward financing and completing one of the great engineering feats of modern times, the Suez Canal. Construction began in earnest in 1866. Toiling workers courageously confronted terrible conditions. Lady Duff Cooper scathingly reported regarding the French-Egyptian collaboration: "Everyone is cursing the French here. Forty thousand men always at work at the Suez Canal at starvation-point, does not endear them to the Arabs" (Gordon 1969, 66). One of the modern wonders of the world, the canal opened in 1869 amid celebrations and festivities. Members of Europe's aristocracy attended, including France's Empress Eugénie and Austria's Emperor Franz Joseph.[13] After being pressured, Giuseppe Verdi accepted a commission to compose an Egyptian-themed opera to commemorate the canal's completion. *Aïda,* which became one of Verdi's most famous operas, opened at the Cairo Opera House in late 1871 (see Humbert 2003). (The inaugural celebration featured a performance of *Rigoletto*.) The Canal's importance raised Egypt's strategic value exponentially but deepened its enormous debt.

Loans and arrears soared to the point where the khedive decided to sell his shares in the Suez Canal Company. British Prime Minister Benjamin Disraeli's government eagerly sought them and, with the assistance of financier Lionel Rothschild, successfully outbid a French consortium. Disraeli's success in purchasing the shares in 1875 gave the British 44 percent of the Suez Canal Company and, consequently, a deep stake in Egyptian affairs.[14] Most important, the British placed two members on the company's board, which gave them predominant control.

During the following year, the Caisse de la Dette Publique, composed of four foreign commissioners representing the principal bondholding countries (Great Britain, France, Italy, and Austria-Hungary), was inaugurated. Intrinsically intrusive, the Caisse, established as a supervisory financial organization, aimed to protect foreign interests and investments. Furthermore, Great Britain and France imposed a "Dual Control" to manage Egyptian finances. Clearly, the khedive's mishandling of the economy undermined his power and imperiled Egypt's autonomy. His country increasingly belonged to Europe, but not in the way that he hoped.

Isma'il endeavored to free himself from the grasp of the Europeans, especially from the Dual Control. To succeed, however, he needed the support of the sultan, despite the often strained relations between Cairo and Constantinople. When Isma'il assumed an apparent nationalist position, Sultan Abdulhamid II (r. 1876–1908), under European pressure, compelled Isma'il to abdicate. His son Muhammad Tawfiq (r. 1879–1892) became khedive, but Egypt soon slipped into British hands.

The British Occupy Egypt

Isma'il's belated response to European intrusions intensified Egyptian nationalism. The National Popular Party or Watani Party (al-Hizb al-Watani al-Ahli) was formed in 1881. It unified nationalists and coalesced around Col. Ahmad Urabi Pasha, a prominent Egyptian officer. When relations between Egyptians and Europeans worsened, the British and French sent a combined naval task force to Alexandria, but this action provoked rioting.[15] After negotiation failed, the British landed troops and defeated the "Urabists" in

September 1882.[16] This operation, ostensibly meant to provide provisional protection, led to a British occupation and interference in Egyptian affairs, which lasted until 1956, when another Egyptian colonel (Gamal Abdel Nasser) challenged the British.

Once in Egypt, the British stayed; too much was at stake, especially the route to India through the Suez Canal. Evelyn Baring became consul general in 1883 and de facto ruler of the country. Elevated to the peerage in 1892, Lord Cromer was an experienced administrator who had served in India. Marshall Hodgson described Cromer as

> a highly cultured, observant, and dedicated man, [who] represented a clas-sic Modern Western attitude to those peoples who had not participated from within in the Modern Transmutation; to their place in the world, and to their nationalism. He found them (in this case, the Egyptians) a backward race, need-ing to be protected and guided by Europeans for their own good as well as for the safety of the Europeans. (Hodgson 1974, 3:241–242)

To Berque, Cromer was "a liberal in economic matters [and] an autocrat in administration" (Berque 1972, 147). He applied his experience in India or as Berque put it, "Egypt *à l'Indienne*" (ibid., 146–169), efficiently administered Egypt, and placed its finances in order. A new progressive legal code ended imprisonment for debt, a particular relief for the peasantry. The British fa-vored the primary sector, agriculture, and relegated the potentially competi-tive secondary sector, manufacturing.[17] Furthermore, Cromer's government limited educational opportunities. Foreign populations also benefited from extraterritoriality agreements. Ethnically diverse communities, such as the Greeks in Alexandria, also encouraged trade and cosmopolitanism. Ehud R. Toledano perceived that British rule "was *exclusivist* in its approach to the local elites and exploitative economically, in contrast to the *inclusivist* rule of the Ottomans, which also allowed a greater share of the surplus to be spent in Egypt itself" (Toledano 1998, 2:284).

There was also the attitudinal, Orientalist dimension to British imperial-ism in Egypt. Cromer wrote: "I have lived too long in the East not to be aware that it is difficult for any European to arrive at a true estimate of Oriental wish-es, aspirations, and opinions" (Cromer 1908, 1:6–7). He contended that "the want of mental symmetry and precision . . . is the chief distinguishing feature between the illogical and picturesque East and the logical West" (ibid., 1:7).[18]

Fundamentally, Cromer was an imperial technocrat who identified with his idealized (and autobiographical) notion of the Englishman taking up the notion of Rudyard Kipling's "white man's burden": "[The Englishman] was convinced that his mission was to save Egyptian society, and, moreover that he was able to save it" (ibid., 2:124). Perhaps surprising to readers, Cromer rejected the idea of an outright absorption of Egypt into the British Empire and instead foresaw an autonomous state (ibid., 2:564). He envisioned a transcultural Egyptian autonomy,

> one which will enable all the dwellers in cosmopolitan Egypt, be they Moslem or Christian, Ethiopian, or African, to be fused into a self-governing body. That it may take years—possibly generations—to achieve this object is more than probable, but unless it can be achieved, any idea of autonomy, in the true sense of the term, will, in my opinion, have to be abandoned. (ibid., 2:568–569)

In the meantime, the British exercised what Cromer called "paramount influence" in Egyptian affairs (ibid., 2:125).

Wider Consequences of the British Occupation

The British occupation of Egypt also impacted Sudan. As mentioned earlier, Alid Egypt expanded south into Sudan beginning with Muhammad Ali. During Isma'il's reign, Egyptians established a presence along the Somali coast (reminiscent of the ancient Punt relationship). Egyptian efforts to invade Abyssinia failed and included a major defeat in 1876. The rise of a charismatic leader named Muhammad Ahmad (1843?–1885), who professed to be the Mahdi, menaced the Alid influence in Sudan. He aimed to establish an Islamic state. In 1885, the Ahmadiyya or Mahdist movement overwhelmed khedival forces at Khartoum, commanded by the British soldier of fortune, Charles George "Chinese" Gordon, a veteran of the Taiping Rebellion in China. Gordon, a popular figure in Victorian England, became a martyred national hero. Jacques Berque considered Gordon as "unstable, impressionable, trusting his intuitions. He was a mystic, sent by Victorian England to the Sudan to conquer another mystic [Muhammad Ahmad]" (Berque 1972, 143). The British perceived the Mahdist presence along the Nile as a threat to their position in Egypt. At the battle of Omdurman in 1898, Lord Herbert Kitchener defeated the Mahdists, thereby expanding British authority into Sudan. Concurrently, a French expedition had arrived at Fashoda to the south. A confrontation seemed imminent, but the French backed down. The "Fashoda Incident" il-lustrated the implicit dangers of the "Scramble for Africa." Indeed, according to historians, the British takeover of Egypt provoked the "Scramble" (see Robinson and Gallagher 1961). The Anglo-Egyptian conquest of Sudan resulted in 1899 in a declaration of a "condominium" of the territory. An agreement was concluded that called for a shared administration of the vast territory, but, in reality, the British controlled Sudan.

The British occupation of Egypt (and Sudan) and the growing European penetration and interference in the Ottoman Empire and Qajar Persia in-spired the itinerant Islamist, Jamal al-Din al-Afghani, and his principal asso-ciate, the Egyptian Muhammad Abduh, to propagate ideas known as Islamic modernism. From the modernists' perspective, Muslim civilization, especial-ly the Muslim-Arab heritage, required a *nahda* or renaissance. Al-Afghani and Abduh dismissed the notion that Islam and modernism were incompatible. The rise of European power through science and industrialism needed to be appreciated and appropriated by Muslims. Al-Afghani may have been refer-ring to himself when he wrote:

> There is no doubt that in the present age, distress, misfortune, and weakness besiege all classes of Muslims from every side. Therefore every Muslim keeps his eyes and ears open in expectation—to the East, West, North, and South—to see from what corner of the earth the sage and renewer will appear and will reform the minds and souls of the Muslims, repel the unforeseen corruption, and again educate them with a virtuous education. Perhaps through that good education they may return to their former joyful condition. (Keddie 1968, 125)

John Esposito explained: "Afghani maintained that the strength and sur-vival of the *umma* were dependent on the reassertion of Islamic identity and solidarity. He exhorted Muslims to realize that Islam was the religion of rea-son and science—a dynamic, progressive, creative force capable of respond-ing to the demands of modernity" (Esposito 2005, 128). Abduh amplified al-Afghani's ideas by calling for education and a regenerated, enlightened mo-rality. In an article published in *al-Manar* in February 1906, he urged reform

> to free minds from the constraints of imitation [*taqlid*] and to lead them to the universe of freedom of thought and deduction. The object is to teach the art of intellectual production and initiation of scientific movement in the fields of ethics, sociology, religion, language, and philosophical sciences, such as those

that came to being during the flourishing epochs of al-Ma'mun and others. (Moaddel and Talattof 2000, 51)

Abduh evoked a historical consciousness, namely the memory of the *aslaf* or venerated and virtuous forebears of the early generations of Islam. Thus, Abduh's "salafiyya" identified with Islamic modernism and the *nahda*. Furthermore, Mustafa Kamil, a talented journalist and effective ideologue, articulated nationalist arguments, which his anti-British Hizb al-Watani (National Party) amplified. Egypt was stirring.

Egyptian dissatisfaction with the British heightened over the Dinshaway Incident of 1906. A British party hunting pigeons, a local economic staple, infuriated villagers from the village of Dinshaway (Dinshwai), who violently confronted the British. One British officer died of sunstroke and later one Egyptian was beaten to death in reprisal. Retributive British justice resulted in flogging, imprisonment, and four death sentences.

As a result of Dinshaway, nationalist resentment deepened, as expressed by the Hizb al-Watani and the more moderate Umma Party. There was also Egyptian administrative resistance to the prerogatives and policies of Lord Cromer, who resigned after Dinshaway. Nevertheless, the reality was that Egypt was in a colonial status, despite the technical travesty of being under the suzerainty of the Ottoman Empire and local khedival government. By 1914, the British had received international recognition of their occupation.

French Algeria

The first great European imperial "scramble" for territory featured the empire-building of Portugal and Spain in the fifteenth and sixteenth centuries and that of France, the Netherlands, and Great Britain in the seventeenth and eighteenth centuries. The second scramble during the late nineteenth and early twentieth centuries included, as we have seen, the British occupation of Egypt and takeover of Sudan. There is another period of European imperialism, however, that deserves our careful and critical attention—European expansion from the end of the French Revolution to the British occupation of Egypt (1815 to 1882). This era of "quiet imperialism," impelled by Europe's industrial economies, featured the subtle yet relentless global extension of European power and especially involved North Africa, most notably Algeria.

Causes of French Imperialism in Algeria

France historically recognized the Regency of Algiers's de facto independence and had developed strong commercial ties. Nevertheless, North African corsairs threatened French interests and ambitions in the Mediterranean, which led to Admiral Abraham Duquesne's bombardments of Algiers in the late seventeenth century. The immediate cause of the French invasion and takeover of Algiers related to a debt owed to Algerian Jewish exporting commercial firms for shipments of grain to France during the Directory (1795–1799).[19] The deys of Algiers represented their Jewish clients and constantly but vainly requested payment from the French.

The French consul's imperious attitude regarding this matter exasperated Husayn Dey (r. 1818–1830), the last ruler of the regency. In 1827, the dey slapped (or tapped) the consul with a fly whisk. This diplomatic affront resulted in a French blockade of Algiers.[20] At this time the ultra-conservative King Charles X (r. 1824–1830) ruled France and had alienated liberals. In an effort to distract the public's disaffection from his unpopular policies, he ordered the invasion of Algiers. Using plans devised by Napoleon's staff, the French expeditionary force of over 37,000 men sailed, landed, and overwhelmed Ottoman forces in June 1830. On 5 July 1830, the dey surrendered and signed a convention, which transferred his authority to the French, thereby ending the regency. Later that month, the July 1830 Revolution overthrew the unpopular Charles X. His cousin Louis-Philippe became "King of the French" and inherited the "Algerian" situation.

Louis-Philippe was uncertain with regard to the conquest. Therefore, he charged a commission to offer consultation. Its report presented familiar imperialist rationales. Militarily, a presence in Algeria provided tactical advantages by flanking and securing the western Mediterranean in French hands. Economically, Algeria potentially supplied French manufacturers with new markets. The commission posited the altruistic idea of a *mission civilisatrice* or civilizing mission. Most important, the French popularly approved the conquest, an important consideration for the new government and monarch seeking to strengthen legitimacy (see Naylor 2000a, 13–14). In 1834, colonization became the official policy although it was still defined as an *occupation restreinte* (limited occupation) (Heggoy 1981, 153).[21] By 1840, most of Algeria's coastline was in French hands.

Algerian Resistance to the French

French colonial plans confronted unremitting Algerian resistance. The principal opponent was the Emir Abd al-Qadir (1807–1883), a leader of the Qadiriyya brotherhood. His defeat of French forces in 1835 in western Algeria led to the Treaty of Tafna of 1837, which recognized his authority. Abd al-Qadir thereby organized a veritable state in western and central Algeria. The French also faced the resolute opposition of the Ottoman Ahmad Bey of Constantine. One French attempt to storm the city failed in 1836. It finally fell in 1837, but Ahmed Bey continued his resistance from southern Algeria for several more years.

Meanwhile, the conflicting ambitions of the French and the Algerians bred war again in western Algeria and hostilities resumed. Abd al-Qadir's state began to crumble before the army amassed by Marshal Thomas-Robert Bugeaud (108,000 soldiers). The emir (as well as refugees) crossed into Morocco and the French pursued, which provoked the battle of Isly with the sultanate in 1844 (see below). The French defeated the Moroccans and forced them to desist from assisting Abd al-Qadir, who surrendered in 1847; the French subsequently imprisoned and exiled the emir.[22] Despite his enduring resistance, the French respected Abd al-Qadir. Léon Roches, a French adventurer, camped with the emir's forces, became his "secretary," and romanticized the Algerian leader (see Berque 1974, 68–71). General F. F. Duvivier wrote several years before the Algerian leader's capture that "Abdelkader was Amir because Liberty had entrusted him with her sword. . . . He was the man of history; she will never forget him; she will repeat his name. . . . Unhappy son of the desert, future generations will honour your name" (Barbour 1959, 216–217, citing *Quatorze observations . . . du général Bugeaud* [1842]). Duvivier's prediction proved to be prescient.

Bugeaud left Algeria before Abd al-Qadir's capitulation. Nevertheless, the marshal is regarded as the true founder of French Algeria.[23] He mapped out plans for colonization reflecting the contemporary currents of utopian socialism. In addition, he not only mobilized the forces that inevitably overwhelmed Abd al-Qadir, but he also created the "Bureaux arabes." Bugeaud sought to have the bureaux play a mediating role between the settlers and the indigenous population (*les indigènes*). Like the Indian agents of the American West, the officers served as interlocutors between tribes and settlers. Many of the officers were Arabophone/Berberophone and treated the tribes with respect and dignity. Others were simply ignorant and, worse yet, indifferent. The marshal's relentlessly brutal campaigns against Abd al-Qadir and other resisters contradicted his admirable sensitivities toward the indigenous population and toward palliating colonial exploitation. Nevertheless, conspicuous cruelty, including the suffocation by fire and smoke of Algerians hiding in caves, characterized French military operations. Furthermore, resistance against the French took many forms. Nationalists later justifiably argued that Algeria never fully succumbed to France.[24]

The French moved into Kabylia in the 1850s, a Berber region in eastern Algeria, and faced more tough fighting. In the west, the Awlad Sidi Shaykh tribe rebelled during the 1860s. The greatest threat to the French presence occurred, however, with the Great Kabyle Revolt of 1871. The Rahmaniyya fraternal order played an important role in the insurrection. With great difficulty the French finally suppressed the "*indigènes*" and systematically expropriated hundreds of thousands of hectares. French colonialism equated with the confiscation of property and, psychologically, of person.

Colonialism in Algeria

There was a major difference distinguishing Algerian colonialism from other colonial situations in North Africa. From 1848 until 1962, Algeria was integral to France, administratively assimilated and demarcated with three departments. To the French mind, Algeria became an atavism—"Algeria is France."[25] This would have powerful and tragic consequences not only for the colonized population, but also for the colonial European settler (*colon/pied-noir*) community. The *colons* also became popularly known as the *pieds-noirs* or "black feet."[26] Eventually, *pieds-noirs* were identified with European settlers who lived in the burgeoning cities of Algeria, such as Algiers, Oran, and Bône (Annaba) (see Çeylik 1997; Prochaska 1990).

The *colons* tirelessly labored, transformed Algeria, and bonded with the land. Revolts (especially that of 1871) ended in confiscatory legislation, such as the Warnier Law of 1873, which expedited enormous land expropriation. From 1830 to 1940, the colonized experienced the loss of 3,445,000 hectares to the colonialists (Bennoune 1976, 13).[27] Left often with barren or uncultivable land, the dislocated and distraught Muslims suffered enormously, while the *colons* benefited from the most fertile fields.

An administrative struggle between the military and the civilian settler population marked the first forty years of colonial Algeria. The military's "rule of the saber" abruptly ended with the establishment of Prince Napoleon's civilian ministry of Algeria in 1858. Nevertheless, Napoleon III terminated the ministry in 1860 and displayed sensitivity toward the Muslim population, much to the chagrin of the settlers. The quixotic emperor, who also visited Algeria, even referred to the country as an "Arab Kingdom." Any Muslim hope of a qualified colonialism under Napoleon III ended with the disastrous Franco-Prussian War (1870–1871) abruptly ending the Second Empire. The establishment of the Third Republic secured civilian control and intensified the exploitation of Algeria and its people.

In the 1870s, a phylloxera blight ravaged Europe's grapevines. Unaffected by this economic disaster, Algeria expanded its viticulture and became a major wine producer and supplier. Grapevines replaced grain fields in a land where hunger chronically haunted the colonized. In 1880, viticulture covered 40,000 hectares, but by 1940, 400,000 hectares were devoted to wine production (Amin 1966, 1:39).

Viticulture symbolized the severity of colonialism upon the colonized. The physical transformation of the land was also a cultural affront, given Islam's proscription of alcohol.[28] Frantz Fanon, who played such an important role in articulating and analyzing the process of decolonization in Algeria, described how colonialism in general disoriented the colonized's personality, resulting in a "psychoexistential" condition.[29] He meant that colonialism inferiorized the colonized culturally, economically, and racially (Fanon 1967, 11–12). Colonialism not only alienated but also effaced the colonized's identity, resulting in "a feeling of non-existence" (ibid., 139). With their lives disrupted by colonialism, many Algerians faced a socially odious alternative—to emigrate to France to work in factories. French colonialism in Algeria was certainly injurious, but its indifference made it particularly oppressive.

On the other hand, the Church addressed the colonized, but its principal interest initially was in proselytizing rather than in protesting colonial conditions. Christian missionary work in Algeria especially centered among Kabyle orphans.[30] Archbishop Charles Lavigerie established the "White Fathers" in 1868 and the "White Sisters" in 1869. These orders aimed to convert the colonized and became identified with France's imperial enterprises in Africa. Their ambitious objective in Algeria was unsuccessful, although there were some converts. Nevertheless, the White Fathers and Sisters subsequently staffed hospitals, orphanages, and asylums. In addition, they were ardent opponents of slavery.

Although not a White Father, one of the most famous clerics was Charles Eugène de Foucauld, a dissipated cavalry officer, who completely reformed his life after military service in North Africa. He was ordained a priest and lived in a hermitage in the Hoggar Mountains deep in the Algerian Sahara (see Porch 1984, 277–289). De Foucauld failed in his efforts to convert the Tuareg, but his Christian devotion, extreme asceticism, and philology of Tamahaq, the Tuareg language, earned him local and international esteem. Nonetheless, marauding Tuaregs murdered him in 1916.[31]

The Establishment of the Tunisian and Moroccan Protectorates

In comparison with Algeria, Tunisia's and Morocco's shared status as protectorates rather than departments tempered their colonial experiences. Their pre-colonial histories were also similar. European encroachments attempting to protect property and promote economic interests slowly sapped the Tunis Regency's autonomy and Morocco's sovereignty. Unlike Algeria's experience, the establishment of the protectorates was closely linked to European continental diplomatic affairs. Tunisia and Morocco became pieces in the "Greater Game" of late nineteenth and early twentieth century diplomatic power plays.[32] Furthermore, unlike Algeria and Libya, but like Egypt, colonialism in Tunisia and Morocco preserved the pre-colonial administration and even advanced state-formation. During the colonial period, the ruling Husaynids in Tunisia and Alawis in Morocco kept their titles, but French authorities exercised decisive power.

The Tunisian Protectorate

Tunisia's Husaynids valiantly tried to maintain their autonomy, but with the French in Algeria and other Europeans playing greater controlling roles in Tunis's economy, it was a difficult and eventually impossible task. European assertiveness manifested itself after the Napoleonic wars. A French and British show of naval force in 1819 reinforced the protocol agreed upon in 1818 by the European Congress powers stating that piracy would no longer be tolerated.[33] Later, despite Husaynid support against Algiers,[34] a treaty with France in 1830 delivered a blow against the beylik's autonomy by creating a capitulations system providing preferential economic privilege and extra-legal protection to Europeans and their dependents. On the other hand, the French takeover of the Algiers Regency ended a chronic threat (but substituted another). The modernizing Ahmad I Bey (r. 1837–1855) notably initiated Westernizing military reforms and in 1840 inaugurated a polytechnic college at Bardo. Furthermore, he skillfully counterbalanced the threat of the restored Ottoman presence in Tripolitania with the thinly masked French ambition to absorb Tunisia (see Brown 1974, 238–240). By exercising diplomatic parry and parity with his aggressive neighbors, Ahmad Bey sustained a circumscribed independence.[35] He embodied the difficult transformation of North Africa, as L. Carl Brown assessed: "The would-be military Westernizer did not from time to time indulge his whims in a more comfortable oriental despotism. Ahmad consistently lived and worked according to an uneasy juxtaposition of new ideals and old, traditional habits" (ibid., 313).

After this remarkable ruler, the modernizing beylik continued to address the rapidly changing geopolitics of the region. The September 1857 "Pledge of Security" dealt with equality of Muslims and Europeans before the law and the inviolability of property and persons. It also allowed European acquisition of property (Abun-Nasr 1987, 281). In 1860, the Tunisians framed the first constitution in Islamdom. It created a remarkably liberal constitutional monarchy. Ministers were responsible to a supreme council, which acted as a parliament. The constitutional monarchy existed for only four years, but it illustrated a rising momentum toward reform, despite opposition from the ulama and other traditionalists. The very capable Khayr al-Din Pasha, a Francophile, led the reform movement and dominated Tunisian politics until the late 1870s.

Nevertheless, Tunisia fell deep into dept in the 1860s. Portending the Egyptian experience, an International Financial Commission was established in 1868–1869, which essentially took over the Tunisian economy. Khayr al-Din presided over the commission and Victor Villet, a French administrator, assisted him. As Abun-Nasr observed: "Villet became in fact, if not in form, the Tunisian minister of finance" (ibid., 283). In 1873, Khayr al-Din became prime minister. He reformed the tax system and promoted the economy, especially encouraging olive production. European consuls' opposition to high tariffs dashed his hope of stimulating Tunisian manufacturing (ibid., 285).

Khayr al-Din also founded Sadiqi (Sadiqiyya) College in 1875. Its Western curriculum aimed to prepare Tunisians to face the changing realities of the modern world.[36] Khayr al-Din's principal political task, which proved to be impossible, was to balance consular jurisdiction with the beylik's autonomy. He eventually alienated the French, who had promoted him, and resigned in 1877. Although Khayr al-Din Pasha is often admired as a reformer, Abun-Nasr critically contended that Khayr al-Din "shared with other nineteenth-century Muslim reformers the naïve conviction that cultural borrowing could be restricted to specific areas, so that the Islamic society would be rejuvenated while retaining its religious beliefs and values." Abun-Nasr also reminded: "As prime minister he did not restore the constitution of 1860" (ibid., 285–286).

Tunisia became increasingly strategic and part of the "Eastern Question."[37] The British wanted to keep the beylik linked to the Ottoman Empire, while the French wanted Tunisia to be more independent and thereby more accessible to their influence. Having completed its unification in 1870, Italy projected itself as a Mediterranean power. It entertained expansive designs at the expense of the nearby beylik. The Congress of Berlin of 1878 determined the fate of Tunisia. Otto von Bismarck, who had united Germany in 1870 and seized part of Lorraine and all of Alsace in 1871 (Treaty of Frankfurt), sought to distract France from revenge by encouraging overseas adventure. With Germany's support the beylik was recognized as within the French sphere of influence. Well aware of Italy's ambitions and the growing Italian population in the beylik, France decisively acted.

Claiming that Tunisian tribesmen had raided Algeria, the French mounted an ostensibly retributive expedition that crossed the border; but it headed instead for Tunis. Pressured also by the landing and occupation of Bizerte by French troops, the bey signed the Treaty of Bardo in 1881, which established the protectorate. France maintained the Husaynid beys as nominal rulers. The Marsa Convention of 1883 confirmed Tunisia's colonial status. Although *colons* took over land, which they *bought,* the exploitation, in general, was not as severe as that of Algeria. Furthermore, Paul Cambon as resident minister convinced the French National Assembly in 1884 to ratify the Marsa Convention and assume Tunisia's debt, which terminated the International Financial Commission. In addition, the recently elevated Cardinal Lavigerie petitioned the papacy to have the see of Carthage restored. His request was granted in 1884. Lavigerie also intervened on behalf of Muslims, who he felt were being treated unfairly. By this time White Fathers and White Sisters had shifted their priorities from proselytism to philanthropy (see above).

A group of progressive Tunisian reformers, an embryonic nationalist elite, emerged during the early protectorate. They called themselves the "Young Tunisians" and hoped that the French would hasten modernization. Some of them sought independence. Violence erupted in 1911 caused by the expansion of a stone quarry near Tunis that threatened to violate a Muslim cemetery. While that was the surface issue, underlying grievances related to the protectorate's discrimination against Tunisians in favor of *colon* interests. In 1912, the Young Tunisians' involvement concerning a labor dispute led to their dissolution by the protectorate. Nevertheless, by that time an incipient nationalism had emerged.

The Moroccan Protectorate

Morocco was not as weak as Tunisia, but it fragmented over the course of the nineteenth and early twentieth centuries. In particular, expansionist French colonialism in Algeria especially pressured the sultanate. Throughout the nineteenth century, the Alawis relied on the friendship of the British as a useful political counterweight. In turn, given their position at Gibraltar, the British desired amicable relations with Morocco.[38] The sultanate supported the Emir Abd al-Qadir's campaigns against the French but suffered a grievous defeat at the aforementioned battle of Isly in 1844. French naval forces also bombarded Moroccan ports (Tangiers and al-Sawira). The sultanate agreed not to help Abd al-Qadir, but it sympathized with the emir's struggle. France's effrontery increasingly worried Morocco's government.

Consequently, the sultanate dispatched a diplomatic mission in late 1845 to affirm Morocco's goodwill and to assess French intentions. Muhammad al-Saffar, one of the diplomats, provided a memoir of the Moroccan initiative. Like al-Tahtawi, al-Saffar was impressed by French science and technology, especially railways, telegraphy, and lithography.[39] After watching troops in review, he recounted:

> So it went until all had passed, leaving our hearts consumed with fire from what we had seen of their overwhelming power and mastery, their preparations and good training, their putting everything in its proper place. In comparison with the weakness of Islam, the dissipation of its strength, and the disrupted condi-

tion of its people, how confident they are, . . . how capable in war and successful in vanquishing their enemies—not because of their courage, bravery, or religious zeal, but because of their marvelous organization, their uncanny mastery over affairs. (al-Saffar 1992, 194)

Concluding that France remained a serious threat, the sultanate tightened relations with Great Britain.

By the Treaty of Tangier of 1856, the British received a preferential position in the economy, including the ownership of property. Furthermore, the sultanate awarded capitulations permitting extralegal privileges for British subjects. The sultanate modeled this treaty to other European countries, inviting cordial relations. Nonetheless, besides France, Spain refused since it entertained its own territorial ambitions.

In 1848, Spain seized three islets off Zaffarin. It still possessed presidios at Ceuta, Melilla, Peñon de Velez, and Alhucemas. Madrid wanted to expand into the Rif and found the sultanate's conciliatory offer of more land around Melilla inadequate. Spanish troops landed at Ceuta and marched against Anjara tribesmen and took Tetuan in February 1860. The peace treaty in April 1860 enlarged Melilla and Ceuta, gave Spain ambiguously delineated territory along the southern Moroccan Atlantic coast, eventually demarcated as the enclave of Ifni (Santa Cruz de Mar Pequeña), and imposed a large indemnity (100 million pesetas). The Spanish later reclaimed territory in the south along the Western Saharan coast (see Chapter 3) and in 1884 named it Rio de Oro, which became the Spanish Sahara.[40] To Moroccans, this region was part of the sultanate's traditional *bilad al-siba,* which portended future post-colonial problems.[41]

Spanish aggression signaled the sultanate's weakness. Under Mawlay Hasan (r. 1873–1896), Morocco belatedly attempted to modernize. Nevertheless, this strategic country, like Tunisia, inevitably became a pawn in the "Greater Game" of European diplomacy and alliances. In addition, it must be reiterated that industrialism, which forged a new, revolutionary global economic system, profoundly affected political policies. Regarding Morocco, for example, Edmund Burke III stated that "the incorporation of Morocco into the world capitalist system . . . slowly undermined the viability of the old society" as well as its "traditional structures and institutions . . . at the local level" (Burke 1976, 210, 212). As we have observed, other North African polities mirrored Morocco's vulnerable condition.

European military, political, and economic predations compounded the internal disintegration of the sultanate's authority. Berber tribes and individuals acted with impunity. For example, a sharif, Ahmad al-Raysuni, kidnapped Ion Perdicaris, a wealthy Greek-American, and his son-in-law from their home in Tangier in May 1904 and demanded a ransom and a district governorship. He received both, but Europeans forced Sultan Abd al-Aziz (r. 1894–1908) to dismiss al-Raysuni, who, nonetheless, resumed his kidnappings and harassments.[42]

Imperial Germany exploited Morocco's instability as an opportunity to assess the viability of the Dual Entente concluded in 1904 between Great Britain and France. At this time, Europeans generally assumed that Morocco's future correlated with France's colonial intentions. Kaiser Wilhelm II conducted a provocative tour of Morocco and baited the French by pledging German support of Moroccan independence. His behavior provoked the First Moroccan Crisis in 1905. Germany learned, however, that Great Britain supported France, thus demonstrating the strength of the entente. President Theodore Roosevelt intervened and brokered the Act of Algeciras of 1906 that clearly placed Morocco in France's sphere of influence.[43] The death of a national in 1907 supplied the French with an excuse to send in troops to Oujda (Wujda) from across the Algerian frontier. During that same year, the French also took over Casablanca and began to invest in its infrastructure. Subsequent violence in Casablanca and its surrounding region led to greater French military intervention.

In 1911, Germany again incited another incident when the warship *Panther* sailed into Moroccan waters as the sultanate's authority fell apart. The Second Moroccan Crisis was resolved when France exchanged Camerounian territory for Germany's recognition of its dominant authority in Morocco. Meanwhile, Sultan Mawlay Abd al-Hafidh (r. 1908–1912), who had rebelled against and replaced his brother Abd al-Aziz, failed to prevent the dismemberment of the country.[44] When rebels marched on Fez, the sultan asked for French assistance. By the Treaty of Fez of March 1912, Morocco became a French protectorate; Spain received a portion of northern Morocco amounting to a third of the country and a zone (Tarfaya) in the south.[45] The Alawi continued as figurehead sultans, which probably saved the dynasty, but a French resident general controlled affairs.

The first resident general was the remarkable General Hubert Lyautey, who served at that post from 1912 to 1925. He believed that a French officer had a special mission, a *devoir social,* or social duty. His colonial service in Indochina and Madagascar highly influenced his concept of service. Indeed, he intertwined *devoir colonial* (colonial duty) with *devoir social.* In 1900, he published an article in the *Revue des Deux Mondes* in which he described France's "providential mission," which was "to open to the peoples of color the industrial, agricultural, and economic way of life, and also . . . a higher moral life, a life more complete" (Lyautey 1900, 318). He wrote that French soldiers in colonial service had discovered an identity mirroring that of Roman legionnaires (ibid., 327). In this context, he wanted to ensure that Moroccan society and culture would not suffer from colonialism like Algeria. Therefore, he monitored French activities closely. As Gwendolyn Wright pointed out: "The protectorate wanted to control the French *colons,* the speculative developers, provincial bourgeoisie, and urban proletariat, none of whom inspired much confidence or respect in Lyautey. . . . Safeguards over the Moroccans' culture and well-being showed a paternalistic superiority, to be sure, but also a recognition of the racism that prevailed in the French community" (Wright 1991, 142).

The resident general encouraged separate development of the European and Moroccan communities as a way to protect the colonized's cultural heritage and identity, while ensuring French domination. This was effectively disclosed in the urban planning projects of "architect-urbanist" Henri Prost. For example, the new city of Rabat surrounded the old, traditional city—a telling metaphor by the circumscription of space as a form of French power (see Rabinow 1989, 277–319). A similar initiative was undertaken in Fez, where a colonial "Ville Nouvelle" arose. Lyautey understood the power of forms and aesthetics and aimed to use it to enhance the French position. As in Tunisia, Morocco received a modern infrastructure, highlighted by the development of Casablanca.

Lyautey believed in supporting the sultanate in collaboration with military and civilian colonial cadres who would administer Morocco's affairs indirectly. As William A. Hoisington concluded, Lyautey's "method continued to provide a purpose to empire building that captivated the idealist, the romantic, the humanist and the missionary in [him]" (Hoisington 1995, 53). Yet he also practiced separate development among the colonized Arabs and Berbers, in part to keep them politically divided. Most important, Lyautey ensured that Morocco maintained its identity or, more accurately, his perception of Moroccan identity. The resident general's proprietary and moral perspective regarding Morocco's welfare resembled Lord Cromer's Egyptian "burden." Nonetheless, Lyautey's earnest enterprise tempered the inevitable colonial exploitation of Morocco.

Italy Takes Tripolitania (Libya)

Fearing further European predations in North Africa after the French ended the Regency of Algiers and imposed conditions on Tunis's beylik, the Ottomans undertook an exceptional initiative by resuming their direct rule in Tripolitania in 1835. Extending their authority into the interior, they faced fervent Islamist opposition, namely the revivalist Sanusiyya brotherhood established by the "Grand Sanusi," Muhammad al-Sanusi (1787–1859), a native Algerian.[46] The Sanusiyya was principally located in Cyrenaica and spread to the west and south mobilizing support through their *zawaya* (lodges). Indeed, the *zawaya* also played a commercial role promoting and protecting Saharan trade (Anderson 1986, 106). Italy's determined ambitions, however, principally threatened the Ottomans.

History and geography profoundly influenced Italy's interest in North Africa. Ancient Rome inspired Italy, flushed with pride from its recent national unification. The new nation immediately sought to assert itself among European powers. In particular, Italian governments envisaged overseas expansion as an outlet to relieve Italy's pressing population problems. France's takeover of Tunisia, especially coveted by Italy, forced it to look elsewhere for African territory. Italy's attempt to conquer Abyssinia (Ethiopia) disastrously ended at the battle of Adowa in 1896. Nonetheless, with the Ottomans sliding in steep decline, Italy opportunistically provoked a war over "Tripolitania" (Libya) and invaded in 1911.[47] Technologically overmatched, the Ottomans still held on and received considerable tribal support. In May 1912, the Italians seized Rhodes and the Dodecanese Islands. A successful Italian offensive in 1912 concurrent to the troubling development of the hostile Balkan League forced the Ottomans to sue for peace. Italy acquired Tripolitania, the coast of Cyrenaica and its immediate hinterland, and a portion of Fezzan (as well as the captured Aegean islands).[48] During World War I, the Italians, principally preoccupied by their European front, also battled Sanusis, Tripolitanian tribes, and Ottomans. By the end of the war, the Muslims had bottled the Italians into coastal cities. The Treaty of London of 1915 guaranteed Italy's position in North Africa. Nevertheless, Tripolitania, Cyrenaica, and Fezzan remained restive and rebellious (see Chapter 7).

The Italian occupation had serious political consequences for Libya. As Lisa Anderson pointed out: "The precolonial administration was destroyed, and with it, the networks of clientele that had grown around it" (Anderson 1986, 10). The Italians had little knowledge of Arabic culture. Their principal interests were "to maintain the appearance of Great Power status and to find an outlet for the country's burgeoning population" (ibid., 186). The Italians first considered indirect rule through local leaders, but when the Fascists came to power in 1922, policy swerved significantly. Benito Mussolini's government encouraged colonization, but it also confronted a tenacious resistance.

Conclusion

The takeover of North Africa by European powers was unprecedented—an exceptional historical and transcultural experience. The Europeans introduced their culture and institutions, which conflicted and coalesced in varying degrees with those of the North Africans. As Berque perceived: "The *colon* had intruded as a third party in the centuries-old rivalry between city and Bedouin life. And this third party was a stranger, an expropriator" (Berque 1972, 56). It was a traumatic yet transformative transcultural event.

Controlling North Africa affirmed Orientalism and the European-perceived preeminence of their civilization. To Edward Said: "The essence of Orientalism is the ineradicable distinction between Western superiority and Oriental inferiority" (Said 1979, 42).[49] Pictorial photography especially reinforced Orientalism's "positional superiority" by propagating stereotypes, such as submissive, sensual women. In Algeria, colonial photographers especially eroticized women, an unseemly, dehumanizing voyeurism (see Alloula 1986). Furthermore, there was a political message conveyed by colonial photography: "In its illusive dissolution of actual resistance, the colonial postcard offers a view of a pacified reality" (ibid., 64). Malek Alloula concluded: "Colonialism is indeed the final morality of Orientalism and exoticism. But it is the morality of a procurer and a bawd" (ibid., 122). The European expropriation of Egyptian antiquities and histories exemplified not only Orientalism, but also another form of subtle (quiet) imperialism (Reid 2002). European (and American) travel accounts disparaged North African society, culture, and history.[50] Colonial sociological studies of indigenous North Africans created divisive ethnographic discourses, such as the "Berber Myth" that elevated Berbers over Arabs (see Lorcin 1995). Exhibitions such as those in Paris in 1867 and 1889 reinforced distorted Orientalist depiction. Representation became reality (see especially Çelik 1992). Timothy Mitchell reflected: "In the end, the European tried to grasp the Orient as though it were an exhibition of itself" (Mitchell 1992, 310). Indeed, Khedive Isma'il visited and stayed in the Egyptian palace at the 1867 Exposition Universelle, thereby becoming, as Timothy Mitchell pointed out, "part of the exhibition" (ibid., 293).[51] This skewed reception and perception of North African history, society, and culture has had enduring consequences.[52] Nevertheless, colonialism's pretensions and exploitations ensured an inevitable resistance. As important as colonialism was in the modern historical development of North Africa, it lasted merely decades for the protectorates and Libya. Egypt freed itself from the British after about seventy-five years of varying degrees of occupation. Algeria suffered the longest, and its decolonization would be North Africa's most intense and violent.

European colonialism in North Africa (and elsewhere) created social hybridities and especially dualities, such as the modern and native cities and the modern and traditional agricultural sectors.[53] Frantz Fanon referred to the colonial condition as "Manichaean." Yet colonialism was not only an exclusive binary but also, in some ways, a blurred exploitation. While the construction of highways, dams, ports, railways, and airports enhanced and enriched colonialist interests, it also endowed independent North Africa with modern, if limited, infrastructures.[54] European public health policies and interventions decreased death rates but increased populations, which colonialism, in turn, was not prepared to support. Archaeologists, tourists, and public historians despoiled Egypt and other regions of North Africa (see Raven 1993, xxx–xxxi). Nevertheless, they also salvaged and preserved artifacts in European-initiated museums.

Furthermore, European historical interest in North Africa was infectious and contributed to the creation of national consciousnesses. For example, before the British occupation, al-Tahtawi composed a history of pre-Islamic Egypt, which was published in 1868. Decades before, Muhammad Ali and al-Tahtawi tried to protect Egyptian antiquities from foreign predation (see above), signaling also an inchoate cultural nationalism (see Reid 2002). Jamal al-Din al-Afghani and Muhammad Abduh patriotically associated the glories of ancient Egypt with the modernizing potential of the country (ibid., 119). Al-Tahtawi's successors, Ali Mubarak, Ahmad Kamal, and Claudius Labib (a Copt) all strove to raise the historical consciousness of Egyptians by referring to and by reappropriating the ancient glorious past. Historicism emerged as an important means to legitimate and to lambaste colonialism.

On 23 February 2005, the French Parliament passed legislation calling for educators to present a positive assessment of colonialism in North Africa. This initiative received popular public support. The Algerian government, not surprisingly, denounced this measure. To understand colonialism, it must be studied in its entirety, including its spatial relationships, its fashion, and its ornamentation. Its physical accomplishments, principally attained and sustained for metropolitan economic interests, were certainly outweighed by colonialism's insidious as well as conspicuous inhumanity. Colonialism oppressed through representation, the imagination of the other, as well as by systemic repression. Berque wrote that the relationship between the colonialists and the colonized was "a mystery. . . . Their mutual relation was, at the same time, one of aggressive awareness and one of defensive obscurity" (Berque 1972, 70). In many ways, cultural confiscation by historical misrepresentation and misperception were as damaging as economic expropriation and political domination. Fundamentally, as Berque noted, imperialism destroyed peoples' histories (Berque 1964b, 156).[55] On the other hand, Malik Bennabi contended that North Africans' condition of colonizability occurred centuries earlier with their intellectual and moral decline, which eventually left them susceptible to European incursion and imperialism. To Bennabi, colonialism was opprobrious, but it also offered a regenerative opportunity for the colonized (see Naylor 2006a). Colonialism's transcultural consequences were complex, contradictory, and ultimately conflictive.

CHAPTER 7

The Decolonization of North Africa

The different forms of the European colonialism in North Africa resulted in a diversity of decolonizations. With the exception of Spanish (Western) Sahara, North Africa was decolonized by 1962.[1] Nevertheless, as observed in the Introduction, Ibn Khaldun reminds that there is a "surface history" and a history of "inner meaning." A closer examination indicates that independence once attained was a surface achievement. Colonialism had destructured, dislocated, and disrupted North African societies to such degrees that liberation was often incomplete, which augured post-independence difficulties and even "post-colonial decolonizations" (as in the case of Algeria; see Chapter 9).[2] Nevertheless, there were commonalities in these struggles. The hybrid profiles of native elites melded imported European ideologies, such as liberalism, constitutionalism, and nationalism, as well as Islamism, notably the Salafiyya movement, which arose from Islamic modernism. Elites' reconciliation of these ideologies on the personal and national levels was difficult and often deferred to the post-colonial period. Thus, decolonization meant more than a transfer of power; it inevitably involved the reimagination of self as well as state and society.

Egypt's Struggle for Independence

Egypt's colonial situation was an anomaly. Although the British occupied Egypt in 1882, arguably inciting the scramble for Africa, it was nominally still part of the Ottoman Empire. During World War I, the British declared Egypt a protectorate. Yet the nationalist movement developed rapidly and asserted itself soon after the war, creating a limited independence in 1922, which was extended in 1936. It would take until the Suez Canal crisis and conflict of 1956 to free Egypt from British colonial and imperial power and pretension.

World War I and Its Aftermath

The Ottoman Empire joined the Central Powers of Germany and Austria-Hungary in late October 1914. The British responded by declaring war against the Ottomans in early November and proclaiming Egypt a protectorate in December.[3] The Ottomans launched ineffective attacks against the Suez Canal, although Ottoman-backed Sanusi strikes from Cyrenaica necessitated a substantial British troop deployment on the western frontier. The British encouraged the "Arab Revolt" featuring T. E. Lawrence and, most significantly, numerous diplomatic perceptions and misperceptions (the controversial Husayn-McMahon correspondence of 1915–1916), which engendered the tragic Arab-Jewish (later Israeli) conflict.

The administrative change to a protectorate meant stricter British control marked by martial law and the suspension of Egyptian political expression. (Egypt officially became part of the British Empire.) The British also imposed forced labor and conscription. Requisitions deepened Egyptian resentment, but expectations also grew. President Woodrow Wilson's idealism, such as the principle of national self-determination, inspired the nationalists. When the war ended, Sa'd Zaghul, who identified with the Umma Party, planned to lead a *wafd* or delegation to discuss the end of the protectorate in London and then proceed to Paris to plead for Egyptian independence. The British arrested Zaghul and imprisoned him in Malta.[4] This action provoked Egyptian protests and rioting that forced the British to reconsider their treatment of Zaghul. The "Revolution of 1919" impressed the Egyptians with their political potential. Women also played a distinctively dynamic role in the unrest.[5] The violence claimed approximately eight hundred Egyptian and fifty British lives. Zaghul was freed and allowed to discuss his case for independence at the Paris Peace Conference and then in London. Although he received no assurances, Zaghul emerged as a national hero and the British knew that they had to adapt to changing realities in Egypt.

A Qualified Independence

Conditions within Egypt remained tense.[6] High Commissioner Edmund Allenby, a hero of the Middle Eastern campaigns, advised London to terminate the protectorate and formulate a new relationship with Egypt. In February 1922, Egypt acquired a qualified independence.[7] Sultan Fuad became King

Fuad and a constitution was constructed which gave the monarchy significant political power. A bicameral parliament was also instituted. The upper
house had half of its members appointed; the lower house was elected indirectly. Universal manhood suffrage was proclaimed. In a subsequent accord
articulating what would be known as the "Reserved Points," the British retained their bases, Sudan, lines of communication, and their traditional role
as protector of minorities. Nevertheless, it took fourteen years to define the
limits of British influence in Egypt. During that time, the monarchy, the Wafd,
which became the principal nationalist party, and the British contested and
conflicted. Zaghul became prime minister in 1924. Meanwhile, intermittent
violence flared, including the assassination in 1924 of the governor general of
Sudan, Sir Lee Stack. Zaghul constantly challenged the king and the British
and finally resigned; he eventually received the honorific presidency of the
lower house.[8] In 1930, Fuad proclaimed a new constitution, which gave his
monarchy more power, but Wafd opposition and British anxiety over Egypt's
political instability led to the restoration of the 1923 constitution in 1935.

Premier Mustafa al-Nahas of the Wafd negotiated with Sir Anthony Eden
a treaty in 1936, which finally defined the new Anglo-Egyptian relationship.
Egyptians enthusiastically welcomed the new agreement. Although Great
Britain preserved control of the Suez Canal and maintained military bases in
the Canal Zone, the treaty terminated capitulations (affirmed by the Montreux
Convention of 1937) and called for the inclusion of Egypt into the League of
Nations in 1937.

The interwar years illustrated Egypt's vibrant society.[9] In 1929, Hasan al-
Banna (1906–1949) created the *Ikhwan* or Muslim Brotherhood. An Islamist,
but not a revolutionary, al-Banna considered blind imitation (*taqlid*), Sufism,
and the Westernization (or more accurately Europeanization) of Egypt as culturally destructive. In particular, he condemned "Western nations" for their
materialism, a principal source of immorality:

> The Western way of life—bounded in effect on practical and technical knowl-
> edge, discovery, invention, and the flooding of world markets with mechanical
> products—has remained incapable of offering to men's minds a flicker of light,
> a ray of hope, a grain of faith, or of providing anxious persons the smallest path
> toward rest and tranquility. . . . Man has become tired of purely materialistic
> conditions and desires some spiritual comfort. But the materialistic life of the
> West could only offer him as reassurance a new materialism of sin, passion,

drink, women, noisy gathering, and showy attractions which he had come to enjoy. Man's hunger grows from day to day: he wants to free his spirit, to destroy this materialistic prison and find space to breathe the air of faith and consolation. (Donohue and Esposito 2007, 60)

The Brotherhood "recruited among the effendis [middle class, see below] and the workers much more than in religious circles [and] tended to gather under their jurisdiction the functions of mobilization and infra-political practices, formerly the province of craft guilds, Sufi brotherhoods, and self-help associations. This was a *sociological opposition*" (Roussillon 1998, 341). Hasan al-Banna emphasized the need to reclaim traditional (and consoling) Islamic values before approaching, adapting, and appropriating modernization.

On the other hand, Taha Husayn's (1889–1973) writings exemplified a Westernized Egyptian. He wrote in *The Future of Culture in Egypt:*

To defend our country, with its geographical situation, against aggression necessitates adopting European weapons and technique. Our religion, I feel, will be best maintained by doing as our ancestors did and keeping it responsive to contemporary needs. ... I cannot be justly accused of advocating loss of Egyptian identity since I am merely asking that the preservatives of defense, religion, language, art, and history be strengthened by the adoption of Western techniques and ideas. (McNeill and Waldman 1983, 421)

Taha Husayn embodied a transcultural epitome. He believed that Egypt's cultural heritage and character were a composite of three legacies—ancient Egypt, foreign influences (especially Greek), and the Arabs (especially their language) (see Hourani 1991a, 341–342).

In addition, a nationalist and imperialist Young Egypt movement also arose, claiming that Sudan should be incorporated into a Greater Egypt. The Egyptian "Green Shirts," worn by members of Misr al-Fatat (Young Egypt), displayed fascist tendencies. Feminist movements also emerged.[10] Huda Sha'rawi (1878–1947) was a pioneering feminist. Fatma Nimat Rashid organized the Egyptian Feminist Party in 1944 and Durriya Shafiq formed the Bint al-Nil (Daughter of the Nile) Union in 1948. Another influential woman, Zaynab al-Ghazali favored Islamism. Furthermore, the music and voice of Umm Kulthum, called by Berque "a sacred wonder" and "a moral symbol as well as a fabulous artist," stirred all of Egypt and the Arab world (Berque 1964a, 227; see Danielson 1997). She personified a dynamic Egyptian woman, who also exercised considerable political influence, especially after Gamal Abdel Nasser seized power.

Egyptians increasingly identified with ancient Egypt as highlighted by Mahmud Mukhtar's monumental sculpture, "Egypt's Renaissance," which he completed in 1928. Fayza Haikal analyzed the sculpture: "Egyptianizing in its size, material and symbolism, this huge red granite statue represents a sphinx, symbol of the grandeur of pharaonic civilization, rising at the side of a woman, Egypt, proudly raising her veil to reveal the awakening of the nation" (Haikal 2003, 175). In his work *Thawrat al-Adab* (The Revolt of Literature) (1933), Muhammad Husayn Haykal reflected upon the need to study the ancient past:

> No part of the history of a country can be deleted from the total sum that forges its identity. As European culture developed without breaking its links with Christianity or ignoring the classical age, so too the changes in language and religion that have taken place in Egypt should in no way sever its present culture from its past. There is no point in denying this spiritual thread which links the past with the present to continue forever into the future, defining Egypt's historical specificity. (Haikal 2003, 167)

Banknotes, Sa'd Zaghul's mausoleum (d. 1927), and Naguib Mahfouz's early novels also illustrated the appeal of Egypt's illustrious ancient past.[11]

The class structure included the Europeanized upper bourgeoisie, the middle class, known as the *effendiyya,* the urban working class, and the peasantry. Egyptian cities, growing rapidly at this time, had a cosmopolitan flavor to them. Furthermore, education, mandatory at the elementary level since 1925, was emphasized during this period, in contrast with the Cromer era.

Literary contributions featured the poetry of Ahmad Shawqi, Hafiz Ibrahim, Ahmad Rami, Khalil Mutran, and Zaki Abu Shadi. Collectively, Egyptian poetry expressed romantic, nationalist, and deeply personal tropes. Umm Kulthum was not only admired for her voice, but also for her precisely articulated poetic recitations in her music, including the verse of Shawqi and Rami (see Danielson 1997). Muhammad Haykal is credited with the introduction of a new, modern form of Arabic novel (*Zaynab* [1914]). The short stories and novels of Mahmud Taymur and Yahya Haqqi were marked by social criticism.

Agriculture continued to dominate the economy, but many farmers remained at the subsistence or sub-subsistence level. Furthermore, price fluctuations, especially during the Depression, added distress. The Bank Misr was founded in 1920 to assist Egyptian entrepreneurs as Egypt inexorably entered the modern global economy. Berque explained: "An important stage had been reached in the history of Egypt's civilization; she had reintegrated the effort of her workers and the product of her soil by means of the most up-to-date technology. Even if the performance was a feeble one by Western standards, even if European machines had to be bought and European specialists called in, this weakness was a purely quantitative one" (Berque 1972, 343). Egyptian-owned enterprises especially profited during World War II, given the risks faced by Mediterranean commerce (Jankowski 2000, 123).

King Faruq (r. 1936–1952) became king as the Anglo-Egyptian Treaty of 1936 neared completion. He was popularly received and many nationalists hoped that he would lead the country to full independence. Unfortunately, Faruq was a libertine and failed to live up to national expectations. Egypt also suffered from political instability as Isma'il Sidqi, a palace favorite, and Mustafa al-Nahas continually competed for influence and power as World War II loomed.

North Africa was one of the major theaters of World War II and deeply involved Egypt. The Axis powers of Germany and Italy under the command of General Erwin Rommel drove deep into the country in 1942 and paused only 100 kilometers from Alexandria. The hard-pressed British perceived the Egyptian government as Axis-oriented and forced Faruq to dismiss Prime Minister Ali Mahir and replace him with Mustafa al-Nahas of the Wafd Party. This "coup" illustrated the embarrassing perpetuation of British political influence in "independent" Egypt. Wafd collaboration with the British also discredited that nationalist party. Meanwhile, the British under generals Harold Alexander and Bernard Montgomery launched a counteroffensive against Rommel. The British victory at El Alamein in October 1942 ranks as one of the decisive battles of World War II. With the British driving from the East, the Americans landed in the west in Morocco and Algeria in November 1942. After putting up a fierce resistance (Kasserine Pass) in Tunisia, German forces withdrew to Italy in 1943.

Egypt endured an intense and eruptive political environment during the postwar period. It resented the ongoing and anachronistic British military bases, an affront to national sovereignty. Furthermore, the proclamation of the state of Israel in 1948 and the military failure of Arab states, including Egypt, to prevent it militarily, alienated the population from Faruq and the government. Reports of defective munitions provided to the Egyptian soldiers deepened public anger. A more militant Muslim Brotherhood joined public demonstrations. The assassination of Prime Minister Mahmud Fahmi al-Nuqrashi provoked the murder of Hasan al-Banna in 1949.

The lack of governmental leadership led to greater problems with the British over their presence, the one issue that unified Egyptians. Back in office as premier, al-Nahas repudiated in October 1951 the Anglo-Egyptian Treaty of 1936 and the Condominium of 1899 regarding Sudan. On 25 January 1952, British troops and Egyptian police fought each other. Violence continued on the next day, "Black Saturday," with rioting in Cairo including the destruction of Shepheard's Hotel, a favorite location of European tourists. In July 1952, "Free Officers" led by General Muhammad Naguib and Colonel Gamal Abdel Nasser overthrew King Faruq and his government. A veteran of the 1948 campaign against Israel, Nasser principally plotted the coup. As Faruq sailed away on his yacht toward exile, native Egyptians governed their country for the first time since the sixth century BCE.[12] Nevertheless, the military takeover also meant the end of a liberal political era, which "had failed to achieve political freedom, civil rights, true independence, or economic development" (Botman 1998, 2:308). The alienated Egyptians looked toward the Free Officers with rising expectations. In 1954, Nasser outmaneuvered Naguib, took control of the government, and soon confronted the British over the Suez Canal.

The Suez Canal Crisis

In several ways, Nasser identified with the legacies of Muhammad Ali and Khedive Isma'il regarding accelerated modernization and, in particular, one great public works project, the Aswan Dam. Unlike the pasha and khedive, Nasser gave up any territorial expectations or concessions regarding Sudan by signing an agreement with the British in 1954, which allowed for Sudan's independence in 1956. The Anglo-Egyptian Treaty of October 1954 was concluded and called for the gradual withdrawal of British troops from the Suez Canal Zone (by June 1956), thereby easing bilateral tension. Yet Nasser was under pressure from nationalists and other Arabs. Nationalists believed that Nasser was too accommodating to the British, while Arabs thought that Nasser should take a more militant position toward Israel. In 1953, after an attack by Palestinian guerrillas from Egyptian-held Gaza, Israelis retaliated in a large-scale raid, which killed thirty-eight Egyptians.

Relations with Great Britain and the United States concurrently deteriorat-

ed. Nasser refused to join the Baghdad Pact, a Middle Eastern treaty organization, supported by the United States. Its members included the United Kingdom, Iran, Iraq, Turkey, and Pakistan. Its aim was to contain possible Soviet
threats.[13] Instead, Nasser signed an arms deal with Communist Czechoslo-
vakia in September 1955. This agreement, compounded by his Baghdad Pact
renunciation, his active public participation in the non-aligned movement
(highlighted by his attendance at the conference at Bandung, Indonesia, in
April 1955), and his negotiations with the Soviet Union to finance the Aswan
Dam alienated the United States, specifically Secretary of State John Foster
Dulles. On 19 July 1956, Washington informed Cairo that the United States
would not fund the Aswan Dam project. The dam was crucial to Nasser's plans
to increase agricultural land and also generate energy for industrialization.
Thus, Nasser nationalized the Suez Canal on 26 July 1956 in order to collect its
tolls and to assert Egyptian independence.

Prime Minister Anthony Eden, who negotiated the Anglo-Egyptian Treaty
of 1936, plotted revenge.[14] He found willing collaborators in France and Israel. France considered Nasser an enemy given his support of Algerian revolutionaries (see below). The Israelis vilified Nasser as an inveterate adversary
determined to destroy their new nation. According to the allied plan, Israel
would attack Egypt and threaten the canal. The British and French would
subsequently intervene and secure the canal allegedly to protect it. The allies hoped that the crisis would topple Nasser. They launched their operation
in late October 1956. The Israelis swept across the Sinai and, as scripted, the
British and French declared their intention to protect the canal by issuing an
ultimatum calling for a cease-fire. The Israelis agreed subject to Egyptian approval, but the Egyptians refused and rallied behind Nasser. The British and
French then dispatched their troops on 5 November, attacked Egyptian positions, and seized Port Said. The United States, the Soviet Union, and the United Nations perceived this operation as anachronistic imperialism. Underlying
Anglo-French strategy, the British still coveted control over the Canal and the
French intended to continue their colonial presence in North Africa. Never-
theless, the world and North Africa were changing. The superpowers, in a rare
display of unanimity, forced the British and French to accept a cease-fire on 7
November; they withdrew by the end of the year. The Israelis finally evacuated
Egyptian territory in March 1957. Nasser emerged as an international hero as
Egypt secured Suez and genuinely reclaimed its independence.

Libya Becomes Independent

In 1912, Italy acquired the last Ottoman territory in North Africa. Nevertheless, the Italians still faced stiff resistance in Cyrenaica, especially from the Sanusis. During World War I, the Sanusis, local Tripolitanian tribes, and Ottomans forced the Italians to withdraw from the hinterland to the coastal cities of Tripolitania and Cyrenaica (see Chapter 6). The Sanusis, supplied by the Ottomans, also subsequently attacked western Egypt, forcing the British to organize a counteroffensive in 1916 (see above). At this time, the "Grand Sanusi" or *muqaddam* of the order was Sayyid Ahmad al-Sharif. After the failure of the Sanusi campaign, Sayyid Ahmad chose exile.[15] He delegated his authority to his cousin, Sayyid Muhammad Idris, who was pro-British.

The Italians negotiated with Idris, who signed the Akrama ('Ikrima) Agreement of 1917. The agreement gave the Italians the shoreline of Cyrenaica, while Idris received autonomy and control of the interior (with less population and economic resources). Idris was also recognized as the emir of Cyrenaica. The Italians encountered major problems in Tripolitania. Local leaders asserted their authority, notably the rivals Ahmad al-Mrayyid and Ramadan al-Suwayhili (Sawayhli).[16] During the war, the Ottomans under Nuri Bey tried to unite Tripolitanians, as did Abd al-Rahman Azzam, an Egyptian nationalist.[17] In 1919, Azzam pressed the Italians by proclaiming a republic led by a council of Tripolitanian leaders. Italian officials quickly negotiated and concluded an agreement with republican leaders that led to the Italian parliament passing the "Fundamental Law" (*Legge Fondamentale*) or "Statute" (*Statuo*), which on paper was remarkably liberal. It called for an Italian governor but also provincial assemblies and local councils in Tripolitania and Cyrenaica where Libyans could exercise considerable influence and autonomy. Opportunities for Italian-Libyan citizenship were also offered.[18] This Italian initiative satisfied the nationalists and the republic was dissolved. Nonetheless, Azzam along with Khalid al-Qarqanni and Uthman al-Gharyania organized the National Reform Party. In October 1920, Idris signed the Rajma Agreement, which reaffirmed the earlier Akrama negotiation, and recognized him as a hereditary emir. The Italians remained concerned, however, that Sanusi *zawaya* had not disarmed. Idris argued that he could not control all the Sanusi *zawaya* scattered throughout Cyrenaica and Fezzan. A month later, Tripolitanian leaders met at the Gharyan conference to create a unified front regarding relations and to negotiate with Italy.

On the other hand, Rome also seemed disinclined to implement its agreements despite Libyan pressures (including direct lobbying in Rome). In July 1922, the Tripolitanians decided to put more pressure on the Italians by offering Idris the opportunity to become emir of Tripolitania as well as Cyrenaica. Idris, a reluctant political leader, delayed his decision as long as possible. In November, he grudgingly realized that he had no choice but to agree for religious as well as national reasons, although his decision risked alienating the Italians and contradicted the Akrama and Rajma agreements. After accepting the Tripolitanian offer, Idris promptly announced his emigration to Egypt and delegated his authority to Sanusi leaders. By that time, relations between the Italians and the Libyans had rapidly deteriorated. The arrival of Governor Giuseppe Volpi in late 1921 decisively shifted Italian policy. There would be no negotiation but pacification.

After Benito Mussolini took over the government in October 1922, he abrogated the Fundamental Laws. Envisioning Italian North Africa as a region that would provide economic and social opportunities for Italy, Mussolini planned a large-scale colonization. What was not anticipated was the well-organized Sanusi resistance commanded by an elderly shaykh, Umar al-Mukhtar. His military leadership featured guerrilla operations in Cyrenaica and Fezzan. The modern Italian military could not control the countryside until it initiated a strategy to confine the guerrillas. The Italians constructed an approximately 300-kilometer-long barbed wire fence to isolate the insurgency and to expedite the *Riconquista*. The Fascists forced villagers to abandon their homes and herded them into resettlement/concentration camps (see Ahmida 1994, 139; Ahmida 2005, 43–46). The resistance still sustained itself until the capture of Shaykh Umar, who was immediately tried and hanged in September 1931. After his death, Sanusi resistance disintegrated.[19] The Italian government officially proclaimed its intention to appropriate tribal lands, if there was no objection by the indigenous population. Ignorant of this coy legal process, Libyans found themselves receiving "compensation" for their "renunciation" of their lands (Abun-Nasr 1987, 401).

The principal architect of Italy's colonial enterprise was the energetic Italo Balbo, who arrived in Libya in 1935. Reminiscent of Hubert Lyautey, Balbo was "an organizer and leader capable of inspiring fierce loyalty and devotion" (Segrè 1974, 84). Unlike Lyautey, Balbo aspired to integrate Libya's northern coastline as a "fourth shore" complementing Italy's Adriatic, Ionian, and Tyrrhenian shores (ibid., 88).[20] A dedicated Fascist, Balbo strove to contribute to Italy's dream of a reconstituted Roman Empire.[21] The colonial government dug wells, built highways and railways, and modernized port facilities. Balbo envisioned agricultural projects to attract colonists. In 1939, Rome decreed that Libya was an integral part of Italy. Furthermore, a surprisingly liberal initiative (when compared to the French in Algeria) offered qualified Italian citizenship without the loss of Muslim status to the Libyans.[22] As World War II broke out, over 100,000 Italian colonists had settled in Libya.[23]

The war ravaged Libya. In particular, battles raged over the strategic port of Tobruk in 1941 and 1942. Cyrenaica received the brunt of the warfare, destroying much of the Italian colonial achievement.[24] Sayyid Idris supported the British and was promised that Cyrenaica would not be returned to the Italians after the conflict.[25] Instead, Great Britain, Italy, and France offered to the fledgling United Nations a stewardship plan in the immediate postwar period. According to the tripartite proposal, the three main regions of Libya—Tripolitania, Cyrenaica, and Fezzan—would be administered by Italy, Great Britain, and France, respectively. The United Nations rejected the plan, created its own trusteeship, and expedited Libya's independence in 1951.[26] Sayyid Idris became King Idris, who became the ruler of the country. He relied heavily on British and American advisers and was a loyal ally during the Cold War. In 1953, the British concluded a twenty-year pact with Libya, giving them military access. The United States paid $42 million, covering the period 1954 to 1971 for its use of Wheelus Air Force Base.

Despite its impressive constitutional trappings, King Idris's government was an oligarchy that supervised a fractured federal system. Indeed, a theme of post-colonial Libya has been its hesitation if not "avoidance" to form a state (see Chapter 8; Anderson 1986 and Vandewalle 2006). From a geostrategic perspective, Libya was a rather insignificant country during its immediate postcolonial period, but that situation changed dramatically by the end of the 1950s.

The French Protectorates Gain Their Independence

Tunisia and Morocco maintained their figurehead monarchies and their identities and were spared the worst abuses of French colonialism. Nevertheless, they were still exposed to French exploitation. Improvements in the infrastructure, while substantial and impressive, were still meant to benefit French interests and investments. Furthermore, France dispatched Tunisians and Moroccans (as well as Algerians) to the Western Front during World War I, where they distinguished themselves with their bravery and sacrifice.[27] Tunisians and Moroccans became increasingly conscious of the limits imposed upon them by their "protectors." Nationalism stirred, inevitably generating independence movements.

Tunisia Becomes Independent

In its first two decades, the protectorate provided greater administrative efficiency compared to the pre-colonial "rule by consuls." Resident Minister Paul Cambon successfully managed and eliminated Tunisian debt (see Chapter 6). Nevertheless, despite Tunisian protest, the protectorate opened lands (Beylical Decree of 1896), including those of the *hubus* (land endowed to religious foundations), to settlers who were given privileged access and opportunities. The protectorate eagerly recruited French *colons* to neutralize the large population of Italians. In 1911, the commune of Tunis had 69,500, inhabitants with 17,800 French and 34,200 Italians. The general European population grew from 19,000 in 1881 to 143,000 (88,000 Italians and 46,000 French) in 1911 to 255,000 in 1956 (180,00 French, 67,000 Italians) (Nouschi 1970, 313, 315). Tunisia benefited from the discovery of phosphates in 1885 and the promotion of an olive industry. Nevertheless, agriculture suffered from depression from 1888 to 1900.

Resentment over land expropriation coupled with the rising influence of Islamic modernism resulted in an incipient nationalism.[28] Led by Abd al-Aziz al-Tha'alibi, the French-educated "Young Tunisians" called for reforms and more educational and economic opportunities, but within the framework of the protectorate. Protests over the Tripolitanian War and complaints stemming from protectorate abuse and indifference led to violence in 1911 (see Chapter 6). Changing his political position over time, al-Tha'alibi traveled to Paris in 1919 to plead the Tunisian case for independence at the peace conference. Like Saʻd Zaghul, he failed to achieve his objective, but he co-organized the Destour Party in 1919–1920, which modified nationalist objectives. Arguing that the French protectorate had disrupted Tunisian modernization, the Destour Party demanded the reinstitution of the Constitution of 1860.[29] It presented a program of moderate reforms, which did not call for unconditional independence. The party failed to mobilize popular support or persuade the bey; Destour's leaders were arrested. Nevertheless, Tunisian workers broke from French unions and inaugurated the Confédération Générale des Travailleurs Tunisiens (General Confederation of Tunisian Workers [CGTT]) in 1924. The protectorate impeded nationalist agitation in 1926 with measures limiting political activity and restricting the press.

Tunisia also experienced a cultural florescence as reflected in the poetry of Abu-l-Qasim al-Shabbi (1909–1934). His lyricism and exploratory verse reached far beyond the protectorate's borders. Mustafa Khurayyif's (1900–1967) works celebrated Tunisian history; his poetry represented a form of cultural nationalism. The great novelist Mahmud al-Masʻadi (Masadi) (1911–2004) also emerged during this decolonizing era.

Political nationalism roused again in May 1930, when a Eucharistic Congress convened in Carthage. Its presence (complemented by the construction of a large statue of Cardinal Lavigerie) upset Muslim sensibilities. Habib Bourguiba, the charismatic father of modern Tunisia, regarded the congress as the decisive determinant in the development of Tunisian nationalism. In 1934, Bourguiba resigned from the Destour Party and established the Neo-Destour Party. According to Lorna Hahn, the party was a transcultural and ideological admixture: "Neo-Destour was drawn from the egalitarianism of Mohammed and the democracy of Voltaire and Rousseau" (Hahn 1960, 19). Its support cut across classes and occupations and it featured a sophisticated patronage network. Riots in April 1938 led to Bourguiba's arrest and detention in France. During World War II, the Germans dispatched Bourguiba to Italy, hoping that the young nationalist would endorse the Axis powers against France. Nevertheless, Bourguiba refused and remained an adamant advocate of the Free French and General Charles de Gaulle.

Tunisia suffered grievously during the war. The Husaynid figurehead, Munsif Bey, surprisingly asserted a "Destourian" position by proposing reforms of the protectorate to include a consultative parliamentary body. The Vichy government rejected his initiative. The bey also called for a reorientation of the economy, an introversion toward manufacturing to benefit the Tunisian people. The Free French removed Munsif from office for being an "Axis" collaborator, yet the real reason was his nationalist agenda. Tunisians also fought with distinction in Free French forces.

After the war, Tunisian nationalism intensified. Co-sovereignty became a major issue. The activist Farhat Hached organized the Union Générale des Travailleurs Tunisiens/General Union of Tunisian Workers (UGTT) in 1946, which introduced a new nationalist variable into the increasingly violent climate. In 1952, *fellaghas* or guerrilla fighters began operations in the south against Europeans. The assassination of Hached in December 1952 provoked more protests, which resonated throughout the Maghrib, resulting, for example, in a general strike in Morocco. Its troubles compounded by the Indochinese disaster and the Algerian War, Paris did not want to deal with another convulsive colonial situation. On 22 April 1955, Bourguiba concluded an agreement that granted Tunisia autonomy, though it caused a nationalist rift (see Chapter 8). In 1956, France accorded full independence and in the following year, the anachronistic Husaynid dynasty ended.

Morocco Becomes Independent

The establishment of the protectorate failed to bring order to Morocco. The country proved difficult "to pacify," to use the French euphemism. In the early 1920s, Abd al-Karim (Abdel Krim) defeated the Spanish in the north and proclaimed an independent Rif Republic ([Dawla] Jumhuriyya Rifiyya).[30] He eventually assaulted the French from his redoubt in the High Atlas. At one point in the war, the Rifs campaigned within 25 kilometers of Fez. To defeat the rebels the French mustered 325,000 men and the Spanish 100,000 and deployed aircraft and armor (Abun-Nasr 1987, 381). Abd al-Karim surrendered in May 1926 but Morocco remained restive. As William A. Hoisington pointed out: "The rebellion had exposed the shortcomings of the Lyautey method in the most public, dramatic, and undeniable of ways. Despite fourteen years of pacification and indirect rule, Moroccans continued to resent and resist the French presence" (Hoisington 1995, 2004). In the 1930s, the Foreign Legion still needed to secure southern Morocco. Furthermore, the French resorted to a divide-and-rule policy in order to take advantage of Moroccan historical rivalries, notably traditional Berber and Sufi resistance to the sultanate.

Nevertheless, on 1 August 1926, soon after Abd al-Karim's surrender, Mo-

hammed Bennouna of Tetuan, who recently returned from Egypt, shared
with friends his observations of Egyptian nationalism. That discussion is
regarded as the beginning of the Moroccan independence movement. Other
conversations took place in other cities like Fez. One of the participants was
Allal al-Fasi, the eventual leader of the Istiqlal (Independence) Party. The improbable leader of the nationalist movement, however, was a shy ruler that
the French enthroned in 1927. The French selected Muhammad bn Yusuf (r.
1927–1961) as sultan since he had lived a closeted life and seemed to be passive and malleable. Their estimation of the sultan proved to be an extraordinary miscalculation.

Although the French protectorates maintained historic monarchies, the
Tunisian Husaynids hardly captured the imagination of their "subjects" as
had the Alawis in Morocco. Abun-Nasr pointed out that the "sultanate remained the symbol of Morocco's Islamic identity. To use the sultanate as the
instrument of French control, instead of reconciling the Muslim leaders of
Morocco to the protectorate, was considered a religious outrage and the sultan was viewed as a victim of French policy rather than a collaborator" (Abun-
Nasr 1987, 382). This perception endowed the sultanate with a political advantage during Moroccan decolonization.

The Salafiyya also influenced Morocco, yet another example of Egypt's influence in the Maghrib. After studying in Egypt, Abu Shu'ayb al-Dukkali returned to Morocco infused with the ideas of Muhammad Abduh, where he
earned the sobriquet "Shaykh Abduh of the Maghrib" (see Berque 1974, 173–
176). The Salafi founded "free schools" to promote Islamic modernism. They
also opposed the French-supported Tijaniyya and the Kittaniyya orders. The
French also patronized the powerful Berber leader lording near Marrakesh,
Thami al-Glawi, who opposed the Alawi sultanate. The French practice of divide and rule was symbolized by the Berber *zahir* (*dahir*) or royal decree of
1930, which brought Berber regions under French jurisdiction.[31] This was an
insult, since it removed the Berbers' Muslim legal status as derived from the
Shari'a. Reminiscent of the "Berber Myth" popularized in colonial Algeria (see
Lorcin 1995), the decree "was based on the twin assumptions that the Berbers
were racially close to Europeans, and that their Islamization was but a thin
veneer in contrast with that of the Arabs" (Hahn 1960, 66). Actually, the Berbers were under the jurisdiction of the sultan by the Treaty of Fez. The decree
incensed politicized Moroccans, leading to the development of the National

Group (al-Jama'at al-Wataniyya). The National Group's leaders called themselves the "Zawiya." By the early 1930s, the National Group became known as the Kutlat al-Amal al-Watani (National Action Bloc).

Sultan Muhammad signed the controversial *zahir* of 1930, but the French found it surprising that he willingly listened to delegations protesting the decree. To the nationalists, the sultan's actions signaled that the young monarch harbored sympathies in regard to their aspirations. When touring in 1934, nationalists organized demonstrations supporting the sultan. It was during this period when Allal al-Fasi emerged as a prominent nationalist. Imbued with Salafi values, he also linked Morocco's future with the sultanate.[32]

In 1934, the Comité d'Action Marocaine (Moroccan Action Committee [CAM]) (derived from the Kutlat) produced a "Plan of Reforms," a detailed 134-page document. It listed demands and suggested significant changes to the protectorate, such as the inauguration of local assemblies. Although not calling for full independence, it asked for the protectorate to model itself after a League of Nations mandate.[33] It also wanted to end the power of *qa'ids,* as exemplified by Thami al-Glawi, who were subsidized and supported by colonial authorities. The French administration ignored the document. Concurrently, the Kutlat organized a conference in October 1936. The protectorate thwarted plans for a second meeting and the Kutlat reconfigured itself as the National Party for Realizing the Reforms (Demands) (al-Hizb al-Watani li-Tahqiq al-Matalib).[34] The National Party hoped to attract disaffected Moroccan workers, who were not allowed to unionize (notably phosphate miners), and the sorely distressed (and dispossessed) peasantry. Violent protests and demonstrations occurred in 1937 (especially in Meknès), resulting in suppression and the arrest and exiling of nationalist leaders. The new Resident General Charles Noguès, mentored by Lyautey, intensified reforming efforts, which aimed to conciliate popular concerns including tariff autonomy for the protectorate and the termination of extraterritorial protection. He also promoted irrigation initiatives and the revival of artisanal crafts. Raising consumption taxes also effectively transferred costs to the European population (Pennell 2003, 244–245; see also Hoisington 1984, 74–103, 120–135).

During World War II, the sultan resisted Vichy pressure to persecute Jews, claiming that it was his responsibility to shield them, since they were "People of the Book" and technically *dhimmis* or protected ones. The Jewish population at that time was about 400,000. Morocco was an Allied landing site, along with Algeria, during World War II.[35] At the Casablanca Conference in 1943, Sultan Muhammad had an opportunity to discuss Morocco's future with President Franklin Delano Roosevelt. Apparently, the meeting resulted in mutual admiration. Reportedly, Roosevelt supported Moroccan self-determination. In 1944, the Istiqlal (independence) Party was organized in Rabat with the exiled Allal al-Fasi receiving the honorific title of *za'im* or leader (rather than president). The party's Charter criticized the protectorate's "direct and oppressive rule," recognized the sacrifice of Moroccan troops for the Allied cause, and resolved "to demand the independence of Morocco" (al-Fasi 1954, 217). Nevertheless, the reassertion of French authority slowed nationalist momentum.[36] In 1947, while delivering a speech in Tangier in the presence of the resident general, the sultan praised Morocco's Arab bonds but snubbed its French ties. The sultan's obvious attachment to Istiqlal's objectives provoked French authorities and their Moroccan allies, principally Thami al-Glawi.

General Alphonse Juin, a Free French hero of World War II, was now resident general. He aimed to temper the sultan's activism. Pressured also by Thami al-Glawi, the sultan renounced the party in February 1951, but he did not specifically mention Istiqlal's name. In hindsight, this was a delaying tactic, since Sultan Muhammad proceeded to write to the president of the Fourth Republic in March 1952 urging the end of the protectorate and the establishment of Moroccan independence. The French government rejected the sultan's request. Meanwhile strikes and demonstrations incited violence throughout the country in 1951–1952, resulting in several hundred Moroccan and some European deaths (Pennell 2003, 160).[37]

The nationalist movement was now inextricably linked to the Moroccan monarch to the point that the protectorate and its native allies forced the sultan's deposition in August 1953 and his exile to Madagascar.[38] Being regarded by the French as a subversive, however, heightened the exiled Sultan Muhammad's prestige. In the meantime, Allal al-Fasi, then in Egypt, appealed for armed resistance. Sultan Muhammad's successor, Sultan Muhammad bn Arafa, survived assassination attempts. In addition, nationalists organized protests, finally forcing the protectorate to announce that Muhammad's return was imminent. Sultan bn Arafa abdicated on 1 October. The next day a self-proclaimed "Liberation Army" began operations. As in Tunisian decolonization, France could not afford additional colonial conflict, given its deepening distress in Algeria. Muhammad returned in November 1955. In a dramatic show of obedience, Thami al-Glawi kissed the sultan's feet. Morocco received its independence on 2 March 1956 and Sultan Muhammad ruled as King Muhammad V.

Algeria Fights for Its Independence

The story of Algerian independence is harrowing and heroic. To review, Algeria was a part of France, just as Alaska is integral to the United States, although it is not contiguous. This psychological atavism that "Algeria is France" added a roiling variable to the struggle for independence. In particular, Algerians not only had to liberate themselves from the French, but also liberate themselves from colonialism's psychoexistential condition (see Chapter 5)—a feeling of inferiority and a lack of identity, of non-existence. Frantz Fanon equated decolonization in general with "the veritable creation of new men" (Fanon 1968, 36).

The Development of Algerian Nationalism

The "Young Algerians," like the "Young Tunisians," were hardly nationalists but modernizers. They were *évolués,* assimilated and French-educated elites. In the late nineteenth and early twentieth centuries, they pointed out the contradictions between French ideals and French colonialism to officials and even directly lobbied Paris. One of their principal demands was the abolition of the Code de l'Indigénat, which dispensed arbitrary, summary justice. They also called for wider access to education and to French citizenship with its privileges. On the other hand, some conservative Muslim leaders, referred to by their detractors as the "Vieux Turbans" (Old Turbans), rejected colonialism to the point of leaving Algeria for the Levant in the early twentieth century.

During World War I, France imported about 120,000 Algerians to work in French factories to replace the workers who went off to the Western Front. In addition, 25,000 Algerians died fighting in the war. Their commitment inspired Georges Clemenceau to initiate reform measures to promote Algerian participation in government as well as civil society through the acquisition of citizenship. *Pied-noir* (European settler) resistance diluted the changes as expressed in the Jonnart Law of 1919 and left the settler position unassailable, although the Code de l'Indigénat was mitigated, special duties paid by the colonized eliminated, and representation in local assemblies increased.

This general failure to recognize and reward the service of Algerians stirred Emir Khaled, a grandson of the renowned Abd al-Qadir and a veteran. He proposed radical changes including equal representation in colonial assemblies, compulsory education in Arabic as well as French, and citizenship without the loss of Muslim status. What Khaled asked for was not only assimilation, but also democratization—in other words, radical reform and, by implication, the end of colonialism. French authorities deported Khaled in 1923.

Three important nationalist tendencies developed after Khaled's departure.[39] Messali Hadj called for complete independence and, after a brief ideological liaison with international Communism, advocated Pan-Arabism. Ferhat Abbas appealed for assimilation and accommodation with France. Shaykh Abd al-Hamid Ben Badis, highly influenced by Egypt's Muhammad Abduh and the Salafiyya movement, encouraged a revival of Muslim values and the Arabic language. The shaykh was more of a cultural rather than political nationalist. The convening of a Muslim Conference in 1936 prompted one of the most important initiatives by the French government—the Blum-Viollette legislation. Presented in 1936, it aimed to provide French citizenship, without loss of Muslim status, to approximately 20,000 Algerians. Colonialists prevented this initiative from even coming to the floor of the National Assembly. This disappointment especially disillusioned Ferhat Abbas.

In February 1943, Abbas produced the Manifesto of the Algerian People, which called for an autonomous Algeria. General Charles de Gaulle, the Free French leader, offered the Ordinance of March 1944, which finally granted citizenship to tens of thousands of Algerians without depriving them of their Muslim status. The nationalists regarded de Gaulle's gesture as politically anachronistic. Abbas then sought to unify the nationalist movement by mobilizing the Association des Amis du Manifeste et de la Liberté (Association of the Friends of the Manifesto and of Liberty [AML]). In March 1945, the AML chose Messali Hadj as its leader. In turn, the government declared its plan to deport Messali. This decision provoked a seminal event that led to Algerian independence—the Sétif riots. In May 1945, during V-E (Victory in Europe) parades in Sétif and Guelma, Algerians displayed nationalist placards, which incited violence and severe reprisals against the colonized (estimated between 5,000 and 10,000 fatalities).[40] The brutality of the colonialists profoundly influenced the increasingly impatient younger elite.

Algerian alienation deepened with the reputed reform known as the Organic Statute of 1947, which actually featured fixed elections muting nationalist voices. A paramilitary movement called the Organisation Spéciale (Special Organization [OS]) mobilized in 1947, associated with Messali's new party, called the Mouvement pour le Triomphe des Libertés Démocratiques (Movement for the Triumph of Democratic Liberties [MTLD]).[41] Colonialist police eventually broke up the OS and arrested its leaders in 1950, but some of its members later became the core of the Comité Révolutionnaire pour l'Unité et l'Action (Revolutionary Committee for Unity and Action [CRUA]) in 1953 and then the Front de Libération Nationale (National Liberation Front [FLN]) the following year.

The War of Liberation

The FLN's Proclamation of 1 November 1954 declared the beginning of the War of Liberation. It remains a remarkable document that held together the fractious FLN and fixed its attention on the overriding objective of independence. The FLN suffered from endemic internal dissension and tragic fratricides, but it still maintained its integrity. The Proclamation called for the restoration of an Algerian state and the internationalization of the liberation struggle. The FLN's military wing, the Armée de Libération Nationale (Army of National Liberation [ALN]), managed to present a security threat throughout the war, despite the French Army's effective counterinsurgency operations.

The war began on 31 October–1 November 1954. In general, French governments implemented a strategy that sought a military solution while addressing neglected social and economic problems. In 1955, Governor General Jacques Soustelle introduced the idea of "integration," a categorical political and economic amalgamation of Algeria with France. Soustelle hoped that this policy would unequivocally tie France to Algeria; but it implied democratization, which alarmed the *pieds-noirs*. In August 1955, the ALN perpetrated atrocities in the region of Philippeville (today's Skikda). Appalled by the brutality, Soustelle allowed indiscriminate French retribution based on "collective responsibility." French revenge alienated moderate Muslims and many, like Ferhat Abbas, gravitated toward the FLN.

At its Soummam Conference in August 1956, the FLN fashioned an administration and a wartime strategy. The conferees decided to initiate an urban guerrilla campaign in Algiers. Using terror tactics, including bombs deliv-

ered by attractive Algerian women passing as Europeans, the civilian government relinquished its power to the Army and in particular, General Jacques
Massu's *paras* (paratroopers). French interrogators resorted to torture to acquire information in regard to the FLN's organization and operation. France
eventually won the Battle of Algiers of 1956–1957, but the brutality of its Algerian War, especially the use of torture, was publicized worldwide. Consequently, the FLN achieved a crucial objective—the internationalization of the
conflict.

Nevertheless, by the end of 1957, the FLN had severely fractured. Important "historic chiefs" (leaders) who had founded the organization had been
killed or captured. At the Soummam Conference, Ramdane Abane asserted
strong leadership, but he alienated the ALN by insisting upon civilian control over the military. He also advocated the primacy of the "internals," political and military cadres within Algeria, over the "externals," counterparts
operating outside of Algeria. Abane was killed in December 1957, a victim of
intra-elite violence. In addition, the FLN steadily eliminated its rival, Messali
Hadj's Mouvement National Algérien (Algerian National Movement [MNA]),
as evidenced by the Mélouza massacre in May 1957.[42] Despite the fratricidal
factionalism, the FLN persevered.

Algeria's independent neighbors played important supporting roles and
provided havens for the ALN and supplies. For example, King Muhammad V
offered an airplane to carry several of the FLN's leaders to a conference in
Cairo in October 1956, but the French skyjacked it, provoking international
protest. The French also constructed the "Morice Line" along the Tunisian
border to prevent the infiltration of ALN soldiers. The French bombing of a
Tunisian village (Saqiyat [Sakiet] Sidi Youssef) led to American and British
diplomatic intervention to repair relations between Tunis and Paris.[43] The
fear of international interference piqued the politicized French army, which
feared another humiliating defeat such as it had endured in France in 1940
and in Indochina in 1954.[44] Worse yet, the military thought that Paris contem-
plated negotiating with the FLN, which was unacceptable.

In May 1958 the Army, with settler support, took over Algiers. It formed a
"Committee of Public Safety" and appealed for General de Gaulle to come to
power. De Gaulle had saved France's honor during World War II and many
of the soldiers in Algeria had fought with him. As the civilian control over

the Fourth Republic faded, de Gaulle assumed power. At first, de Gaulle pursued Fourth Republic initiatives, which the military supported, to secure his power. He proclaimed the Constantine Plan in October 1958, which called for a vast transformation of Algeria fueled by recent hydrocarbon discoveries in the Sahara. His principal objective was to preserve a French presence. As these difficult years passed, de Gaulle had to redefine the nature of that presence.

In September 1958, the FLN formed the Gouvernement Provisoire de la République Algérienne (Provisional Government of the Algerian Republic [GPRA]) and chose Ferhat Abbas to be its president. It rejected de Gaulle's proposal in October 1958 for a cease-fire, termed a "Peace of the Brave," as well as a "special place" for Algeria within the French Community. In September 1959, de Gaulle announced during a televised speech that his government would pursue self-determination. Frustrated *pieds-noirs* set up barricades in January 1960, but de Gaulle's persuasive rhetoric averted civil strife.

Concurrently, French armed forces under General Maurice Challe conducted very effective airmobile operations (deploying troops by helicopters) against the ALN, which significantly reduced its operations. In June 1960, de Gaulle invited the FLN to begin negotiations, which were briefly held later that month at Melun, outside of Paris. In November, de Gaulle spoke the words "Algerian Algeria." *Pieds-noirs* and politicized officers equated de Gaulle's statement with abandonment. When de Gaulle visited Algeria in December to garner support for a self-determination referendum, he noticed that the colonized rather than the settlers greeted him. Violence between the communities also escalated.

De Gaulle's policy was now clearly decolonization, which he announced in another televised speech in April 1961. Later that month, four generals, including Challe, rebelled against the government from Algiers. This time the result was not that of May 1958. De Gaulle called on military units to remain loyal to him and his government, and the vast majority of them obeyed that order. Generals Challe and André Zeller surrendered, but the two others, Raoul Salan and Edmond Jouhaud, entered the ranks of the recalcitrant Organisation de l'Armée Secrète (Secret Army Organization [OAS]) that futilely sought to preserve *Algérie française* (French Algeria).

The Evian Accords and the Transfer of Power

Negotiations between the FLN and the French government began in Evian, France, in May. A month later, talks broke down over sovereignty of the Sahara, which the French claimed was not really part of Algeria, and the political status of the settler community in the future independent state. Anarchic violence raged in Algeria and in France, marked especially by the savage suppression of an emigrant worker protest in Paris, which left approximately two hundred dead in October 1961.

In February 1962, negotiations resumed in the Jura Mountains at Les Rousses, bordering Switzerland, and resulted in an agreement. Final discussions occurred in Evian in March. The subsequent Evian Accords proclaimed a cease-fire and provided for Algerian political independence while preserving a French presence through "cooperation." France also retained control of the Sahara's hydrocarbon fields and, provisionally, military bases, but it agreed to continue massive social and economic aid. After three years, *pieds-noirs* would have to choose between French and Algerian citizenship.

Meanwhile, the OAS conducted a scorched earth campaign compounded by terrorist assaults, one of which tragically claimed the life of the renowned Kabyle novelist, Mouloud Feraoun. In turn, the ALN retaliated against the *pieds-noirs*. In this frightful atmosphere, *pieds-noirs* fled the country, leaving land and property. The French government expected "repatriations," but it did not anticipate that approximately 80 percent of the European population would immediately return—about 800,000 settlers. This caused severe logistical problems. The settlers continued to leave even after the FLN and the OAS signed an accord in June ending their hostilities. On 3 July, de Gaulle proclaimed Algeria's independence, and two days later, the 132nd anniversary of the French capture of Algiers, Algerian officials declared national liberation.

But who was in charge? The split between the FLN's and ALN's "internals" and "externals" widened. During the war, the French had managed to block and isolate Algerian external forces, which had mustered and trained in Tunisian and Moroccan havens. After hostilities ceased, they marched into Algeria. Col. Houari Boumedienne, the ALN Chief of Staff, opposed the GPRA and sided with Ahmed Ben Bella, one of the skyjacked FLN leaders; they formed the Political Bureau. Ben Youssef Ben Khedda had replaced Ferhat Abbas as the president of the GPRA in August 1961 and attempted to assert his authority. Conflicts broke out between internal guerrillas and external forces. Civil war loomed, but the Union Générale des Travailleurs Algériens (General Union of Algerian Workers [UGTA]) organized mass protests which prevented further fratricide. Given the superior military resources of the Political Bureau, Ben Bella became Algeria's first premier in September 1962.

Boumedienne repeatedly claimed that 1.5 million Algerians died in the War of Liberation. David C. Gordon contended that one million perished (Gordon 1966, 84). Benjamin Stora placed the figure at 500,000 (Stora 2001, 111). Belkacem Krim, who negotiated the Evian Accords, stated that 300,000 died (Horne 1987, 538). All agree that Algeria's freedom came with a heavy cost. Furthermore, the last wartime FLN congress (convened in Tripoli, Libya) recognized that the Evian Accords' neocolonial stipulations illustrated that despite liberation, decolonization was incomplete.

Conclusion

The decolonization of North Africa redefined not only the political status of the colonized states, but also those of the colonizers. Great Britain's loss of the Suez Canal ended its colonial era and expedited the decolonization of its colonies in Africa. Italy's hopes of retaining Libya after World War II were frustrated. The decolonization of the Moroccan and Tunisian protectorates and the loss of Algeria symbolized national decadence to many in France. To Charles de Gaulle and others, however, decolonization represented an opportunity to redefine France and correlate its policies to changing realities. When surveying the vast history of North Africa, it is important to remember that colonialism represented a relatively short period of time. Nevertheless, the colonial experience was intense and had profound post-colonial significance.[45]

Decolonization denoted much more than the expulsion of Europeans from North Africa. It meant dealing with imported ideologies and reconciling modernization with liberation (see Berque 2001, 3:149). To North Africans, decolonization also involved consequential questions of personal as well as national identity. Berque and Bennabi understood the importance of the "interior" in the decolonizing struggle. The post-colonial paradox, as Berque perceived, was that the ex-colonized "having freed himself from the Other and his resentment against the Other, will find the Other deep in himself" (Berque 1964b, 170). The Other's presence persisted in varying ways—habits, language, clothing, even cuisine. Bennabi affirmed: "To liberate oneself from colonialism[,] . . . it is necessary to liberate oneself from its cause—colonizability" (Bennabi 1954, 81).[46] Nagging questions remained. Did the departure of the Europeans really end colonialism? Correlating Bennabi's thought, was "post-colonial man" still "colonizable"?

CHAPTER 8

Post-Colonial and Contemporary North Africa

Egypt, Libya, and Tunisia

The transfer of power and the attainment of independence were historic achievements. Nevertheless, the post-colonial period challenged the countries of North Africa in manifold ways. Political, economic, and social instability wracked these developing nations. In addition, cultural questions regarding Islam and modernity became increasingly important in post-colonial North Africa. It became evident that there was a need to restore a sovereign self as well as a state. That imperative remains a paramount contemporary issue.

This chapter surveys post-colonial and contemporary Egypt, Libya, and Tunisia. Chapter 9 continues by covering Algeria, Morocco, and Western Sahara.

Egypt

The post-colonial period in Egypt began after the Suez Canal crisis and conflict of 1956, which is considered to be the last act of European imperialism. By repelling the British, French, and Israelis, with the support of the superpowers, and maintaining its sole hold on the Canal, Egypt asserted its independence. Furthermore, Egypt's success resonated positively, especially among the countries of the Arab and emerging Third Worlds. President Gamal Abdel Nasser became the most charismatic North African and Arab of his generation. His influence and Pan-Arab ideology especially inspired revolutionary Algeria—a cogent modern example of Egypt as a transcultural hinge. Egypt's post-colonial era also featured wars with Israel, domestic repression, and Islamist suppression. Economically, Egypt could not muster the resources or provide jobs for its teeming population—now at (or over) 80 million (and expected to reach more than 100 million by 2020 [UN 2002, 37]). It became increasingly reliant on foreign aid. A post-colonial heritage of authoritarian government currently challenged by rising expectations of democratization

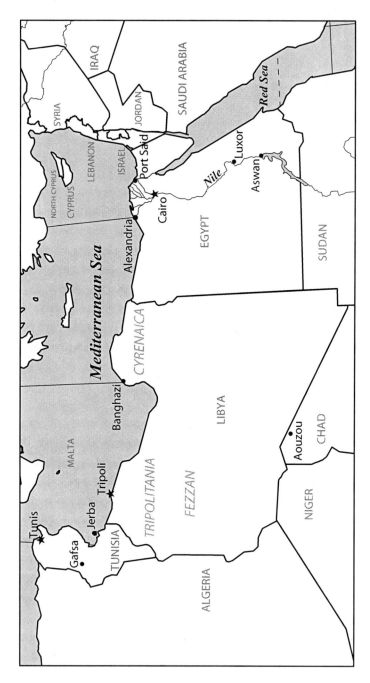

Contemporary Egypt, Libya, and Tunisia

has to be resolved eventually. Given Egypt's enduring and historic geopolitical significance, that resolution will inevitably influence North Africa and the wider world.

Nasser since Suez: From Triumph to Disaster

Nasser's prestige soared as a result of the successful conclusion of the Suez Canal affair. His espousal of Pan-Arabism, the unification of Arabs, resulted in the brief integration of Syria with Egypt as the United Arab Republic from 1958 to 1961. His amalgamation of Egyptian nationalism and his own brand of socialism melded as "Nasserism," which appealed to the rising postcolonial elites of North Africa and the Arab world.[1] Nevertheless, the United Arab Republic of Egypt and Syria eventually failed. Egyptian administrative domination alienated the Syrians. Furthermore, Nasserism's ambiguous socialist economic policies (including state appropriation of properties) had mixed results. Land reform admirably redistributed considerable property and wealth, but it had not threatened ownership rights. Industrial projects faltered, except for the building of the Aswan Dam (officially inaugurated in 1971). The Soviet Union's active participation in Egypt's development, especially at Aswan, established a Communist presence on the African continent and the Mediterranean—a consequence of the strategic myopia of the United States. Nasser permitted a rather free press in the 1950s, but he tightened state censorship in the 1960s. His government dissolved opposition parties such as the Wafd and denied other expressions of dissent. Afaf Lutfi al-Sayyid Marsot reflected upon the irony that even with Egyptians ruling their own country after centuries of foreign domination, the public remained alienated "because the governments that came after 1952 were too insecure to adopt a truly representative government, and so opted for authoritarian and repressive rule which ended by representing vested interests rather than the interests of the majority" (Marsot 2007, ix).

The Muslim Brotherhood was an opponent of Nasser's rise to power and reportedly preferred General Naguib. It was held culpable for perpetrating an assassination attempt of Nasser in 1954. Advocating an Islamic revolution, the leader of the Muslim Brotherhood, Sayyid Qutb, one of the most influential Islamists of the twentieth century, was arrested. He had coined the phrase "jahiliyya of the twentieth century," implying the illegitimacy of authoritarian states that claim to espouse Muslim values (Roussillon 1998, 342). *Jahiliyya* refers to ignorance, heterodoxy, and, specifically in Islamic history, the period before Muhammad's reception of Islam's revelatory message. Nevertheless, Qutb believed that *jahiliyya* continued to confront contemporary Islam. He asserted: "We are surrounded by *jahiliyya*. Its nature is the same as during the first period of Islam and it is perhaps a little more deeply entrenched. Our whole environment, people's beliefs and ideas, habits and art, rules and laws is *jahiliyya*."[2] Evoking the principles of the Salafiyya, he urged that "we must return to that pure source from which the first generation derived its guidance, free from any mixing or pollution. . . . From the Koran [Qur'an] we must also derive our concepts of life, and our principles of government, politics, economics, and all other aspects of life." He advocated an active, offensive as well as defensive jihad: "The purpose of *jihad* in Islam is to secure complete freedom for every man throughout the world by releasing him from servitude to other human beings so that he may serve Allah" (Rubin and Rubin 2002, 30–31). His unwavering, absolute conviction that toxic foreign influences poisoned Muslim society attracted a wide range of international Islamists.[3] Qutb was executed in August 1966. In the following year, disaster struck Egypt and the Arab world.

Nasser's animosity toward Israel was profound and personal (dating from his battle experience against the Israelis in 1948). His vitriolic oratory against the Jewish state echoed throughout the Arab world. After serious border fighting between Israel and Syria, Nasser was widely criticized for not being more supportive of his Arab brothers. With reluctance, Nasser attempted to live up to his rhetoric but badly miscalculated the Israeli response. He forced UN peacekeepers to withdraw from the Egyptian side of the border with Israel and blockaded the Straits of Tiran and the Israeli port of Eilat, a bellicose act.[4] With Arab armed forces mobilizing and massing on its borders, an anxious Tel Aviv launched a preemptive assault. Perceiving Egypt as its greatest and most dangerous enemy, Israel immediately attacked, destroying Egypt's air force while it was still on the ground. Concurrently, Israeli armor swept through the Sinai. By the time hostilities ended, the Israelis had taken over the Sinai and were camped along the Suez Canal. Egypt's allies also suffered substantial territorial losses.[5] Nasser offered his resignation, but it was refused. During the next three years, he endured the fracturing of the Arab world. The Palestine Liberation Organization (PLO), supported by Nasser, had been organized in 1964. After the 1967 catastrophe, King Hussein and his government perceived PLO activities in Jordan to be subversive. He feared the PLO wanted to overthrow his monarchy. This threat resulted in "Black September," a period of intense civil strife between Palestinians and Jordanians. The ailing Nasser strove to end this tragedy in 1970. Nevertheless, as a result of his strenuous yet successful role as conciliator, he exhausted himself and died of a heart attack. His death sorrowed Arabs worldwide. Nasser was repressive and often ruthless; nevertheless, his charisma distinguished his rule and his appeal. Marsot pointed out: "His slogan 'We are all Nasser,' found a responsive echo in the heart of the people. . . . He stands as the only ruler of Egypt who did anything for the mass of the population, notably the poorer, working classes. He created a welfare state that raised the living standard of millions of Egyptians, who, to the present day, adulate Nasser" (Marsot 2007, 153–154). His immediate successor lacked that acute political and social sensibility, a fatal failure.

Anwar Sadat's Perilous Policies

Nasser's longtime associate, fellow "free officer," and vice president, Anwar Sadat, came to power. Observers found it difficult to gauge Sadat, since Nasser had towered over the Egyptian political scene for years. Yet Sadat was a risk taker and visionary, which resulted in the pursuit of perilous policies. The Constitution of 1971 replaced that of 1956 and changed the nation's official name from the United Arab Republic to the Arab Republic of Egypt. His principal objective was to confront Israel over its capture of the Sinai Peninsula and have it returned to Egypt. Since 1967, Egypt engaged Israel in a stalemated low-level conflict along the Suez Canal, such as launching commando attacks or lobbing artillery shells at positions. Sadat hoped to order an overwhelming assault against the Bar-Lev Line, Israel's Sinai fortifications.

To achieve this objective, Sadat needed to galvanize domestic consensus, which was a difficult task.[6] He recognized the alienation of Islamists and sought to elevate his political and public image as a Muslim. He piously led Friday prayers and loosened state restrictions. He also outmaneuvered rivals, thereby securing his power. In 1972, he informed Soviet technicians, officers, and consultants that their services were no longer needed in Egypt.[7] This decision received public approval since it represented an act of national self-reliance as well as independence from foreigners. Sadat renewed Egypt's alliance with Syria and planned a war to reclaim its territory and to avenge its 1967 humiliation.

In October 1973, Egyptian forces crossed the canal and surprised the Israelis. Furthermore, Egyptian air defenses effectively anticipated the Israeli air response. With Syria attacking in the north, Israel found itself hard-pressed.[8] The Soviet Union vehemently protested as the United States rushed supplies to Israel. The war threatened to escalate and involve the superpowers. Reeling but recovering from its initial shock, and with its superior forces reinforced by arriving American logistical assistance, Israel recovered and the momentum shifted. An Israeli division outmaneuvered the Egyptians and crossed the Suez Canal and threatened the Nile Valley. Sadat, satisfied with the progress of the war up to that point and increasingly worried by the Israeli thrust toward the Nile, accepted a cease-fire. Secretary of State Henry Kissinger "shuttled" between capitals and peace was restored. Kissinger also expedited contacts between Israelis and Egyptians, resulting in subsequent disengagement agreements.

Although on the brink of a possible disaster, given the Israeli counteroffensive west of the canal, Sadat portrayed the war as a victory. Indeed, Egyptian forces had performed well, especially in the beginning of the war. He hoped for more territorial concessions rather than a strip along the east bank of the canal. On the other hand, Kissinger and Sadat developed a close rather than just a cordial dialogue. Relations between Washington and Cairo almost ruptured during the Nasser years, but substantially improved under Sadat. The Egyptian president hoped for American and European investment, a fundamental aspiration of the postwar liberalizing policy known as the *infitah* or "opening" of the economy. Furthermore, the president impatiently expected a change in Israel's behavior toward Egypt. Concluding that another war was too hazardous and aware of an increasingly restless public, he took another risk.

The astonished Israelis learned that the president of Egypt intended to visit their country in order to launch a peace initiative. Sadat arrived in November 1977 and displayed his disarming charm but also his determination. He wanted the Sinai back and was willing to negotiate for it. President Jimmy Carter encouraged and expedited Sadat's subsequent discussions with Prime Minister Menachem Begin, culminating in the Camp David framework agreements of 1978. One agreement charted a course to peace in the Middle East and focused on the Israeli-Palestinian relationship. The second agreement was a bilateral peace between Egypt and Israel. In March 1979, the formal bilateral peace treaty was signed, providing for the phased withdrawal of Israeli forces from the Sinai and the exchange of ambassadors (i.e., diplomatic recognition). A letter attached to the treaty aimed to start negotiations regarding the Palestinians. Nevertheless, the latter initiative was stillborn because of Israeli intransigence and the Arab reaction to the treaty. A "Front of Steadfastness," including Libya and Algeria, condemned Egypt's diplomacy toward Israel. Egypt, which had played such an important role in the formation of the Arab League in the 1940s (meetings in Alexandria [1944] and Cairo [1945]), was expelled from it. The headquarters of the Arab League was transferred from Cairo to Tunis. One by one, Arab nations broke relations with Egypt. Sadat stood alone. Indeed, his policy toward Israel also estranged many Egyptians, although most favored the prospect of peace.

To radical Islamists, Sadat's courtship of the United States and Western Europe and accommodation with Israel were symptomatic of the poisonous effect of the president's Westoxification. The economy was also in crisis; the *infitah* failed to attract substantial foreign investment.[9] On the other hand, the economy benefited from the reopening of the Suez Canal and the recuperation of the Sinai oil fields.[10] (Remittances from Egyptians living in foreign countries also helped the balance of payments.) Nevertheless, economic growth was uneven and consumerism widened class differences, which opponents rhetorically exploited.[11] While projecting a liberal image internationally, Sadat's domestic policies relentlessly repressed proliferating Islamism and the political opposition. Sadat was gunned down by Islamist soldiers in 1981 while reviewing a military parade commemorating the October 1973 War.[12] The world mourned this risk taker and peacemaker, but also wondered why Egyptians did not widely share its grief.

Hosni Mubarak and the Search for Stability

Vice President Hosni Mubarak took over the government and remains in power. He has maintained relations with Israel, although they have often been strained. Furthermore, he has suppressed Islamists. The repressive political system has ensured the domination of Mubarak's National Democratic Party (NDP) in legislative and presidential elections.[13] Mubarak notably achieved the gradual reacceptance of Egypt in Arab circles, including its formal reentry into the Arab League in 1989. By that time, Arab states had restored diplomatic relations with Egypt. Mubarak decided to join the United Nations coalition in the Gulf War of 1991.[14] He also mediated Israeli-Palestinian discussions in the 1990s. He questioned and opposed the American invasion of Iraq in 2003.

Mubarak's principal political interests have been domestic. Amnesty International and other human rights organizations have reproached his government for the brutality of its security forces, especially against militant Islamists.[15] In turn, the Jama'at Islamiyya (Islamic Group) claimed responsibility for attacks on tourists in Cairo and Luxor in 1997.[16] The latter assault resulted in 70 deaths, including 58 tourists. Mubarak condemned the 11 September 2001 suicide attacks in New York City and Washington, D.C., and referred to 9/11 to justify his suppression of Islamist radicalism in his country. Nevertheless, extremist Islamist groups detonated bombs that killed scores of Egyptians and foreigners in attacks in Taba in October 2004 and in Sharm al-Shaykh in July 2005.

Egypt's constitution stipulates multi-party political participation, although elections and referendums during the Mubarak era have guaranteed the success of his NDP. Other political organizations include the New Wafd Party, the Socialist Labor Party (SLP), the National Accord Party (Hizb al-Wifaq al-Qawmi), and the Arab Democratic Nasserist Party. Islamism as a political ideology has been an Egyptian tradition since the founding of the Muslim Brotherhood in 1928. Among the most significant Islamist organizations are the Muslim Brotherhood; Islamic Jihad (Jihad al-Islami), whose leader, Dr. Ayman al-Zawahiri, is attached to Usama bin Ladin's al-Qa'ida; and Jama'at Islamiyya, which proclaimed a cease-fire in 1999 in its campaign to overthrow the government. The current Greater Middle East Initiative by President George W. Bush's administration has called for greater democratization. (American politicians and pundits have especially targeted Mubarak's authoritarianism.) The September 2005 presidential election featured multiple candidates for the first time. Mubarak won handily, but the emergence of new parties, such as Kafiya (Enough), attracted regional and global attention, as well as the imprisonment of Ayman Nour in December, the leader of the El-Ghad (Tomorrow) Party and opposition presidential candidate.[17] Political intimidation and widespread fraud marked the November 2005 parliamentary elections. Nevertheless, with its candidates running as "Independents," the Muslim Brotherhood continued to be the strongest opposition party, capturing 88 out of 444 seats. In February 2006, political protest, especially from Islamists, forced Mubarak to postpone local elections scheduled for April. Amendments to the constitution, which notably prohibited parties based on religion, passed by referendum in March 2007. The electorate's meager participation in this measure signaled resignation and alienation.[18] Egypt faces difficult and dangerous times, encapsulated by the question: who will succeed Mubarak?[19]

Egypt's Economy and Society

According to the International Monetary Fund (IMF), from 1961 to 1980 economic growth averaged 6 percent a year.[20] During the 1980s and the 1990s it dropped to 4.8 percent. From 2001 to 2004 it slowed to annual rate of 3.5 percent. These positive though falling indicators of an expanding economy belie a lower per capita income than other regional non–oil producing countries (IMF 2005a, 15).[21]

Egypt's burgeoning population of 80 million consumes enormous resources.[22] As earlier chapters illustrated, Egypt relied upon agricultural exportation. Now it must import much of its alimentary needs, such as wheat. The primary (first) sector, agriculture, accounts for only about 16 percent of the annual Gross Domestic Product (GDP). The Aswan Dam's regulation of flooding (and Lake Nasser) permits perennial irrigation and expansion of agricultural areas, such those in the Western Desert. The unexpected rise in the water table and salinity, however, has deterred the extension of arable terrain. Urban sprawl has also stymied reclamation projects. Furthermore, silt loss has affected the watershed in three ways. First, without the deposit of silt and its nutrients, farmers, if they can afford it, have bought fertilizers, which create other ecological problems. Second, silt also nourished fish, which have disappeared along with fisheries.[23] Third, without silt accumulation, the Mediterranean has encroached on and eroded the Nile delta (Marsot 2007, 167). Cotton remains the principal crop and is labor-intensive, which helps relieve the unemployment, officially estimated at 10 percent. Egypt remains one of the world's largest exporters of long-staple cotton. Rice and sugar are also important crops. Avian flu ravaged Egyptian poultry in 2006 and 2007.

The secondary sector includes food-processing, textiles, and especially hydrocarbons. Egypt is self-sufficient in oil and natural gas. In the mid-1990s, Egypt pumped 900,000 barrels per day (bpd), but in 2002–2003 production of crude oil, condensate, and liquefied petroleum gas averaged 719,000 bpd. National consumption averaged 461,000 bpd, leaving only 258,000 bpd for net exports (a net exporter since 1975). Egypt averages about 590,000 bpd (IMF 2005a, 34). It is a modest producer and not a member of the Organization of Petroleum Exporting Countries (OPEC). On the other hand, Egypt expects to be a significant gas exporter (ibid., 34–35). Egypt already produces petro-chemical fertilizer, and more plants are projected. As planned, the Aswan Dam provides hydroelectric power for Egypt's heavy industry, which includes steel and aluminum production.

The tertiary (third) sector features tourism, which provides about $4 billion annually. Thus, the firefight at Luxor in 1997 and the bombing at Sharm al-Shaykh in 2005 targeted the economy as well as the government. Despite the terrorist threat compounded by chronic regional instability, Egypt's historic appeal and its sedimentary civilization continue to attract visitors. The Aswan Dam's completion exponentially increased the country's electrification.

The Suez Canal provided $3.6 billion in revenue in 2006. Although hydro-carbon pipelines compete with tanker transport, increasing commerce from India and especially China has increased traffic and revenue (German and Taylor 2007, 365).

The most serious problems currently faced by the economy are trade and budgetary deficits, unemployment, and foreign debt (approximately $30 billion). Historically, wages have also not risen with inflation, consequently im-poverishing the working class and impeding middle class entrepreneurship. That situation improved in the 1990s when the inflation rate dropped to single digits but, as implied above regarding population growth and per capita as-sets, disposable income has considerably dropped since the 1970s (Jankowski 2000, 182–183). Government subsidies have also been significantly reduced, such as in fuel, which have had an inflationary effect (12 percent in early 2007 [German and Taylor 2007, 359]). On the other hand, beneficial reforms were implemented earlier this decade regarding personal and corporate taxation. A pressing political and economic question is reducing deficits while main-taining the social protection system (IMF 2007a). Egypt benefited financially from its participation in the Gulf War with debt forgiveness provided by the United States and the IMF's greater liberality regarding stand-by credits. The

Paris Club also rewrote and rescheduled debts. On the other hand, the war displaced hundreds of thousands of Egyptians working abroad. In 1989, total remittances reached $4.2 billion, which equates with the current flow (German and Taylor 2007, 360, 374). There are approximately 4 million expatriate Egyptian workers.

Egypt remains reliant upon foreign aid. The United States is a major donor since bilateral relations thawed after the October 1973 War. Despite reservations regarding political suppression and repression, the United States appreciates and rewards Egypt as a moderate, mediating voice in the volatile Middle East. Since 1975, American aggregate aid has totaled approximately $50 billion (Levinson 2004). Egypt's most important commercial clients are the United States and the European Union.

Socially, Egypt is still one of the most diverse countries in North Africa and the Arab world. This is because of its traditional transcultural character and its role as a historical hinge linking peoples, commodities, and ideas. This is reflected in the literature of the Nobel Prize winner Naguib Mahfouz and, more recently, Alaa al Aswany and Nawal el-Saadawi (see Conclusion).

There have been important strides toward gender equality in Egypt. In 2001, an amendment to the Family Law, based on a liberal interpretation of a hadith, gave women more rights regarding divorce, thereby tempering men's patriarchal authority. Women can now ask for and be granted a divorce. For a brief time, Nawal el-Saadawi (see Chapter 9) ran for the presidency in 2005, a particularly important symbolic act.

Egypt's geopolitical position and historical (and transcultural) legacy necessitate its close observation and appreciation. Given its political, economic, and social significance, Napoleon's assessment of Egypt as the most strategic country in the world remains compelling.

Libya

During the post-colonial period, Libya has had only two rulers, King Idris and Col. Muammar Qadhafi. Their leadership styles were markedly different. The king relied upon advisers and was a reluctant ruler. The colonel, inevitably called mercurial to the point that it is now practically an epithet, is still in power. Since he seized power in 1969, Qadhafi has assumed multiple "personas"—the dashing military officer, the figurative Bedouin, the "Supreme

Revolutionary Leader," the global terrorist, and the Pan-Arabist and Pan-Africanist. Qadhafi's erratic behavior and enigmatic personality coupled with his ambiguous ideology and his access to Libya's oil wealth have often propelled him prominently and controversially onto the world stage.

Despite their contrasting manners and personalities, there is a common theme shared by Libya's two post-colonial governments and leaders. It is an aversion, an "avoidance," according to Lisa Anderson and Dirk Vandewalle, to forming a state and constructing a nation (thematic in Anderson 1986 and Vandewalle 2006). Without bureaucracies, ministries, and simply an effective governmental apparatus, Libya is an anomaly of being a stateless country with three distinct regions: Tripolitania, Cyrenaica, and Fezzan. On the other hand, Ali Abdullatif Ahmida contends that Libyans identify a centralized state with colonialism and that there was a heritage of state formation ("tribal-peasant confederations" and Sanusi institutions) despite the apparent "stateless" condition (Ahmida 1994, 5–6; Ahmida 2005, 74). Regardless of the degree of Libya's perplexing statelessness, Libya's post-colonial history has global as well as regional significance.

Idris I's Reign

Throughout his life, Idris was principally a Sufi leader. His grandfather was the first "Grand Sanusi," Muhammad al-Sanusi, whose Islamism inspired resolute resistance to Italian invasion and colonialism. During World War II, Idris supported the British against the Italians and was later awarded by the United Nations with the rather artificial kingdom of Libya. As we considered earlier, the kingdom's three territorial components, Tripolitania, Cyrenaica, and Fezzan, had distinctive geographical and cultural characteristics and histories. Idris exercised his greatest influence in Cyrenaica. Despite the appearance of a constitutional monarchy, the king had dominant power. In particular, the United States and the United Kingdom supported Idris's government. Each ally possessed military installations in Libya, notably the Americans' Wheelus Air Force Base, a strategic asset in the global effort to contain the Soviets.[24] Nevertheless, Idris occasionally asserted himself. For example, he ignored his traditional close relations with the British and refused to have the Suez task force anchor in Libyan waters in 1956. Indeed, Nasser's refusal to repudiate his decision to nationalize the canal, despite foreign invasion, inspired Libyans, notably Muammar Qadhafi (Pargeter 2000, 54). In 1967,

American support of Israel provoked protests at Wheelus and at the American embassy.

By this time a septuagenarian, Idris was a tired king who had witnessed dramatic and traumatic changes in Libya. At independence, Libya had *seven* university graduates. Its three principal exports were cuttlefish bone, esparto grass, and battlefield scrap (Parker 1987, 65). The discovery of oil in 1959 stimulated the striking transformation of the country's economy. Nevertheless, Libya had few institutions and instead the monarchy depended on "a group of favored individuals, families, and tribes it judged necessary for its own survival" (Vandewalle 2006, 73). When Muammar Qadhafi and the Revolutionary Command Council (RCC) deposed Idris in 1969, the king harbored little ill will and may have felt relief. Qadhafi was an unknown figure, and, given his subsequent capricious comportment, remains inscrutable today.

Qadhafi's Behavior: Recurrent Themes

Despite the difficulty in understanding Qadhafi's conduct over the decades, there are some recurrent themes. He believes in political unity. This was illustrated in numerous efforts to integrate Libya with other countries. A Pan-Arabist, who initially identified closely with Nasser, Qadhafi sought unification with Egypt. Eventually, hostility arose between Qadhafi and Anwar Sadat, provoking violence along the border in 1977. During Mubarak's presidency, relations with Egypt significantly improved. Morocco and Libya, two contrasting countries, declared a qualified unity by the Treaty of Oujda in 1984; but that agreement fell apart in 1986.[25] Libya is a charter member of the Union du Maghreb Arabe (Arab Maghrib Union [UMA]), which was inaugurated in 1989.[26] Most recently, Qadhafi has called for unity with sub-Saharan Africa and is a supporter of the African Union (AU) (ex-Organization of African Unity [OAU]) and the ideal of a United States of Africa. Thus, he has evolved from a fervent Pan-Arabist to an ardent Pan-Africanist.

Qadhafi confronted foreign oil companies in 1970 and 1971, resulting in higher posted prices and royalties. His actions influenced and emboldened the Algerians to nationalize French concessions in the Sahara in February 1971. From late 1971 into 1974, Libya ordered the limited nationalization of major foreign concessionaires (giving Libya 50 or 51 percent of the controlling interest), thus expanding the Libyan National Oil Company's (LNOC) participation in the sector.

During the 1970s, Qadhafi, as self-appointed "Leader of the Revolution" (*qa'id al-thawra*), inaugurated a Cultural Revolution featuring the publication of a three-volume *Green Book,* which appeared between 1975 and 1979. An ambiguous amalgam of socialism and Islamism, the *Green Book* aimed at mobilizing the population. It projected a new ideological direction, referred to as the "Third Universal Theory,"[27] which was reflected in administrative changes in the country—committees and congresses on local, regional, and national levels. The RCC became the General Secretariat. Despite the proliferation of assemblies and popular mobilization, Qadhafi refrained from consulting public opinion or sharing governing responsibility. The name of the country was changed to the Socialist People's Libyan Arab Jamahiriyya. "Jamahariyya" is a neologism and refers in this context to a mass assembly.[28] Arguably, this ideological initiative was the greatest example of "statelessness—the avoidance of creating a modern state" (Vandewalle 2006, 1; see also Anderson 1986, 251–269). Qadhafi's reluctance to develop state institutions and complementary bureaucracies ironically correlated to the political practice of the Sanusi monarchy. On the other hand, Ali Abdullatif Ahmida argued that Qadhafi's initiative took into account Libyan social, cultural, and political realities: "By appealing to the rural ideology of statelessness and fear of the urban-centered state (seen as the colonial state), Qadhafi destroyed institutions of the old monarchy and, at the same time, created the Jamahiriyya institutions legitimizing a strong state acceptable to most Libyans in the hinterland" (Ahmida 2005, 72).

To Vandewalle, the *Green Book*'s "ideas are simple and, with their insistence on egalitarianism and lack of hierarchy, reflect a tribal ethos" (Vandewalle 2006, 103). Qadhafi implemented a socialist program that eliminated capitalism and private enterprise, and consequently reduced the middle class. With oil revenues pouring into the treasury, Qadhafi imported or provided social services for his population, which rose from being one of the poorest countries in the world to one of the wealthiest. Anderson referred to Qadhafi's policies as "distributive," making people reliant upon the regime's "largesse" (Anderson 1986, 268–269). Nevertheless, these policies did not result in popular mobilization; instead, Libyans became comfortable and complacent. Qadhafi eventually allowed private enterprise to stimulate the economy (and the population); the first of several liberalizing *infitahs* was announced in March 1987.

Qadhafi's vision for Libya did not receive unanimous approval. In 1975, university students protested and there was also a coup attempt. Exiled Libyans in opposition to his government were ruthlessly tracked down and targeted. From 1980 to 1987, approximately twenty-five Libyans were assassinated overseas (Lawless 2007, 771). There have been recurrent, although not well documented, internal (as well as external) attempts to overthrow him, especially in the 1990s. Qadhafi now faces an Islamist threat and has responded by incorporating elements of the Shariʻa in Libyan law.[29] His decision in December 2003 to accommodate international demands for dismantling weapons of mass destruction (WMD) facilities has served Qadhafi well. After decades of diplomatic isolation compounded by economic sanctions,[30] Libya is receiving renewed attention and new contracts, which are sure to benefit Qadhafi politically and personally (see below).

Qadhafi Plays a Dangerous Game

Rebuffed regarding his unity initiatives and regarded as an eccentric by Arab and world leaders, Qadhafi resorted to supporting a wide range of controversial and radical organizations, especially in the 1970s and 1980s. These included extremist Palestinian organizations, the Baader-Meinhof Gang of West Germany, the Red Brigades of Italy, and the Irish Republican Army (IRA). His support of terrorism led to direct confrontation with the United States during Ronald Reagan's presidency.

In August 1981, American carrier-based jets from the Sixth Fleet shot down Libyan fighter planes over the Gulf of Sirte. Rumors then circulated that Libya had sent a "hit squad" to assassinate the American president. In March 1985, the Sixth Fleet's maneuvers in the Gulf of Sirte provoked Libyan SAM (surface-to-air missile) attacks. The Americans responded by destroying the missile and radar installations as well as four Libyan patrol boats. An explosion on 5 April at a discotheque in Berlin frequented by American soldiers resulted in the death of one American and a Turkish woman. Investigation proved that Libyan agents perpetrated the bombing. On 15 April, American aircraft from the United Kingdom and the Sixth Fleet bombed selected targets in Tripoli and Benghazi. Qadhafi's residence was struck, killing an adopted infant daughter. In January 1989, two more Libyan aircraft, assessed as threats to the Sixth Fleet, were destroyed.

Qadhafi received little support or sympathy from the Arab world or the Soviet Union, his arms supplier, regarding these confrontations with American forces. Indeed, Qadhafi's government was implicated in two horrendous acts of terror. In December 1988, 259 people aboard a Pan American Boeing 747 (Flight 103) perished when a bomb detonated in flight over Lockerbie, Scotland. A French UTA passenger aircraft was also blown up over the Sahara in September 1989, killing 170. This explosion was also linked to Libya. The United Nations imposed sanctions. With Libya's assets already frozen in the United States since 1985, Washington added secondary sanctions. After years of negotiation, the two Libyans held responsible were tried by Scottish judges in the Netherlands in 2000. In January 2001, the Scottish judges rendered their decision. One of the defendants was freed, but the other was sentenced to life imprisonment. In August 2003, a compensation package for the Lockerbie victims' families was concluded ($2.7 billion) and began to be distributed. The UN subsequently lifted its sanctions. In January 2004, a similar compensation agreement was reached with the UTA victims' families.

Qadhafi also intervened in African affairs. A border dispute with Chad (Aouzou Strip), dating from the colonial period, led to an eight-year military involvement in that country that culminated in Libya's defeat in 1987. Libya agreed to the International Court of Justice's decision in 1989 to award the Aouzou Strip to Chad. Qadhafi also had supported the 1971 military coup against King Hassan II of Morocco and eventually backed the POLISARIO, the Sahrawi liberation organization, in its struggle to attain Western Sahara's independence (see Chapter 9). Nevertheless, his assistance to the Sahrawis was erratic and he mended his relations with Morocco to the point of signing the aforementioned Treaty of Oujda. In 1980, Tunisian dissidents, apparently expedited by Qadhafi, crossed the frontier and attacked Gafsa in an attempt to destabilize Habib Bourguiba's government. Nevertheless, by the end of the decade, Libya had made peace with its neighbors, symbolized by its joining the UMA.[31]

Qadhafi Surprise Announcements

It was well known that Qadhafi sought chemical and nuclear weapons. A reputed mustard gas plant mysteriously caught fire in 1980, presumably the work of Western intelligence services. In December 2003, the United Kingdom and the United States announced that Libya intended to disclose and destroy its WMD facilities. Although Libya did not have atomic weapons, it was developing capabilities for them. Libya's decisions resulted in the lifting of most of the American sanctions. (UN sanctions had been lifted earlier.) Why did Qadhafi pursue this startling change of policy?

Washington argued it was because of its invasion of Iraq in 2003, which demonstrated American intolerance for WMD (weapons of mass destruction) threats. The display of American power convinced Qadhafi that he might be next on the Bush administration's list, since the principal official reason for the Iraq war was to find and eliminate WMD. Notwithstanding the Bush administration's rationale, the Libyan government's decisive reason seemed more related to economic concerns as well as growing internal unrest. Furthermore, Qadhafi's condemnation of the 11 September 2001 attacks already signaled a more cooperative attitude. His opposition to Islamism is well known and controversial.[32]

Qadhafi's accommodation of the Pan Am 103 families' claims and the termination of his WMD program ameliorated relations with the United States. There also were reports of intelligence sharing. In 2004, Libya agreed to compensate victims of the Berlin discotheque bombing, and the United States ended its economic sanctions. With full diplomatic relations restored in 2006, Libya was no longer regarded as a state sponsor of terrorism. Indeed, American oil companies hoped to resume business in Libya.

Libya's Economy and Society

Libya's transformation from the poorest country in the world to one of the richest has had enormous political, economic, and social consequences for its six million citizens. Qadhafi's handling of this wealth has been controversial. While social services are available, much of the country's work is done by foreign labor. The public sector employs 75 percent of the working population. Private investment has been calculated at a very low 2 percent of the Gross Domestic Product (GDP); therefore job creation in the private sector is minuscule (IMF 2005b, 5), although the government is in favor of joint enterprises (EIU 2007c). Qadhafi's spontaneous invitation to Africans on the continent to come and work in Libya created multiple problems regarding finding jobs and housing. In addition, the arrival of the immigrants to take advantage of Qadhafi's quixotic initiative incited animosity to the point where Sub-Saharan Africans were asked or forced to leave Libya.[33] The government has requested foreign companies, especially in the hydrocarbons sector, to hire Libyans.

Libya's over reliance on hydrocarbons has exposed the economy to dan-

gerous price fluctuations, such as the plunge in the mid-1980s. From 1999 to
2003, the oil sector accounted for 50 percent of GDP, 97 percent of Libya's export revenues, and 75 percent of the government's revenues (IMF 2005b, 5).[34]
The real GDP grew by 9 percent in 2003 (IMF 2005c, 5). The average real GDP
growth from 2002–2006 was 5.0 percent (EIU 2007b).[35] Hydrocarbon prices
are at record levels as of this writing and, given the restoration of relations
with Washington, American companies hope to participate in the sector. Nevertheless, the high petroleum prices also create false expectations. Hydrocarbons, like other sectors and markets, go through cycles. Qadhafi has understood the need to diversify the country's rentier, distributive economy, but he
has not decisively or effectively acted.

In 1983, Qadhafi inaugurated an extraordinary and ambitious public works
project entitled the "Great Man-Made River" (GMR). It recalls the technology
of the Garamantes of antiquity, who irrigated using underground water channels (*foggaras*) (see Introduction; Chapter 2). Like the Garamantes, Qadhafi
aspired to tap the aquifers and vast underground basins in the Sahara and
channel water to the north in order to promote agriculture. Several phases
have been implemented, but the "river" remains occasionally dammed by
contractual and technological issues and historically by the fluctuating hydrocarbon revenues which primarily fund its construction. Nevertheless, by
the mid-1990s, Benghazi and Tripoli received GMR water. The ambitious national water grid is yet to be completed as well as the agricultural aspirations
associated with it. Qadhafi prefers dramatic transformations (or personal
transmutations), such as the GMR, and ignores or is unappreciative of more
modest and practical initiatives, such as the development of a Libyan fishing
industry. Instead, foreign trawlers are hauling in profits from the rich catch
offshore.

Qadhafi remains acutely apprehensive of internal upheaval. The sanctions created numerous social and economic problems. Their lifting may also
inspire rising expectations, which could also destabilize the Jamahariyya.
Furthermore, Ahmida observes: "The regime seems to have exhausted its revolutionary zeal and faces major domestic problems, including a lack of institutionalization, weakened civil associations, brain drain of the best-educated
Libyans, and an inability on the part of its leadership to deal with a changing,
complex international system" (Ahmida 2005, 72). Although Qadhafi's recent
policy of accommodation has ended Libya's isolation, his caprice keeps the

world wondering. Ronald Bruce St. John believes that "[Qadhafi] is more likely to introduce changes designed to consolidate his pre-eminent position in the political system he created. . . . With no formal mechanism in place to ensure a smooth transition of power, the post-[Qadhafi] era can be expected to be a time of tension and uncertainty, with numerous socioeconomic and political groups vying for power" (St. John 2008, 67).[36]

Tunisia

Habib Bourguiba, a courageous, contradictory, and controversial figure in modern North African history, created one of the most secular states in the Muslim world. He provided unparalleled rights for women and established a legal system based on Western models. Yet he also became increasingly authoritarian, which led to opposition featuring a rise of Islamism. Refusing to consider retirement while enduring debilitating health problems, the "grand old man" was respectfully removed from the presidency. Bourguiba's successor, Zine el-Abidine Ben Ali, after signaling political liberalization, also resorted to authoritarianism, while Tunisia experienced impressive economic growth.

Bourguiba to Ben Ali

Bourguiba's gradualist course to independence alienated two important nationalists. Salah Ben Yusuf equated autonomy with compliance with the French. He also believed that Bourguiba ignored Tunisia's Arabic-Islamic heritage. Ahmad Ben Salah, the secretary-general of the UGTT, did not agree with the integration (and loss of independence) of the national union with the Neo-Destour Party. He later reconciled his differences and became Bourguiba's principal minister in charge of Tunisia's socialist policies of the 1960s. As for Salah Ben Yusuf, he remained an adamant opponent of Bourguiba's to the point of mobilizing a guerrilla force in the south. He later went into self-exile in Tripoli, then Cairo. Tunisian agents likely assassinated him in August 1961 in Frankfurt, West Germany.

   With his political opposition either co-opted or removed, Habib Bourguiba imposed his will on Tunisia. He was highly influenced by French culture and values. He produced the Personal Status Code of 1956, one of the most secular in the Muslim world. It rejected polygamy, provided equal rights regarding divorce, and gave mothers the right to have custody of their children. The Personal Code also raised the minimum age for marriage to eighteen years for men and fifteen for women. The government appropriated public *hubus* (land holdings of Islamic foundations) in 1956 and abolished private *hubus* a year later. In 1958, an educational program was launched to accelerate literacy. The Institut des Hautes Etudes, established in 1945, became the University of Tunis in 1960.

Bourguiba supported Third World liberation and especially accommodated Algerian nationalists with havens. The French bombing of the Tunisian village of Saqiyat (Sakiet) Sidi Yusuf in 1958 eventually led to the events in May 1958 in Algiers that precipitated the end of the Fourth Republic.[37] Bourguiba mistakenly tried to force the French out of their naval and air base at Bizerte in 1961, which incited violence resulting in more than 1,000 Tunisian deaths. The French withdrew from Bizerte in October 1964. His efforts to redraw the border between Algeria and Tunisia, in order to take advantage of nearby hydrocarbons, failed.

In 1964, Bourguiba changed the name of the Neo-Destour Party to the Parti Socialiste Destourien (Destourian Socialist Party [PSD]), which indicated the ideological direction in which Bourguiba aimed to lead his country. Charged with implementing a socialist system, Ahmad Ben Salah collected a number of ministerial portfolios such as finances, education, and planning. At independence, *colons* still controlled sizeable agricultural land. Bourguiba nationalized French property in 1964 and 1965, much to the chagrin of the French government, which reduced cooperation (assistance programs/foreign aid) with Tunisia. The resistance of Tunisian farmers to Ben Salah's socialist initiatives eventually convinced Bourguiba to sack his powerful minister (and potential rival). Ben Salah was accused of treason and convicted in 1970 to a ten-year prison sentence. He escaped in 1973 and went into exile.

The Chamber of Deputies recognized Bourguiba as "president for life" in 1974, alienating members within his party and the public. A nationwide general strike on 26 January 1978 ("Black Thursday"), protesting the government's handling of the economy, led to scores being killed (possibly two hundred deaths). Parliamentary elections in 1981 featured an alliance between the PSD and the trade unions, creating a National Front, which resulted in a sweeping victory. This election engendered a new opposition, however: the Islamists of the Mouvement de la Tendance Islamique (Islamic Tendency

Movement [MTI]). Rioting in 1984 was attributed to the MTI and led to its suppression. Major opposition parties boycotted the parliamentary elections in 1986 that the National Front dominated by default. In October 1987, an ailing Bourguiba selected Zine al-Abidine Ben Ali as his premier. Bourguiba was soon declared unfit to rule (implementing Article 57 of the Tunisian Constitution), and Ben Ali assumed the leadership of the country.[38]

In an effort to secure legality and power, Ben Ali promised a transition to democracy. The "National Pact" was signed in 1989 and political parties were legalized, but not the MTI, now called al-Nahda (Renaissance). Shaykh Rashid Ghannushi (Ghannouchi), the principal Islamist leader, was forced into exile.[39] National elections in 1989 resulted in the unopposed Ben Ali continuing as president with the Ralliement Constitutionnel Démocratique (Democratic Constitutional Rally [RCD]), the successor of the PSD, taking every seat in parliament.[40] In 1990, success in local elections by Islamists led to a crackdown that continues to this day. Token parliamentary opposition was allowed in the 1994 elections. Ben Ali was also reelected president in 1999. After voicing criticism of the restrictive political conditions, several opposition leaders were detained in 1995. In 2003, al-Nahda (Ennahda, the French transliteration) issued a communiqué calling for opposition solidarity and a "national pact of opposition" (Communiqué 2005, 329–331). Ben Ali continues to exercise, however, authoritarian power.[41] As Kenneth Perkins perceived, Ben Ali's latest reelection in 2004 has made him Tunisia's "second 'president for life'" (Perkins 2004, 202, 212). The lack of political freedom portends serious future problems.

Tunisia's Foreign Relations

Neighboring Algeria's socialist direction and general popularity throughout the Third World influenced Bourguiba's decision to pursue similar policies in Tunisia. Although Tunisia eventually rejected socialism, relations remained cordial with Algeria in the 1970s and 1980s. In 1983, Tunisia and Algeria concluded a friendship treaty. From the Tunisian perspective, a close relationship with Algeria was necessary, especially after Libya sponsored an attack by three hundred guerrillas at Gafsa in 1980. Relations with Libya have improved since Ben Ali took power. Tunisia also joined the UMA in 1989.

Clearly aligned with the West during the Cold War, Tunisia also played an important role in the Arab world during the 1980s. Tunis became the headquarters of the Arab League after Anwar Sadat's divisive peace with Israel. The Tunisian government also agreed to host the Palestine Liberation Organization (PLO) after the Israeli invasion of Lebanon in 1982. The PLO stayed in Tunisia until 1994.

Terrorism has also targeted Tunisia. In 2002, an explosion outside a synagogue on Jerba killed twenty-one and wounded twenty others. The casualties were mostly tourists. Al-Qa'ida, which considers Tunisia an apostate polity, perpetrated the atrocity. On the other hand, al-Nahda's Rashid Ghannushi has condemned Islamist extremism and violence.

Tunisia's Economy and Society

With a population of ten million, Tunisia has the most balanced economy in the Maghrib. Each sector has important strengths. The primary sector's produce includes grain, citrus fruits, and especially olive products. Approximately two-thirds of Tunisia's land is arable. The secondary sector features textiles and phosphate production. Tunisia's oil and natural gas production almost covers the nation's needs. Tourism highlights the third sector. Remittances from Tunisians living overseas, especially in Europe, also are economically beneficial. In addition, Tunisia has cemented its ties with Europe by negotiating the first Association Agreement with the European Union (EU), which went into effect in 1998. France remains Tunisia's principal commercial partner. By the Agadir Treaty of 2004, Tunisia, Egypt, Jordan, and Morocco agreed to establish a free trade zone. According to the IMF, Algeria represents "Tunisia's largest untapped sources for trade in the world" (IMF November 2004, 20). Unfortunately, the UMA's aspirations for greater regional trade remain unfulfilled. Despite Tunisia's strong economy, unemployment is estimated to be 14 percent. Nevertheless, Tunisia's current GDP growth is estimated at an impressive 5 percent, which should remain at this level or slightly above in the short term (EIU 2007f). Inflation dropped from about 10 percent in the early 1990s to 1 percent in 2005 (IMF 2007c, 4). Tunisia has one of the most liberalized economies in North Africa and the Arab world.

Tunisia's expansive economy developed under President Ben Ali's authoritarianism, but questions persist. Given his personal domination over the country, how will Tunisia's relative prosperity be affected after Ben Ali? How vulnerable is the economy and society to political unrest?

CHAPTER 9

Post-Colonial and Contemporary North Africa

Algeria, Morocco, and Western Sahara

This chapter continues the survey of post-colonial and contemporary North Africa with a second group of closely linked countries—Algeria, Morocco, and Western Sahara. Although the latter's international political status as a "country" remains unresolved, Western Sahara's international importance deserves and receives particular consideration.

Algeria

The history of post-colonial Algeria discloses an existential engagement, a search to build and define a nation wracked from colonialism and war. From 1962 until 1988, the army and the FLN dominated Algerian politics. Riots in October 1988, however, led to rapid political and economic liberalization. The rise of the Islamist Front Islamique du Salut (Islamic Salvation Front [FIS]) and its success in elections provoked a coup in January 1992 against the government by military and civilian elites, resulting in the cancellation of the second round of parliamentary elections, which would have brought the FIS to power. The consequences of the coup were enormous—a bloody *fitna* or trial of the Algerian nation resulting in widespread civil strife and an estimated 150,000–200,000 deaths. Beginning in the mid-1990s President Liamine Zeroual carefully calibrated a policy of political redemocratization and reinstitutionalization, enhanced by the political craftwork of his successor, Abdelaziz Bouteflika, who has pursued important national reconciliation initiatives. Algeria has regained its political stature and civil strife has significantly ebbed, despite bombings in Batna and Dellys in September 2007 and Algiers in December 2007 resulting in scores killed and wounded.

Algeria is one of the major hydrocarbon producers in the world. Although its oil production is significant, it is one of the world's largest natural gas pro-

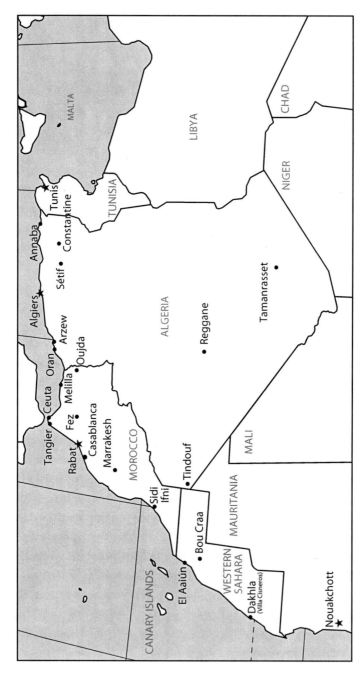

Contemporary Algeria, Morocco, and Western Sahara

ducers. The EU is especially dependent on Algerian gas. Furthermore, the United States has recently emerged as Algeria's principal trading partner, thereby reinforcing an increasingly close political relationship, especially since the 11 September 2001 attacks in New York City and Washington, D.C. In March 2006, Algeria and Russia agreed to a significant military contract, and there is growing cooperation (and possible collaboration) regarding natural gas exportation. The signing of economic and strategic agreements with the People's Republic of China in November 2006 underscores Algeria's global interest and initiative.

The ideals of the Revolution as expressed in the Proclamation of 1 November 1954 still resonate in Algeria, despite *al-hagra* (*al-hogra*), the painfully chronic social alienation and exclusion especially afflicting the youth. Kabyle protests in 2001 threatened the destabilization of the government, and Amazighism (Berberism) is ascendant. President Bouteflika easily won reelection in 2004, but he suffered a serious health problem in late 2005. Algeria's parliament passed a previously shelved constitutional amendment, which portends the institutionalization of an authoritarian "presidential regime."

Ahmed Ben Bella: The Difficult First Years (1962–1965)

The Algerian War of Liberation ended with a power struggle between the GPRA (provisional government), which had negotiated the Evian Accords, and the Political Bureau, an opposition group headed by Ahmed Ben Bella with the powerful support of the army chief, Col. Houari Boumedienne. The Political Bureau was victorious, but the bloodshed stained the heroic revolutionary image of the FLN. A National Assembly with constituent powers was elected and selected the veteran nationalist Ferhat Abbas as its president. Ben Bella became the premier.

Ben Bella faced the consequences of 132 years of colonialism and the brutal War of Liberation. The flight (*exode*) of the *pieds-noirs* also meant the loss of important cadres and managers. France responded with massive aid ("cooperation"), including technical and cultural *coopérants,* technicians and teachers. The preservation of a French presence, including military bases, contradicted Algerian independence, but there was no alternative for the governing elite. Inherent in the French-Algerian post-colonial relationship was a sustained paradox of conflict and cooperation (see Naylor 2000a). The Evian Accords defined the future relationship, but they were immediately chal-

lenged by changing and dramatic historical events. The meticulous stipulations to protect the settlers in independent Algeria became anachronistic
given the *pied-noir* flight. Furthermore, the Tripoli Program framed a socialist program for independent Algeria that implicitly targeted France's perpetuated interests, especially in the hydrocarbons sector. Although Algeria
faced multiple dislocations, the principal problem was existential. Ben Bella
and his successors posited directly and indirectly that Algeria still needed to
free itself from foreign political, economic, social, and cultural influences in
order to create an authentic national identity. Thus, in some ways, Fanon's
psychoexistential condition persisted in the post-colonial era.[1]

Exclusion rather than inclusion has characterized Algerian post-colonial
politics. The FLN became the only legal party as affirmed by the Algiers Charter of 1964. Regarding labor relations, the UGTA also came under the control
of the party, mirroring the relationship between the Neo-Destour Party and
the UGTT. A constitution framed in 1963 provided for a dominant presidency.
Subsequently, Ben Bella was elected to a five-year term as Algeria's first president. His authoritarianism alienated Ferhat Abbas, who resigned in protest
from his presidency of the National Assembly. Another prominent nationalist, Mohammed Khider, left his post as secretary-general of the FLN and went
into exile, reportedly with a sizeable amount of the party funds. Hocine Ait
Ahmed, a Kabyle and, like Khider, one of the FLN's founders, launched an
armed rebellion with his Front des Forces Socialistes (Socialist Forces Front
[FFS]) in 1963. The specter of Arab vs. Berber communal conflict loomed as a
serious and destabilizing threat.

While the Kabyle insurrection spread, relations with Morocco deteriorated rapidly. The GPRA had signed an agreement (negotiated by Ferhat Abbas)
with the sultanate in 1961 to address the border situation as soon as independence was attained. Ben Bella ignored the agreement. King Hassan II decided
to force the Algerian government to consider the frontier issue by advancing
Moroccan troops toward the border. Fighting erupted with the Moroccans
displaying their military superiority. Given the national crisis caused by the
brief "War of the Sands" (November–December 1963), one of Ait Ahmed's chief
lieutenants reconciled with Ben Bella. This loss of leadership seriously weakened the revolt, which was quelled in 1964; Ait Ahmed was imprisoned but
later escaped. The commander of the Algerian armed forces, Mohamed Chaabani, rebelled in 1964. He questioned Ben Bella's socialist direction, which

seemed to subordinate Algeria's Muslim character. Chaabani was captured and executed.

Although politically threatened, Ben Bella and his rivals strove to end the French neocolonial presence in Algeria. The government appropriated abandoned or vacated properties in 1962 and 1963, upsetting repatriated *pieds-noirs* and the French government.[2] The Evian Accords ensured that oil companies would preserve their privileges in the Sahara, but Ben Bella inaugurated SONATRACH, an Algerian national enterprise to contend with the international companies in the Sahara.[3] Furthermore, Ben Bella led an independent foreign policy supporting national liberation movements. He also embraced Nasser's Pan-Arabism, and Arabization began in primary school classes. The Evian Accords had allowed the French to maintain military bases (including atomic testing sites), but they pulled out of the Sahara as Pacific Ocean testing facilities became available.

The relationship between Ben Bella and Boumedienne was never close. Boumedienne criticized Ben Bella's capricious behavior. When Ben Bella methodically attempted to eliminate Boumedienne supporters from his cabinet, the colonel acted. On 19 June 1965, Boumedienne overthrew Ben Bella and suspended the constitution.

Houari Boumedienne: The Building of a State (1965–1978)

Boumedienne's serious temperament contrasted with Ben Bella's spontaneity, but they shared the objective of completing Algeria's decolonization and socialization. The Algiers Accords of July 1965 redefined the French hydrocarbon position in the Sahara. In addition, France agreed to help Algeria industrialize.[4] Boumedienne also began state-planning. The first "pre-plan" was inaugurated in 1967. A more substantial Four-Year Plan was introduced in 1970. The emphasis was on the secondary sector—industry and manufacturing ("industrializing industries").

In February 1971, after an arduous and frustrating negotiation, Boumedienne nationalized the French hydrocarbon concessions in the Sahara. This was the principal example of "post-colonial decolonization." The French-Algerian relationship declined precipitously. By July 1973, when Foreign Minister Abdelaziz Bouteflika visited Paris, both countries knew that they needed each other. For example, there were about one million Algerians living in France who were vital to the French economy. In addition, their remittances

were crucially important to Algeria's balance of payments. Soon after Bouteflika's visit, however, violence against the Algerian community in France led
to Boumedienne's decision to stop emigration. By that time, the decision was
moot, given the stagflated French economy and rising unemployment.

The Agrarian Revolution, officially proclaimed in 1971, extended socialism into the primary sector. It aimed to construct 1,000 socialist villages
and reclaim and redistribute land. The initiative especially targeted absen-
tee ownership. Concurrently, the government launched the Cultural Revolution, which correlated with the acceleration of Arabization in education and
society.[5] Although influenced by Fanon's ideas, Boumedienne also perceived
the political as well as cultural importance of Islamism.[6] For example, he
changed Algeria's weekend from the Western Saturday and Sunday to the
Muslim Thursday and Friday.

Boumedienne insisted that Algeria play a very active international role.
Algeria joined the Organization of Petroleum Exporting Countries (OPEC),
and his nationalization of the French companies in the Sahara enhanced the
country's image as a revolutionary state. He supported the PLO and later condemned Anwar Sadat's peace initiative. In 1974, Algeria sponsored a special
United Nations session addressing North-South relations, focusing on the
economic inequality between the developed and developing worlds. Boumedienne's Algeria also played a prominent role among the "Group of 77" developing nations.

Early in his rule, Boumedienne faced serious threats, including an assassination attempt. The murders of potential rivals Mohammed Khider (d. 1967)
and Belkacem Krim (d. 1970) (the latter led the FLN negotiating team leading
to the Evian Accords) were most likely perpetrated by Algerian special services. By the early 1970s, Boumedienne exercised total control and had earned
international prestige.

In April 1975, French President Valéry Giscard d'Estaing visited Algiers,
a seemingly remarkable gesture of reconciliation. Nevertheless, inadequate
French hydrocarbon imports to address trade imbalances, but most significantly, Paris's apparent support for the Madrid Accords of 1975, which
partitioned Spanish Sahara between Morocco and Mauritania, dashed the
prospects of lifting the relationship to a privileged level. Boumedienne subsequently gave massive aid to the POLISARIO, the Sahrawi liberation organization (see below).

The Algerian government promulgated a National Charter in 1976, which defined Algeria as a socialist and Islamic state. It was accompanied by a new constitution that provided the president overwhelming power but allowed for an Assemblée Nationale Populaire (National Popular Assembly [ANP]). The FLN remained, however, the only legal party.

With social and economic revolutions and new institutions, the existential post-colonial project seemed to be addressed, but was it fulfilled? Boumedienne had many notable achievements, but he still perpetuated an exclusive rather than inclusive political system. He built a state, but was it a nation?[7] In December 1978, he died from a rare blood disease.

Chadli Benjedid: Transformation, Turbulence, and Tragedy

Algeria's new institutions, inaugurated by the Constitution of 1976, ensured the smooth succession of the presidency after Boumedienne's untimely death. His successor, Chadli Benjedid, was less ideological. Although initially committed to Algeria's socialist orientation, he began a prudent liberalization. Benjedid's government's First Five-Year Plan from 1980 to 1984 significantly gave agriculture more attention, given Algeria's increasing population and dependence on alimentary imports. The secondary sector continued to receive important allocations. Clearly, Benjedid wanted to balance sectoral development, as evidenced by the Second Five-Year Plan, scheduled from 1985 to 1989. The Agrarian Revolution was abandoned and agriculture privatized. Plunging petroleum prices in the mid-1980s, which also had a deleterious effect on natural gas pricing, shocked the economy. In 1986, Algeria began its liberalization of the hydrocarbon sector to attract foreign investment.

Benjedid's economic reorientation also related to foreign policy. Algeria's international prestige, built especially by Ben Bella and Boumedienne, placed the country in a useful strategic position to serve as an intermediary. Algeria played an important role in resolving the 444-day hostage crisis between the United States and Iran (1979–1981). Its efforts to mediate the Iran-Iraq War cost the life in 1982 of Foreign Minister Mohamed Benyahia, who died in a plane crash. Benjedid met with King Hassan II in 1983 and in 1987, which contributed toward the restoration of relations in 1988 (broken over Western Sahara [see below]) and assured the inauguration of the UMA in 1989. Friendship treaties with Tunisia and Mauritania in 1983 illustrated Benjedid's interest in regional rather than global affairs. Relations with France improved markedly, beginning with President François Mitterrand's visit to Algeria in November 1981. For the next several years, accords were concluded promoting "co-development" in a variety of sectors, especially in hydrocarbons (natural gas accord of February 1982). Although relations declined in the mid-1980s, they improved with financial and natural gas accords in January 1989 and a short visit by Mitterrand in March.

Decentralization was also a theme of the Benjedid years. The *wilayat* or provinces increased from thirty-four to forty-eight, which allowed for greater local participation. The government also restructured state enterprises, such as SONATRACH. Despite these important changes, the "enriched" National Charter of 1986 repeated the socialist axioms of the original; there was a change in style rather than in substance. The Charter added a historical section, however, which acknowledged the efforts of nationalists in creating the nation, including Messali Hadj. In addition, the government posthumously rehabilitated the reputations of Ramdane Abane, Mohammed Khider, and Belkacem Krim.[8]

During the 1980s, the public generally approved Benjedid's prudent and deliberate liberalization. There were signals, however, that all was not well in Algeria, which had prided itself on its stability. Within the FLN elite, there was opposition to liberalization. Critics contended that veering from socialism renounced the Revolution. Feminists successfully resisted a conservative family code in 1981. Nevertheless, in 1984, one was passed, which reinforced patriarchy and the role of the Shari'a in Algerian jurisprudence. Islamism also became insurrectionary. The Mouvement (Algérien) Islamique Armé (Armed Islamic [Algerian] Movement [M(A)IA]) led by Mustapha Bouyali foreshadowed the violence of the 1990s. Bouyali condemned the secular nature of the state and started an insurgency, which ended with his death in 1987. Arabization and the emphasis on Algeria's Arab identity, as reinforced by the Cultural Revolution, led to major conflict in 1980 in Berber Kabylia, with other violent episodes erupting in 1982 and 1986.[9]

Algeria's annual budgetary allocation toward education was admirable, but it also engendered a frustrated, educated young population with few hopes of employment. This lack of economic and social opportunities compounded by political exclusion produced alienation and contempt (*al-hagra*). Youth in Algeria, as in Tunisia and Morocco, turned toward Islamism as the only viable alternative means of dissent. The collapse of oil prices also had manifold negative social as well as economic consequences. The government attempted to implement austerity by reducing subsidies, which led to protests and strikes. National discontent and distress incited and impelled rioting in Algiers in October 1988, which spread throughout Algeria. The brutal response by the government resulted in heavy casualties.[10] The October 1988 riots represented a watershed in the history of Algeria. The government's political legitimacy was called into question as well as the FLN's revolutionary legacy.

The *Fitna*: Algeria's Trial as a Nation

In Arabic, *fitna* can mean trial, temptation, and strife. The word's multiple meanings apply to Algeria since 1988. After the riots, Benjedid initiated reforms highlighted by a new constitution in February 1989, which allowed the legalization of opposition parties. The FLN's political monopoly ended. The government allowed freedom of expression, which resulted in a proliferation of publications. Algeria became the freest country in the Arab world.[11] Parties were officially recognized, including the Islamic Salvation Front (FIS) in September 1989. Hocine Ait Ahmed, who had lived so long in exile, returned in December and his Socialist Forces Front (FFS) was also formally accepted. Ben Bella arrived in 1990. A constellation of parties posted candidates in the remarkably free local elections of June 1990. The Islamist FIS astonished Algeria and the world by handily winning these elections. On the other hand, the government cancelled parliamentary elections slated for June 1991 because of unrest. Authorities arrested the FIS leaders, Abassi Madani and Ali Benhadj. The rescheduled elections for December–January 1991 also startled the country and the international community. In the first round, the FIS dominated, ensuring its control of the National Popular Assembly (APN) and, given constitutional changes, the government. Alarmed over the prospects of an Islamic government, civilian and military cadres overthrew Benjedid's government in January 1992 before the second round of elections guaranteed the FIS's victory.[12]

The new government, called the Haut Comité d'Etat (High State Committee [HCE]) immediately cancelled the elections and outlawed the FIS in March. The head of the HCE was a repatriated FLN revolutionary leader and cofounder of the FLN, Mohamed Boudiaf. Renowned for his integrity, Boudiaf attempted to mobilize support for his government. He also aimed to eliminate corruption. His initiative and intentions resulted in his assassination in June. Although blamed on Islamists, Boudiaf's reforms also threatened the "Pouvoir"—or the oligarchic power establishment dominated by the army. Ali Kafi, a respected veteran of the War of Liberation, replaced Boudiaf, but he did not possess his charisma. Meanwhile, civil violence had already started. The MIA reorganized and the Armée Islamique du Salut (Islamic Salvation Army [AIS]), the military arm of the FIS, mobilized. In 1993, the Groupe Islamique Armé (Armed Islamic Group [GIA]) appeared and targeted foreigners. The violence escalated as well as the atrocities.

To call this period a civil war would be a mistake. This was not a binary struggle contested as the state (or secularism) versus Islamism.[13] There were conflicts within the conflict, some of them communal. Islamists also fought each other. Nevertheless, the violence is popularly referred to as and reduced to a civil war in the press and in publications. Its human cost has been enormous—150,000 to 200,000 deaths (and counting, given current sporadic violence). An effort was made in January 1995 by opposition parties to create a united front to end the strife. Meeting at the Sant'Egidio community in Rome, the parties produced a document seeking to reconcile all sides.[14] The Algerian government refused to have a solution imposed upon it and created its own agenda.

In January 1994, the HCE had dissolved and Liamine Zeroual, the defense minister, became president. He initiated a deliberate process termed a "redemocratization" of Algeria beginning with presidential elections in November 1995, which featured multiple candidates and high voter turnout. The FIS was not allowed to participate, but moderate Islamist parties were permitted. Zeroual received a mandate; however, his rule was torn between those, like himself, who wanted to conciliate the insurgents, and others within the Pouvoir who wanted them eradicated. A new constitution in 1996 returned much power to the presidency, reinstituted the National Popular Assembly (APN), and added an upper house, the Conseil de la Nation (Council of the Nation [CN]), sometimes referred to as the "Senate." With financial aid through the International Monetary Fund (IMF) and the rescheduling of public and private foreign debt during the mid-1990s (the Paris and London clubs, respectively), the government escalated its operations against the insurgents. France provided particular support.[15] Horrific violence occurred in late 1997 and early 1998, which attracted greater international scrutiny. The European

Union and the United Nations sent investigative teams which presented inconclusive reports. The government's carefully monitored redemocratization and reinstitutionalization continued with parliamentary elections in June 1997 and local elections in October. Zeroual's party, the Rassemblement National Démocratique (National Democratic Rally [RND]), dominated these contests.[16] Notwithstanding these electoral successes, the political toll on Zeroual led to his decision to announce in 1998 his retirement before the end of his term. Presidential elections were scheduled for April 1999.

Abdelaziz Bouteflika: Restoration and Reconciliation

Seven candidates ran for office, but electoral irregularities emerged right before the election. Six candidates withdrew, leaving Abdelaziz Bouteflika, Houari Boumedienne's foreign minister and protégé, as the remaining single candidate. Thus, Bouteflika's presidency began with controversy. Nevertheless, from the start of his presidency, Bouteflika pursued two principal objectives—the restoration of Algeria as an international force and national reconciliation. Although considered as the favorite of the Pouvoir (especially the army), Bouteflika endeavored to promote civilian control, which equated with increasing his personal power. He presented a "Civil Concord" proposal and legislation, which offered amnesty to insurgents in the field who had not committed atrocities. It received a 98 percent affirmative vote in a September 1999 referendum with 85 percent of the electorate participating. By that time the AIS had already concluded a cease-fire, taken advantage of Bouteflika's amnesty, and disbanded. The GIA and a splintered group known as the Groupe Salafiste pour la Prédication et le Combat (Salafist Group for Preaching and Combat [GSPC]) refused the offer and continued to fight against the government. Nevertheless, by 2000, it was apparent that the insurgency had significantly weakened.

Bouteflika also reasserted Algeria's international presence. In June 2000, he was accorded the first state visit to France by an Algerian president.[17] He helped negotiate peace between Eritrea and Ethiopia later that year. In 2001, Bouteflika visited Washington twice and was among the first to offer sympathy and assistance to the United States after the 11 September attacks. He hosted the Arab League's meeting in Algiers in 2005, which seemed for the moment to reanimate the UMA, given his cordial conversations with King Muhammad VI of Morocco. Relations subsequently declined over Western Sahara.

Bouteflika also faced serious challenges to his authority. In April 2001, a Kabyle youth died while in police custody, which provoked violence resulting in more than one hundred deaths.[18] The Kabyles were especially incensed over the imposition of Arabization, a symbolic repudiation of their language (Tamazight) and culture. Their grievances became part of the Kseur Platform of June 2001, which called for the removal of the despised national police from Kabylia, the promotion of Tamazight as a national and official language, and an extension of social, economic, and political opportunities. Aspects of the Kseur Platform reverberated nationally.[19] In November 2001, flash floods claimed approximately 750 lives in Algiers. Citizens blamed their government for not having the sewer system in proper condition to handle the flooding. In May 2003, an earthquake east of Algiers resulted in 2,250 deaths and 10,500 injuries. The slow governmental response to this tragedy also tainted Bouteflika's presidency.

Nevertheless, the public appreciated Bouteflika's general success in restoring Algeria's prestige internationally and his efforts to reconcile the country. Another restoration occurred, that of the FLN returning to dominant political power, as evinced in the parliamentary and local elections in 2002. In the presidential elections of April 2004, Bouteflika received 85 percent of the vote—an unexpectedly strong mandate. In November, while commemorating the fiftieth anniversary of the beginning of the War of Liberation, he proposed another amnesty.

In August 2005, Bouteflika detailed a "Charter for Peace and National Reconciliation." It projected an amnesty for all insurgents who were not involved in mass killings or severe violence since the end of the Civil Concord amnesty of 1999. (It also protected security forces involved in counterinsurgency operations from prosecution.) A referendum took place on 29 September 2005. With 80 percent of the electorate participating, the charter received 98 percent approval. In March 2006, the Algerian parliament ratified the charter and Islamists were released from prison. According to many critical observers, Bouteflika's conciliatory policies have fostered a forgive-and-forget mentality, rather than promoting transparency regarding the causes, courses, and consequences of the continuing *fitna*. (See Tlemçani 2008, 15.) In early 2007, the GSPC, now renamed Al-Qa'ida in the (Land of the) Islamic Maghrib (AQ[L]IM), escalated its operations and perpetrated shocking suicide bombings in Algiers in April and December 2007, killing and wounding scores.

Clearly, Islamist extremism remains a threat to Algeria's stability. In addition, the poor participation in the national legislative election of May 2007, with only 36.5 percent of the electorate taking part, illustrated, according to one report, "widespread despair and apathy" (Ouali 2007; see also Whitlock 2007). Local and provincial elections in November attracted 44 percent participation and also signaled a weakening of the FLN's predominant political position at the expense of its close ideological rival, the RND.

Pursuing national reconciliation has distinguished the Bouteflika presidency. In particular, he has reduced the influence of the army in Algerian political life. Nevertheless, the growth of Bouteflika's authoritarianism also raises concern. It is expected that the currently shelved constitutional amendment allowing him to run for a third term will be presented soon. Observers wonder, however, if his health will permit a third term.

Algeria's Economy and Society

Hydrocarbons dominate the Algerian economy. Approximately 95 percent of Algeria's export receipts are acquired through hydrocarbon sales (supplying 25 percent of the European Union's imports [EIU 2007d]). The high price and demand for oil and natural gas resulted in an approximately $100 billion surplus in currency reserves by the end of 2007. Algeria has also impressively reduced foreign debt below $5 billion. Inflation dropped from 32 percent in 1992 to under 2 percent in 2005 (IMF 2007f, 11). Algeria still must import much of its alimentary needs, but there have been improvements reported in the primary sector (e.g., hard wheat, potato production [see IMF 2007e, 11]). The tertiary sector, especially housing and water supplies, remains a critical concern. It is anticipated that Algeria will eventually join the World Trade Organization (WTO). Algeria also signed an Association Agreement with the European Union in December 2001.

Algeria's real GDP rose from 3.2 percent in 1999 to 6.9 percent in 2003 (IMF 2005d, 3). GDP growth is expected to continue to grow impressively at a 6 percent rate from 2008–2011 (EIU 2007a). Oil production (and substitutes) reached 62.5 million metric tons in 2005, compared to 40.6 million in 2001. In addition, gross production of natural gas increased from 173.2 billions of cubic meters in 2001 to 193.2 in 2005 (IMF 2007e, 7–8). Before the late 2008 economic downturn, Algeria enjoyed a booming economy fueled by hydrocarbons. This prosperity offered a strategic opportunity to prepare, plan, and implement projects to ensure sectoral development.[20] There is a pressing need, however, for reforming financial and regulatory services to expedite diversification and private enterprise to encourage domestic private investment, increase trade openness, and improve investment climate. Infrastructure, especially housing, remains a chronic problem. Despite the country's wealth, there is an underclass, which is underemployed or unemployed. The unemployment rate was usually pegged between 20 and 25 percent of the working population, although it is now officially claimed to be considerably lower, which the IMF corroborates.[21] This is due to general economic growth, public sector investment in construction and public works, and private sector job creation. Nevertheless, many of these jobs are temporary rather than permanent (IMF 2007f, 19). The population of Algeria today is approximately 32 million and its growth rate has significantly slowed. Nevertheless, the variables that caused the October 1988 riots are latent and dangerous. Martin Evans and John Phillips refer to "an anger that will not go away" (the title of their book's "Afterword") and conclude: "Algerians feel angry and frustrated because the system offers no future" (Evans and Phillips 2007, 297). Tempering this anger represents Algeria's greatest challenge.

Morocco

It is difficult to assess how Morocco's post-colonial era would have evolved, if not for the untimely death of King Muhammad V. His astute political skill and his appealing personality would be missed. His son and successor, King Hassan II, although very capable politically, became a repressive ruler, despite a liberalizing "opening" in the last decade of his rule. The government controlled or contained the opposition. In foreign policy, Hassan II strongly sided with the West, which appreciated Moroccan "stability." Nevertheless, two attempted coups dramatically disclosed the military's discontent. In part to reorient the military, Hassan embarked upon taking over Spanish or Western Sahara in order to realize the popular aspiration of a "Greater Morocco."

His son, King Muhammad VI, impressively inaugurated his rule by freeing political prisoners and permitting a more open civil society. Nevertheless, he has subsequently limited political inclusion and maintained the monarchy's dominant political role. The question remains: How effective will he be in the historical role of the king as an "arbiter" of power (see Waterbury 1970)?

King Hassan: *Baraka* and Ambition

The prestige accrued by Sultan Muhammad during decolonization gave him unassailable influence and power in the immediate post-colonial period. As King Muhammad V of independent Morocco, he sympathized with the Algerian Revolution, but he prudently measured his support not to alienate the French, who provided foreign aid and technical assistance. He secured his independent state by suppressing Berber insurgents in 1957, by integrating the Army of Liberation into the Forces Armées Royales (Royal Armed Forces [FAR]) or by disarming its irregulars, and by reforming the Sufi orders. The king ensured that he controlled the most important ministries. He also encouraged a multi-party system, rather than a one-party state. This maneuver protected the monarchy against the possibility of a powerful united opposition. In 1959, Istiqlal split between Muhammad Allal al-Fasi and the left-oriented Mehdi Ben Barka, who formed the Union Nationale des Forces Populaires (National Union of Popular Forces [UNFP]). The unexpected death of Muhammad V brought Crown Prince Hassan to the throne.

Hassan was well educated and adept in politics. During his reign, he framed five constitutions for Morocco (1962, 1970, 1972, 1992, 1996). His efforts to demarcate or redraw borders with Algeria in 1963 provoked the inconclusive "War of the Sands," which ended bilateral "fraternal" feelings (see above). Mehdi Ben Barka became an incisive critic of the monarchy, but in 1965, Moroccan agents kidnapped him in Paris and subsequently killed the opposition leader. This event created a rift between Rabat and Paris. Ben Barka's death did not eliminate opposition, but a new constitution promulgated in 1970 reinforced the king's political predominance.

Hassan had played a direct role in developing the FAR dating from 1957, but he faced two attempts on his life mounted by the military in 1971 and 1972. His survival was popularly perceived as *baraka,* meaning blessedness or luck.[22] After purging the armed forces, Hassan took advantage of Spain's weakening condition and engaged his country and his military in a popular adventure, which led to diplomatic isolation, but also secured his monarchy.

Morocco and Western Sahara

Morocco's interest in Spanish Sahara related to its imagination of itself as a state. Traditionally and historically, Morocco considered Spanish Sahara as part of the *bilad al-siba*. A historic, if transitory, Moroccan presence there corresponded to earlier Sa'di and Alawi expansions resulting in tribal allegiances.[23] In June 1956, Allal al-Fasi stated: "If Morocco is independent, it is not completely unified. The Moroccans will continue the struggle until Tangier, the Sahara from Tindouf to Colomb-Bechar, Touat, Kenadza, and Mauritania are liberated and unified. Our independence will only be complete with the Sahara! The frontiers of Morocco end in the south at Saint-Louis-de Sénégal" (Hodges 1983, 85). Istiqlal's party newspaper, *Al-Alam,* published a map of Greater Morocco. The monarchy embraced this idea. Spain returned Tangier in 1956 and relinquished the Tarfaya zone in southern Morocco in 1958. Meanwhile, Morocco laid claim to Ifni, Spanish Sahara, and Mauritania in 1957.

After his accession to the throne, Hassan II moderated the Greater Morocco ambition and exercised admirable pragmatism and patience with Spain. He met with Spanish dictator Francisco Franco at the Barajas airport near Madrid in 1963 and established a cordial relationship. Two years later Hassan joined Franco during a hunting party in Andalucía. Hassan's prudent policy (besides authoritarian affinity) with Franco paid off with Spain's cession of Ifni in 1969. During that same year, Hassan and Houari Boumedienne reconciled their differences at Ifrane, Morocco. The signing of two conventions in 1972 aimed to resolve border contentions (Tindouf recognized as Algerian; mutual exploitation of iron deposits). Algeria ratified the agreements but Morocco refrained.[24] Rabat normalized relations with Nouakchott in 1970, seemingly renouncing the idea of a Greater Morocco that incorporated Mauritania.

In July 1974, Spain announced its intention to institute an internal autonomy in Spanish Sahara, which startled Morocco, since it indicated Madrid's willingness to pursue a self-determination process. Rabat's anxieties were well founded. In August, Spain declared that it planned to organize, in conjunction with the UN, a referendum in the first six months of 1975. Although Morocco, Algeria, and Mauritania had repeatedly called for Spanish Saharan self-determination and backed UN resolutions, the political climate within the territory had changed. Morocco assumed that the Sahrawis would opt for territorial integration with the sultanate. Nevertheless, a popular nationalist movement, the POLISARIO (Frente Popular para la Liberación de Saguia el Hamra y Río de Oro/Popular Front for the Liberation of Saguia el Hamra and

Río de Oro) had organized in 1973 and sought independence (see below). Morocco invited the International Court of Justice (ICJ) to consider the legal history of Western Sahara. This initiative, backed by Mauritania, was supported by a UN resolution charging the ICJ to offer an "advisory opinion." Algeria also voted in favor of the resolution.

In October, King Hassan hosted an Arab summit. Apparently, he reached an agreement with President Mokhtar Ould Daddah of Mauritania to divide Spanish Sahara between them. Respecting Algeria's obvious contiguous interest in the region, President Boumedienne was informed in executive session of the Moroccan-Mauritanian plan. According to a tape produced by Mauritania, Boumedienne concurred. Ambassador Richard Parker assessed that Boumedienne may have thought that Spain would never allow a partition or that Rabat and Nouakchott would never cooperate with each other (given the ideal of a "Greater Morocco" which enveloped Mauritania). Boumedienne later claimed he never consented to the plan (Parker 1987, 109–110). After talks between King Hassan and Foreign Minister Abdelaziz Bouteflika, however, Morocco and Algeria seemed to have come to an agreement as worded in a general communiqué in July 1975. It suggested that Algeria would support the partition of Spanish Sahara in exchange for Morocco's recognition of Tindouf and a conclusive settlement of border issues (i.e., the ratification of the 1972 convention).[25]

Nonetheless, Boumedienne apparently changed his mind (or Bouteflika exercised too much latitude) and adamantly opposed the idea of partition. Perhaps Boumedienne personally identified with the POLISARIO, since its resistance reminded him of his own experiences in the Algerian struggle for independence. An Algerian foreign policy tenet called for the support of national liberation movements. To repudiate the POLISARIO, which identified with the wartime FLN, equated with renouncing Algeria's ideological principles and its revolutionary heritage. Rabat's determined pursuit of a Greater Morocco also alarmed Boumedienne. Furthermore, Morocco had not ratified the 1972 conventions.

In October 1975, the International Court of Justice recognized the historic existence of "legal ties of allegiance" between tribes and Morocco as well as "some rights relating to the land, which constituted legal ties" with Mauritania. Nevertheless, the ICJ also concluded that there was no established "tie of territorial sovereignty between the territory of Western Sahara and the Kingdom of Morocco or the Mauritanian entity" (Jensen 2005, 27). To Hassan, this assessment was still enough to legitimize Morocco's takeover of the territory. American Ambassador Richard Parker recounted: "He went on the air and informed his people that they had won—the court had found that the Sahara had ties of allegiance to Morocco and under Islamic law allegiance was tantamount to sovereignty, since it meant loyalty and faithfulness to the sovereign" (Parker 1987, 111).[26]

By this time, Hassan had prepared for a spectacular political move. The government mobilized 350,000 unarmed Moroccans to march into Spanish Sahara and claim it. Hassan's actions galvanized the Moroccan public, now raised to a nationalist fervor. In early November Moroccans strode eleven kilometers into the Spanish Sahara and then stopped; this was called the "Green March." Ignoring its negotiations with the POLISARIO (see below), the Spanish government, paralyzed by Franco's rapidly declining condition (comatose after a series of heart attacks), agreed to an expedient devolution of power. Spain, Morocco, and Mauritania quickly resolved the crisis by concluding the Madrid Accords of November 1975, which divided Spanish Sahara between Morocco and Mauritania. Algeria was alienated and angry. In turn, it provided havens for Sahrawi refugees and guerrillas and substantial logistical and political support to the POLISARIO. The struggle for Western Sahara commenced and remains unresolved today (see below).

Western Sahara has been a political paradox for Morocco. On the one hand, the conflict's irresolution has isolated Morocco from other countries. When the Spanish officially withdrew on 27 February 1976, the POLISARIO formally proclaimed the Sahrawi Arab Democratic Republic (SADR). Algeria recognized the SADR and Morocco immediately severed diplomatic relations (restored in 1988). Morocco withdrew from the OAU in 1984 after it recognized the SADR as an official member. On the other hand, the quest to annex Western Sahara has unified parties on the Left and the Right. There have been few national voices that have opposed or protested the Western Saharan policy.[27] Above all, the effort to realize "Greater Morocco" has strengthened the monarchy and its prestige. On the other hand, the war and administration of occupied Western Sahara have been costly, exacerbated by falling phosphate prices. Unrest in the Moroccan zone as well as domestic discussion, evoked in part by Sahrawi students enrolled in Moroccan schools, may affect the dominant national discourse regarding Western Sahara.

Muhammad VI Comes to the Throne

After the "leaden years" of the 1980s, which featured severe repression and in-famous detention,[28] King Hassan permitted a deliberate "liberalization" in-cluding reforms and amnesties during the 1990s. A new constitution in 1992 led to parliamentary elections the following year, which were flaunted as the freest since independence (see Munson 1999). An amendment to the consti-tution in 1996 created a bicameral parliament and new elections in 1997. In a manner reminiscent of the pageantry of Ahmad al-Mansur, the great Sa'di sultan (see Chapter 5), King Hassan II also "restaged" his monarchy, creat-ing a new image aiming to be politically and socially inclusive and receptive to the concerns of the disadvantaged and alienated. Even if symbolic rather than substantial, strides were made, for example, on behalf of women. This recasting of the monarchy was exemplified by the celebratory opening of the immense King Hassan II mosque in 1993 that clearly sought to unify the state and enhance the status of the monarchy (see Combs-Schilling 1999). A year be-fore King Hassan died, Susan E. Waltz noted: "Morocco's political problems are far from having disappeared, but there appears to be new willingness to expand parliamentary powers and tolerate dissent" (Waltz 1999, 301).

The funeral of King Hassan in July 1999 brought many dignitaries to Mo-rocco who were impressed by the poise of his son and successor, Muham-mad VI.[29] There was great domestic expectation that he would share preroga-tive and power (see Ferrié 2002; Howe 2005). He announced the formation of a Human Rights Council to investigate abuses such as arbitrary deten-tion. He allowed Abraham Serfaty, a Marxist critic who supported the self-determination of Western Sahara, to return from exile. He also sacked Driss Basri, the influential and repressive minister of the interior, who was regard-ed as the *éminence grise* or power behind the throne. In 2000, the king freed Shaykh Abdessalam Yassine of the Islamist Jama'at al-'Adl wa-l-Ihsan (Justice and Charity Group) from house arrest, although he was kept under surveil-lance.[30] The shaykh had challenged Hassan's legitimacy as "commander of the faithful" (*amir al mu'minin*) and promptly suggested that Muhammad VI pay off the national debt with royal funds. The new king recognized the growing Ber-ber movement by establishing the Royal Institute for Amazigh Culture in 2000.

The king also stated that he would not change Morocco's position toward Western Sahara. He parried President Bouteflika's proposals for summit talks. They briefly met at the Arab League Summit in Algiers in March 2005, but the meeting was courteous rather than substantial. Their polarized positions regarding Western Sahara prevented further discussions.

In May 2003, terrorist bombings in Casablanca, targeting tourist and Jewish sites, killed 45 people. The perpetrators were native Moroccans. This was a shock since Morocco has historically practiced cultural tolerance. It was believed that terrorism occurred elsewhere, rather than in Morocco, and certainly not in cosmopolitan Casablanca. The distress deepened when it was learned that Moroccans were principally involved in the terrorist attacks in Madrid in March 2004 that killed 191 people and wounded 1,800. Suicide bombers detonated explosives in Casablanca in March and April 2007, which resulted in injuries rather than deaths.

Islamism is a threat to the Moroccan monarchy even with its sharifian heritage. Parliamentary elections for the Chamber of Representatives in September 2002 revealed the strength of the moderate Islamist Parti de la Justice et du Développement (Justice and Development Party [PJD]), which became the third most powerful party in the Chamber of Representatives.[31] Five years later, the PJD came in second to Istiqlal in parliamentary elections, which were marked by a distressing record-low turnout (37 percent of the electorate). Shaykh Yassine and his daughter, Nadia, also continue to articulate their opposition. Muhammad VI has demonstrated that he possesses political sensibility, but would he be willing to share some of his predominant political power?[32] What is his political threshold?

Morocco's Foreign Policy

Although Morocco eventually secured most of Western Sahara, its international status declined. Algeria's prestigious international influence helped the SADR acquire a privileged status position in foreign circles. Approximately sixty countries recognized the SADR by the 1980s.[33] Morocco protested and withdrew from the Organization of Africa Unity (OAU) when it formally recognized the Sahrawi republic in November 1984. King Hassan attempted with difficulty to isolate Western Sahara within its foreign policy. The restoration of relations with Algeria in 1988 occurred as a result of summit meetings (sponsored by King Fahd of Saudi Arabia) between King Hassan and President Chadli Benjedid. (The bilateral relationship between Rabat and Algiers seems founded on the principle "to agree to disagree.") The escalating Islamist insurgency in Algeria during the 1990s especially worried Morocco. When violence surged over the frontier in 1994, the border closed, which has had a particularly negative effect upon the Moroccan economy. The border with Algeria remains closed as of this writing. Despite differences and difficulties over Western Sahara, Moroccan-Algerian diplomatic relations endure.

Morocco maintains traditional close relations with the United States. Although the United States claimed to have not supported the Green March and the tripartite Madrid Accords, it was difficult to believe that without American approval (Algeria's contention), Hassan would have acted so dramatically and decisively in 1975. Recently, Jacob Mundy disclosed documentation illustrating Washington's complicit support of Morocco regarding the takeover of Western Sahara (see Mundy 2006). Furthermore, the United States provided liberal military assistance, especially during the Cold War era. The selection of former Secretary of State James Baker to lead the UN's efforts to resolve Western Sahara signaled that the United States would not be totally disinterested concerning Moroccan ambitions (see below).

In the tradition of his father, Muhammad V, Hassan also protected the Jewish community, despite the intensified Arab-Israeli conflict. The king hosted Shimon Peres in July 1986, ostensibly to offer his mediating service. The decreasing Moroccan Jewish community viewed the visit as an important gesture, as did Israel and the United States.[34] The attendance of Prime Minister Ehud Barak at Hassan's funeral in 1999 illustrated Israel's esteem for Morocco and its religious toleration.

King Hassan's relations with France eventually improved after the Ben Barka affair. During the 1970s, President Valéry Giscard d'Estaing viewed the Moroccan king as a *copain* (pal). Giscard sympathized with Morocco's position regarding the Sahara and intervened militarily on behalf of Mauritania (see below). President François Mitterrand initially focused greater attention on Algeria rather than Morocco. Nevertheless, Paris eventually had to play a parity game between Rabat and Algiers, especially during the 1980s, given its special interests with each country. With the United States giving greater attention to the Maghrib in the 1990s and early 2000s, President Jacques Chirac asserted France's traditional regard in the region. He did not hold the same kind of close personal relationship with Hassan, but Chirac's policies mirrored those of Giscard.[35] Relations between France and Morocco remain strong and supportive today, especially regarding Western Sahara.

In general, Spain's policy has reverted from its expedient "de-administration," permitting the Sahara's partition, to supporting once again Sahrawi self-determination. Thus, relations between Madrid and Rabat have often been contentious. In addition, the presidios of Ceuta and Melilla have compounded this complex relationship.[36] The rising problem of clandestine trans-Saharan migration (a Maghribi and Sahelian as well as Moroccan issue) has also seriously affected the bilateral relationship, as illustrated in September and October 2005 when thousands of Sub-Saharans tried to breach the barbed wire and fences at Melilla (and hundreds concurrently at Ceuta). The tragic consequences resulted in thirteen deaths and one hundred wounded (de Larramendi and Bravo 2006, 167; see also Gold 2000, 120–150). Furthermore, illegal Moroccan immigration is another critical issue resulting in tens of thousands of annual expulsions.[37] The Spanish are very critical of lax Moroccan border surveillance. The involvement of Moroccans in the May 2004 terrorist attacks in Madrid further strained the relationship, even with the realization that there must be greater security cooperation and collaboration between Rabat and Madrid.[38]

The impasse over the presidios and their future (also a stressful domestic issue for Madrid), security issues, and chronic disputes over fishing and catch will continue to perturb political relations. Furthermore, there is a lingering Spanish regret, a feeling of "bad faith," over the way it relinquished Western Sahara.

By agreeing to the surprising Treaty of Oujda in 1984 with Libya, King Hassan hoped to end Libyan support of the POLISARIO and possibly receive financial aid. Col. Qadhafi cut off aid to the Sahrawis, but he declined to offer substantial assistance to Morocco. Indeed, this relationship, technically a unity agreement, could not have worked given the contrasting personalities and ambitions of King Hassan and Col. Qadhafi. Morocco and Libya terminated the agreement in 1986 but maintained friendly relations.

Morocco's Economy and Society

When Morocco became independent, its primary sector exported grain.[39] With today's population of 32 million, Morocco must import most of its alimentary needs. In the last few years, drought has afflicted the country and affected produce exports, such as citrus fruit. The estimated GDP real growth from 2006 to 2011 will be between 4.5 and 5 percent growth (EIU 2006). Morocco is the world's largest phosphate exporter; however, prices chronically fluctuate.[40] In 2000, oil was mistakenly reported in eastern Morocco and eagerly publicized, which discredited the government. There is the potential of offshore deposits (and in and offshore Western Sahara). Fishing is an important part of the economy. In 2005, an accord with the European Union regarding catch and remuneration was concluded (EIU 2005). Asian competition has significantly harmed Morocco's textile industry. Tourism greatly helps the economy, which has chronic trade deficits. In addition, workers' remittances account for about 9 percent of the GDP, compared to about 5 percent annually before 2000 (IMF 2004b, 32).[41] Like Tunisia and Algeria, Morocco concluded an Association Agreement with the EU, which went into effect in 2000. In 2004, Morocco signed a Free Trade Agreement (FTA) with the United States. The IMF is concerned about Moroccan debt, yet Rabat has fulfilled or is fulfilling IMF criteria, and most analysts are positive about Morocco's direction toward freeing the economy. The government is aware of the dangers of liberalization and the elimination of subsidies, given the memory of the tragic Bread Riots of 1981 in Casablanca, which unofficially left hundreds dead.[42] Approximately 20 percent of the working population is unemployed. Student unrest is always a threat, as disclosed by riots in 1994. Finally, investment in Western Sahara and the maintenance of troops there have also affected budgets and expenditures, to the consternation of domestic critics who believe that those allocations should be allotted within the kingdom.

Moroccans often speak several languages and have the reputation of providing great hospitality. These positive qualities are being tapped, especially in Casablanca, which is emerging as a high-tech center. Yet the gap between the wealthy and the impoverished has widened. Morocco has high illiteracy, estimated in 2003 at 49.3 percent of the population over age fifteen (60.6 percent for women) (CIA, Morocco). Feminists and activists contributed to a revision of the Family Code in 2004 and quota systems to ensure the political inclusion and participation of women in parties and in elections. Women make up 10.8 percent of the Chamber of Representatives. Nevertheless, entrenched patriarchy also has profound political and cultural ramifications regarding reformist and Islamist agendas. Social as well as economic conditions will be significant determinants regarding Morocco's political future.

Western Sahara

Western Sahara should not be merely studied in the context of Algerian foreign policy or Moroccan territorial ambition. The Sahrawis have a political identity and the SADR is currently recognized by forty-four countries. Furthermore, the importance of Western Sahara's irresolution has manifold international consequences.[43]

Who Are the Sahrawis?

The Sahrawis are a social composite. Sanhaja Berbers dominated the region until the Awlad Hassaniyya (especially the sub-group Awlad Dulaym) of the Banu Ma'qil arrived in the thirteenth century (see Chapter 3). In the sixteenth century, a powerful new nomadic tribe, the Reguibat (Rgaybat), emerged in Western Sahara. Its principal ethnic background was Sanhaja, but the group was galvanized by a sharif from southern Morocco, Sidi Ahmad al-Rgaybi. The Reguibat divided between western and eastern clans. Collectively, the Sahrawis often engaged in internecine conflict.

Compounding these matters, occasional Moroccan expansion into Western Sahara (conceived as a component region of the *bilad al-siba*) led to oath-taking (*bay'a*) by Sahrawis, equivalent to pledges of fealty. In the colonial period, the Reguibat crossed into Algeria and assaulted Tindouf. It took until 1934 for the French to secure Tindouf and "pacify" the far-flung Reguibat. Spanish authorities paid little attention to the Western Saharan hinterland until pressured by the French. Madrid's perspective changed, however, given militant regional activities of the mid-1950s.

A Moroccan "Army of Liberation" mobilized in response to the deposal and exile of Sultan Muhammad. It initially aimed to liberate Morocco. After Moroccan independence, the army remained active, despite the sultanate's efforts to integrate its members with the FAR. By this time, the army had radicalized and sought to free the far Maghrib (*maghrib al-aqsa*) from all colonial control. Guerrillas attacked Ifni and mounted operations in Mauritania and especially Spanish Sahara. Illustrating their politicization, many Sahrawis enlisted in the Army of Liberation's ranks. The hard-pressed Spanish withdrew from the Western Saharan interior to its coastal cities. Then in collaboration with the French, the Spanish launched a counterinsurgency campaign (Operation Ouragon) in February 1958 that successfully forced the army into southern Morocco, where the guerrillas were disarmed. With its ranks depleted, the army disintegrated, but the idea of liberating Spanish-held territory remained. Furthermore, the Spanish Sahara began to attract international attention. The United Nations adopted a resolution in 1965 urging the decolonization of Spanish Sahara. A year later, the OAU also called for the territory's "freedom and independence" (see Pazzanita and Hodges 1994, xxii).

The Rise of Sahrawi Nationalism

It was internationally assumed that Morocco would eventually incorporate Western Sahara. The rise of an authentic Sahrawi national movement was unexpected. As indicated earlier, Sahrawi enlistees in the Army of Liberation signaled an incipient nationalism. Under the leadership of Mohammed Sidi Ibrahim Bassiri, a well-educated Sahrawi, a nationalist organization known as the Movement of the Liberation of Saguia el Hamra and Oued ed-Dahab (Río de Oro) (MLS) formed as an underground group. In September 1970, the party joined a public protest against Spanish colonial authority, which became infamous as the "Massacre of Zemla." Colonial authorities brutally suppressed this demonstration, resulting in several deaths and many wounded. In turn, Bassiri was seized and disappeared. Nevertheless, Bassiri embodied the "new Sahrawi."

On 10 May 1973, young Sahrawis, principally educated in Morocco and conscious of Third World liberation movements, organized the POLISARIO under the leadership of El-Ouali Mustapha Sayed. The POLISARIO commenced its guerrilla war against Spanish colonialism ten days later. By mid-1974, the POLISARIO was determined to attain total independence. Its growing support among Sahrawis neutralized the Djemaa, the Spanish-controlled assembly, and the Partido de la Union Nacional Saharaui (Party of Saharan National Union [PUNS]), a party promoted by colonial authorities. In May 1975, a UN mission visited Spanish Sahara and concluded that the POLISARIO "appeared as a dominant political force" (Pazzanita and Hodges 1994, 165). In September, the Spanish government, recognizing the POLISARIO's strength, negotiated prisoner releases and considered plans to hand over authority to the movement in exchange for long-term fishing and phosphate privileges. It was at this time when King Hassan mobilized the "Green March." Morocco's intentions to integrate the territory incited Sahrawis, even those in the compliant Djemaa and the PUNS, to support the POLISARIO. In domestic crisis, given General Franco's rapidly failing health, and under Moroccan pressure, Spain reversed its position and signed the Madrid Accords. When Spain officially pulled out from the territory in early 1976, the Sahrawis proclaimed the SADR.

The Struggle for Western Sahara

As the Moroccans and Mauritanians moved into Western Sahara to claim their portions of the partitioned territory, the POLISARIO resisted the invaders. Nevertheless, its initial objective was to resettle tens of thousands of Sahrawi refugees. They were grouped into camps near Tindouf, Algeria. The exiled Sahrawis developed their own administration in the camps featuring significant social and political roles for women. Over the years, the camps' organization and operation impressed a growing number of interested international officials and reporters.

The military campaign intensified. The POLISARIO judged correctly that Mauritania was much more vulnerable than Morocco. With this in mind, the Sahrawi raiders in Land Rovers left their havens in Algeria and attacked Zouerate, the iron ore mining center, and the capital Nouakchott. An expedition against Nouakchott in June 1976 led by el-Ouali, although a successful operation, also cost the life of the POLISARIO's charismatic leader. Under military cooperation provisions, French Jaguar aircraft intervened to protect the Mauritanians in 1977. Nevertheless, Mauritania, one of the poorest countries in the world, could not sustain the unpopular war. In 1978, President Ould Daddah was overthrown and a cease-fire was declared. Given the stipulations of its agreement with the POLISARIO negotiated in Algiers in 1979, Mauritania recognized the SADR and ceded its allotted portion of Western Sahara to it. Morocco quickly occupied it, however, extending its occupation of the territory.

The Sahrawis then campaigned against the Moroccans, including raiding southern Morocco. As the POLISARIO's operations emboldened, Morocco reacted by building "The Sand Wall"—a 650 kilometer berm to keep Sahrawi guerrillas from the most "useful" (*utile*) areas of Western Sahara. Eventually, the berm was extended and now reaches approximately 1,000 kilometers. After stunning Sahrawi operations in 1983 reaching Smara in Western Sahara and also Lemsid in southern Morocco, the war devolved into one of attrition, notwithstanding UN-sponsored "proximity talks" held by intermediaries and rare meetings between the antagonists. In 1988, Secretary-General José Pérez de Cuéllar offered a plan to resolve the struggle to Morocco and the SADR in 1988, which was agreed upon in principle by each side. In December, the POLISARIO announced a unilateral cease-fire. It sent representatives in January 1989 to meet with King Hassan in Marrakesh. The king condescendingly referred to the Sahrawi nationalists as a group who had "gone astray." Instead of advancing the prospect of conciliation, as apparently anticipated by the Sahrawis, the king alienated the POLISARIO, which resumed operations against the Moroccans. In 1991, an official cease-fire (a de facto one was already in operation) was agreed upon by which the UN would implement a "Settlement Plan" and organize a national self-determination referendum. The institution in charge of planning the referendum was introduced, the UN's Mission for the Referendum in the Western Sahara (MINURSO). Questions over who would vote stymied progress toward a resolution throughout the 1990s until former Secretary of State James Baker, under UN auspices, persuaded both sides, through the Houston Accords of 1997, to resume voter identification. The Houston Accords also framed procedures for prisoner of war and detainee releases, troop confinement, and conduct during the referendum campaign (e.g., use of the media). Again, differences over voter identification impeded progress toward a referendum. In 2000, Baker offered a "third way" calling for autonomy and then a self-determination vote. Pressured by Algeria, the POLISARIO agreed to the "Baker Plan's" third iteration in 2003, which allowed for a significant Sahrawi administrative presence in a five-year transition toward a self-determination vote; but Morocco rejected this latest version. Consequently, Baker resigned in 2004 (see Zoubir and Benabdallah-Gambier 2004). Although MINURSO remained extant, there was increasing international sentiment that Western Sahara should be resolved by individual nations' negotiations (which should include the SADR to be effective) rather than through the UN. Morocco and the SADR accused each other of prisoner abuse. In August 2005, the Sahrawis released all its Moroccan prisoners. The SADR and Algeria have asked Morocco to reciprocate by freeing Sahrawi prisoners.[44]

If Morocco forcibly incorporates the territory, even with international backing, or if Algeria abandons the Sahrawis, Western Sahara would continue as a historic *bilad al-siba*.[45] Resentment and resistance would be the consequence rather than resolution. Although the cease-fire holds, the POLISARIO contends that there is an *intifada* occurring in the occupied zone (see Shelley 2004, 81–107). The POLISARIO, and its supporters within the occupied zone, will only be satisfied today by a national self-determination referendum.[46] That will not take place, however, without a negotiated settlement with Morocco, which views Western Sahara as an integral territory of the kingdom.

The Consequences of an Unresolved Western Sahara

Western Sahara is hardly an irrelevant geopolitical problem involving a remote and desolate region with a sparse population. It has always had important "international dimensions" (see especially Zoubir and Volman 1992). Indeed, its significance has grown given current international relations. The United Nations has invested financially as well as politically in an effort to achieve a legitimate decolonization. The failure of its iterated plans has harmed its reputation. Although MINURSO continues to be renewed, the UN's credibility is at stake. The UMA will never be able to explore its potential in achieving regional integration until Western Sahara is settled. The UMA's future is closely linked to the prospects of a positive Moroccan-Algerian relationship. Their bilateral relations will remain acutely sensitive until Western Sahara is resolved. The importance of a strong relationship is crucial to the stability of the Maghrib. By occupying portions of Western Sahara, Morocco has not only attempted to realize the dream of an imagined "Greater Morocco," it has also repudiated borders circumscribed by colonial powers. Nevertheless, those borders are held as sacrosanct by the African Union. Morocco's precedent could inspire other countries to imagine or realize a historic "boundary," provoking more violence in a war-torn continent. There is also the humanitarian aspect of refugees and human rights issues regarding detained and released prisoners. Furthermore, there is growing international interest in Western Sahara's potential mineral and metal wealth as well as phosphates.[47] Islamist extremism and its potential in the neighboring Sahel is also worrisome to the international community.[48] Clearly, the irresolution of Western Sahara impedes North Africa's (and the Sahel's) stability, as well as its progress, prosperity, and potential.

Recently, the UN considered proposals from the POLISARIO and Rabat for resolving Western Sahara (see "Morocco and Polisario Agree to Talk"; "UN Calls for Talks on Western Sahara"). On 30 April 2007, the Security Council voted unanimously (Resolution 1754) to promote direct talks ("negotiations without preconditions") between Morocco and the POLISARIO. The Moroccans continue to offer autonomy but not sovereignty. The nationalist Sahrawis view the talks as a means to reanimate negotiations for a self-determination referendum, which would offer a choice of complete independence. (Algeria is also supportive.) MINURSO and a small peacekeeping force have also received new mandates. The Security Council's resolution represents the most important international initiative regarding Western Sahara since 2003. It is imperative that its sponsors, the United States, France, Spain, Russia, and the United Kingdom, remain interested and engaged.[49] Although direct talks between Morocco and the POLISARIO in June and August 2007 reiterated conflicting positions and were inconclusive, the fact that both sides engaged in direct talks was positive and hopeful. Talks again in January 2008 disclosed that the impasse remains regarding Moroccan sovereignty equated with autonomy and a self-determination resolution with an option of independence. The POLISARIO has threatened a resumption of hostilities. With the AQI(L)M operating in Algeria and Mauritania, there is a growing international concern with the region, which may impose a solution on Western Sahara, which could, in turn, foment other problems.[50]

Conclusion

The countries of post-colonial North Africa share many themes. Politically, authoritarian leaders have asserted themselves. Tentative democratization has occurred in several countries, but political systems are exclusive rather than inclusive. Local, regional, and parliamentary institutions and elections pose few threats to executive power. Furthermore, institutions are not independent, such as the judiciaries. John Waterbury concluded a decade ago: "What does appear unavoidable is a situation in which governments and regimes can no longer legislate by decree and in which they must bargain with the constituted interests—economic, religious, and ethnic—of their societies. That is enough of a break with the political status quo of past decades to stir cautious optimism" (Waterbury 1997, 170). Although there is general political disaffection from Egypt to Morocco, there have been changes regarding, for example, greater participation of women in political and civil society (see Aït-Hamadouche 2008). Abdelaziz Bouteflika's managing Algeria's return to civilian rule and King Muhammad VI's sensitive initiatives early in his reign

inspired rising expectations, which have since been deflated. In general, a coercive "robust authoritarianism" dominates North Africa. Eva Bellin states:
"The Middle East and North Africa lack the prerequisites of democratization.
The lack of a strong civil society, a market-driven economy, adequate income
and literacy levels, democratic neighbors, and democratic culture explains
the region's failure to democratize" (Bellin 2004, 141). The contemporary
prospects for genuine regional democratization are remote. If democratization does occur, it may be the result of changing economic conditions.

Nevertheless, North Africa faces many economic challenges with considerable political ramifications. Observers reiterate that there is a need
for accountability and transparency not only in the politics, but also in the
economies of the region. Yet there are daunting difficulties inherent in simultaneous political and economic reform and liberalization.[51] Countries
also need sectoral diversification. While Libya and Algeria accrued lucrative
profits from soaring petroleum prices, given the current economic downturn, their rentier economies (based on non-renewable resources) risk sharp
declines because of their dependence on hydrocarbon sales (also Morocco's
predicament regarding phosphate exports).[52] Furthermore, both countries
have experienced the difficulties in reconciling *thawra* (revolution) with *tharwa* (wealth).[53] Unemployment and underemployment as well as in equitable
economic distribution are concerns in all these countries. Globalization
also poses problems. As a result of trade agreements with the EU (notably the
Euro-Mediterranean Partnership [EMP]) and the United States, the anticipated Mediterranean Free Trade Area (MEFTA) (via the "Barcelona Process") to
be implemented in 2010, as well as expected memberships to the WTO, North
African countries face insistent demands for liberalized economies featuring
fiscal and institutional reforms. Thus, this vertical integration poses complicated political as well as economic challenges.[54] Traditionally, North African
countries prefer political and economic opacity, thereby obfuscating corruption and patronage networks. In addition, the perceived interference of
foreign control over local economies has provoked North African protest and
mobilization (see Khiari 2005, 113–125).[55] On the other hand, competition
will eliminate inefficient local industries. The great regional aspiration is to
attract investment; but foreign interest evokes memories of the nineteenth-
century's "quiet imperialism" that overwhelmed the Tunisian and the Egyptian governments. The exponential growth of the Internet and cellular com-

munication has profound economic (and political) significance. Population growth and the demographic shifts from rural to urban areas, compounded by infrastructure inadequacies, present enormous difficulties. Furthermore, pollution and desertification threaten natural resources, such as Mediterranean fisheries and fragile agricultural and pastoral areas. For example, Algeria's hydrocarbon industry's discharges have polluted coastal waters. Algerian initiatives to stem erosion and desertification, e.g., the *Barrage Vert* (Green Barricade) program of the 1970s, have had mixed results. In addition, overuse has exhausted precious arable fields or pastures. Land reclamation and restoration are major concerns shared by North African countries. To its credit, Tunisia was the first Arab country to institute a ministry of the environment. The imperatives of economic development and environmental protection are daunting concerns for contemporary North Africa.

Socially, feminists have demanded important changes to family law in Morocco and Algeria.[56] Women have run for president in Algeria and Egypt and Moroccan parties must have their complement of women candidates and representatives. Yet patriarchy remains a powerful force and assiduously and fallaciously equates itself with Islam. The youth of North Africa, often alienated by *al-hagra,* encounter ideological influences competing for their loyalty. Chronic economic problems also limit their social prospects. Benjamin Stora observes: "Many of today's young Maghribis consider emigration to be the most effective means of social mobility" (Stora 2007, 5). Drug addiction is a serious problem; AIDS also threatens this especially vulnerable population.

Underlying the post-colonial period is the legacy of colonialism. Post-colonial North Africa's reconciliation of the past with the present has proven to be exceedingly demanding and difficult.[57] Regarding the Maghrib, although this also relates to Egypt, Jamil M. Abun-Nasr blamed colonialism for "narrow[ing] the options which the leaders of the independent states . . . had for consolidating their authority" (Abun-Nasr 1987, 408). A new generation is emerging, which has found its options and opportunities "narrowed" by "consolidated" authoritarian post-colonial systems. North African youth need political, economic, social, and cultural enfranchisement.[58] With an ageing North African leadership in Egypt, Libya, Tunisia, and Algeria, they may very well demand it.

John Voll's assessment remains applicable: "At the moment we are seeing an epochal transition. The current conflicts are no longer simply over tactics or various strategies of modernization. There is now a struggle for control of the very concepts of political life, for control of the way people think about politics, and the way that we can talk about polity and society" (Voll 1997, 15). Jacques Berque's observations, made over forty years ago regarding Egypt, reflecting Maghribis as well as Mashriqis, remain relevant, if not prescient. He perceived Maghribis and Mashriqis as "absorbed by that dispute between the authentic and the effective which undoubtedly constitutes the profoundest debate in which they have been involved since their conversion to Islam. For this reason, according to one . . . interpretation of the term *jihad,* holy war, their fight is not against the Other as against themselves—against a certain aspect of themselves" (Berque 1967, 394–395). Complementing Berque, Malik Bennabi believed that North Africa and the Muslim world needed to realize the importance of an Islamic and historic "authenticity" serving as a "social dynamic" to promote genuine "efficacity."[59] Islamism and its many expressions offer a variety of alternatives, including democratic ones. One of Mark Tessler's conclusions in his groundbreaking polling in Oran and Rabat is that "Islam appears to have less influence on political attitudes and behavior than is frequently suggested by students of Arab and Islamic society." His research indicates that "Islam is not the obstacle to democratization that some Western scholars allege it to be" (Tessler 2003, 118–119). John Entelis, a longtime observer of Maghribi Islamism, maintains that "the democratic imperative in North Africa needs no Islamic qualifier. . . . Islamists are the most committed to the democratic project. As long as all actors play according to the democratic rules of the game, then none should be excluded from participation" (Entelis 2008, 24). Another dynamic, transnational Amazighism, also must be taken into greater account regarding twenty-first century national identities (see Maddy-Weitzman and Zisenwine 2007; Willis 2008).[60] Who will take over for ageing or fragmenting elites? Who will be the new actors? North Africa is in another transformation, which is fraught with peril as well as promise. As this book goes to press, a global recession looms that will have multiple regional consequences beyond plunging petroleum, falling phosphate prices, and sagging GDPs.

The Peril and Promise of North Africa

As this book concludes, consider these questions: How would Ibn Khaldun's *asabiyya* apply to modern North Africa? What would represent "group feelings" in the modern and contemporary periods? Would they be mobilizing ideologies such as nationalism, socialism, and Islamism?[1] If so, can we expect them to evolve or devolve as did the states and dynasties that Ibn Khaldun studied? Socialism certainly no longer captivates as it did in the 1960s. Nationalism remains an ideological force, but the nationalist imagination of the state has also changed during the post-colonial period and is now challenged by Islamism. Hugh Roberts contends that Algeria, for example, is in a "post-nationalist" era (see Roberts 2003). How different are North Africans today compared to those analyzed by Ibn Khaldun?

Turning to Malik Bennabi, would he find the North African today, the "post-colonial man," as colonizable as the "post-Almohadean" man? I believe he would, provisionally. Over thirty years ago Abdallah Laroui lamented that Maghribis "are too preoccupied with the present—economics, sociology, politics; they look on the study of the past as a largely unprofitable investment and leave this task to foreigners without stopping to ask whether the resulting picture of their past may not in the long run shape their present" (Laroui 1977, 5). There is still a lack of historicism in North Africa, which is a principal cause of "colonizability." Jean Déjeux referred to Assia Djebar's first novel, *La Soif* (1957), regarding the need to recognize and transcend constrictive atavisms. Djebar wrote: "Worst of all is the lethargy, the somnolence. We hear only of settlers and colonialism. But the real evil is our mentality of the colonized, of colonizables. That is what must be changed, that is what we have to tell them in our own language" (Déjeux 1973, 23, quoting Djebar, 70–71). Yet there is also a need for ex-colonialists and European and American scholars to question their learned and often comfortable reception and perception of post-colonial and contemporary North Africa. This is what makes Jacques

Berque's *oeuvre* particularly appealing; he questions his vantage point. Historians can only present "a dimension of the real" or of the "virtual" (see Berque 1964b, 35).

From Berque's perspective, the reconciliation of North African society with industrial (or globalized) civilization remains an unfulfilled and complex existential project. He wrote regarding Egypt that the

> Other was not an individualized exploiter such as Britain or France but rather, more anonymously, industrial civilization, whose influence was general enough, and even necessary enough, to disturb and jeopardize Egypt's sense of identity. This could only be established through a transformation which, in many respects, meant deformation. Thus, by an apparent contradiction, in order to maintain her identity Egypt had to exercise her specific characteristics, hindering thereby her adaptation to the general trend of the world. (Berque 1972, 502)

On the other hand, Malik Bennabi contends in his writings that an archetypal Muslim identity must first be re-instilled and then an authentic adaptation can occur. His response to challenges of the modern and contemporary world, repeated in his works, is a favorite Qur'anic ayat: "Verily, God changes not what is in a people until they change what is in themselves [their souls]" (13:11). Of course, Egyptians and Maghribis have recognized and engaged this redemptive struggle involving power, identity, and resistance.

Naguib Mahfouz, Egypt's greatest modern novelist, won the Nobel Prize for Literature in 1988. His novels and short stories provide incisive and insightful views on Egypt's past and present. Alaa al Aswany ('Ala' al-Aswani), a dentist and a writer, published *The Yacoubian Building* (2004), in which his character studies offer metaphorical commentary upon the inherent contradictions and complexities in modern Egyptian society and politics. Nawal el-Saadawi, an Egyptian feminist and sociologist (and briefly a presidential candidate in 2005), has examined gender issues and how identity is conceived by others (for example, by Americans). The Libyan writer Ahmad Ibrahim al-Faqih has produced a sweeping trilogy covering Libya's dramatic transformation from the reign of Idris to the rule of Muammar Qadhafi. While al-Faqih's works are placed in urban and foreign settings, Ibrahim al-Kuni narrates domestic Libyan rural life (see Ahmida 2000). Albert Memmi, a Tunisian Jew, produced cogent sociological and psychological studies of colonialism and identity. Another Tunisian, Bashir Khurayyif, like many North African

authors, has described the effect of modernism on traditional life. Muhammad al-Hadi ben Salih addressed the corruption of the PSD. Tunisian women
authors, such as Hind Azzuz and Laila ben Mami, have examined issues like
abortion and sexuality. Moufida Tlatli's films have dealt with feminist as well
as political themes. In Algeria, Kateb Yacine wrote in French and in Arabic
with a keen sense of Algeria's history. Mouloud Feraoun described Kabyle life
and chronicled his impressions during the War of Liberation. Assia Djebar
has written about Algerian women in time and space and is also a film director. She is mentioned as a Nobel Prize candidate. Tahar Djaout, a victim of
the civil strife of the 1990s, feared that ideology whether secular or religious
could close the human imagination. The principal characters in Merzak All-
ouache's prescient film, *Bab El-Oued City* (1994), act as metaphors of Algeria's
post-colonial history. Morocco's Driss Chraïbi and Tahar Ben Jelloun represent two of the Maghrib's greatest novelists. Ben Jelloun won the prestigious
Prix Goncourt in France for *La nuit sacrée* (1987; *The Sacred Night*) (the first
North African bestowed with this honor) and the 2003 International IMPAC
Dublin Literary Award for the English-translated *The Blinding Absence of Light*
(*Cette aveuglante absence de lumière* [2000]) (Ben Jelloun, 2006), regarding
the brutality suffered by Moroccan political prisoners (see Chapter 9; Howe
2005, 187–188). Fatima Mernissi is a renowned sociologist and feminist who
has courageously defended and pursued the rights of women in Morocco. For
example, she explores gender geographies and boundaries in *Dreams of Tres-
pass: Tales of a Harem Girlhood* (1994) (see Fayad 2000, 88–95). Another Moroccan, Abdelkebir Khatibi, questions post-colonial binaries, subjectivities, and
dialectics and concludes that "it is necessary to listen to the Maghrib resonate in its plurality (linguistically, culturally, politically)" (Khatibi 1983, 39).[2]
Indeed, that appeal applies to all of North Africa. Chapters 8 and 9 surveyed
the perils associated with North Africa's post-colonial period, which continue today: political authoritarianism, economic distress, and social upheaval.
These women and men selected from so many others voice the polyphonic
promise of North Africa, the collective courage and critical engagement
of its people (see also Mortimer 2007). Furthermore, they serve as cultural
links between Arabs and the rest of the world. In particular, Maghribi social
and cultural hybridity located at the interstices of the "West" and the Arab-
Berber world offer the possibilities of exceptional opportunities for intra-
civilizational commutative communication and comprehension.[3]

Social criticism and historicism represent means of ending "post-colonial colonizability." There is another liberating variable—transcultural-ism. North African civilizations reached their greatest heights when they were open to transcultural encounter and interaction. This was highlighted by al-Andalus's *convivencia*, but this was also illustrated in Alexandria, Carthage, Qayrawan, Cairo, Tunis, Algiers, Tlemcen, Sijilmasa, Marrakesh, and Fez, as well as Cordoba. Contemporary Islamism, especially in its extreme forms, is often xenophobic, anti-historical, and to the vast majority of Muslims, anti-Islamic.[4] Bennabi, whose Islamist credentials are well known (and unimpeach-able to most), bridged Algeria, France, and Egypt without any kind of Fanonist psychoexistential colonial or post-colonial complex. He exemplified the his-toric transcultural North African, as did Ibn Khaldun centuries earlier.[5]

Bennabi, Laroui, and others have exhorted North Africans to remember accurately and assiduously their history, since their illustrious past *could* be their present.[6] Historical consciousness would assert their independence rather than undermine it with a transmuted colonizability. For North Afri-cans (as well as Europeans and North Americans) to understand who they are, they must understand who they were. For Jacques Berque, an outsider yet insider regarding North African history and sociology, there was a constant need to dialogue with documentation, the other, and the self. His conscious-ness was inherently transcultural. Albert Hourani admiringly wrote: "Berque has taught us to distinguish the different rhythms of history; that which for-eign rulers have tried to impose upon the Arab Muslim countries they have ruled, and that which those peoples have produced from within themselves" (Hourani 1991b, 5). Questioning Eurocentric modernization theories and interpretations of state-building, Ali Abdullatif Ahmida offered an alterna-tive approach "recovering the social history of the indigenous society, par-ticularly the history of resistance and various strategies for survival. . . . We need to look at history from below and understand groups such as peasants, tribesmen, women, and outcast groups . . . focusing on production, class for-mation, gender, and popular culture" (Ahmida 1994, 143). Algeria's Rachid Boudjedra's *Les 1001 années de la nostalgie* (1979) features a protagonist trying to rediscover his family's identity after being dispossessed by colonialism. He imagines himself as kin to Ibn Khaldun. Throughout the novel Boudjedra calls for an honest appraisal of Muslim history and its demystification. Simi-larly, in *Petit éloge de la mémoire: Quatre mille et une années de nostalgie* (2007),

Algerian Boualem Sansal offers a concise yet sweeping exploration from pharaonic Egypt to contemporary Algeria (see Mortimer 2008). He implores: "To read history is not enough, it is necessary to search within oneself and imagine" (Sansal 2007, 51). This book appeals to North Africans (and to us) to appreciate their rich history. The colonial period, in particular, has been termed an interruption in history and a suppression of memory (see Harlow 1986, xx–xi; Lorcin 2006). Yet contemporary intolerance associated with political authoritarianism and extremist Islamism also menace the restoration of memory and the reconciliation of the past with the present. The past, present, and future need to be rhymed or, from Bennabi's perspective, there must be a synergy of man, land, and time. North Africa faces the manifold dangers of political and cultural obscurantism[7]; hypocrisy and denial of history represent the region's greatest peril.

Writing in the context of the Cold War and decolonization, Lorna Hahn wrote: "The North Africans . . . need us, but we need them also" (Hahn 1960, ix). North Africa should be regarded as more than just a strategic region for expedient political and economic purposes. There are other compelling reasons to study the region. In Kateb Yacine's *Nedjma*, we find a style that evokes William Faulkner; in Tahar Djaout, George Orwell. In Umm Kulthum's singing we find Bessie Smith; in Khaled, the king of Rai, Elvis. We are not so different and certainly should not be so indifferent. Instead of a dualistic, binary othering, we must appreciate the play between self and other or selves and others.[8] Jacques Berque reflected that modern man "must reconcile his specific personality and his universal humanity, both within himself and in the eyes of the Other" (Berque 1972, 30). That project remains exciting and attainable as long as we learn and listen.

Fernand Braudel wrote: "My favourite vision of history is as a song of many voices" (Braudel 1972–1973, 2:1138). We are literally beginning to realize Braudel's vision and his song. After reading about it (see Introduction), I bought Robert Plant's *Mighty Rearranger*. The instrumentation on the compact disc includes the bendir, a large-frame drum used in the Maghrib, and the tehardant, a three-stringed lute-like instrument used by the Tuareg. If you listen carefully you will hear a transcultural meld of the sounds of the Sahara with those of the Mississippi Delta, celebrated poignantly by Plant, a Briton, and his band.[9]

There is promise.

NOTES

Introduction

1. The Arabic word *ra'y* means opinion. "Rai" is the usual transliteration appearing in the English language press. The "King of Rai" is Cheb Khaled (see Naylor 2006, 311, 389–390). See also Schade-Poulsen 1999.

2. The author initially introduced the transcultural ("trans-cultural") perspective in the *Wider West* program designed for his Western Civilization students at Marquette University (see Naylor 2000b, 2001).

3. The term *al-maghrib* also translates as the "west" or the "place where the sun sets" and is also the name for Morocco. According to Richard B. Parker, a former American ambassador with service in Algeria and Morocco, President Habib Bourguiba of Tunisia demarcated the Maghrib from the Mashriq (*al-mashriq*, the east or where the sun rises) "where the people stop eating rice and start eating couscous, the staple starch of North Africa. That line runs through Derna, in eastern Libya" (Parker 1987, 1). Occasionally *al-maghrib* is further delineated as *al-maghrib al-aqsa* or the far west meaning Morocco, *al-maghrib al-awsat* meaning the middle west or Algeria, and *al-maghrib al-adna* or the near west meaning Tunisia and Libya (and sometimes Algeria).

4. Sahel (*sahil*) in Arabic means coast or shoreline. In our geographic context, it refers to the belt of semiarid land separating the Sahara from tropical Africa. It often does not refer to Sudan (and occasionally Chad), but from our standpoint, the coastline stretches as far as the Saharan "sea"; thus, the Sahel includes from west to east Mauritania, Senegal, Mali, Niger, Chad, and Sudan. As several maps illustrate in this book, "Northern Africa" would include North Africa and the Sahel (see narrative).

5. French historians refer to the "Maghreb" (French transliteration often used in English) as Morocco, Algeria, Tunisia, and often Libya and Mauritania (thus generally subscribing to the aforementioned demarcation of the *jazirat al-maghrib*).

6. I am momentarily excluding Egypt. Its anthropological origins seem to be an admixture of West Asian, Black African, and Berber peoples. See Brett and Fentress 1996.

7. An *Amazigh* is a male Berber and a *Tamazight*, a female Berber. Tamazight is the general term for the Berber language, which features many dialects. "Amazighism" today equates with Berber cultural nationalism.

8. In the predynastic period, skeletal remains indicate "a mixture of racial types (negroid, Mediterranean, and European)." On the other hand, "the beginning pharaonic period" indicates an influx of "a different physical type from Syria-Palestine." The contention was whether this group was a result of conquest or of "gradual infiltration" (Shaw 2000a, 315). Given Egypt's history of the Intermediate Periods, the latter interpretation seems more convincing.

9. Libyan is derived from Libou, a prehistoric people who migrated from the east and mixed with the indigenous population of the Maghrib (Abun-Nasr 1971, 7).

10. Carthage was a Phoenician colony that became a powerful independent state that eventually rivaled Rome for control of the western Mediterranean. See Chapters 1 and 2.

11. Hamitic refers to an Afro-Asiatic language group of northeastern Africa. Berber dialects are also included in the Afro-Asiatic group, along with ancient Egyptian and Semitic languages.

12. North Africa's Mediterranean climate and topography mirrored those of West Asia's Fertile Crescent, thereby expediting the transfer and implementation of the latter's Neolithic "package" (see Diamond 1999).

13. As for the Sahel, cattle domestication may have occurred independently or with the introduction of West Asian cattle (Diamond 1999, 98).

14. Dwarf crocodiles are still found in pools in the Ennedi (Archeï) region (de Villiers and Hirtle 2002, 100, 141).

15. In the 1950s, Henri Lhote examined in detail the Tassili paintings, while Fabrizio Mori studied a similar "gallery" in the Acacus Mountains of Fezzan in the 1960s (see Wellard 1967, 39–46).

16. The idea of Western civilization being geographically "tri-continental," including West Asia and North Africa besides Europe, is thematic to Naylor (2000b).

17. The *Reconquista* is the name for the Spanish Christian reconquest of the Iberian peninsula from the Muslims. The surrender of Granada in 1492 marked the end of the *Reconquista,* although the expulsion of Andalusian Muslims from Spain sporadically continued for well over a century. Historian Ahmad Tawfiq al-Madani termed the specific conflict between the Regency of Algiers and Spain as a 300-year struggle (al-Madani 1968).

18. The *Muqaddima* introduces the *Kitab al-Ibar,* Ibn Khaldun's universal or world history, part of which is translated as the *Histoire des Berbères* (see Ibn Khaldun 1968–1969).

19. See Franz Rosenthal's description of *asabiyya* ("Translator's Introduction" in Ibn Khaldun 1967, 1:xxviii). Marshall G. S. Hodgson referred to it as "group solidarity or party spirit" (Hodgson 1974, 2:481). Calling the term "elusive," Muhsin Mahdi related *asabiyya* as a "communal ethos, community of sentiment, or social solidarity [the

latter being Mahdi's preferred term]" (Mahdi 1964, 196). Albert Hourani added that *asabiyya* was "a corporate spirit oriented towards obtaining and keeping power" (Hourani 1991a, 2). *Asabiyya* depended upon the identification of one's destiny with those of others, for example, the willingness to serve and sacrifice for the good of the group. In his study of *asabiyya*, Ibn Khaldun examined the role of many social variables such as religion, demography, environment, and especially the rivalry between nomadic and sedentary societies. Architecture was also viewed as an important indication signaling the strength and solidarity of group feeling. Ibn Khaldun's presentation of *asabiyya* is an exceptional analysis of political and social psychology and power.

20. Bennabi elaborated upon colonizability in his work *Vocation de l'Islam* (1954).

21. The battle of Siffin symbolized strife or *fitna* within the Muslim *umma* or community. It was fought between Caliph Ali (656–661) and his rival, the governor of Syria, Mu'awiya (see Chapter 3). During the battle, Mu'awiya's soldiers tore off pages of the Qur'an and placed them on their lances, demanding arbitration. Ali complied but the rivalry continued. After Ali's assassination, Mu'awiya took over the Muslim empire and inaugurated a dynasty, the Umayyads, ending the elective caliphate. See Chapter 3.

22. Bennabi provides the metaphor of an engine running out of gas (Bennabi 1954, 26). He viewed religion rather than rationalism as a greater deterrent preventing a civilization's degeneration. Bennabi's stages of civilization evoke Georg Friedrich Hegel's concept of an epochal *zeitgeist* or spirit of an age. Unlike Hegel, Bennabi viewed history as cyclical rather than teleological. See also Boukrouh 2006.

23. Islamism is an ideology. In general, its adherents share political, economic, and social beliefs, which aim to reform, revive, and renew society on an Islamic basis.

24. He amorously reflects upon the beauty of "Zohra" (see the autobiographical Berque 1989).

25. Dale F. Eickelman noted that dating from "the 1930s Berque's writing indicated a subtle awareness of the nature of the colonial situation that he experienced" (Eickelman 1998, 42).

26. Wilfrid J. Rollman pointed out that scholars and students contend that occasionally Berque's "use of language and imagery [is] paternalistic, even as they applaud his rejection of 'Orientalist assumptions' and 'revolutionary history,' or his contributions to the development of local identity and self-critique" (Rollman 1997, xxii).

27. Braudel's magisterial *The Mediterranean and the Mediterranean World of Philip II* (1949, 1966, trans. 1972, 1973 [vol. 2]) takes into account North Africa's important role during this period. His distinction between "conspicuous"/"conjuncture" and "submerged"/"structure" histories relates to Ibn Khaldun's "surface" and "inner meaning" approach. To Braudel history was a "dialogue between structure and conjuncture, the moment in time and the long or very long term" (Braudel 1972–1973, 2:757). Furthermore, their approaches were similar. Ibn Khaldun would have appreci-

ated Braudel's contention that "history accepts and discovers multidimensional explanations, reaching, as it were, vertically from one temporal plane to another. And on every plane there are also horizontal relationships and connections" (Braudel 1972–1973, 1:16). Berque implemented a similar methodology. Andrew C. Hess questioned Braudel's conception of a unitary Mediterranean (see Hess 1978, 1–10) (see Chapter 5). Braudel taught in Algeria from 1923 to 1932.

28. Continuing the significant contributory intellectual tradition of North Africa in the post-colonial period, Abdelkebir Khatibi, a Moroccan sociologist, critic, and novelist, offers critiques of Ibn Khaldun, Malik Bennabi, and Berque, but he affirms their pluralist approaches to regional and civilization studies in *Maghrib pluriel* (1983).

29. Led Zeppelin often experimented with North African/Middle Eastern rhythms. Consider the guitar riffs in "The Immigrant Song," "Kashmir," and "Over the Hills and Far Away." Plant along with guitarist Jimmy Page journeyed to Morocco intending to tape-record Berber music in the mid-1970s. Their exploration of the country was impeded by the events surrounding the "Green March" and the partition of Spanish (Western) Sahara (see Chapter 9). Military blockades diverted their travels (Davis 1997, 253–254). Umm Kulthum, the greatest modern Egyptian singer, also influenced Plant's remarkable vocals (Davis 1997, 309–310). For more information on Umm Kulthum see Danielson 1997.

30. Plant released his ninth solo album, titled *Mighty Rearranger,* in 2005. In particular, two songs on that album, "Somebody's Knockin'" and "Takamba," illustrate North African influences. Plant also listens to the Algerian performer Rachid Taha, who melds rock and roll with North African music (see http://www.rollingstone.com/news/story/_/id/7287549/ledzepplin). Taha's *Tékitoi* (2004) is an album that features his transcultural musical meld of the Clash's "Rock the Casbah" with notable guest Brian Eno.

Chapter 1

1. Scholars debate which writing system developed first, Sumer's cuneiform or Egypt's hieroglyphics.

2. In contemporary geopolitical orientation, Canaan stretched from southern Syria to the Palestinian Authority's Gaza.

3. This event occurred during Napoleon Bonaparte's occupation of Egypt (see Chapter 5).

4. Dates differ among sources regarding ancient Egypt and should be regarded as approximate. I have relied upon Shaw 2000b.

5. Imhotep may be the first recorded polymath (a person with extraordinary breadth of knowledge). He served as Djoser's principal minister and was also an architect and a physician.

6. The Middle Kingdom tale "The Story of a Shipwrecked Sailor" attests to Egyptian Red Sea trade. As early as the 5th Dynasty (2494–2345 BCE), Egypt engaged in the Red Sea trade to the Somali coast. There is some controversy regarding Punt's location. Scholars believe that its location may have been in southern Sudan or in Eritrea. In addition, there may have been complementary expeditions from the Nile overland to Punt. The last indication of an expedition to Punt appeared to occur during the reign of Ramesses III (r. 1184–1153 BCE) (see Shaw 2000a, 322–324). For more information on the expedition see Tyldesley 1996, 145–146; Welch 1972, 24–27.

7. Historians often refer to Akhenaten's religion as a form of monotheism, but monolatry, the belief in one god without denying belief in other deities, is a more accurate representation of the pharaoh's faith.

8. The Sea Peoples destroyed the Hittite Empire.

9. Egyptologists also include concurrent kings ruling as the Twenty-third Dynasty (818–715) and Twenty-fourth Dynasty (727–715). Even with the Kushite conquest, Libyans still exercised significant local power.

10. The eschatological explanation presented in the narrative is simplified for the reader. There are also other interpretations, especially regarding the role of the *akh*. For further information, see this helpful University of Chicago web site—http://oi.uchicago.edu/OI/DEPT/RA/ABZU/DEATH.HTML.

11. Nnamdi Elleh perceives a diffusion of Egyptian architectural styles beyond Sudan and the kingdom of Kush to Aksum, Ethiopia, and West Africa (Elleh 1997, 47–48).

12. See O'Connor and Reid 2003. Regarding transculturalism, see especially Folorunso 2003, 77–92, and MacDonald 2003, 93–106. Lady Duff Gordon believed in the mid-nineteenth century that the "*real* difference" between "Orientals" and "Western Christians" was found less in religion but "consists in all the class of notions and feelings . . . which we derive—not from the Gospels at all—but from Greece and Rome, and which of course are altogether wanting here [in Egypt]" (Gordon 1969, 173). Those sympathizing with Bernal's ideas and interpretations would find Gordon's observations amusingly ironic.

13. Spain's natural resources, such as tin, silver, lead, copper, and iron, especially attracted the Phoenicians and later their colonial inheritors, the Carthaginians.

14. B. H. Warmington questions if the Phoenicians reached Britain (Warmington 1969, 77), although earlier in his book, he contends that there was trade between the "Tartessians" of coastal western Iberia and Britain and Ireland (ibid., 24).

15. Stéphane Gsell offers the founding dates 814–813 BCE (Gsell 1920–1928, vols. 1–2). See Warmington 1969, 26–31.

16. Horses probably arrived from Egypt and Libya, a most significant transcultural transaction.

17. Acculturated Berbers are sometimes referred to as "Libyphoenicians."

18. The year 480 was very important in Greek history. That was the same year that the Greeks decisively defeated the Persians at Salamis. Given the important role that the Phoenicians played in Persian forces, historians have wondered if the Carthaginians coordinated their campaign against the Greeks. Warmington argues: "It is hardly to be thought that the quarrel of a distant and minor power like Carthage could have had any influence on the Persian plans" (Warmington 1969, 52). Remember that "tyranny" in antiquity meant rule by one person, who usually exercised power justly rather than cruelly.

19. Greek success against the Persians led to the establishment of Athens' Delian League, which controlled the eastern Mediterranean, thereby limiting Carthaginian commercial opportunities. Hanno's reorientation toward Africa was transformative, according to Dio Chrysostom, a first century CE historian. The Carthaginians evolved "from Tyrians into Africans" (Raven 1993, 11).

20. This was especially true with acculturated Berbers. On the other hand, Carthaginians often resorted to violence in order to exact tribute from neighboring tribes.

21. Agathocles convinced Ophellas, the Macedonian governor of Cyrenaica, to ally with him. Their conflicting ambitions led to the murder of Ophellas (see Abun-Nasr 1971, 19).

22. Punic is derived from the Greek and the Latin word for Phoenician.

23. The Carthaginians reportedly sacrificed hundreds of children to Baal for protection when Agathocles campaigned in North Africa.

24. Sufet equates with the Hebrew "shophet" or judge in the context of a leader (as in the Book of Judges) (Warmington 1969, 140).

25. Their Greek enemies also mustered armies composed of "men of very diverse origins" (Gsell 1920–1928, 2:389).

26. Hanno may have been interested in refounding or reviving old Phoenician outposts along the Atlantic (ibid., 1:507).

27. These enterprises probably occurred between 500 and 450 BCE.

28. The Sahara was not as desiccated as it is today.

29. The camel arrived in Egypt with the Assyrian conquest in the seventh century BCE (Hitti 1970, 22). Richard W. Bulliett provides meticulous information regarding the camel's introduction in North Africa (Bulliett 1975, 111–140). He sides with scholars who believe that the Romans were principally responsible for the camel's introduction as a pack animal. He distinguishes between earlier "encounters" reported by textual evidence and the actual systematic introduction of the animal. For example, the camel's presence in western Libya in the third century is well documented (ibid., 113). He writes: "When the Romans finally did obtain access to camels in some quantity, probably beginning in the first or second century A.D., they had to decide what, if anything, to do with them. . . . Ideas gleaned from Egypt and Syria may have been

influential in adopting the animal as a beast of burden, and the South Arabian saddle was probably introduced along with the North Arabian saddle to facilitate this" (ibid., 139). Bulliett reminds the reader that Berbers used the camels for milk as well as riding and that there was at this time "no major caravan trade." He states that the Garamantes' isolation inhibited their adoption of the camel (ibid.); however, it is conceivable that once they realized the military and economic advantages provided by the animal, they played a role in its introduction to the wider Sahara. Galbraith Welch assessed the camel's profound importance: "No animal ever played so decisive a role in history. The camel created a continent—or rather gave a continent to the rest of the world" (Welch 1972, 137–138). The camel expedited commerce but also "gave the nomad a devastating mobility in his ceaseless pressure on settled lands" (Hillenbrand 1976, 41).

30. The Carthaginians reportedly sent expeditions to Arabia and to South Asia, although Hellenistic Egyptian merchants monopolized these routes and commerce (see below).

31. In philosophy, there were Carthaginian Pythagoreans. In addition, a Carthaginian named Hasdrubal studied with Carneades at Athens's Academy in the mid-second century BCE. Hasdrubal became renowned as Clitomachus and eventually headed the famous school (Momigliano 1975, 5).

32. According to Abun-Nasr, the Carthaginians often bartered, and when they did purchase commodities, transactions were made "with the money which they obtained from the sale of their wares" (Abun-Nasr 1971, 21).

33. They included Euesperides (Benghazi), Barce, Teuchira, and Apollonia. The Greeks established themselves in the region of what is known today as the Jabal Akhdar (Green Mountains), a region of plateaus and hills and Libya's wettest area.

34. According to tradition, runners set out from Carthage and Cyrene and headed toward the others' city with the understanding that borders would be established where they met. The distance covered by the Carthaginian runners astounded the Cyrenes. The Carthaginian brothers who participated in this event swore that they had not cheated and demanded, as a question of honor, to be buried alive at the demarcation of the border. This was done and the brothers became exemplars of Carthaginian virtue, earning also the respect of the Greeks (see Sallust 1967, 111–112).

35. Egypt exercised a precarious independence from 404 to 343 BCE, given Persia's problems with its western satrapies, namely the Greeks. Under Artaxerxes III (343–338 BCE), the Persians finally reasserted direct control. According to Alan B. Lloyd, Alexander's appearance terminating the Persian presence "was lamented by no one" (Lloyd 2000, 395).

36. Ptolemy also reportedly managed to secure the corpse of Alexander the Great, which was embalmed and preserved in a glass coffin. Alexander's remains added to Ptolemy's legitimacy.

37. Plato's Academy and Aristotle's Lyceum in Athens inspired these Ptolemaic institutions. The Museum housed the Library (Lloyd 2000, 405).

38. Aristarchus organized *The Iliad* and *The Odyssey* into twenty-four books.

Chapter 2

1. Former enemies Syracuse and Rome offered assistance to Carthage.

2. The reasons for this depreciation are unclear (see "Introduction" to Livy 2006). Harsh winter conditions and assaults by Alpine tribes probably played important roles in reducing the invasion force (Dupuy and Dupuy 1977, 63).

3. Although Hannibal provoked dread and terror among the Romans, Tom Holland recounted that "the Romans never forgot that in Hannibal, in the scale of his exertions, in the scope of his ambition, they had met the enemy who was most like themselves. Centuries later statues of him were still to be found standing in Rome" (Holland 2005, 8).

4. Cato the Elder (234–149 BCE) infamously ended his speeches in the Senate with the words "Carthage must be destroyed."

5. For more information on the Berbers and Masinissa see Kaddache 2003, 37–52.

6. One of the reasons Syphax shifted allegiances was that he reputedly fell in love with Sophonisba, the daughter of the Carthaginian commander, Hasdrubal, who strategically married her to the Berber chieftain. Livy describes Sophonisba as "a woman of outstanding beauty and in her prime" (Livy 2006, 576). The Romans captured Syphax, but Sophonisba entered the court of Masinissa, who married her. The Romans, fearing Sophonisba's Carthaginian influence, demanded that she be surrendered to them. Respecting Sophonisba's wish never to be handed over to the Romans, Masinissa sent her poison delivered by a servant, which she willingly accepted. According to Livy she said: "I accept this wedding gift. It is not unwelcome, if my husband has found it impossible to give his wife a greater one. But tell him this: my death would have been more acceptable had my marriage not coincided with my funeral" (Livy 2006, 580). It is possible that Livy added this drama for literary purposes, but the story also reveals the complexity of shifting Carthaginian-Roman-Berber politics.

7. The renowned poet and essayist Jean Amrouche (1906–1962) correlated the Numidian king with a modern Algerian identity in *L'Eternal Jugurtha* (1943).

8. Troops loyal to Sulla and commanded by Pompey executed Hierbas, the losing brother.

9. Caesar's autobiographical *African War* presents his perspective. Caesar, like Hannibal, had the ability to command "Syrians and men of divers races" (Caesar 1955, 175).

10. Caesar calculated that his forces had "killed ten thousand of the enemy and routed a large number" while he had "fifty soldiers missing and a few wounded" (ibid.,

281). Even if Caesar's reckoning exaggerated his success, there is no question regarding his brilliantly crafted campaign in Numidia. Military historians record that Caesar suffered less than 1,000 casualties, while the combined Pompeian-Numidian army of 60,000 lost 10,000 dead and approximately 10,000 wounded and captured (Dupuy and Dupuy 1977, 111).

11. Ironically, Caesar began his *Alexandrian Wars* by noting that "Alexandria is well-nigh fire-proof, because its buildings contain no wooden joinery and are held together by an arched construction and are roofed with rough-cast or tiling" (Caesar 1955, 11). Of course, interiors were flammable. Warehouses crammed with "priceless books," or the Library, may have been destroyed. As Tom Holland points out, "Christians and Muslims have also been blamed" for this immeasurable loss (Holland 2005, 319). The Emperor Theodosius issued an edict in 389 that led to the destruction of the "Sister Library" in Alexandria. Philip Hitti notes that the story that Amr ibn al-'As stoked fires with the ancient manuscripts seized at the Library "makes good fiction but bad history. . . . At the time of the Arab conquest [in the seventh century] . . . no library of importance existed in Alexandria" (Hitti 1970, 166). John Paul Russo also refutes the idea of Muslim culpability and states that "it was destroyed by two or three centuries of neglect" (Russo 2005, 66). Sosigenes, an Alexandrian scholar, helped calculate Caesar's "Julian" calendar (Ritner 1998, 3).

12. Antony had suffered military defeat at the hands of the formidable Mesopotamian Parthians, who had also destroyed legions under Crassus's command in 53 BCE.

13. The death of King Bocchus of Mauretania in 33 BCE ended the dynasty. Romans ruled Mauretania until Juba II took over as a Roman client king.

14. He also established a second court at Volubilis (in Morocco).

15. This hydrology also relates to Muammar Qadhafi's contemporary "Great Man-Made River" project (see Chapter 8).

16. Balbus, an Iberian from Gades (Cadiz), received Roman citizenship for his campaign (Pliny 1942, 245). Balbus's success earned him a triumphal parade in Rome, the first for a foreigner (see Wellard 1967, 66).

17. Besides Balbus, Suetonius Paulinus traversed the Atlas Mountains and entered the western Sahara. Septimius Flaccus and Julius Maternus also entered the Sahara by the end of the first century CE. Flaccus may have reached the Tibesti Mountains in today's Chad (Raven 1993, 63; see also Pliny 1942, 229–231). The Romans knew of the Niger River (see Pliny 1942, 251).

18. Candace approximates *kandake,* the Meriotic term for queen (see Ritner 1998, 11). Pliny adds regarding Meroe "that it is ruled by a woman, Candace, a name that has passed on through a succession of queens for many years" (Pliny 1942, 477). In Acts 8:26, Candace is referred to as "Queen of the Ethiopians."

19. The Numidians and other North African farmers also stored grain in subsoil vaults to protect it and conserve it in case of conflict (Caesar 1955, 247).

20. Local recruitment for the legions increased during the second century CE. Thus, Berbers eventually manned the Third Augustan (see Albertini et al. 1937, 1955, 66–67; Ayache 1964, 49).

21. Carthage rivaled Alexandria and Antioch in sophistication and size. It is estimated that Carthage had approximately 300,000 to 400,000 inhabitants. Once again, it became a cosmopolitan city.

22. Augustine studied there and recounted: "I found myself in the midst of a hissing cauldron of lust" (Augustine 1961, 55). Nevertheless, years later he opened a school in Carthage (ibid., 120)—a stage in his colorful life before his Christian conversion (see below). Many wealthy North Africans also sent their children to study in Athens or Rome. North African women also received exceptional educational opportunities compared to other regions in the empire.

23. The Emperor Nerva (r. 96–98 CE) authorized the founding of Djemila and Sitifis (Sétif). The Romans founded Timgad in 100 CE during the reign of Trajan (98–117 CE). Today Timgad features one of the most impressive sites of Roman ruins.

24. Thysdrus (El Djem) in Tunisia possessed an amphitheater rivaling Rome's Colosseum. Cities also had acting companies. Timgad's theater had seating for 3,700 (Ayache 1964, 65).

25. Timgad featured a remarkable water system including thirteen public baths and constantly flushing latrines.

26. North Africa had a large slave economy. The wife of Lucius Apuleis (see below) gave her children four hundred slaves. Before she entered a monastic life in the beginning of the fifth century (and eventual sainthood), Melanie reportedly freed thousands of slaves from her African properties (Ayache 1964, 55).

27. Although Egypt was also an important market in the wild animal trade, the Maghrib still had elephants and "big cats," such as lions and leopards, during this period (Raven 1993, 5). Indeed, cheetahs still existed in Algeria until the early 1970s (according to a sign posted in the National Zoological Park in Washington, D.C.).

28. The Silk Road from China to the West included a route to India, which Hellenistic traders took advantage of and profited from. Pliny worried about balance of payments with India as he calculated "that in no year does India absorb less than fifty million sesterces of our empire's wealth, sending back merchandise to be sold with us at a hundred times its prime cost" (Pliny 1942, 417). This trade imbalance was insignificant, however, given the volume of the empire's economy.

29. Strabo adds that Memphis "consists of mixed races of people, like those who have settled together in Alexandria" (Strabo 1949, 89). Although it was usually stable,

riots broke out in Egypt between Jews and Greeks during the reign of the Emperor Caligula. Communal violence recurred from 115 to 117 and the consequent severe suppression almost eliminated the Jewish presence there.

30. Quietus can be observed on Trajan's Column leading the bareheaded Berber cavalry.

31. Charles Finch argues that Egyptian religion significantly influenced the development of "historical Christianity," such as the revivified and resurrected Osiris (see Finch 1991). Whether Finch's insistent interpretation of Christianity's African roots is accepted or not, Christian beliefs significantly correlated with Egyptian religious traditions.

32. Christine Mohrmann recognized that "Christian Latin literature first came into existence" in North Africa. She maintained: "It must however be considered very improbable that the Latinizing process of the Christian community did not begin very early in Rome too" (Mohrmann 1961, 109–110). The Christianization of Latin, as amplified by North Africans, also widely disseminated that language. Of course, in Egypt, Coptic and Greek also had profound Christian significance. North Africa's importance in the history of early Christianity is especially consequential.

33. An imperial decree in 391 declared paganism illegal.

34. Egyptian Christians especially popularized iconography. Peter Brown notes the "Coptic adaptation of Isis suckling the infant Horus" (Brown 1971, 143).

35. The claims and counter-claims of apostasy leading often to intra-Christian terrorism and violence are reminiscent of the controversies and conflicts of contemporary North African Islamism.

36. Diocletian (r. 284–305) conceived this complicated system, which aimed to end chronic succession crises and conflicts. It actually compounded succession troubles and intensified rivalries. Furthermore, it led to the division of the empire between western and eastern halves. During the civil war, a rival destroyed Cirta, but Constantine rebuilt it. Renamed in his honor, it remains an urban testament in Muslim Algeria to the first Christian Roman emperor. Diocletian also administratively reorganized North Africa west of Egypt into a reduced Mauretania, Tingitana (soon to be abandoned), Caesariensis, and Sitifensis. The Romans governed Numidia as Cirtensis in the north and Militiana in the south. Africa Proconsularis was renamed Zeugitana in the north, Byzacena in its central region, and Tripolitania in the east.

37. Augustine viewed history as teleological, ending with the Parousia or Second Coming of Christ. He composed *The City of God* from 413 to 427.

38. Constantine convened the Council of Arles in 314 to deal with the Donatists, but it was ineffectual.

39. By that time, the empire had divided between the Western Empire with its capi-

tal in Rome and the Eastern Roman Empire with its capital at Constantinople. Significantly, Rome became increasingly dependent on the Maghrib for its grain, since Egyptian grain supplied the new capital at Constantinople (Warmington 1954, 59).

40. Byzantine refers to Byzantium (Byzantion), the city which the Emperor Constantine renamed Constantinople. It is known today as Istanbul.

41. After their conquest, the Byzantines incorporated Vandals into their army, including a special unit called the "Vandals of Justinian" (Procopius 1953, 333). Furthermore, the Byzantines enlisted Berbers to help patrol North African frontiers (Diehl 1966, 1:323).

42. Diehl 1966 (vol. 1) provides detailed diagrams of Byzantine ramparts. In addition, Tunisia features outstanding examples of Byzantine mosaics.

43. The Byzantine "re-Romanization" of North Africa featured a major cultural difference: "The language of newly revived Roman administration was Greek, a foreign tongue that had never been widely spoken in the area before: it must have made the imperial authorities seem more like alien invaders than restorers of past glories" (Kennedy 2007, 202).

Chapter 3

1. Abraham is regarded as the father of the Arabs through Isma'il (Ishmael), the son he sired with Hagar.

2. From verse (*ayat*) 24:36: "Light on light, God guides to His light whom He wishes."

3. The Hijra also marked the beginning of the Muslim calendar.

4. Patriarchy within Arab society principally derives from atavisms and traditions rather than from Islam.

5. Muslims recognize Jewish and Christian sacred texts. Nevertheless, Muhammad's message is regarded as the perfection of previous revelation, which, from a Muslim perspective, was misinterpreted and misapplied.

6. Muslims believed that Abraham constructed the shrine to honor God.

7. There is the notion that the fall of the Holy Land to Islam launched the Western European Crusades. Actually, Muslims ruled the Holy Land for well over 400 years before European Crusaders captured Jerusalem in 1099. The rise of the Seljuk Turks and its disastrous effect upon Byzantine power (the battle of Manzikert [1071]) was an important cause of the Crusades. Byzantine Emperor Alexius I (1081–1118) requested assistance.

8. Emperor Heraclius introduced "Monotheletism" in 624, which compounded Orthodox Christianity's fractious Christology. Monotheletism attempted to reconcile Orthodox and Monophysite Christians by arguing that Christ had a human and a di-

vine nature but *one* will. Neither side adopted Monotheletism, and the Third Council of Constantinople condemned it in 680.

9. John, the late seventh century Coptic bishop of Nikiu and hardly an apologist for the Muslim conquest of Egypt, noted regarding Amr's legacy: "He exacted the taxes which had been determined upon, but he took none of the property of the Churches, and he committed no act of spoliation or plunder, and he preserved them throughout all his days" (John 1916, 200).

10. The population of Egypt gradually converted to Islam over centuries, although a sizeable Monophysite or Coptic community continued to exist. Cairo, founded in the tenth century as a consequence of the Fatimid conquest (see below), eventually enveloped Fustat. The Muslims also entered Sudan and negotiated a treaty with Christian Nubia in 652 (see Hitti 1970, 168).

11. A less liberal attitude characterized later Muslim expansion in South Asia. Hindu idolatry appalled Muslims. In the history of Islam in the West, when persecution occurred against privileged "People of the book," it usually resulted from economic distress or war rather than from religious policy (see Hourani 1991a, 118–119).

12. Abun-Nasr 1987, 30. Nevill Barbour subscribes to the traditional interpretation that Uqba reached the Atlantic (Barbour 1966, 41). Ibn abd al-Hakam places Uqba in Morocco. He also recounts how Uqba prayed for help when he and his men were dying of thirst. His horse then began to dig with its hoof and uncovered stones bursting with water (al-Hakam 2004, 222–223).

13. Zuhayr was killed at Barqa (in eastern Libya) by Byzantines in 688 or 689.

14. Ibn Idhari refers to al-Kahina as a *malika* or a queen. The resistance of Kusayla and al-Kahina remains important regarding contemporary Berber-Arab cultural controversies, such as the use of the Berber language, Tamazight. See also El-Aroui 1990.

15. Philip Hitti credited the Arabs' Semitic (refers to language not ethnicity) kinship with the Phoenicians in expediting their relations with the Berbers who still spoke Punic in some regions: "This explains the seemingly inexplicable miracle of Islam in Arabicizing the language and Islamizing the religion of these [Berbers] and using them as fresh relays in the race toward further conquests" (Hitti 1970, 214). On the other hand, a significant number of bishoprics remained in North Africa three hundred years after the conquest (ibid., 361). Regarding Arabization, see also the section on the Banu Hilal in this chapter. Musa's trust in Tariq illustrated an exceptional sensibility between Arab and Berber, which obviously expedited the campaigns in the far Maghrib and Iberia.

16. Historians, such as Edward Gibbon and Henri Pirenne, regarded this battle as seminal in the development of European civilization. Actually, the Byzantines faced the greater onslaught. The first Muslim siege of Constantinople occurred in 669 and

recurred intermittently in the 680s. The Umayyads launched a massive assault against the Byzantine capital in 717 and 718. If the Byzantines had failed to stop the Muslims, European history would certainly have changed—as it did after the Ottoman Turks captured Constantinople in May 1453, a severe psychological blow. Politically, the Balkans already had fallen under Ottoman control. Regarding the battle of Tours, W. M. Watt concluded: "What the battle showed was that the Muslims had come to the limit of profitable raiding expeditions. The manpower they could spare to send into central France was insufficient to overcome the opposition they were likely to meet there" (Watt 1972, 9). On the other hand, there is the interpretation that Muslims (specifically Musa bn Nusayr) sought to overrun Western Europe (see Karsh 2007, 60–61). The armies specifically engaged at Moussais la Bataille north of Poitiers (Kennedy 1996, 22). Bernard Lewis compares the "Battle of Tours and Poitiers" to the assaults on Constantinople (Lewis 1982, 18–20). He states: "There can be little doubt that in disregarding Poitiers and stressing Constantinople, the Muslim historians saw events in a truer perspective than the later Western historians. The Frankish victors at Poitiers encountered little more than a band of raiders operating beyond their most distant frontiers, thousands of miles from home" (ibid., 19).

17. Referring to the work of Ibn Butlan (eleventh century), Elizabeth Savage notes that "the ideal slave was a Berber woman who from the age of nine had spent three years in al-Madina, three in Mecca, and then nine in Iraq," where she received a musical and literary education. Savage states: "Though some Berber women became famous singers, they were also highly regarded for housework, sexual relations, and childbearing" (Savage 1997, 68).

18. North Africa and al-Andalus would also contribute to the intellectual achievements of Islamdom (see below and Chapter 4). Nevertheless, we must recognize some names from the Mashriq here: Ibn Sina (980–1037), the great physician and scholastic philosopher, who was born in Bukhara; al-Razi (865–?930), the greatest medical mind in medieval Western history, from Persia; al-Khwarizmi (780–?850) the outstanding mathematician; Umar Khayyam (1038–1123), a poet and mathematician from Persia; Abu Hamid al-Ghazali (al-Ghazzali) (1058–1111), the most renowned Muslim theologian; and the polymath al-Biruni (973–1048) from Central Asia, the celebrated astronomer, geographer, philologist, and historian of India. Notice the ethnic and intellectual diversity. The Abbasid period marks one of the greatest eras of intellectual achievement in the history of Western civilization, a testament to transculturalism.

19. The Romans may have established themselves in Sijilmasa or in the surrounding area (Howe 2005, 41). The city referred to here was founded in 758. The Midrarids were Khariji.

20. The palace featured a pool of quicksilver (mercury) with floating inflated leather cushions (Hitti 1970, 454).

21. "Ikhshid" refers to Muhammad Ben Tughji's Central Asian familial roots and is considered a royal title.

22. As Robert Hillenbrand pointed out: "From the time of Ibn Tulun onwards, a Turkish military presence was never long absent from Egyptian soil" (Hillenbrand 1976, 24).

23. There were also very close links with the Mashriq, notably Basra in Iraq. Neighborhoods in Tahart were renowned for their Basran and Kufan merchants (Savage 1997, 40). Ibadis remain renowned for their commercial acuity.

24. He is referred to as a Shi'i by Ibn Khaldun (Ibn Khaldun 1967, 1:49). Idris claimed descent from Hasan, a son of Ali and Fatima, and brother of the martyred Husayn.

25. His father Idris I is also credited with founding the city in 789 (see Brett 1999, 59). Idris II moved his capital from Volubilis to Fez in 809 where he built contiguous neighborhoods, a new settlement.

26. Jacques Berque provides a brief but informative survey of medieval Fez (see Berque 1974, 35–47).

27. The years 698 or 732 are usually given regarding the building of the original structure.

28. Efraim Karsh reminds that the Aghlabids often had Christian support in their Sicilian and Italian campaigns. In this case, the Aghlabids helped repulse the duke's rival. In turn, the Neapolitans allied with the Aghlabids in a campaign against Messina (Karsh 2007, 70).

29. Frederick II promoted scholarship and education. According to Philip Hitti: "This almost modern spirit of investigation, experimentation and research which characterized the court of Frederick marks the beginning of the Italian Renaissance" (Hitti 1970, 611).

30. The Isma'ilis followed the family of the seventh imam, Isma'il, who died before his father, the sixth imam Ja'far al-Sadiq. Most Shi'a recognize Isma'il's younger brother, Musa al-Kazim, as the eighth imam, thus continuing the imamate until the twelfth imam, Muhammad al-Muntazar, who disappeared and who, according to adherents, will return as the Mahdi, the rightly guided one or redeemer. The Fatimids followed descent from Fatima. They had missions (*da'wa*) throughout Islamdom. They established communities from Sind (Pakistan) to the Maghrib and from Daylam (south of the Caspian Sea) to Yemen (although the Zaydis dominated).

31. According to Ibn Khaldun, the Abbasids ordered Aghlabid and Midrarid clients to seize Ubayd Allah (Ibn Khaldun 1967, 1:42). He was disguised as a merchant and kept in contact with Abu Abd Allah al-Shi'i (Halm 1997, 9–10).

32. Succession disagreements also weakened the imamate. The Ibadis migrated to the northern Sahara and set up new communities and cities, which still exist today in the Mizab of Algeria.

33. As much as Ubayd Allah fiercely opposed the Aghlabids, the geographer al-Bakri (from al-Andalus) recounts that the Fatimid leader admired their engineering and architecture. Referring to Aghlabid hydrology in Tunis and fortifications (Qasr al-Bahr) in Raqqada, the Mahdi asserted: "I saw in Ifriqiya two incomparable things that I did not see in the East" (al-Bakri 1965, 26–60).

34. The Fatimids invaded again in 919 and campaigned until 921 before being repelled by the Abbasids, who had toppled the Tulunids and reinstated their authority in Egypt in 904–905.

35. Muslims plundered Genoa in 934.

36. Caliph al-Walid ordered Musa to return to the Mashriq along with Tariq. Musa appointed his sons to high office—Abd al-Aziz as governor of al-Andalus and Abdallah as governor of North Africa. Al-Walid died soon after Musa arrived and his brother Sulayman became caliph. The new caliph questioned Musa's policies in North Africa and al-Andalus and accused him of financial misdeeds. Musa paid a large fine and apparently reconciled with the caliph to the point that they decided to travel to Mecca together. Musa died along the way. On the other hand, Hugh Kennedy wrote that Musa's death occurred while he was "probably still in confinement" (Kennedy 2007, 314). Abd al-Aziz was assassinated and Abdallah replaced. Tariq was considered as a candidate for the governorship of al-Andalus, but, as explained by Abdulwahid Taha: "The Umayyad caliphate feared the increase of the Berber's influence in Spain" (Taha 1989, 101–102). Tariq's life in the Mashriq is unknown.

37. Yahya bn Yahya al-Laythi played a most important role in this achievement (see Berque 1974, 41–42).

38. Converts did not pay the *jizya* (head tax). There were also social restrictions placed on Jews and Christians. Nevertheless, conversions were also sincere and Islam enthusiastically embraced.

39. Charlemagne also had important relations with the Abbasids, notably Caliph Harun al-Rashid (see Einhard and Notker 1969).

40. For a detailed description of the mosque and its evolution over the centuries see also al-Makkari 2002, 1:217–231.

41. In Europe, only the Byzantine emperors of the powerful Macedonian dynasty matched Abd al-Rahman III's dynamism, culture, and capital city. Otto the Great (r. 936–973) inaugurated the Holy Roman Empire in Germany, but it did not project the sophistication of Umayyad Iberia or Byzantium. The contemporary Buyids (945–1060) dominating the Abbasid caliphate in West Asia and the Fatimids in North Africa (and West Asia) also exercised considerable power and influence.

42. According to Ibn Khaldun: "The fleets . . . constantly attacked each other's countries . . . and . . . thoroughly devastated coastal regions." He notes that under Abd al-

Rahman III, the Umayyad and Fatimid fleets each numbered about 200 vessels (Ibn Khaldun 1967, 2:40). The Muslims dominated the Mediterranean, although Byzantine power surged during the ninth and tenth centuries marked significantly by the reconquest of Crete.

43. Former French Ambassador Marcel Peyrouton, citing Jacques Risler, *La Civilisation arabe* (p. 80), reminds that four centuries later, King Charles V (the Wise) (r. 1337–1380) possessed, in comparison, about 1,000 books (Peyrouton 1966, 113). For further description of this scholarly caliph, see al-Makkari 2002, 2:169–170.

44. Despite the lack of central authority, individual Party Kingdom leaders demonstrated impressive political and military prowess. Ibn Khaldun notes that Mujahid al-Amiri from Denia seized Sardinia in 1014/1015 (Ibn Khaldun 1967, 2:41).

45. Maliki ulama, such as the jurist Abu al-Walid al-Baji (1012–1081), regarded Ibn Hazm as heterodox and polemically opposed him (Berque 1974, 42).

46. Nevertheless, Ibn Khaldun writes that there were travel restrictions: "The Spanish Umayyads . . . prevented their people from going abroad to fulfill the duty of the pilgrimage. They were afraid they might fall into the hands of the Abbasids. . . . The pilgrimage was (again) permitted . . . only after the Umayyad rule had come to an end" (Ibn Khaldun 1967, 2:100).

47. The Spanish scholar Julian Ribera computed that Abd al-Rahman III was 0.39 percent Arab and 99.61 percent Spanish! Wilfrid Knapp qualified that "intermarriage must have become the exception, except for those rich enough to own slaves" (Knapp 1977, 20).

48. Although the Isma'ilis had significant power, the Buyids had impressively asserted themselves in West Asia and dominated the Sunni Abbasids, who remained as figurehead caliphs. The Buyids were also Shi'a but *Ithna Ashari* ("Twelvers").

49. Jawhar, the commander of the successful Fatimid invasion of Egypt, was of Slavic background (see Walker 2002, 35) or Greek (*Encyclopedia of Islam*).

50. Norman A. Stillman writes: "Only after the Fatimid conquest of Egypt and the establishment of the caliphal seat of government in . . . Cairo in 972 did Egypt become a prominent center of Jewry, even as it became a political, economic, and cultural center of the Islamic World" (Stillman 1998, 201).

51. Jews also played an important social role in Fatimid Ifriqiya. For example, Ishaq bn Sulayman al-Isra'ili (d. 932), a renowned physician, lived in Qayrawan. In the tenth and early eleventh centuries (when the Fatimids especially prospered), European Jews, especially those in Italy, played important roles in commerce with North Africa and West Asia.

52. The revitalization of the Red Sea as a route to the Indian Ocean and South Asia negatively affected the rival Buyids and their Persian Gulf trade network.

53. Regarding the Italian trade, Karsh reminds: "Venice became the largest slave market in Central Europe, selling even Christian slaves to the Muslims" (Karsh 2007, 69).

54. The Norman Sicilian kings commissioned Fatimid artists to paint the stalactite ceiling of the Cappella Palatina in Palermo. Reflecting the Normans' transcultural proclivity, the building also features Byzantine mosaics (Hillenbrand 1976, 28).

55. Occasional persecutions and Arabization contributed to the gradual conversion of the Christian Egyptians to Islam (see Wilfong 1998, 183–187).

56. Nonetheless, Heinz Halm writes: "Even the reproach that al-Hakim was unpredictable and erratic and that he used to countermand instructions he had just given cannot be confirmed from the sources" (Halm 1997, 35). In general, Halm presents a sympathetic interpretation of al-Hakim and underscores his efforts to reconcile Sunni and Shi'a. Halm claims that al-Hakim's order to destroy Christian religious buildings, including the Church of the Holy Sepulchre, aimed "to contain the rise of anti-Christian sentiment among Muslims" and that "there was no general persecution of Christians, as has been falsely maintained time and time again" (ibid., 37). Abbas Hamdani contends: "What the hostile writers think was his insanity, may have been an enthusiastic purposefulness. What they call his fanaticism may have been his genuine desire to promote Ismailism which the Fatimid State had not up to now seriously taken up, because of the pressing problems of consolidation. . . . His cruelty and ruthlessness may have been his sincere attempts, however mistaken, to root out all corruption and meet the dangers of famine, plague and rebellion" (Hamdani 1962, 38–39).

57. During al-Hakim's reign, two Isma'ili missionaries named Darazi and Hamza ibn Ali proselytized the Mashriq in what would be southern Lebanon. They eventually projected al-Hakim as a "divine incarnation." When the caliph mysteriously disappeared (or was murdered), they interpreted his absence as a period of seclusion. The Druze emerged from this caliphal cult (see Esposito 2005, 47–48).

58. According to Yves Lacoste, the Fatimids were bibliophiles and their renowned library collection in Cairo had two million books, including 1,200 copies of al-Tabari's history (Lacoste 1969, 232).

59. Sadly, unpaid officials and soldiers pillaged the Dar al-'Ilm and other libraries in late 1068. Although many works survived, others perished, a loss comparable in context to that of the Hellenistic Museum and Library. A new Dar al-'Ilm opened in 1132, but a religious charge apparently circumscribed its collection and activity (see Halm 1997, 84–85). Fortunately, Ibn al-Tuwayr, a late Fatimid and early Ayyubid chronicler (as quoted by al-Maqrizi), mentions that collections were re-assembled. The Little (western) Palace had a large hall, which reportedly housed more than 200,000 books (Halm 1997, 91–92).

60. Hammad bn Bulukkin (r. 1014–1028) founded the dynasty. Although confronting formidable invaders, namely the Banu Hilal, the dynasty survived and flourished under al-Nasir (r. 1062–1088) and his son al-Mansur (r. 1088–1104).

61. Al-Mu'izz also patronized the renowned rival poets, who later reputedly became close friends, Ibn Rashiq and Ibn Sharaf.

62. The invading Bedouins did not establish their own states.

63. The principal Hassaniyya group in Western Sahara was the Awlad Dulaym. Hassaniyya also settled in the Sahel (Mauritania, Senegal, Mali, Niger). See Norris 1986.

64. In 1194, Saladin vainly requested naval help against Crusader strongholds such as Acre and Tyre from the powerful Almohads (see Chapter 4), but he did not receive it (see Ibn Khaldun 1967, 2:44–45). On the other hand, in the *Ibar,* it is mentioned that the Almohads eventually dispatched warships to aid the Ayyubids (Ibn Khaldun 1968–1969, 2:215–216) (see Chapter 4). (Furthermore, the rise of the Almohads dislocated Egypt's traditional access to West African gold. This was important since Saladin expended his gold resources.) The Crusaders actually achieved considerable success against Saladin and secured the Palestinian-Syrian littoral and Cyprus, despite the Third Crusade's failure to recapture Jerusalem.

65. Although Egypt in general prospered, Saladin's liberal financial policies led to a loss of revenue. Furthermore, war against the Crusaders and his efforts to eliminate the Fatimid cultural presence through new coinage as well as educational institutions resulted in repeated near state bankruptcies.

66. As mentioned earlier, the Fatimids had also established madrasas. Nevertheless, the Ayyubids especially promoted these educational institutions. Saladin and his successors also patronized religious foundations or *waqfs,* which in turn helped fund Sunni scholarship and education (see Chamberlain 1998, 231–232).

67. An impressive hospital had also been established earlier under Ahmad ibn Tulun.

68. Driven westward by the Mongol onslaught, the Khwarizmis (Khwarizmians) had invaded Iran and threatened Mesopotamia. Furthermore, the Seljuk Turks also menaced Ayyubid holdings in the north.

69. The Karimi probably organized during the Fatimid period.

70. With regard to Western Islamdom, the Umayyads in al-Andalus, the Fatimids in the Maghrib and Egypt, and the Abbasids (Buyids) in the Mashriq represented another example of Muslim trilateral power and parity. Concurrently, the Christian Byzantine Empire also exercised impressive and competitive authority and influence. In Western civilization's tenth century, for example, we can geopolitically conceive of a quadrilateral parity of power of highly sophisticated comparative and correlative states.

Chapter 4

1. Ibn Khaldun also recognized contemporary decline and decadence in the *Muqaddima* (see below).

2. The Barghawata (Berghawata) were Masmuda (others believe they were Zanata) Berbers, who adapted Khariji and Shi'i Islam, Christianity, Judaism, and animism to Berber culture. Their spiritual leader was Salih bn Tarif, who proclaimed himself a prophet in c. 744. Barghawata beliefs featured their own prophetic tradition and holy book (see Ibn Khaldun 1968–1969, 2:125–133). Regarded as heretics, they faced over centuries the hostility of the Idrisids, Umayyads, the Fatimids, and the Zirids. Richard B. Parker refers to their beliefs as a "Berberized Islam" (Parker 1981, 3–4).

3. Yusuf Ibn Tashfin is also often credited with the founding of Marrakesh.

4. The Almoravids subsequently implemented an impressive irrigation system at Fez.

5. Abun-Nasr states that the use of this title was meant "to stress the religious character of their authority" (Abun-Nasr 1987, xiv). The title also implied the authenticity of their belief.

6. The Hammadids expanded westward and took Tlemcen in 1102–1103.

7. Over the centuries the Saharan trade was renowned for its route from Sijilmasa to Taghaza (the site of a salt mine) to Walata. Along the way, salt would be traded for gold (see Chapter 1). Almoravid and later Sa'di (sixteenth century) incursions failed to monopolize the trade. The Portuguese also sought the source (Wanqara/Wangara) of West African gold. Al-Bakri provided an invaluable contemporary impression of Awdaghust (Awdaghost), a cosmopolitan city. Although Awdaghust's allegiance was to the animist kingdom of Ghana, there was a liberal spirit in the city. He noted its many mosques. Furthermore, the city attracted people from all over Ifriqiya and other important Muslim cities. He commended the cuisine of the women, which included *qataif* and other sweets (al-Bakri 1965, 158/300). Al-Bakri condemned the Almoravid raid on Awdaghust (ibid., 168/317). Furthermore, he also questioned Ibn Yasin's morality and practices (ibid., 169–170/318–320). Al-Bakri probably never visited Ghana and relied upon resources available to him in al-Andalus.

8. Renowned for his defense of Valencia against the Almoravids, El Cid actually spent more time serving Muslims rather than Christians. *The Poem of the Cid,* composed several decades after his death, illustrates the crusading ethos of the *Reconquista* (see *The Poem* 1975).

9. C. R. Pennell complemented Messier's interpretation: "The empire decayed not only because of a weakness at its centre, but because of the problems of its periphery. The effective division of the empire between its Saharan and Maghribi parts, from the late eleventh century onwards, deprived Marrakesh of manpower, although trade con-

tinued unfettered. Al-Andalus was a further drain both on manpower and finances" (Pennell 2003, 47–48).

10. The dissemination of Andalusian art and architectural styles in the Maghrib was marked notably by the "outrepassé, or horseshoe, and cusped, or foliated, arches which are the hallmarks of Moorish architecture to most westerners" (Parker 1981, 14). The Almoravids' buildings were built with brick and pisé-concrete.

11. Historians agree that Ibn Tumart's supposed meeting with al-Ghazali was apocryphal, but he was familiar with his ideas. On the other hand, Ibn Khaldun stated that Ibn Tumart had met al-Ghazali (Ibn Khaldun 1968–1969, 2:163).

12. According to Ibn Khaldun, Ibn Tumart "adopted the tenets of the Ash'arites [the followers of the scholastic al-Ash'ari] and criticized the Maghribis for having deviated from them by returning to the ancestral tradition of rejecting allegorical interpretation of explicit statements of the religious law, a rejection that leads to (anthropomorphism)" (Ibn Khaldun 1967, 1:471). Charles-André Julien agreed that Ibn Tumart was influenced by the Ashari(te) school of Sunni jurisprudence of "figurative" rather than literal interpretation (Julien 1970, 94).

13. The Muminids had a consultative council of fifty Almohad tribal members.

14. The Almoravids also simultaneously faced surging Christian offensives in al-Andalus.

15. Genoese attacks had weakened the Hammadids.

16. Abd al-Mu'min was preparing for a major Andalusian campaign before he died.

17. Ibn Khaldun notes that Ibn Tumart "set the precedent of coining square dirhams and engraving a square on the round dinar. He covered one side of the coins with the formulas: 'There is no God but God' and 'Praised be God,' and the other with a legend of several lines containing his name, (which was replaced by) his successors with their names" (Ibn Khaldun 1967, 2:57).

18. Ibn Khaldun wrote that the Almohad "fleet was of a size and quality never, to our knowledge, attained before or since." Saladin sent Karim bn Munqidh to lead an Ayyubid delegation to Ya'qub al-Mansur to ask for naval assistance. Reportedly, since the Ayyubids did not address the caliph as "Commander of the Faithful," they did not receive aid although they were "treated . . . with great kindness and honor" (Ibn Khaldun 1967, 2:43–46. In the *Ibar* it is mentioned, however, that al-Mansur eventually dispatched eighty ships that helped the Ayyubids prevent Christian attacks against Syria (Ibn Khaldun 1968–1969, 2:215–216). See Chapter 3.

19. See chapters in Bovill 1995 regarding European trade relations with Maghribi states.

20. Hafsid expansion significantly included the capture of Ceuta and Sijilmasa.

21. The Aragonese Christians were close allies of the Zayyanids—an illustration of

the complexity of political relations among the post-Almohadean Berber states. Catalonians also served the Hafsids.

22. Intra-dynastic perfidy also occasionally plagued the Hafsids and Marinids.

23. Abu'l-Hasan was known as the "Black Sultan" since his mother was an Abyssinian (Ethiopian). The Marinids were dynamic, but as C. R. Pennell points out, they "never solved the problem of having too few men, because the dynasty was essentially a tribal state" (Pennell 2003, 64). The viability of their state relied on "kinship and tribal alliances" rather than "political unity out of a common religious message" as with the Almoravids and Almohads (ibid., 75).

24. According to Marshall Hodgson: "The Spanish Christian hostility to Islam (and to Judaism) was monumental; a vast section of the population of the peninsula was driven out on refusal to convert to Christianity, including many of the most industrious classes. In the course of the following [sixteenth] century, the Muslims and the greater number of the Jews fled for asylum to Muslim territory by the hundred thousands, many of them perishing on the way" (Hodgson 1974, 3:117). Displaced Andalusian Muslims dispersed throughout the Maghrib. Important populations emerged in Fez, Tlemcen, Algiers, and especially Tunis.

25. On his way back to Morocco, Ibn Battuta stopped again in Tlemcen and visited the tomb of Abu Madyan (Ibn Battuta 1929, 307). Note that Ibn Khaldun was familiar with Ibn Battuta's travels and critically assessed them. An acquaintance warned Ibn Khaldun: "Be careful not to reject such information about the conditions of dynasties, because you have not seen such things yourself." Although contemporaries, Ibn Battuta and Ibn Khaldun apparently never met (see Ibn Khaldun 1967, 1:369–371).

26. Given Ibn Battuta's description, this is most likely the Maristan al-Mansuri (see Chapter 5).

27. Berque characterizes Ibn Khaldun's life as a "*vie vagabonde.*" See his critical analysis of Ibn Khaldun (Berque 1974, 48–64).

28. Muhammad ibn Arafa (al-Warghani [1316–1401]) was a renowned Maliki scholar teaching and writing in Tunis. When Ibn Khaldun returned to Tunis in late 1378 and resumed teaching, Ibn Arafa discovered his students gravitating to Ibn Khaldun's classes, which irritated the Maliki scholar. Ibn Arafa may have resented Ibn Khaldun's pluralist methodology (see Ibn Khaldun 1967, 1:lvii.).

29. Fez, Tlemcen, and Tunis had their great scholars, but their principal interest was theology. Science, literature, and history no longer received attention as before. In addition, the *Reconquista* resulted in the destruction of priceless Andalusian libraries.

30. To reiterate, all the dynasties mentioned in this chapter used Christian troops or had Christian allies. The historian Ibn Athir recounted that Christian troops betrayed the Almoravids and allowed the Almohads to seize Marrakesh (Ibn Khaldun 1968–1969, 2:577).

31. Although usually associated historiographically with the sixteenth century (see Chapter 5), the hardening religious and political positions in the Mediterranean world occurred earlier.

32. Historians question the sincerity of his conversion, and some believe that Hasan reconverted to Islam later in his life.

Chapter 5

1. The Il-Khanids attempted to secure European alliances against the Mamluks. See a fascinating account of an Il-Khanid diplomatic initiative led by a Nestorian Christian named Rabban Sawma (fl. thirteenth century) (Budge 1928). In 1271, English crusaders arrived in Acre and received some assistance from the Il-Khanids. Nevertheless, the strategic collaboration achieved little except to raise Mamluk geopolitical anxieties.

2. Although initially stopped in 1260, the Mongols surged again and seized Damascus in 1295 and occupied it for about a year.

3. Regarding the tribes, they often rested in Egypt before traversing the North African littoral.

4. At the time of the battle of Ayn Jalut, the Mamluks asked the Crusaders to join their forces. They chose to be neutral.

5. As Marco Polo and Ibn Battuta indicated in their writings, the Mongols encouraged transcultural relations and were receptive to foreign ideas as well as wares.

6. The distinction between privateer and pirate was often imperceptible.

7. The name "Barbarossa" technically refers to the red beard of one of them, Khayr al-Din, although Aruj has also been referred to as Barbarossa. Another brother, Ilyas, apparently perished at the hands of pirates in the Aegean. His death occurred before the Barbarossas' North African exploits.

8. The number of Greeks serving the Ottomans, including Turghut (see below), led Fernand Braudel to conclude that "in the first decades of the sixteenth century there began a fresh phase of Greek expansion over the whole of the Mediterranean" (Braudel 1972–1973, 1:116).

9. Andrew C. Hess reminds: "Each of the provinces maintained Ottoman institutions and a respect for the culture of the empire: this web of cultural and institutional ties gave substance to imperial unity in the age of decentralization" (Hess 1978, 112).

10. Bernard Lewis and others see this battle as blown out of proportion by Europeans—"a minor setback" since the Turks quickly launched new ships (Lewis 2002, 11). The Ottoman grand vizier stated that the empire could fit a fleet with "silver anchors, silken rigging and satin sails" (Lewis 1982, 43–44). The Italians were especially pleased with the results at Lepanto. Anti-Ottoman songs were made up, such as the one regarding Uluj Ali: "You have no more galleys, no more fleets to go a-raiding; all your men are slaves. Listen, swinish brute, if Heaven is closed to you, so is the Earth

and even Hell, peopled with beasts like yourself, will refuse you; where then will you roam?" (Heers 2003, 112). Andrew Wheatcroft wrote: "In Spanish political mythology, Lepanto symbolized the decisive shift of power in the struggle for control of the Mediterranean. This triumphalism was enhanced by the close association of the house of Habsburg with Lepanto. . . . Both Ottoman and Spanish naval power continued, but the process of aggressive expansion was halted" (see Wheatcroft 1995, 66). Miguel de Cervantes, the author of *The Adventures of Don Quixote,* severely injured his hand and arm at the battle. In 1575, an Algerian corsair captured him. Uluj Ali expedited his ransom and return to Spain. In *Don Quixote,* Uluj Ali ("Aluch Ali") is described as "a good moral man, [who] treated his prisoners with great humanity" (Cervantes 1966, 354). Of course, Christian corsairs also seized Muslim ships. As mentioned in Chapter 4, Hasan bn Muhammad was captured in 1519 and became renowned as Leo Africanus. Thus, the corsairs and their diverse crews and captives also played transcultural literary roles.

11. The Ottoman government respected the corsairs as leaders or consultants regarding naval affairs (see Imber 2002, 299).

12. The corsairs initially vied for power through their *ta'ifa,* or group of corsair captains.

13. The Lazarist, Trinitarian, Mercedarian, and Capuchin orders played important humanitarian and even political roles, notably in Algiers (and Tunis). See also "The Captive's Tale" in *Don Quixote* (Cervantes 1966, 345–380).

14. Wheatcroft reminds us of the vast Ottoman commercial network that included North Africa: "From the hinterland of Asia, Europe and North Africa flowed a torrent of goods: wool, leather, furs and cambric through Constantinople. . . . The empire stood astride all the traditional trade routes from East to West, and controlled a coastline of more than 3,000 miles, which encompassed some of the greatest ports of the Mediterranean" (Wheatcroft 1995, 71). In addition, see Braudel 1972–1973.

15. Reflecting transculturalism, Husayn bn Ali, the founder of the Husaynids, was an Ottoman of Greek descent whose mother was Ifriqiyan (Tunisian).

16. Furthermore, the conclusive expulsion of Moriscos from Spain in 1609 diffused Muslims and Jews throughout the Maghrib. The refugees found Tunis, Algiers, Fez, Marrakesh, and Rabat especially attractive.

17. The Levant refers to the eastern Mediterranean, specifically today's Lebanon, Israel, and parts of Syria and Turkey.

18. In the fourteenth century, the capital was moved from Kanem to Birni Ngazargamu in Bornu. The state is often called Bornu. As a polity, (Kanem-) Bornu lasted from the ninth to the twentieth century.

19. The Banu or Awlad Muhammad paid tribute to the Ottomans, especially if strong authority emanated from Tripoli; if not, they refused. The Banu/Awlad Muham-

mad earned revenues from Saharan caravans. Illustrating the breadth of the Sahara's political, economic, and social networks, a Moroccan sharif and shaykh, Muhammad al-Fasi, inaugurated a dynasty for this "tributary state" that existed from about the mid-sixteenth century to 1811, when Murzaq (Murzuq), the capital of Fezzan, was captured by Yusuf Qaramanli's troops. With his revenues falling in the Mediterranean, Yusuf hoped to recover financially by exploiting the wealth of Saharan commerce. According to Ali Abdullatif Ahmida, the assertive existence of the Banu/Awlad Muhammad and later the activity and resistance to colonialism of the Sanusiyya disclosed incipient state formation (thematic in Ahmida 1994).

20. Ahmad Qaramanli was a *kulughlu,* meaning his background was mixed Turkish-native.

21. Barbary refers to the littoral from Tripolitania to Morocco.

22. It is estimated that 10,000 slaves arrived in North African markets annually (Morsy 1984, 62). An inestimable number perished along the way.

23. Concurrently, Barbary attracted the operatic imaginations of Mozart in his *Abduction from the Seraglio* (1782) and Gioacchino Rossini's *Italian Girl in Algiers* (1813).

24. The founder of the Darqawiyya was Abu Hamid al-'Arabi al-Darqawi (1760–1823), who was born north of Fez. According to Magali Morsy, the emergence of the Darqawiyya reflected "a popular reaction against wealth and complexities of modern life and its irreligiousness" (Morsy 1984, 26). Abd al-Qadir al-Jilani (Jilali) (1077?–1166) was born in Iran and taught in Baghdad. He founded the Qadiriyya in the twelfth century. Its *tariqa* or ritual emphasized devotion, generosity, and asceticism. Founded by Ahmad al-Tijani (1738–1815) in Algeria, the Tijaniyya could not affiliate with other brotherhoods. Although the Tijaniyya often collaborated with the governing authority, the order occasionally took up arms against it and rival brotherhoods. It was egalitarian compared to the more aristocratic Qadiriyya. Its headquarters eventually was situated in Fez. Under the leadership of al-Hajj Umar (1794?–1864), the Tijaniyya aspired to establish a Muslim state in Senegambia and stoutly resisted French encroachments.

25. Europeans also raided the Western Saharan coast beginning in the early fifteenth century to the point that by the end of the century Spain planned to construct presidios. Nevertheless, by the Portuguese-Spanish Treaty of Cintra of 1509, Spain gave up its coastal claims except for Santa Cruz de Mar Pequeña (founded by Diego García de Herrera in 1468), which was assaulted by tribes and abandoned in 1524. (Spain's interest at this time was focused on the Western Hemisphere.) (See Mercer 1976, 75–90.) Although the Spanish left the Western Sahara, the memory of their presence persisted, as evinced in Chapter 6.

26. See also Ernest Gellner (1969) regarding the historic anthropological as well as political relationship between government and tribes, e.g., social structure ("segmentation") and the role of tribal proximity to urban areas and central government.

27. For details and tactics see Smith 2006, 39–42.

28. The sultan proposed that Spanish colonies with warmer climates be given to the Moroccans! (ibid., 139).

29. This was also a rationale for Portuguese expansion along the Atlantic coast. Al-Mansur also was known as al-Dhahabi, the Golden One.

30. For tactical details see Smith 2006, 111–114.

31. Moroccans remained in the western Sahel (the "Sudan" of West Africa) and ruled as independent pashas. They intermarried with Songhay families, forming their own ethnic group known as the Arma (see ibid., 154–155).

32. While politically unstable, this period also had a vital intellectual life. See Berque 1982.

33. Although Moroccan corsairs operated from the sixteenth to the early nineteenth centuries, privateers were especially active and adventuresome from the 1620s to the 1640s. In 1624, corsairs cruised off the coast of Newfoundland. The Rabat-Salé fleet numbered between forty and fifty ships in 1637. Austrian warships deterred renewed privateering by bombarding Larache in 1828 (see Pennell 2003, 94–96, 114).

34. *Abid* can mean slaves or servants, or from the Moroccan context, Black Africans. (Mawlay Isma'il was half-Black.) Historians approximate their numbers from 70,000 to 150,000. Statistics are especially challenging regarding the trans-Saharan slave trade. Ralph Austen's study is particularly noteworthy. His approximations, derived from "direct and indirect evidence," estimated that trans-Saharan routes exported 9,387,000 slaves to North Africa from the seventh century to the end of the nineteenth century (given estimated mortality [20 percent] and "desert edge retention" [5 percent], approximately 7,450,000 slaves arrived) (Austen 1979, 66). Morocco and Egypt especially imported slaves for their militaries. In the modern period, "Egypt, Tunisia, and Algeria seem to have received most of their black servile population as secondary imports from neighboring North African countries" (ibid., 37).

35. As Magali Morsy pointed out, "'Alawi rule and policy had developed on the basis of two apparently contradictory principles: the development of a strong army to control Morocco, expel the Christians, and ward off the threat of foreign invasions, and, at the same time, the need to obtain from Europe the wherewithal to do this, both in terms of revenue and equipment. The dynasty was, in fact, able to reconcile the two by well-nigh absolute royal control over foreign affairs" (Morsy 1984, 68). The same observation could be made regarding the Alawis' dynastic predecessors, the Sa'dis.

36. The idea of seizing Egypt was a popular one and Napoleon had apparently entertained the idea since 1797, given the new French geopolitical and economic position attained in Italy. Talleyrand included Egypt in his plan for a revived French colonial policy (Dykstra 1998, 116; Cole 2007, 12–14). Great Britain also had a strategic plan dating from 1795 regarding seizing Alexandria, Cairo, and Suez. As a counterpoise to the

French invasion, the British set up a base in 1799 on the island of Perim, in the Bab el-Mandeb strait, leading later to its occupation of Aden (see Morsy 1984, 77).

37. Stuart Harten viewed the Egyptian campaign as "part of a much larger process of Continental and overseas expansion that began with the Directory. The desire to compensate for the loss of Saint-Domingue and challenge Britain's hegemony of the seas was what provoked France into a desperate series of colonial and imperial ventures" (Harten 2003, 40–41).

38. Napoleon's attempt to co-opt Egyptian leaders included the formation of an advisory "Diwan." The French employed Copts in important financial and bureaucratic positions, which raised fears of a Christianization of Egypt (see Cole 2007, 103.) Juan Cole assessed: "Behind a façade of lawmaking and reasonableness visible in Bonaparte's correspondence crouched the grim realities of corruption, power, and terror" (ibid., 104).

39. During the French Enlightenment, the Baron de Montesquieu considered the Ottoman sultan despotic, while Voltaire used his play *Mahomet* as a vehicle to attack institutionalized religion, although he admitted his portrayal was unfair. Bonaparte also criticized Voltaire's perspective on the Prophet (Cole 2007, 141). Regarding the French expedition, Juan Cole reminds that the ulama as well as Europeans criticized superstitious Islamic rites. Furthermore, "bilingual Egyptians of the middle strata were probably the chief interpreters to the French of the meaning of popular religious practices, and they probably transmitted some of their own disgust with them to the Europeans. Far from being a sole creation of European Orientalism, this image of popular Islam was a joint production" (ibid.).

40. A second revolt occurred in March 1800 (see below).

41. Napoleon left Egypt in command of General Jean-Baptiste Kléber. Kléber concluded a convention with the British and Turks in January 1800 to allow the evacuation of his army from Egypt. The British broke the agreement and hostilities resumed. A major Egyptian revolt broke out in March 1800 and General Kléber was assassinated in June 1800. Egyptian resistance continued, compounded by an outbreak of the plague. The French army finally disembarked in September 1801. Juan Cole pointed out that Napoleon's Egyptian expedition influenced his future policies more than historians have appreciated. For example, Napoleon's negotiation with the papacy, producing the Concordat of 1801, evoked his conciliation with the Egyptian ulama. In addition, his self-perception as a sultan in Egypt would be reimagined as Napoleon elevated himself as an emperor in 1804. In this sense, he was "Ottomanized" (see Cole 2007, 244; reiterated by Cole at the New American Foundation, 24 August 2007, Booktv.com, C-Span 2).

42. There were only two archaeologists. Most of the scholars were engineers (see Russell 2001, 11–12).

43. The *Description* was an exceptional work of scholarship featuring, as Stuart

Harten details, "some 7,000 pages of text, 837 copper engravings, and over 3,000 il-lustrations in total. Judged both by its encyclopedic pretensions and its monumental size, the *Description* provided a powerful ideological justification for what was ulti-mately an unsuccessful colonial venture" (Harten 2003, 34).

44. Maya Jasanoff observed that the *Description*'s frontispiece featuring "confis-cated antiquities" was framed by the names of Napoleon's victories in Egypt and "car-touches containing a star and a bee, Napoleon's personal emblems. This is not just Orientalism. It is Bonapartism, French national and imperial ambition rolled into one. Considered as a whole, the *Description* is a monumental attempt to compensate for loss—a vicarious collection and an intellectual one" (Jasanoff 2005, 222).

45. Al-Jabarti denounced those who revolted in October 1798 as well as the French repression of the insurrection (al-Jabarti 1975, 93–108).

46. On the other hand, Malik Bennabi and especially Egypt's Muhammad Abduh (see Chapter 6) welcomed that interaction and believed in modernism's compatibility with their religious beliefs.

47. For example, Marseilles merchants impeded peaceful Muslim and Jewish trad-ers. Eventually the French dominated the western Mediterranean, including the trade between Tunis and Iberia (Valensi 1977, 58–59).

48. Bernard Lewis states that a "factor which would certainly have discouraged the Muslims from traveling in western Europe was the ferocious intolerance of its rulers and peoples. . . . The fate of the Jews in medieval Europe would not have encouraged followers of other non-Christian religions to settle or even travel in these lands" (Lew-is 1982, 91). In addition, European merchants, such as those in Marseilles, prevented Muslim commercial enterprise, which threatened their economic interest. Thus, con-stricted contact and commerce created mutual misperceptions tainting transcultural relations.

49. Valensi also list travelers' accounts and other memoirs that contributed to this epistemic shift (1977, xxi–xxii).

50. On the other hand, Morocco was the first country to recognize the sovereignty of the United States in 1777. The bilateral Treaty of Peace and Friendship concluded in 1786 remains the longest unbroken treaty in American history. There was an innocu-ous "war" between the United States and Morocco in 1802–1803, another chapter in the "Barbary Wars" (Parker 2004, 156–157). Relations with the Tunis Regency were usu-ally cordial except when Hamuda Bey threatened war over compensation regarding the capture of a Tunisian naval vessel and two prizes during the American blockade of Tripoli. A show of American force in Tunis's harbor ended the crisis. To reinforce cordial relations, Hamuda Bey dispatched an ambassador to Washington. As Richard Parker notes, Suleiman Mellimelli was "the first ambassador from the Muslim world . . . and was an instant social success" (Parker 2004, 152–154).

Chapter 6

1. The allied fleet subsequently threatened Tunis and Tripoli.

2. The *Description de l'Egypte,* which began publication nearly ten years after the French withdrew from Egypt, reinforced this altruistic perspective.

3. According to Fred H. Lawson, Muhammad Ali's military campaigns had important domestic political ramifications. The government's conscription of agricultural workers "weakened Egypt's larger agricultural landholders" by controlling the numbers of laborers available in the sector and thereby "precluded the reemergence of a landed military elite" (Lawson 1992, 141). Of course, "Egyptianizing," as well as modernizing, the armed forces had momentous consequences, creating social opportunities for promotion and education.

4. A gunpowder factory was constructed on Rawda Island. Egyptians extracted saltpeter, necessary for gunpowder, by cooking refuse (al-Jabarti 1994, 4:360). This was another illustration of Muhammad Ali's intention to become as autarkic as possible.

5. Muhammad Ali urged Constantinople to recognize Greek independence in principle (Fahmy 1998, 2:159). Concurrently, Britain and France sought to increase their influence within Egypt. Maya Jasanoff perceived: "In a paradoxical twist, Britain and France found themselves joining forces to contain Muhammad Ali outside Egypt, while each was working to strengthen its own position—along with the pasha's—within Egypt" (Jasanoff 2005, 277).

6. Referring to Muhammad Ali in 1817, al-Jabarti concluded: "The ruler had no vocation other than exerting his energy, his mind, and his wits to acquire money and profit by curtailing people's livelihoods, by restricting and monopolizing all their means of subsistence" (al-Jabarti 1994, 4:379).

7. The British were also concerned about Muhammad Ali's intentions in Yemen, where instability led to an Egyptian expedition in 1833. At risk, in part, was the coffee trade (at Mocha), a particular British commercial interest (Ibrahim 1998, 202–204). By the Treaty of London of 1840, Muhammad Ali had lost his possession of Syria, Crete, and the Hijaz. On the other hand, the pashalik (position of pasha) would be hereditary.

8. For British assistance against the Alids, the Ottomans agreed to the Treaty of Balta Liman (Anglo-Turkish Convention) of 1838, which significantly reduced import tariffs throughout Ottoman territories, including Egypt. Specifically, the agreement forced a reduction of tariffs to 8 percent and prohibited state monopolies, thereby undercutting Muhammad Ali's development plans (Owen 1993, 115). The Anglo-Turkish Commercial Convention of 1841 underscored the Ottoman Empire's and Egypt's peripheral, subordinate status. British "free trade" actually meant protecting British global commercial monopoly given the unmatched output of its factories.

9. The pasha left office in 1848 because of his failing health.

10. Marsot wrote that Muhammad Ali "had given the . . . fallah [peasant], who fought in his armies, a sense of pride at having beaten the Ottomans, and a sense of achievement that went a long way to giving him a positive self-identity even though he hated the army and sought to get out of conscription" (Marsot 2007, 77). Anouar Abdel-Malek's erudite study details the period from 1805 to 1892, an era of remarkable transcultural encounter, as crucially important in defining a modern Egyptian identity (see Abdel-Malek 1969).

11. This rivalry also arose in Tunisia (see below).

12. Zachary Karabell describes de Lesseps as "a potent combination of vision, pragmatism, and will" (Karabell 2004, 7).

13. The "guest list" also included Emile Zola, Eugène Fromentin, and Henrik Ibsen. The famous Algerian Emir Abd al-Qadir also attended (see below).

14. By this time, Egypt's importance as a commercial partner had grown regarding the British economy. From 1848 to 1860, Egypt rose from twenty-sixth to twelfth place as an export market and from 1854 to 1860, its position as an import supplier changed from tenth to sixth (Owen 1993, 116).

15. In 1881, there were more than 90,000 Europeans in Egypt compared to 8,000 to 10,000 in 1838 (ibid., 117).

16. Charles Edwin Wilbour, an American Egyptologist, saddened by the destruction in Alexandria, came upon "a young Englishman" who asked "why there were so few marks of fire. . . . I said: 'Why, you goose, this was knocked down by your shells; why should it show any signs of fire?' He seemed convinced. Years will pass, I think, before Alexandria will be rebuilt" (Wilbour 1936, 179–180).

17. Cromer achieved solvency "albeit at the expense of Egyptian industry, and had transformed agriculture into a monoculture, cotton, to feed the mills of Lancashire" (Marsot 2007, 93).

18. Cromer's attitude toward the East was probably affected by his linguistic limitations. Although he had a "fair acquaintance with Turkish," he was not an Arabist (Cromer 1908, 1:7).

19. The contract dated from 1796.

20. Given Paris's close relations with Cairo, the French entertained a plan of having Muhammad Ali seize or later administer Algiers (see Abun-Nasr 1987, 250).

21. Reflecting upon France's imperial atavism, as well as its recent Egyptian experience, Maya Jasanoff wrote: "Arguably, France would never have moved to conquer Algeria had it not already established itself, in some sense, in Egypt. To an extent, the invasion of Algeria resembled Napoleon's invasion of Egypt: both were not new projects, but extensions of something old. Here was vivid testament to the strength and persistence of French imperial ambitions in the East" (Jasanoff 2005, 286).

22. Abd al-Qadir believed that the French would allow his exile to the Mashriq. In-

stead, he was imprisoned in France until freed by Louis Napoleon in 1852. He subsequently lived in Bursa (Turkey) until 1855 and then Damascus until his death in 1883. In 1860, he reportedly saved twelve thousand Christians in Damascus during sectarian violence, earning him official and popular French esteem. He also attended the opening of the Suez Canal. Although there were occasional rumors of Abd al-Qadir playing a client role for Napoleon III in the Mashriq or even in Algeria, the emir preferred writing and study. His book *Rappel à l'intelligent* (1858) illustrated his interests in philosophy, religion, ethnology, philology, and history. Despite his resistance to French colonialism, the exiled Abd al-Qadir hoped to facilitate mutual understanding between Muslims and Europeans. His writings also suggest an incipient Islamic modernism.

23. The "French Possessions" in North Africa became officially known as "Algérie" in 1839.

24. Julia Clancy-Smith especially recounts the subtle complexity of Algerian-French colonial resistance and concludes that "rebellion and uneasy accord" were equally significant and "intimately related" (Clancy-Smith 1994, 254).

25. In 1892, Jules Ferry, a principal advocate of French imperialism, recognized the reality that Algeria was not assimilative despite being part of France: "Algeria is not the extension of France[;] it is a colony" (Peyrouton 1966, 199). According to Peyrouton, Islam prevented French assimilation (ibid., 268), although colonialism's inherent divisive discrimination obviously played a determining role as well as the persistent resistance of the Algerians.

26. Historians contend that the term *pied-noir* may have been derived from the Algerians referring to the settlers' shoes. The term also refers to the French settlers in Tunisia and Morocco; but it is most often identified with the French of Algeria.

27. A hectare equals 2.47 acres.

28. The transformative effect of colonialism on the land and especially its social and economic consequences is reminiscent of Banu Hilal's invasion and subsequent introduction of transhumance (see Chapter 3).

29. Although *Black Skin, White Masks* was about the social conditions in the French Antilles, Fanon's subsequent writings about Algeria mirrored these ideas. He wrote in *Wretched of the Earth* that colonialism was "violence in its natural state" (Fanon 1968, 61). The colonized incurred colonial violence in many ways. The psychoexistential dilemma evinced a metaphysical violence against the colonized.

30. There were also Protestant missionaries active in Kabylia.

31. The Catholic Church beatified Father de Foucauld in November 2005.

32. The "Great Game" principally referred to the Eastern Question (see below). By this time, European diplomacy's "game" was "global," thereby "greater."

33. Given the diversity of the beylik's economy, privateering was not a significant economic variable.

34. Support of France also was a means to assert Tunisian independence from the Ottoman Empire.

35. Julia Clancy-Smith details how the beylik's deft diplomacy was also exercised on the shores of the Mediterranean, where the government leased or loaned seaside villas as "an astute stratagem for maintaining alliances and politically savvy ties" (Clancy-Smith 2008, 7).

36. In 1896, Sadiqi graduates and liberal Protectorate officials established the Khalduniyya (named after Ibn Khaldun) to complement students' Islamic studies at Zaytuna with a European-based education. Of course, the curricular objectives of both institutions differed as they competed for the loyalties of Tunisians.

37. The Eastern Question dealt with the weakening position of the Ottoman Empire and the growing strength of Imperial Russia. Great Britain feared that the eastern Mediterranean, crucial to its links to India, could be threatened by Russian ambitions. Thus, the British supported the Ottomans, as demonstrated during the Crimean War (1853–1856).

38. Gibraltar was added to the British Empire as a result of the War of Spanish Succession (1700–1714).

39. Al-Saffar mentions Egyptians "sent [to France] by Muhammad Ali to learn the sciences" (al-Saffar 1992, 179).

40. The Spanish claimed a swath of land between Cape Bojador and Cape Blanco. A Franco-Spanish agreement in October 1904 defined Spanish borders regarding southern Morocco and Rio de Oro.

41. Sultan Mawlay Hasan attempted to neutralize the Spanish by appointing a Sufi shaykh, Ma-l-Aynayn, to be his representative in the Sahara. The post-colonial government would claim that such an action represented traditional Moroccan sovereignty over Western Sahara.

42. The government also permitted al-Raysuni to assume the governorship of Asila.

43. Roosevelt won the Nobel Peace Prize for his successful mediation, ending the Russo-Japanese War of 1904–1905. His prestige expedited his diplomatic efforts regarding the "First Moroccan Crisis." The Act placed Moroccan finances and internal security under de facto joint French-Spanish control, reminiscent of the Egyptian and Tunisian pre-colonial experiences.

44. Opposition to Morocco's territorial disintegration included that of Abd al-Kabir al-Kittani, the founder of the Kittaniyya order. Al-Kittani initially supported Abd al-Hafidh until the latter agreed to abide by the Act of Algeciras, in order to obtain European recognition of his sultanate. Al-Kittani's hostility toward Abd al-Hafidh resulted in the shaykh's execution in 1909.

45. A treaty in 1912 between the protectorate powers delineated the Spanish territories.

46. Al-Sanusi (1787–1859) inaugurated the Sanusiyya in 1837. Its *tariqa* aimed to purify Islam and promote Muslim unity. The shaykh was more of a reflective *mujadid* than a rebellious *mujahid*. Nevertheless, given the lack of central or strong government in Libya, the Sanusiyya inevitably asserted a political as well as religious role.

47. Italy was already well invested in Tripoli. According to Claudio G. Segrè: "Italians operated the largest commercial bank, and in 1907 Italian shipping lines controlled 45 percent of the commerce entering the port" (Segrè 1974, 41; see also Ahmida 1994, 105). During the colonial period, Italy identified its North African territory with the ancient name Libya (see Chapter 7).

48. By this time, the Ottomans were in terrible political condition. The Young Turks had taken over the government in 1908 and begun modernizing reforms, but their initiatives also created problems, especially among subject peoples. Infused with intense nationalism, the Balkan states aimed to realize territorial ambitions and redeem irredentist populations at the expense of the Ottoman Empire, which contributed to the Balkan Wars of 1912–1913. The Arabs were also restless in West Asia and had their territorial ambitions and aspired for independence from the empire. The Ottomans could not afford to mount a determined defense against the Italians—a territory of only nominal value. By the Treaty of Lausanne (1912), the Ottomans preserved a spiritual rather than secular authority in Libya, which had serious political ramifications. Wary of alienating Muslims, the Italians allowed the sultan to appoint the qadi of Tripoli. It was not until the Treaty of Lausanne (1923) that Turkey ended its spiritual and indirect political presence in Libya (see Khadduri 1963, 12).

49. Besides the aforementioned *Description de l'Egypte* (see Chapter 5), Edward Said points out Edward William Lane's *Account of the Manners and Customs of the Modern Egyptians* (1836) as another salient Orientalist work. Referring to contemporary "Egyptomania" in films (e.g., *The Prince of Egypt* [1998], *The Mummy* [1999], and *The Mummy Returns* [2001]) as an "offshoot" of Orientalism, Tayseer Gomaa writes: "In the postcolonial age, the stereotyping of Egypt in visuals has gone beyond . . . merely tying the country to the magnificent accomplishments of its ancient civilization. It has reached the point where it involves trivializing these accomplishments by binding them to a picture of an Egypt that is seen as merely a source for provoking terror and fear. As for Egyptians, they are seen as unjust and cruel slavemongers in antiquity, and as bringing up the rear in the parade of culture in modern times" (Gomaa 2002, 101–102; see also MacDonald and Rice 2003). Consult also AlSayyad, Bierman, and Rabbat 2005.

50. Saharan explorers, namely Heinrich Barth in the 1850s, Alexandrine Tinné and Gustav Nachtigal in the 1860s, and Erwin von Barry in the 1870s, also contributed to a growing interest in North Africa and eventually an imperialist enterprise, e.g., Paul Flatters's expeditions in 1880–1881 (see Porch 1984; de Villiers and Hirtle 2002).

51. On the other hand, Zeynep Çelik argues: "Both Isma'il Pasha and [Ottoman]

Sultan Abdülaziz used the opportunity to convince European powers of their commitment to modernization and hence their desire to become part of the European system. Their presence made a difference vis-à-vis the public, shattering romantic beliefs and demystifying certain stereotypes" (Çelik 1992, 36).

52. Zachary Karabell noted: "When Europeans examined the cultures of the world in the nineteenth century, they avoided looking themselves in the mirror" (Karabell 2003, 53). He added: "The states of the West were expanding unchecked throughout the globe. They had no need to grapple with the cultural complexities of their adversaries. The same was not true on the other side" (ibid., 54). Edmund Burke III links sociological studies to the political environment in colonial Morocco (see Burke 1972, 175–199). Dale F. Eickelman states that works on Morocco prior to and in the early period of the protectorate "constitute one of the best collections of colonial ethnography to be found anywhere. One reason for the quality of this research, in contrast to most of that conducted in Algeria, was a conscious decision on the part of the French, at least in principle, to preserve and enhance indigenous institutions" (Eickelman 1998, 33). To Berque, imperialism made the colonized an "object rather than a subject of history" (Berque 1964b, 163).

53. Dislocation and pauperization forced North Africans to emigrate to find work. In particular, large Maghribi communities arose in France, resulting in a hybrid society suspended between North African and European cultures. By 1954, there were 400,000 Algerians living in France. Usually considered as alienated communities, these communities are viewed in the Conclusion as precious populations poised strategically at social and cultural interstices that could enhance mutual understanding by their ability to bridge between traditions and heritages.

54. For example, the construction of the first Aswan Dam in 1902 had several important consequences, as Michael Sorkin explained: "By stabilizing the river's banks, not simply was Egyptian agriculture rescued from the historic cycle of flood and drought, but extensive urban development along the shore was enabled, leading to a westerly shift in Cairo's center of gravity away from the medieval city to the east of the floodplain" (Sorkin 2001, 45). Baron Edouard Empain, a Belgian urban developer, was responsible for the construction of the Cairo Electric Railway and the city of Heliopolis north of the capital (eventually incorporated into it). Sorkin notes that Empain hoped "to create a largely self-sufficient town in the desert with both a lavish resort component as well as an industrial base. With this in mind, a wide range of housing types was planned, although their internal layouts were essentially European. The architecture—arcaded and elaborate—achieves a kind of orientalist sublime, and the generous apartments in the original buildings are much sought after today" (48–49).

55. In a collection of essays entitled *L'Eté* (Summer), Albert Camus noted the transcultural character of Algeria, but not necessarily its history: "The softness of Algiers is

rather Italian. The cruel glare of Oran has something Spanish about it. Constantine, perched high on a rock above the Rummel Gorges, is reminscent of Toledo. But Spain and Italy overflow with memories, with works of art and exemplary ruins. . . . The cities I speak of, on the other hand, are towns without a past" (Camus 1970, 143). Although an admirer of Camus's writings, Ahmed Taleb Ibrahimi criticized his lack of historical consciousness (Taleb [Ibrahimi] 1966, 76–77; for Camus and Algeria's War of Liberation see Le Sueur 2001, 87–127). Pierre Claverie, a *pied-noir* who eventually became bishop of Oran in the post-colonial period, reflected how he grew up in a "colonial bubble" without recognizing the colonized other. The Algerian War of Liberation "burst the bubble" (Pérennès 2000, 32). Claverie reflected during his ordination as bishop of Oran that "I had lived like a foreigner throughout my youth" (J'ai vécu en étranger toute ma jeunesse) (ibid., 109). As Fanon emphasized in his writings, colonialism also had a deleterious effect upon the colonialist. See also Rivet 2002.

Chapter 7

1. The Spanish Sahara's decolonization will be covered in Chapter 9. It represents an incomplete decolonization, which remains a major post-colonial problem.

2. To Berque, colonialism involved the "dispossession" of the colonized's personal and natural environment (Berque 1964b, 105–106). Thus, decolonization was a process of manifold repossession. He spoke of the need of countries "recovering" from colonialism and about the need to rediscover their "nature" as well as their culture (*renaturer leur culture et reculturer leur nature*) (Berque 2001, 2:349). Bennabi referred to "colonization" as "a regression in human history" (Bennabi 1949, 90). To Bennabi, whose ideas are very similar to Berque's regarding colonialism and decolonization, colonizability was not only compelled from the "exterior," but also impelled by the "colonizables'" indolent "interior."

3. The British, apprehensive over the Ottoman call for a jihad, attempted to portray the protectorate status as a stage toward independence, but according to M. W. Daly, there was a fundamental ulterior motive: "Protectorate status was a wartime improvisation to cut Egypt adrift from the Ottoman empire without inciting Egyptians with the prospect of tightened British control" (Daly 1998a, 2:246).

4. British officials in Egypt, notably Reginald Wingate and General Edmund Allenby, recognized the need to negotiate and compromise with the Egyptian nationalists but not the obdurate British government, which was concurrently embroiled in Irish decolonization.

5. For studies of Egyptian women during the nationalist and post-colonial periods, see Badran 1995 and Baron 2005.

6. The British blamed Zaghul for the continuing violence and deported him in 1921 to the Seychelles Islands, where he remained in exile until the following year.

7. Although the continuing British presence limited independence, there were important cultural consequences. Independence "allowed Egypt to keep the entire contents of Tutankhamun's [recently discovered] tomb, pass far stricter controls on exporting antiquities, begin Egyptianizing the museums and Antiquities Service, emphasize pharaonic history in the schools, found a state university, and open programs to train Egyptian Egyptologists, classicists, and specialists in Islamic art history" (Reid 2002, 293).

8. To Afaf Lutfi al-Sayyid Marsot, Zaghul's political influence "was not always for the better. He had introduced a system of patronage into political life, and a system of violence and of public demonstrations as a weapon against the opposition. Through his autocracy he had alienated the most brilliant brains, and had set up a personal form of rule" (Marsot 2007, 102). As Marsot recognized, Zaghul's political legacy continues to affect political life in contemporary Egypt.

9. See Berque 1972 for particularly insightful observations, especially "As Others See Us," 466–483.

10. Hind Nawal established *al-Fatah* (The Young Woman), the first women's newspaper, in 1892.

11. Mahfouz's *Thulathiyya* (Trilogy) recounts the ferment of the interwar years, although it was published in 1956–1957.

12. The monarchy was officially abolished in June 1953. There were occasional insurrections resulting in intermittent periods of independence during the Persian era.

13. The Baghdad Pact or CENTO (Central Treaty Organization) was meant to complement the North Atlantic Treaty Organization (NATO) (1949) and the Southeast Asia Treaty Organization (SEATO) (1954).

14. In deference to Eden, Egypt printed a stamp with his face on it after the Anglo-Egyptian Treaty was concluded in 1936. Eden served as foreign minister in Winston Churchill's cabinet during World War II. He identified Nasser with Hitler, a misreading of the actual historical conditions regarding Egyptian national aspirations. British troops had left their bases in June, as stipulated by the aforementioned 1954 agreement.

15. The complicated World War I period was also marked by factional strife. The Sanusis also tried to expand their influence and power in Tripolitania in 1916, but Ramadan al-Suwayhili's forces defeated them.

16. Al-Suwayhili asserted his independence by declaring a republic at Misrata. Although not recognized, it foreshadowed the events of 1919.

17. Azzam later became the first secretary-general of the Arab League.

18. Separate Fundamental Laws were issued for Tripolitania in June and Cyrenaica in October 1919. Governor Giacomo di Martino attempted to implement these liberal initiatives, which aimed to establish indirect rule. Regional incompatibility and na-

tive national aspirations prevented di Martino's pursuit of a coherent colonial policy. After his death in late 1921, Italian policy hardened and headed toward pacification even before the Fascist takeover in 1922.

19. Nevertheless, al-Mukhtar's legacy remained inspirational (see Nassar ad Boggero 2008, 201–217).

20. Mirroring Algeria's colonial administration, Balbo intended that Libya's interior be under military rule. The northern region would be, like Algeria's, assimilated as part of the nation.

21. Plans sought to restore the Roman archaeological sites of Leptis Magna and Sabratha (Pitock 2005, 103). Land was cleared in Tripoli to highlight the Arch of Marcus Aurelius (Fuller 2000, 134). Archaeology deeply interested Balbo (Nickerson 1968, 127). Derived from the ancient Greek name for the people of the region (see Chapter 1), the name "Libya" was assigned to the colony during the colonial period.

22. Although the colonial government did not intend to raise the colonized's status to full citizenship with equal civic and economic opportunities, Balbo insisted on cultural sensitivity, prohibiting, for example, the sale of alcoholic drinks during Ramadan (Abun-Nasr 1987, 402).

23. Despite colonial ambitions, only 12 percent of Libya's Italian population directly engaged in agrarian life (Hourani 1991a, 323).

24. Balbo perished when Italian anti-aircraft fire mistakenly shot down his plane. He opposed the German alliance.

25. While under British occupation during the war, Italian settlers agitated for the postwar resumption of Italian rule. The creation of an anti-British "Republican Fascist Party" in 1944 led to arrests. Of course, Libyans also opposed the reestablishment of Italian rule (Khadduri 1963, 82).

26. There were Libyan nationalist groups exiled in Egypt, which promoted a variety of positions including support for/rejection of a Sanusi monarchy and Pan-Arabism (see Baldinetti 2003, 80–82).

27. Driss Maghraoui estimated "roughly 63,748 Moroccans participated" in World War I and that the "percentage of recruitment . . . was more than 6 percent" of the male population (Maghraoui 2004, 7). The Germans also hoped to incite desertion among the Allied Muslim troops by propagandizing the idea of an Ottoman-proclaimed jihad against France. Nevertheless, the support of Sultan Mulay Yusuf and the brotherhoods for France decisively influenced recruitment (ibid., 10–16).

28. Muhammad Abduh visited Tunisia in 1884–1885 and 1903.

29. *Dustur* means constitution in Arabic.

30. Abd al-Karim had great success against the Spanish. At the battle of Annual in 1921 he overwhelmed a Spanish army, inflicting approximately 15,000 casualties. He also obtained ransoms for captives. According to Allal al-Fasi, the renowned Moroc-

can nationalist and Salafi, the Rif National Program calling for independence and a constitutional system was "the goal of all Moroccan nationalists since the beginning of the twentieth century" (al-Fasi 1954, 105). Abd al-Karim also advocated Salafi educational goals in Rifi schools and exploited the labor of Spanish prisoners-of-war to build roads and a telephone system (Pennell 2003, 146).

31. To Gellner: "This decree triggered off modern Moroccan nationalism" (Gellner 1969, 18). In addition, there was the fear that the decree represented a "step in the attempt to convert the Berbers from Islam" (ibid., 18–19). The decree arguably related to "a genuine element of romanticism" in French protectorate policy, "a concern with the preservation of tribal institutions" (ibid., 23–24).

32. According to al-Fasi, the Salafiyya "aimed at the reform of the individual as a prerequisite for the perfection of society. The success of the movement, it was realized, hinges upon the acceptance of an 'open mind' towards innovations and their critical evaluation" (al-Fasi 1954, 114).

33. Under the mandate system, mandatory powers were required to publish reports regarding their activities in the mandates, which resulted in an internationally monitored and tempered "mandate colonialism."

34. Illustrating a fractured nationalist elite, Mohamed Hassan Ouazzani, hoping to play a leading role in the National Party, founded the Hizb al-Amal al-Watani (National Action Party). At this time, the principal nationalists in the Kutlat/National Party were Ahmad Belafrej, Omar Abdeljalil, Allal al-Fasi, and Mohammad al-Fasi and his wife Malika.

35. Like other Maghribis, Moroccans heroically served in the French army during World War II (see Gershovich 2000, 185–186, 192–193).

36. Writing in early 1947, Berque perceived that the "dynasty aspires to independence." He considered the protectorate as administratively anachronistic to changing social and historical realities—a "legal exoticism" (Berque 2001, 3:46).

37. Concurrently, Europeans founded Présence Française, a terrorist group targeting Moroccans, which aimed to preserve the French establishment in Morocco.

38. According to Lorna Hahn, the Berber demonstrations or show of force outside of Rabat and Fez supposedly against Sultan Muhammad were caused by "reasons given them [which] ranged from receiving vaccinations to partaking in a great festival" (Hahn 1960, 93).

39. Although simplified here, Algerian nationalism like that of other North African movements was complex and competitive and sought to appropriate representative authority and discursive authenticity. See McDougall 2006.

40. Others estimate the fatalities at 15,000 to 20,000. There were 103 European deaths.

41. The MTLD is often referred to as the PPA/MTLD or MTLD/PPA. The Parti du Peuple Algérien (PPA) was a Messalist party that the French banned in 1939.

42. Messali Hadj founded the MNA in December 1954. The MNA and FLN also competed and conflicted in France. Hugh Roberts reminds that the FLN was not a party but "a political movement fighting a revolutionary war for nationalist purposes which from the outset was at odds with all pre-existing political organizations in Algeria and determined to outflank and eliminate them" (Roberts 1993, 118).

43. Dating especially from the private meeting between Sultan Muhammad and President Roosevelt, colonialists in the Maghrib viewed the United States' position as intrusive and pro-nationalist.

44. Jane S. Nickerson states another consequence of the French failure in Indochina: "Two-thirds of the 28,000 prisoners of war released by the Viet Minh after the Armistice in 1954 were North Africans; and they returned home not only with the memory of the humiliating French withdrawal, but also with a thorough indoctrination by their captors in Communist principles" (Nickerson 1968, 133–134).

45. The enduring effect of colonialism has also played an important role in the reformulation of relations between former colonial powers and their colonies in the post-colonial period. Regarding Algeria, see, for example, Stora 1991, Naylor 2000a, Ruedy 2005, and Lorcin 2006.

46. Writing in the immediate post-colonial period, Bennabi stated that "the most revolutionary act is that which decolonizes man himself" (Bennabi 1989, 44). Abdelkebir Khatibi examines sociological discourses and "logocentric" tropes and concludes that there is a need to decolonize as well as deconstruct "Arab sociology" (see Khatibi 1985).

Chapter 8

1. Escalating nationalism also alienated foreign communities in Egypt. Nationalism also increased tendencies toward stereotyping others. After the Suez Canal crisis, the Egyptian government deported aliens, while others departed on their own (see Marsot 2007, 137). The disappearance of foreign communities also meant the end of important transcultural interaction.

2. Qutb clarified: "This Jahiliyyah is based on rebellion against God's sovereignty on earth. It transfers to man one of the greatest attributes of God, namely sovereignty, and makes some men lords over others. It is now not in that simple and primitive form of the ancient Jahiliyyah, but takes the form of claiming that the right to create values, to legislate rules of collective behavior, and to choose any way of life rests with men, without regard to what God has prescribed" (Qutb n.d., 11). He asserted: "Any society is

a jahili society which does not dedicate itself to submission to God alone, in its beliefs and ideas, in its observances of worship, and in its legal regulations." Qutb concluded: "According to this definition, all societies existing in the world today are jahili" (ibid., 80). He classified Muslim as well as Jewish and Christian societies as jahili, "because their way of life is not based on submission to God alone. Although they believe in the Unity of God, still they have relegated the legislative attribute of God to others and submit to this authority, and from this authority they derive their systems, their traditions and customs, their laws, their values and standards, and almost every practice of life" (ibid., 82–83).

3. Bennabi was not among them. Indeed, Qutb contended that Bennabi was overly influenced by his colonial past (see Christelow 1992, 69–70, citing *Jalons sur la route de l'Islam (Ma'alim fi al-tariq)* [Paris, 1968], 91–92).

4. Israel successfully insisted that the United Nations Emergency Force (UNEF) be stationed only on the Egyptian side of the border. Marsot considered Nasser's actions to be a "bluff" (Marsot 2007, 147).

5. Syria lost the strategic Golan Heights and Jordan, East Jerusalem, and the West Bank of the Jordan River.

6. Sadat appealed to nationalism as symbolically signaled by the Constitution of 1971. The new constitution, replacing that of 1956, changed the nation's official name from the United Arab Republic to the Arab Republic of Egypt.

7. Sadat's action contradicted the spirit of the Treaty of Friendship signed in 1971.

8. Although Egypt and Syria were the actual Arab combatants, Iraq, Morocco, Algeria, Tunisia, and Sudan also supplied combat/combat support troops and matériel. Libya and Saudi Arabia provided financial assistance.

9. Alain Roussillon explores the historical model between the "developmentalists," namely Muhammad Ali and Gamal Abdel Nasser and Khedive Isma'il and Sadat, who "betrayed or distorted their predecessors' . . . aims and sacrificed the public good and Egypt's independence to mercantile interests of a class of speculators and unscrupulous businessmen that served as a wedge for foreign penetration" (Roussillon 1998, 2:334–336). Roussillon finds the model "simplistic" and concludes: "Within the logic of this paradigm, 'understanding Egypt'—writing its history, describing its social or political systems, and decoding present ideologies—involves highlighting long-term, quasi-ecological continuities linked to the relation between river and desert, while showing how the breaks, apparent or effective, that create the rhythm of this long history—changes in language, religion, foreign masters—recompose the meaning of continuity while confirming it" (ibid., 2:336). From our interpretive perspective, these recurrences are simply layers pressed on Egypt's sedimentary history.

10. Egypt collected $100 million in 1975, which increased to $700 million in 1980 (IMF 2007a, 8).

11. According to Galal Amin, the Revolution of 1952 changed Egypt by transforming the Egyptian economy and its educational system. The impact was revolutionary since it generated unprecedented "social mobility." Amin contends that social mobility, evinced, for example, by the rise of a substantial middle class and significant female emancipation, is the principal cause for Egypt's instability (see Amin 2000).

12. Two Islamist groups principally plotted Sadat's death: Jama'at Islamiyya (Gemaa Islamiyyah) and Islamic Jihad (Jihad al-Islami).

13. Mubarak's presidency began with a referendum on 13 October 1981 after Sadat's assassination. He was reelected in 1987, 1993, 1999, and 2005. Sadat organized the NDP in July 1977.

14. Egypt's participation was not popularly supported given the negative image of the wealthy Kuwaitis and the subsequent devastation of Iraq, a brother Arab nation. On the other hand, given Egyptian collaboration in the United Nations coalition, the United States cancelled Egypt's enormous military debt ($4.5 billion) (see Marsot 2007, 171–172).

15. An assassination attempt targeting Mubarak occurred in 1995.

16. The attack was perpetrated near the tomb of Queen Hatshepsut.

17. Nour was accused of forging petitions. He remains imprisoned as of this writing despite international protest. (Note: Nour was released in February 2009.)

18. According to the BBC, the official participation of the electorate was 27 percent, while other "independent groups" claimed only 5 percent took part in the referendum (BBC 2007).

19. His son, Gamal, is often viewed in the media as a possible successor. Afaf Lutfi al-Sayyid Marsot warns: "Unless a liberal regime is restored, one where the cabinet is responsible to a popularly elected parliament through real, honest elections, and where corruption is rooted out and inefficiency—the result of indifference and loss of hope—is replaced, then the opposition will grow stronger and more militant" (Marsot 2007, 177).

20. Khalid Ikram calculates a growth from 4.5 to 4.7 percent a year from 1965 to 2000 since "national accounts overstate the weight of industry . . . and understate that of agriculture" (Ikram 2006, 278).

21. According to the EIU, from 2002–2006, real GDP averaged 4.3 percent (EIU 2007e). The EIU estimated real GDP growth for Egypt from 2007 to 2012 to be 6.2 to 6.3 percent. Nevertheless, the rising costs of foodstuffs, in particular, are bound to affect performance (as well as the global economic crisis of late 2008) (EIU 2008a).

22. The population is 75.4 million and the population's annual growth is at 1.9 percent (ibid.).

23. In addition, the Egyptian government has not developed the alimentary and fishing potential of the High Dam's Lake Nasser (Marsot 2007, 167).

24. The United States took over the airfield at Mellaha east of Tripoli from the British in 1943, which became Wheelus.

25. Libya was involved in numerous integration initiatives including with Algeria (1973) and Tunisia (1974) (see Vandewalle 2006, 87). Regarding Morocco and Libya, see Parker 1985.

26. The UMA is the latest effort of Maghribi integration. The Constitutive Assembly of the Arab Maghrib was formed in 1958 and followed by the Permanent Consultative Maghribi Committee in 1964. Like the UMA, they also failed to attain a meaningful integration beyond occasional meetings.

27. John Esposito observed that "the bulk of *The Green Book* does not refer explicitly to Islam. Qaddafi defended himself against his Islamic critics by maintaining that the Third Universal Theory . . . is meant to bring about social justice and equality for the entire world, not just Muslims" (Esposito 2005, 177).

28. *Jumhuriyya* means republic; thus, the neologism is meant to relate to, though differ from, this commonly used word in official state titles. Lisa Anderson refers to some of the meanings associated with Jamahariyya—"state of the masses" and "peopledom" (Anderson 1986, 264). In Arabic, the root *jama'a* means to assemble, to gather, to group. *Hurriyya* (from the root *harra*) means independence and liberation. The verb *jamhara,* from which *jumhuriyya* is derived, is synonymous with *jama'a.*

29. The disappearance of Musa Sadr, the mystic Lebanese Shi'i leader, while visiting Libya in 1978 remains a mystery. To many Shi'a, he is regarded to be in a state of occultation but will return (Esposito 2005, 188). For more information on Libyan Islamism see also Ouannes 1999, 178–182.

30. Libya tried to renew diplomatic dialogue with the United States in 1992, but it was shunned.

31. Qadhafi also reportedly provided haven and support for Tuareg insurgents in their struggle against the Malian government.

32. Libya was the first government to issue an Interpol arrest warrant for Usama bin Ladin.

33. Libya reported to the IMF that its foreign worker population dropped from 187,900 in 2001 to 56,900 in 2005 (IMF 2007d, 7).

34. Libya pumped 1,539,000 bpd in 2003, of which 1,184,000 were for export (IMF 2005c, 21). Italy, Germany, France, Spain, South Korea, and Turkey are important commercial clients.

35. The EIU estimated real GDP growth for Libya from 2007 to 2012 to be 5.7 percent. Soaring hydrocarbon prices will increase revenues and GDP, but there will probably be few structural economic changes to Libya's rentier economy (EIU 2008b).

36. There is mention of his son, Sayf al-Islam, as Qadhafi's heir apparent. He is de-

scribed by Mary-Jane Deeb as apparently "less ideologically driven than his father" (Deeb 2007, 453).

37. The French thought that Saquiat harbored Algerian revolutionaries.

38. Bourguiba retired to his home in Monastir and died in April 2000.

39. Ghannushi believes in power-sharing as "a necessity in order to lay the foundations of the social order. This power-sharing may not necessarily be based on Islamic Shari'ah law. However, it must be based on an important foundation of the Islamic government, namely shura, or the authority of the *ummah* (community), so as to prevent the evils of dictatorship, foreign domination, or local anarchy" (Donohue and Esposito 2007, 273). The ideas of Malik Bennabi have also significantly influenced Ghannushi.

40. The elections included other parties, but they were overwhelmed by the RCD, which received 80 percent of the popular vote (see Perkins 2004, 189).

41. On the other hand, Georgie Anne Geyer sympathetically portrays Ben Ali as a prudent statesman following a gradual democratic course (see Geyer 2003).

Chapter 9

1. In part, this was because of the fractured elite and the subsequent establishment of exclusive institutions and organs of government. Writing during this period, Clement Henry Moore observed: "Algeria lacked an elite with shared, concrete purposes" (Moore 1970, 128).

2. Algerians spontaneously seized these properties and initiated an inventive *autogestion* (self-management) system. It was later bureaucratized by the government (see Clegg 1971).

3. Société Nationale pour la Recherche, la Production, le Transport, la Transformation, et la Commercialisation des Hydrocarbures (National Company for Research, Production, Transportation, Processing, and Marketing of Hydrocarbons [SONATRACH]).

4. The French blueprinted many eleventh-hour social and economic programs during the "Algerian War."

5. For example, the street signs were changed from French to Arabic. There was a problem with the change, since most Algerians could not read Arabic.

6. For example, he co-opted some of the ideas of the al-Qiyam (values) group, an organization highly influenced by Malik Bennabi, who was an administrator and professor at the University of Algiers. Boumedienne's government disbanded al-Qiyam in 1966. Bennabi eventually hosted private "seminars" in his home disseminating his Islamism.

7. Writing in the early 1980s, John Entelis described Algeria as a "bureaucratic pol-

ity—a political system in which power and national decision making are shaped almost exclusively by the employees of the state, and especially by the topmost levels of the officer corps, single party organization, and civilian bureaucracy, including the significant socioeconomic class of managers and technicians" (Entelis 1986, 208).

8. Benjedid ordered Ben Bella's release from house arrest in 1979. The former departed for Europe in 1980 and formed an opposition party, the Mouvement pour la Démocratie en Algérie (The Algerian Movement for Democracy [MDA]) in 1984.

9. For a description and analysis of the "Berber Spring" demonstrations and protests in 1980, as well as her personal experience of Berber restiveness in Kabylia, see Goodman 2005, 29–48.

10. The official report of 161 killed and 154 wounded is roundly criticized as inaccurate.

11. Azzedine Layachi pointed out the economic consequences of Algeria's rapidly changing political culture: "The state, after unleashing the forces of political liberalization, found it virtually impossible to implement the economic reforms that were in the past exclusively designed by a limited circle of technocratic and political elites" (Layachi 1996, 147).

12. The Pouvoir (the power establishment) also feared that the FIS would investigate its patronage and corruption (see Martinez 2005, 18).

13. There were many dimensions to this tragic conflict. For example, the strife provided opportunities that economically and socially empowered insurgents, evoking a comparison between Islamist "emirs" and Ottoman corsairs (see Martinez 2000, 137–146).

14. The document framed was the "Platform for a Political and Peaceful Solution to the Algerian Crisis." It is also known as the "National Contract."

15. Violence related to the *fitna* spread to Paris in 1995 and 1996.

16. The revised Constitution of 1996 prohibited parties based on religion. For a survey of Islamist parties and armed groups see Layachi 2005, 54–56.

17. Benjedid visited in 1983, but he was not received at the "state visit" level.

18. The death of the Kabyle singer-activist Lounès Matoub in June 1998 remained a roiling memory in the region (see Silverstein 2003, 101–103).

19. The Kseur Platform remains a basis for discussion between Kabyle activists and the government. The Kseur Platform and its explication are reproduced in Bennadji 2003, 139–145.

20. The government implemented the "Economic Recovery Program and Growth Consolidation Program" in 2001, which has benefited the non-hydrocarbon sector (IMF 2007f, 4–5). The Growth Consolidation Program (2005–2009) is especially targeting the tertiary sector with a public investment program of $140 billion, which also hopes to address unemployment (IMF 2007b, 4–5).

21. In 2004 and 2005, the IMF reported unemployment percentages of the workforce at 17.7 and 15.4 percent, respectively (IMF 2007e, 18). The non-hydrocarbon sector employs 98 percent of the workforce (IMF 2007f, 3).

22. Violent opposition against the royal government continued. In 1972, insurgents detonated bombs at Nador and Oujda. Other devices were disarmed in Casablanca and Rabat. Algiers was implicated, since some of the insurgents apparently crossed into Morocco from Algeria (see Knapp 1977, 310).

23. Of course, one could argue from a Mauritanian/Sahrawi perspective that Morocco was part of the Almoravid empire. To reiterate, the Almoravids were Sanhaja Berbers who came from Mauritania and Western Sahara (see Chapter 4). Ernest Gellner, referring to Robert Montagne, described the ebb and flow of Moroccan power and influence as "oscillation" (Gellner 1969, 4, 64–66; see also Montagne 1973).

24. Morocco ratified the conventions before the formation of the UMA.

25. Algerian "ambiguity," leading eventually to wholehearted support of the POLISARIO, is succinctly analyzed by Hodges 1983, 193–195.

26. Richard Parker was particularly close to these events, serving as the American ambassador in Algiers and then Rabat during this time. Recent declassified documents show that the United States was complicit in Spanish withdrawal and Moroccan takeover (see Mundy 2006). These policy decisions, made at a higher level, were not confided to the ambassador (Mundy 2006, 292).

27. A notable exception was the prominent Marxist Abraham Serfaty (see below).

28. As graphically described in Ben Jelloun 2006.

29. The king met with Abdelaziz Bouteflika. Indeed, Bouteflika also shook hands with Prime Minister Ehud Barak of Israel, an extraordinary event given Algeria's strong support of the PLO.

30. In 1974, Shaykh Yassine sent a 124-page tract to the king to reform and inaugurate a caliphal system chosen by ulama. The shaykh was arrested in 1984 and sentenced to two years in prison. He was placed under house arrest in 1989.

31. Under the 1996 constitution, an upper house, the Chamber of Counselors, was added.

32. Daniel Zisenwine notes: "The monarchy has maintained its position as Morocco's preeminent proactive force because at the moment, no other political institution can match its ability to implement widespread reforms" (Zisenwine 2007, 146). On the other hand, Gregory W. White states that Moroccan "political stability is contingent on economic and social justice. . . . Economic or social promises will soon have to be delivered, or the closing of the political system may become even more pronounced" (White 2008, 105). White argues that Morocco is in a transitional condition that could return to an "era of leniency" (pre–Casablanca bombing of 2003) or tilt toward authoritarianism.

33. As of this writing the SADR is recognized by over forty countries, most of which are in Africa, including recently South Africa and Kenya.

34. The Moroccan Jewish population has declined from 300,000 in the mid-1950s to about 5,000 in the early 2000s (Howe 2005, 41).

35. François Mitterrand gave greater attention to Algeria from 1981 to 1984 and then eventually pursued a more balanced regional policy. Danielle Mitterrand, the French president's wife, engaged politically as a critic of Moroccan policy and as a supporter of the Sahrawis.

36. Other Spanish territories are Peñon de Velez de la Gormera, the islands of Peñon de Alhucemas, and the Islas Charafinas. In July 2002, the deserted rocky islet of Perejil/Leila near Ceuta was "invaded" by several Moroccan soldiers. Spain perceived this maneuver as a threat to the presidio and a brief crisis ensued. Spanish troops arrived to "retake" the island. There was no violence, but the incident exacerbated the presidio problem.

37. From 2000 to 2004, the Spanish annually deported an average 24,107 Moroccans (de Larramendi and Bravo 2006, 159).

38. Since the Madrid bombings in 2004, Spanish authorities have detained many suspected Islamists. Moroccans are especially targeted given their activity and the size of their community in Spain (approximately 500,000). In May 2007, sixteen North Africans were arrested; fourteen were Moroccan and the other two Algerian. They were accused of recruiting volunteers for international extremist Islamist operations and support (Burnett 2007, A9).

39. There was no vast nationalization or expropriation of French property. There were buyouts and compensation packages.

40. Western Sahara's Bou Craa deposits have augmented Morocco's production. There was a price boom concurrent to the Spanish "de-administration" of Western Sahara. From $14/ton in fall 1973, prices rose to $68/ton in early 1975 before declining (Denoeux and Maghraoui 1998, 56). Prices were over $300/ton before declining in late 2008.

41. It is estimated that more than two million Moroccans live abroad.

42. The official toll was 66 dead, but unofficial statistics, including those offered by exile groups, suggest that 600 to 1,000 were killed (Pennell 2000, 354–355).

43. For further details consult Hodges 1983; Damis 1983; Barbier 1982; Dunbar 2000; Pazzanita and Hodges 1994; Lawless and Monahan 1987; Zoubir and Volman 1992; Price 1979; Shelley 2004; Jensen 2005; Ruf 2004; and Mundy 2006.

44. Aminatu Haidar is a Sahrawi woman living in Moroccan-occupied Western Sahara. She has been active in peaceful resistance to the Moroccans and has been nominated for the Andrei Sakharov Prize. The official SADR web site (http://www.arso .org/aminatoucamp.htm) displayed a picture of her bloodied face (accessed September

2005). Although it would be expected for the POLISARIO to publicize the plight of Haidar and other abused Sahrawis, what cannot be ignored is that increasingly Western Sahara is becoming a moral as well as political issue. Morocco has also condemned the POLISARIO for abusing Moroccan prisoners.

45. Toby Shelley noted: "A quarter of a century after the Green March the division between the indigenous and Moroccan populations of towns like Laayoune and Smara is sometimes subtle, sometimes striking, always present" (Shelley 2004, 82).

46. It should be noted that despite the POLISARIO's supratribal image, it is primarily composed of Reguibat, which concerns non-Reguibat Sahrawis (e.g., the Awlad Dulaym) (see ibid., 122).

47. It is expected that Western Sahara has significant deposits of iron ore, vanadium, and titanium (ibid., 77). Furthermore, in 2001, Moroccan energy interests signed contracts with firms to explore for oil off the Western Saharan coast. In turn, the SADR issued exploration licenses in 2006.

48. The United States inaugurated the Pan-Sahel Initiative (PSI) in late 2002 to assist and train forces in Mauritania, Mali, Niger, and Chad as means to counter the GSPC's operations and control Saharan trafficking. In March 2004, PSI-trained Chadian troops reportedly killed forty-three GSPC militants. The PSI was renamed the Trans-Sahara Counter Terrorism Initiative (TSCTI) in 2005 and enlarged to include Algeria, Morocco, Senegal, Ghana, and Nigeria. This collaboration between Maghribi and Sahelian states must take into account perceptions of their shared history, which have not been endearing, namely slavery and racism (see Bensaad 2006, 96–99). American concern has now resulted in the establishment of a US African Command (AFRICOM), which became operational in October 2007. Its principal mission is to provide assistance and training to Maghribi and Sahelian states. Clement M. Henry points out that the Global War on Terror (GWOT) has increased regimes' repression and coercion in Algeria, Morocco, and Tunisia (see Henry 2008).

49. Importantly, Algeria and Mauritania are also involved as observers. Rob Annandale contends that Spain still has a role to play (thereby addressing its aforementioned "bad faith"). He offers an "out of the box" proposal: "By offering to relinquish [Ceuta and Melilla] in exchange for Morocco's willingness to allow a referendum under conditions acceptable to the Polisario, Spain could help clean up the mess it left behind in 1976" (Annandale 2007). The diplomatic impasse needs imagination. Enlarging the discussions from a bilateral to regional negotiation (e.g., borders, border closures, the presidios) could expedite a resolution of Western Sahara. Haizam Amirah-Fernández notes: "Many Spaniards consider that their country has a historical and moral responsibility towards the Sahrawis for having withdrawn hastily from the former colony . . . before having organized a referendum on self-determination for the Sahrawi people, to which they had the right under international law" (Amirah-Fernández 2008, 350).

50. In January 2008, the Paris-Dakar Rally was cancelled because of the threat caused by the AQI(L)M (ex-GSPC), considered the perpetrators in the deaths of four French tourists in Mauritania in December 2007.

51. Azzedine Layachi points out that "economic reforms produce new political and economic alliances and threaten old ones." He adds: "There is no blueprint for successful simultaneous economic and political reforms" (see Layachi 1998, 170–171). Louisa Aït-Hamadouche and Yahia H. Zoubir note regarding Algeria after the October 1988 riots and before the coup of January 1992: "Economic liberalization measures did not presuppose only the end of governmental control but also that of the unofficial monopolies held by various interest groups. This, of course, did not happen" (Aït-Hamadouche and Zoubir 2007, 127). Referring to Libya as a rentier state, although applicable throughout North Africa, Dirk Vandewalle writes: "Economic liberalization and privatization can only take place if internal, national markets either exist or can readily be created" (Vandewalle 1996, 207). These kinds of reform insist upon political will. Authoritarian governments, especially those marked by corrupt patronage or clientage systems, perceive privatization and liberalization as potential political threats. On the other hand, support of these measures correlates to their co-optation by governments.

52. In the 1960s, Rashid al-Barrawi perceived an "oil revolution in Africa," with the Maghrib, notably Algeria and Libya, playing important roles (see al-Barrawi 1963). Given the high price of oil and the subsequent development of more minor Egyptian and Tunisian fields, North Africa is in another revolution. There are continuous searches in Morocco and offshore Western Sahara for oil. Oil production is beginning in offshore Mauritania, raising its economic significance (it possesses large iron ore deposits).

53. In Libya's case, the consequences of *thawra* and *tharwa* were enormous: "The sudden capital inflows allowed the regime to unleash a wave of new economic and political plans and directives. . . . The formal attempts at planning, however, were matched by virtually unrestrained spending: in an effort to maintain those groups that the regime considered its main supporters, it made major outlays through an unbridled program of welfare measures, military purchases, and government contracts" (Vandewalle 1998, 83; see also Vandewalle 1996). *Thawra* and *tharwa* strengthened the state's "distributive" power. A similar experience occurred in Algeria. The fall in oil prices in the mid-1980s had manifold ramifications in both countries, especially in Algeria. Nazih N. Ayubi conceived this play on words (as credited by Professor Vandewalle) in his excellent study of *thawri* and *tharwi* regimes in a broader Middle Eastern context (see Ayubi 1995, particularly 447–448).

54. In November 1995, twelve North African and Middle Eastern countries joined the EU in Barcelona and established the EMP, which plans not only to implement MEFTA, but also to promote security, civil society, and what we may call transcultural interac-

tion, e.g., cultural exchange and cooperation. The Mediterranean Union, inaugurated in 2008, shares these objectives. Horizontal integration, as represented by the UMA, remains an elusive or illusive ideal. Commercial activity among the Maghribi states is negligible compared with that with the EU. Benjamin Stora suggested that there was a need for historical reflection (and transcultural action) regarding potential integration: "In building its unity, the future Maghrib might reconstruct, little by little, the bases of its old inheritance of trans-Mediterranean civilisation; it might thus preserve the possibility of a real dialogue between all those 'Westerners,' Christian, Jewish, or Muslim, who live on both sides of the Mediterranean" (Stora 2003, 33). Nevertheless, neo-liberalism, such as tariff reductions, poses particular problems for weaker North African manufacturing sectors. There are also social risks regarding macroeconomic and microeconomic restructuring. Furthermore, greater attention given to vertical integration affects the potential of the UMA and the prospects for wider intra-Arab economic activity (see Attinà 2004, 149, and Escribano and Lorca 2008).

55. For example, Algeria's SONATRACH has reasserted its monopoly rights in contracts and hydrocarbon transportation and recently slapped a windfall tax on producing companies profiting in the Sahara.

56. The Moroccan Family Code was revised in February 2004, highlighted by raising the minimum age of marriage to eighteen for women, improving property rights for women, and providing court-supervised divorce. The Algerian Family Code was revised in February 2005. The revision fixed marriageable age at nineteen for men and women, maintained polygamy but with the consent of wives, and provided greater assurances to divorced wives and their children. Despite social restrictions, women play impressive professional roles in Algeria (70 percent of the lawyers, 60 percent of the judges). In addition, 60 percent of the university students are women. On the other hand, women account for only 20 percent of the workforce (Slackman 2007, A1).

57. It can be argued concerning Western Sahara that Morocco needs to reconcile or adapt its imagination of its imperial past with its present historical condition as well as with regional geopolitical realities (e.g., Sahrawi nationalism).

58. See Lawrence 2003 for a study of Algerian youth.

59. Thematic in Bennabi 1976.

60. Bruce Maddy-Weitzman, in a study of Moroccan and Algerian Berberist movements, questions whether "dominant national narratives" can accommodate "Amazigh elements" (Maddy-Weitzman and Zisenwine 2007, 66; see also Willis 2008).

Conclusion

1. Dale F. Eickelman contended that "only with group feeling can a religious ideology be practically implemented; thus Ibn Khaldun used the notion to link ideologies to their political contexts" (Eickelman 1998, 28).

2. Khatibi believes that accepting pluralism should be a global engagement (Khatibi 1983, 14). Of course, pluralism is thematic in Berque's writing too (see Berque 1998). See also Mireille Rosello's analyses of "performative encounters" in Maghribi literature that are described as "exceptional moments" where "new subjects-positions, a new language, and a new type of engagement appear at the same time, none of the elements depending on the preexistence of the others" (Rosello 2005, 1–2). Khatibi and several of the authors mentioned above, namely Assia Djebar, are included in her study. For more on Mernissi and Djebar see Fayad 2000, 85–108.

3. I use "intra-" rather than "inter-" civilizational since North Africa and West Asia are component parts of Western civilization (see Introduction). "The West" is a modern historiographic construct that distorts the heritage and reality of interregional history (Hodgson) or, from our perspective, transcultural history (see Hodgson 2000). The potential of the emigrant/immigrant North African community to play an important reconciling social and cultural role has been recognized officially by French governments with the selections of sociologist/author Azouz Begag (of Algerian descent) and Rachida Dati (of Moroccan and French descent) as ministers. As minister of opportunities in the Dominique de Villepin ministry, Begag was especially critical of the government's response to North African youth violence in November 2005. Dati became the first person of North African and Arab descent to hold a major ministry, justice. She was appointed by President Nicolas Sarkozy in 2007. For more information on North African women in France see Keaton 2006 and Killian 2006. Zinedine Zidane, the French soccer superstar of Algerian heritage, has played a reconciling role. He is esteemed in France and Algeria.

4. Marnia Lazreg refers to Islamism in Algeria as a "recolonization because of its targeting of Algerians' cultural space in a manner similar to the French who, in the nineteenth century, attempted to displace local norms and values to suit their political purposes" (Lazreg 2000, 149). Her argument raises interesting questions regarding "colonizability."

5. There are so many others today, such as the renowned choreographer Sidi Larbi Cherkaoui, who is of Moroccan and Flemish descent. Indeed, social, cultural, and intellectual hybridity represents a strategic vehicle toward mutual recognition and understanding. Maghribis, especially those in the arts, are strategically placed to play this increasingly important role.

6. Emphasizing the importance of culture and history, Bennabi wrote: "There is no history without culture, for a people which no longer has its culture, no longer has its history" (Bennabi 1949, 51). Ibn Khaldun would subscribe to that position.

7. Ultimately this means addressing revelation and rationalism. Taking a position of the Ash'ari school of Muslim jurisprudence (and arguably reminiscent of Immanuel

Kant's phenomenal and noumenal epistemology), Ibn Khaldun viewed revelation and rationalism circumscribed yet complementary. Bennabi's oeuvre can be viewed as a reconciliation of reason and revelation. Two other important Maghribi figures involved in examining the roles of humanism and religion in Islamic and Arab intellectual thought include Mohammed Arkoun (see Arkoun 1984), a Kabyle, and Morocco's Mohammed Abed el-Jabri (Muhammed abd al-Jabri) (see al-Jabri 1999).

8. Today we are dealing less with an "Other" but "Others"—for example, the complex historical anthropology of North African communities in Europe as viewed in the literature of Azouz Begag, Leila Sebbar, and others.

9. In late 2006, Plant was preparing a trip to the Sahara to participate in a documentary on blues ("Plant" 2006). Exemplifying his remarkable transcultural consciousness, Plant has added "Sidi Mansour Ya Baba," an Algerian song, within the Led Zeppelin classic "Whole Lotta Love" (ibid.). He has also performed with Tinariwen, a Tuareg group, which has also opened for the Rolling Stones (Goddard 2007). As Andy Morgan rightly relates in his liner notes to Tinariwen's album *Amassakoul,* their sound evokes John Lee Hooker. Another example of North African musical hybridity is the transnational group "Kantara," which features a mixture of Tunisian and Appalachian music (Fenner 2007). The number of similar groups is exponentially expanding.

GLOSSARY

Abid   Moroccan black soldiers (seventeenth and eighteenth centuries) ('abd means slave or servant)

Agha   Ottoman commander

Aguellids   Berber kings

Amazighism   Berberism; primarily a movement to protect and promote Berber culture, although with political ramifications

Amir al-Mu'minin   Commander of the Believers

Amir al-Muslimin   Commander of the Muslims

Arkan   Pillars of Islam (*Shahada* [Testimony of Faith]; *Salat* [Prayer]; *Zakat* [Charity]; *Sawm* [Fast]; Hajj [Pilgrimage])

Asabiyya   "Group feeling"; the social cohesion necessary to start and sustain a state, according to Ibn Khaldun

Asala   Authenticity

Autogestion   Self-management; refers to Algerian policy and program regarding vacated properties in the immediate post-colonial period

Ayat   Verse in the Qur'an

Baraka   To bless; regarding Sufis and marabouts, quality of being favorably blessed

Barbary   The littoral from Tripolitania to Morocco

Bay'a   Act or oath of allegiance

Beylerbey   Ottoman commander of commanders; title of Algiers Regency leaders during the sixteenth century

Bilad   Countryside

Bilad al-Siba   Land of dissidence

Bilad al-Sudan   Land of the Blacks

Capitulations   Economic, cultural, and legal (even extraterritorial) privileges granted to foreigners in Muslim states

Convivencia   Coexistence; Andalusian society especially under the Umayyads

Coopérants   French teachers and technicians

Da'i   Da'wa (pl.); a "caller" who proselytizes Shi'i Islam; missionary (mission)

Dar al-Islam   House of Islam or Muslim lands

Destur   See *dustur*

Devoir social   Social duty of the French colonial officer; epitomized by Hubert Lyautey

Devshirme   Ottoman system of adopting Christian boys for imperial service

Dey   Ottoman governor

Dhimmis   Protected ones; people (as in People of the Book) who pay the *jizya*

Dustur   Constitution

Effendiyya   Egyptian middle class

Evolués   Assimilated, French-educated

Exode   Refers to the *pied-noir* flight and repatriation during Algerian decolonization

Faqih   Fuqaha (pl.); jurisconsult

Fatiha   First sura of the Qur'an

Fellagha   Guerrilla fighter

Fitna   Trial, test, civil strife

Foggaras   Underground irrigation channels

Al-hagra (hogra)   Contempt, exclusion, alienation

Hajj   Pilgrimage to Mecca

Hadith   Collected written accounts of the traditions, customs of the Prophet

Hijra   Muhammad's emigration from Mecca

Hubus   Pious foundations; also known as *waqfs* in the Maghrib

Ibadat   Duties

Ijma   Community consensus in legal matters

Imam   Sunni prayer leader; religious and political leader of Shi'a and Khariji

Iman   Faith; belief

Indigènes   Indigenous population; usually stereotyped as in Algeria

Intifada   Uprising, resistance

Infitah   Opening; in reference to Egyptian economic liberalization

Iqta   Tract of land; a fief

Jahiliyya   Ignorance; period before arrival of Islam

Jihad   Struggle; exertion; holy war

Jizya   Head tax paid by non-Muslims

Kalam   Word; discourse; speech; theology

Kandake   Meriotic (Kushite) term for queen

Kapudan pasha   Admiral of the Ottoman fleet

Khalifa   Successor, deputy; caliph

Khariji(tes)   Seceders; alienated by Caliph Ali's arbitration at the battle of Siffin

Khedive   Viceroy; title used in Alid Egypt

Al-Kitab   The Book; refers to the Qur'an

Kulughlu   Person of mixed Turkish-Maghribi ancestry

Levant   Eastern Mediterranean region including today's Lebanon, Israel, and parts of Turkey and Syria

Litham   Facial scarf of the Murabitun or Almoravids

Maat   Ancient Egyptian moral order

Madhab   Doctrine usually associated with a juridical school or Sufi order

Madrasa   An Islamic school at the secondary or college level

Maghrib   Northwest Africa; North Africa west of Egypt; *al-Maghrib* can mean the West or Morocco

Al-Maghrib al-adna   The near west; Tunisia, Libya (sometimes Algeria)

Al-Maghrib al-aqsa   The far west; Morocco

Al-Maghrib al-awsat   The middle west; Algeria

Mahalla   Traditional tour by Ottoman beys with troops to collect taxes and demonstrate power primarily in Tunisia

Mahdi   Rightly or divinely guided one; redeemer

Mai   Ruler

Malika   Queen

Mamluk   *Mamlukun* (Arabic pl.); slave soldier; a dynasty in Egypt

Marabout   Sufi; holy individual bestowed with *baraka*

Mashriq   The East; the Levant; West Asia and Egypt

Mawali   Non-Arab converts

Mawlay   Honorific title ("my lord") for sharifian Moroccan monarchs

Mubtada   Beginning; causes; causative, formative variables (relates to Ibn Khaldun's thought)

Mujadid   Renewer, as a renewer of Islam; involved in re-Islamization of society

Mujahid   Combatant, freedom fighter; derived from the verb *jahada*, meaning to exert or struggle; especially connotes the individual struggle to become a faithful Muslim

Al-Mulathamun   The veiled ones (Murabitun or Almoravids)

Muqaddam   Leader of a Sufi order or brotherhood

Ojaq   Military corps or caste of Janissaries

Pieds-noirs   French (European) settlers of North Africa, especially Algeria

Porte   Ottoman government (sultanate) in Constantinople

Pouvoir   Algerian power establishment

Presidio   Fortress, enclave

Princips   First citizen of the Roman state (Octavian/Augustus)

Qadis   Magistrates

Qa'id   Local leader

Qanats   Underground water channels

Qataif   A pastry with nuts and honey

Qur'an   Sacred book of Islam

Rasul   Messenger; one who receives revelation

Ra'y   Personal opinion in legal matters

Reconquista   Spanish Christian reconquest of Iberia

Renegade   A Christian convert to Islam

Ribat   Retreat-fortress

Riconquista   Italian conquest of Libya

Salafiyya   A return to the beliefs of the venerable and virtuous early generations of Muslims; identified with the ideas of Islamic modernism of Muhammad Abduh

Sahel   Coast; coastline; the belt of semiarid land separating the Sahara from tropical Africa

Salat   Muslim prayer

Sawm   Muslim fasting

Shahada   Testimony of Faith in Islam

Shari'a   Islamic law

Sharif   *Shurafa* (pl.); descendant of Muhammad

Shaykh   Teacher; leader

Shi'a   Muslims who believe that caliphal succession should be through the family of Ali and Fatima; from *shi'at* Ali or party of Ali

Shirk   Polytheism; sin of ascribing partners to God

Sidi   Honorific title from the Arabic *sayyid*

Sufet   Suffetes; Carthaginian executive magistrate elected annually

Sufi   Muslim mystic

Sunna   Customs, traditions of Muhammad as recounted by hadiths

Sura   Chapter in the Qur'an

Ta'ifa   Group of corsair captains

Tariqa   "Path" or ritual practiced by Sufi orders or brotherhoods

Taqlid   Imitative tradition

Ulama   Religious scholars

Umma   Muslim community, commonwealth; modern sense, nation

Vizier   Principal or prime minister

Wafd   Delegation

Wazir   See vizir

Wilayat   Provinces

Zahir   *Dahir;* Moroccan royal decree

Za'im   Leader

Zakat   Muslim charity

Zawiya   *Zawaya* (pl.); religious study and meditation center or lodge; monastery; hostelry

BIBLIOGRAPHY

Abd al-Qadir. 1858. *Le Livre d'Abd el-Kader intitulé Rappel à l'intelligent, avis à l'indifférent.* Translated by Gustave Dugat. Paris: Benjamin Duprat.

Abdel-Malek, Anouar. 1969. *Idéologie et renaissance nationale.* Paris: Editions Anthropos.

Abun-Nasr, Jamil M. 1971. *A History of the Maghrib.* Cambridge: Cambridge University Press.

———. 1987. *A History of the Maghrib in the Islamic Period.* Cambridge: Cambridge University Press.

Ahmida, Ali Abdullatif. 2005. *Forgotten Voices: Power and Agency in Colonial and Postcolonial Libya.* New York: Routledge.

———. 1994. *The Making of Modern Libya: State Formation, Colonization, and Resistance, 1830–1932.* Albany: State University of New York Press.

Ahmida, Ali Abdullatif, ed. 2000a. *Beyond Colonialism and Nationalism in the Maghrib: History, Culture, and Politics.* New York: Palgrave.

———. 2000b. "Identity and Alienation in Postcolonial Libyan Literature: The Trilogy of Ahmad Ibrahim al-Faqih." In *Beyond Colonialism and Nationalism in the Maghrib: History, Culture, and Politics,* edited by Ali Abdullatif Ahmida, 73–84. New York: Palgrave.

Aït-Hamadouche, Louisa-Dris. 2008. "Women in the Maghreb: Stereotypes and Realities." In *North Africa: Politics, Region, and the Limits of Transformation,* edited by Yahia H. Zoubir and Haizam Amirah-Fernández, 202–226. New York: Routledge.

Aït-Hamadouche, Louisa, and Yahia H. Zoubir. 2007. "The Fate of Political Islam in Algeria." In *The Maghrib in the New Century: Identity, Religion, and Politics,* edited by Bruce Maddy-Weitzman and Daniel Zisenwine, 103–131. Gainesville: University Press of Florida.

Albertini, Eugène, and others. 1937, 1955. *L'Afrique du Nord française dans l'histoire.* Lyon: Editions Archat.

Albrecht, Holger, and Eva Wegner. 2006. "Autocrats and Islamists: Contenders and Containment in Egypt and Morocco." *Journal of North African Studies* 11, no. 2 (June): 123–141.

Alloula, Malek. 1986. *The Colonial Harem.* Translated by Barbara Harlow. Minneapolis: University of Minnesota Press.

AlSayyad, Nezar, Irene A. Bierman, and Nasser Rabbat, eds. 2005. *Making Cairo Medieval.* Lanham, Md.: Lexington Books.

Amin, Galal. 2000. *What Happened to the Egyptians? Changes in Egyptian Society from 1850 to the Present.* Cairo: American University in Cairo Press.

Amin, Samir. 1966. *L'Economie du Maghreb.* 2 vols. Paris: Editions de Minuit.

Amirah-Fernández, Haizam. 2008. "Spain's Policy towards Morocco and Algeria: Balancing Relations with the Southern Neighbors." In *North Africa: Politics, Region, and the Limits of Transformation,* edited by Yahia H. Zoubir and Haizam Amirah-Fernández, 348–364. New York: Routledge.

Anderson, Lisa. 1986. *The State and Social Transformation in Tunisia and Libya, 1830–1980.* Princeton, New Jersey: Princeton University Press.

Annandale, Rob. 2007. "Thinking Outside the Box." Angus Reid Global Monitor: Politics in Depth, 17 June. http://www.angus-reid.com/analysis/view/16152.

Aqqad, Salah. 1966. *Al-Maghrib al-'Arabi: al-Jaza'ir, al-Tunis, al-Maghrib al-Aqsa.* Cairo: Maktab al-Ang(j)lu al-misryiyya.

Arkoun, Mohammed. 1984. *Pour une critique de la raisin islamique.* Paris: Maissonneuve et Larose.

el-Aroui, Abdelmajid. 1990. *La Kahena: Fiction, légende et réalité, ou, La Conquête de l'Ifriquiya par les Arabes: Tragédie en cinq actes.* Tunis: Published by the playwright.

al-Aswany, Alaa. 2004. *The Yacoubian Building.* Translated by Humphrey Davies. Cairo: American University in Cairo Press.

Attinà, Fulvio. 2004. "The Barcelona Process, the Role of the European Union and the Lesson of the Western Mediterranean." *Journal of North African Studies* 9, no. 2 (Summer): 140–152.

Augustine. 1961. *Confessions.* Translated by R. S. Pine-Coffin. New London: Penguin Books.

Austen, Ralph A. 1979. "The Trans-Saharan Slave Trade: A Tentative Census." In *The Uncommon Market: Essays in the Economic History of the Atlantic Slave Trade,* edited by Henry A. Gemery and Jan S. Hogendorn, 23–76. New York: Academic Press.

Ayache, Albert. 1964. *Histoire ancienne de l'Afrique du Nord.* Paris: Editions Sociales.

Ayubi, Nazih N. 1995. *Over-stating the Arab State: Politics and Society in the Middle East.* London: I. B. Tauris Publishers.

Badran, Margot. 1995. *Feminists, Islam, and Nation: Gender and the Making of Modern Egypt.* Princeton, N.J.: Princeton University Press.

al-Bakri, Abu Ubayd (Abou-Obeïd-el-Bekri). 1965. *Al-maghrib fi dhikr bilad ifriqiyya wa-l-maghrib wa huwa juza' min kitab al-masalik wa-l-mamalik/ Description de l'Afrique septentrionale.* In Arabic with French translation by MacGuckin de Slane. Paris:

Librairie d'Amérique et d'Orient, Adrien-Maisonneuve, reproduction of 1911–1913 edition.

Baldinetti, Anna. 2003. "Libya's Refugees, Their Places of Exile, and the Shaping of Their National Identity." *Journal of North African Studies* 8, no. 1 (Spring): 72–86.

Barakat, Halim, ed. 1985. *Contemporary North Africa: Issues of Development and Integration.* Washington, D.C.: Georgetown Center for Contemporary Arab Studies.

Barbier, Maurice. 1982. *Le Conflit du Sahara occidental.* Paris: L'Harmattan.

Barbour, Nevill. 1959. *A Survey of North West Africa (The Maghrib).* London: Oxford University Press.

———. 1966. *Morocco.* New York: Walker and Company.

Baron, Beth. 2005. *Egypt as a Woman: Nationalism, Gender, and Politics.* Berkeley: University of California Press.

al-Barrawi, Rashid. 1963. *Thawrat al-batrul fi ifriqiyya.* Cairo: Dar al Nahdat al-Arabiyya.

Baruma, Ian, and Avishai Margalit. 2004. *Occidentalism: The West in the Eyes of Its Enemies.* New York: Penguin Books.

Bellin, Eva. 2004. "The Robustness of Authoritarianism in the Middle East: Exceptionalism in Comparative Perspective." *Comparative Politics* 36, no. 2 (January): 139–157.

Ben Jelloun, Tahar. 2006. *This Blinding Absence of Light.* Translated by Linda Coverdale. New York: Penguin.

Ben-Jochannan, Yosef. 1991. "Moses: African Influence on Judaism." In *African Origins of Major World Religions,* edited by Amon Saba Saakana, 1–32. 2d ed. London: Karnak House.

Ben Khalifa, Sadok. 1992. *Le Maghreb à la recherche de son unité.* Tunis: Imprimerie de l'U.G.T.T.

Bennabi, Malek (Malik). 1949. *Discours sur les conditions de la Renaissance algérienne.* Algiers: En-Nahda.

———. 1954. *Vocation de l'Islam.* Paris: Seuil.

———. 1976. *Les grands thèmes.* Algiers: Omar Benaissa.

———. 1989. *Pour changer l'Algérie: articles de presse.* Algiers: Société d'Edition et de Communication.

Bennadji, Chérif. 2003. "Chronique politique 2001." *Annuaire de l'Afrique du Nord* 39 (2000–2001). Paris: CNRS, 127–145.

Bennoune, Mahfoud. 1976. "Algerian Peasants and National Politics." MERIP, No. 48: 13–14.

———. 1988. The *Making of Contemporary Algeria, 1830–1987: Colonial Upheavals and Post-Independence Development.* Cambridge: Cambridge University Press.

Bensaad, Ali. 2006. "De l'espace euro-maghrébin à l'espace eurafricain: le Sahara comme nouvelle jonction intercontinentale." *L'Année du Maghreb* (2004). Paris: CNRS Editions, 83–100.

Berkey, Jonathan P. 1998a. "Culture and Society during the Late Middle Ages." In *The Cambridge History of Egypt: Islamic Egypt, 640–1517,* vol. 1, edited by Carl F. Petry, 375–411. Cambridge: Cambridge University Press.

———. 1998b. "The Mamluks as Muslims: The Military Elite and the Construction of Islam in Medieval Egypt." In *The Mamluks in Egyptian Politics and Society,* edited by Thomas Philipp and Ulrich Haarmann, 163–173. Cambridge: Cambridge University Press.

Bernal, Martin. 1987 (1991, 2006). *Black Athena: The Afroasiatic Roots of Classical Civilization.* 3 vols. Rutgers, N.J.: Rutgers University Press.

Berque, Jacques. 1955. *Structures sociales du Haut-Atlas.* Paris: Presses Universitaires de France.

———. 1964a. *The Arabs: Their History and Future.* Translated by Jean Stewart. London: Faber and Faber.

———. 1964b. *Dépossession du monde.* Paris: Editions du Seuil.

———. 1967. *French North Africa: The Maghrib between Two World Wars.* Translated by Jean Stewart. New York: Frederick A. Praeger.

———. 1972. *Egypt: Imperialism & Revolution.* Translated by Jean Stewart. London: Faber & Faber.

———. 1974. *Maghreb: Histoire et sociétés.* Gembloux: Duculot.

———. 1978. *L'Intérieur du Maghreb: XVe–XIXe siècle.* Paris: Gallimard.

———. 1982. *Ulémas, fondateurs, insurgés du Maghreb: XIIe siècle.* Paris: Sindbad.

———. 1989. *Mémoires des deux rives.* Paris: Editions du Seuil.

———. 1998. *Une cause jamais perdue: pour une Méditerranée plurielle (Ecrits politiques [1956–1995]).* Paris: Albin Michel.

———. 2001. *Opera minora.* 3 vols. Paris: Bouchène.

Bhabha, Homi K. 1994. *The Location of Culture.* London: Routledge.

Bierman, Irene A., ed. 2003. *Napoleon in Egypt.* Reading, UK: Ithaca Press.

Bonner, Michael, Megan Reif, and Mark Tessler, eds. 2005. *Islam, Democracy and the State in Algeria: Lessons for the Western Mediterranean and Beyond.* London: Routledge.

Bookin-Weiner, Jerome. 1993. "Corsairing in the Economy and Politics of North Africa." In *North Africa: Nation, State, and Region,* edited by George Joffé, 3–33. London: Routledge.

Botman, Selma. 1998. "The Liberal Age, 1923–1952." In *The Cambridge History of Egypt: Modern Egypt, from 1517 to the End of the Twentieth Century,* vol. 2, edited by M. W. Daly, 285–308. Cambridge: Cambridge University Press.

Boudjedra, Rachid. 1979. *Les 1001 années de la nostalgie.* Paris: Denoël.

Boukrouh, Nour-Eddine. 2006. L'Islam sans l'Islamisme; vie et penseé de Malek Bennabi. Algiers: Samar.

Bourquia, Rahma, and Susan Gilson Miller, eds. 1999. *In the Shadow of the Sultan: Culture, Power, and Politics in Morocco.* Cambridge, Mass.: Center for Middle Eastern Studies, Harvard University Press.

Bourrienne, Louis Antoine Fauvelet de. 1993. "The French View of the Events in Egypt." In *Napoleon in Egypt: Al-Jabarti's Chronicle of the French Occupation, 1798,* excerpted from de Bourrienne's *Memoirs of Napoleon Bonaparte* (Paris and Boston: Napoleon Society, 1895), 1:158–191. Princeton: Markus Wiener Publishing.

Bovill, Edward William. 1995. *The Golden Trade of the Moors.* Princeton, N.J.: Markus Wiener Publishers.

Brace, Richard M. 1964. *Morocco, Algeria, Tunisia* (Englewood Cliffs, N.J.: Prentice-Hall.

Braudel, Fernand. 1972–1973. *The Mediterranean and the Mediterranean World in the Age of Philip II.* 2 vols. Translated by Siân Reynolds. New York: Harper & Row.

Brett, Michael. 1999. *Ibn Khaldun and the Medieval Maghreb.* Aldershot, Hampshire: Ashgate.

Brett, Michael, and Elizabeth Fentress. 1996. *The Berbers.* Oxford, United Kingdom: Blackwell.

British Broadcasting Company (BBC). 2007. "Divisive Egypt Reforms Approved." 27 March. http://news.bbc.co.uk/2/hi/middle_east/6498573.stm.

Brown, L. Carl. 1974. *The Tunisia of Ahmad Bey, 1837–1855.* Princeton, N.J.: Princeton University Press.

Brown, Peter. 1967. *Augustine of Hippo: A Biography.* Berkeley: University of California Press.

———. 1971. *The World of Late Antiquity, AD 150–750.* New York: Harcourt Brace Jovanovich.

Buckler, F. W. 1931. *Harunu'l-Rashid and Charles the Great.* Cambridge, Mass.: Mediæval Academy of America.

Budge, E. A. Wallis, ed. and trans. 1928. *The Monks of Kublai Khan, Emperor of China or the History of the Life and Travels of Rabban Sâwmâ, Envoy and Plenipotentiary of the Mongol Khâns to the Kings of Europe, and Markâs Who as Mâr Yahbhallâhâ III Became Patriarch of the Nestorian Church in Asia.* London: Religious Tract Society.

Bulliett, Richard W. 1975. *The Camel and the Wheel.* Cambridge: Harvard University Press.

Burke, Edmund, III. 1972. "The Image of the Moroccan State in French Ethnological Literature: A New Look at the Origin of Lyautey's Berber Policy." In *Arabs and Berbers: From Tribe to Nation in North Africa,* edited by Ernest Gellner and Charles Micaud, 175–199. Lexington, Mass.: D. C. Heath and Company.

———. 1976. *Prelude to Protectorate in Morocco: Precolonial Protest and Resistance, 1860–1912*. Chicago: University of Chicago Press.

Burnett, Victoria. 2007. "Spain Arrests 16 North Africans Accused of Recruiting Militants." *New York Times*, 29 May, A9.

Caesar, Julius. 1955. *Alexandrian, African and Spanish Wars*. Translated by A. G. Way. Cambridge: Harvard University Press.

Camus, Albert. 1970. *Lyrical and Critical Essays*. Translated by Ellen Conroy Kennedy. New York: Vintage Books.

Çelik, Zeynep. 1992. *Displaying the Orient: Architecture of Islam at Nineteenth-Century World's Fairs*. Berkeley: University of California Press.

———. 1997. *Urban Forms and Colonial Confrontation: Algiers under French Rule*. Berkeley: University of California Press.

Central Intelligence Agency (CIA). *The World Factbook: Morocco*. www.cia.gov/cia/publications/factbook/geos/mo.html. Accessed 29 January 2007.

Cervantes Saavedra, Miguel de. 1966. *The Adventures of Don Quixote*. Translated by J. M. Cohen. Baltimore, Md.: Penguin Books.

Chamberlain, Michael. 1998. "The Crusader Era and the Ayyubid Dynasty." In *The Cambridge History of Egypt: Islamic Egypt, 640–1517*, vol. 1, edited by Carl F. Petry, 211–241. Cambridge: Cambridge University Press.

Christelow, Allan. 1992. "An Islamic Humanist in the 20th Century: Malik Bennabi." *Maghreb Review* 17 (nos. 1–2): 69–83.

Clancy-Smith, Julia. 1994. *Rebel and Saint: Muslim Notables, Populist Protest, Colonial Encounters (Algeria and Tunisia, 1800–1904)*. Berkeley: University of California Press.

———. 2008. "Where Elites Meet: Households, Harem Visits, and Sea-Bathing." Drafted chapter printout presented to author from *Mediterranean Passages: Migrants and Mobilities in Nineteenth-Century North Africa*. Berkeley: University of California Press (forthcoming 2009).

Clancy-Smith, Julia, ed. 2001. *North Africa, Islam, and the Mediterranean World: From the Almoravids to the Algerian War*. London: Frank Cass.

Clegg, Ian. 1971. *Workers' Self-Management in Algeria*. New York: Monthly Review Press.

Clover, Frank M. 1993. *The Late Roman West and the Vandals*. Aldershot, Hampshire, Great Britain; Brookfield, Vermont: Variorum.

Cole, Juan R. I. 2003. "Mad Sufis and Civic Courtesans: The French Republican Construction and Eighteenth-Century Egypt." In *Napoleon in Egypt*, edited by Irene A. Bierman, 47–62. Reading, UK: Ithaca Press.

———. 2007. *Napoleon's Egypt: Invading the Middle East*. New York: Palgrave Macmillan.

Combs-Schilling, M. Elaine. 1999. "Performing Monarchy, Staging Nation." In *In the*

Shadow of the Sultan: Culture, Power, and Politics in Morocco, edited by Rahma Bourquia and Susan Gilson Miller, 176–214. Cambridge, Mass.: Center for Middle Eastern Studies, Harvard University Press.

"Communiqué d'Ennahda publié à l'occasion des rencontres d'Aix en Provence (23–25 mai 2003) et signé par Ameur Laraiedh, chef du Bureau politique d'Ennahda (extraits), traduction Eric Gobe "Revendications et combat pour les libertés en Tunisie: vers un pacte national de l'opposition."" 2005. *Annuaire de l'Afrique du Nord* 41 (2003). Paris: CNRS, 329–333.

Crecelius, Daniel. 1998. "Egypt in the Seventeenth Century." In *The Cambridge History of Egypt: Modern Egypt, from 1517 to the End of the Twentieth Century,* vol. 2, edited by M. W. Daly, 59–86. Cambridge: Cambridge University Press.

Cromer, Earl of (Lord) (Evelyn Baring). 1908. *Modern Egypt.* 2 vols. New York: Macmillan Company.

Daly, M. W. 1998a. "The British Occupation, 1882–1922." In *The Cambridge History of Egypt: Modern Egypt, from 1517 to the End of the Twentieth Century,* vol. 2, edited by M. W. Daly, 239–251. Cambridge: Cambridge University Press.

Daly, M. W., ed. 1998b. *The Cambridge History of Egypt.* Vol. 2, *Modern Egypt, from 1517 to the End of the Twentieth Century.* Cambridge: Cambridge University Press.

Damis, John. 1983. *Conflict in Northwest Africa: The Western Sahara Dispute.* Stanford: Hoover Institute Press.

Danielson, Virginia. 1997. *The Voice of Egypt: Umm Kulthum, Arabic Song, and Egyptian Society in the Twentieth Century.* Chicago: University of Chicago Press.

Davis, Stephen. 1997. *Hammer of the Gods: The Led Zeppelin Saga.* New York: Berkley Boulevard Books.

Deeb, Mary-Jane. 2007. "Great Socialist People's Libyan Arab Jamahiriyya." In *The Government and Politics of the Middle East and North Africa,* edited by David E. Long, Bernard Reich, and Mark Gasiorowski, 432–455. 5th ed. Cambridge, Mass.: Westview Press.

Déjeux, Jean. 1973. "Meeting of the Two Worlds in the Maghrib." In *Man, State, and Society in the Contemporary Maghrib,* edited by I. William Zartman, 21–30. New York: Praeger.

de Larramendi, Miguel Hernando, and Fernando Bruno. 2006. "La frontière hispano-marocaine à l'épreuve de l'immigration subsaharienne." *L'Année du Maghreb* (2004). Paris: CNRS, 153–171.

Denoeux, Guilain P., and Abdeslam Maghraoui. 1998. "The Political Economy of Structural Adjustment in Morocco." In *Economic Crisis and Political Change in North Africa,* edited by Azzedine Layachi, 55–88. Westport, Conn.: Praeger Publishers.

de Villiers, Marq, and Sheila Hirtle. 2002. *Sahara: The Extraordinary History of the World's Largest Desert.* New York: Walker & Company.

Diamond, Jared. 1999. *Guns, Germs, and Steel: The Fates of Human Societies*. New York: W. W. Norton.

Diehl, Charles. 1966 (1896). *L'Afrique Byzantine: Histoire de la domination Byzantine en Afrique (533–709)*. New York: Burt Franklin.

Donohue, John J., and John L. Esposito, eds. 2007. *Islam in Transition: Muslim Perspectives*. 2d ed. New York: Oxford University Press.

Dunbar, Charles. 2000. "Saharan Stasis: Status and Prospects in the Western Sahara." *Middle East Journal* 54, no. 4 (Fall): 522–545.

Dunn, Ross. 1989. *The Adventures of Ibn Battuta: A Muslim Traveler of the 14th Century*. Berkeley: University of California Press.

Dunn, Ross, ed. 2000. *The New World History: A Teacher's Companion*. Boston: Bedford/ St. Martin's.

Dupuy, R. Ernest, and Trevor N. Dupuy. 1977. *The Encyclopedia of Military History from 3500 B.C. to the Present*. New York: Harper & Row.

Dykstra, Darrell. 1998. "The French Occupation of Egypt, 1798–1801." In *The Cambridge History of Egypt: Modern Egypt, from 1517 to the End of the Twentieth Century*, vol. 2, edited by M. W. Daly, 1113–1138. Cambridge: Cambridge University Press.

Dzielska, Maria. 1995. *Hypatia of Alexandria*. Translated by F. Lyra. Cambridge: Harvard University Press.

Economist Intelligence Unit (EIU). 2005. ViewsWire. Morocco Economy: EU Fishing Deal Signed. 24 August. http://proquest.umi.com/pdqweb?did=892279261&sid= 2&Fmt=3&clientId=1953&RQT=309&Vname=PQD.

———. 2006. ViewsWire. Morocco: Country Forecast Summary. 7 December. http:// proquest.umi.com/pdqweb?did=1188627041&sid=3&Fmt=3&clientId=56639&RQT= 309&VName=PQD.

———. 2007a. ViewsWire. Algeria: Country Forecast Summary. 26 April. http:// proquest.umi.com/pdqweb?did=1264629541&sid=2&Fmt=3&clientid=56639&RQT =309&Vname=PQD.

———. 2007b. ViewsWire. Libya: Country Fact Sheet. 24 April. http://proquest.umi .com/pdqweb?did=126407691&sid=9&Fmt=3&clientid=56639&RQT=309&Vname=P QD.

———. 2007c. ViewsWire. Libya: Country Forecast Summary. 24 April. http://proquest .umi.com/pdqweb?did=1264607701&sid=9&Fmt=3&clientid=566639&RQT=309&Vn ame=PQD.

———. 2007d. ViewsWire. Algeria: Country Outlook. 3 April. http://proquest.umi.com/ pdqweb?did=1264634751&sid=2&Fmt=3&clientid=56639&RQT=309&Vname=PQD.

———. 2007e. ViewsWire. Egypt: Country Fact Sheet. 3 April. http://proquest.umi.com/ pdqweb?did=1264533621&sid=11&Fmt=3&clientId=56639&RQT=309&Vname=PQD.

———. 2007f. ViewsWire. Tunisia: Country Outlook. 3 March. http://proquest.umi

.com/pqdweb?did=1264467261&sid=6&Fmt=3&clientid=566636&RQT=309&Vname=PQD.

———. 2008a. ViewsWire. Egypt: Country Forecast Summary. 15 April. http://proquest_.umi_.com/pqdweb_?did=1473231511_&sid=30_&Fmt=3_&clientId=56639_&RQT=309_&VName=PQD.

———. 2008b. ViewsWire. Libya: Country Forecast Summary. 7 April. http://proquest_.umi_.com/pqdweb_?did=1473174311_&sid=2_&Fmt=3_&clientId=56639&RQT=309_&VName=PQD.

Eickelman, Dale F. 1998. *The Middle East and Central Asia: An Anthropological Approach.* 3d ed. Upper Saddle River, N.J.: Prentice Hall.

Einhard and Notker the Stammerer. 1969. *Two Lives of Charlemagne.* Translated by Lewis Thorpe. New York: Penguin Books.

Elleh, Nnamdi. 1997. *African Architecture: Evolution and Transformation.* New York: McGraw-Hill.

Encyclopedia of Islam. Database: http://www.encislam.brill.

Entelis, John P. 1986. *Algeria: The Revolution Institutionalized.* Boulder, Colo.: Westview Press.

———. 2008. "Democratic Desires and the Authoritarian Temptation in the Central Maghreb." In *North Africa: Politics, Region, and the Limits of Transformation,* edited by Yahia H. Zoubir and Haizam Amirah-Fernández, 9–30. New York: Routledge.

Entelis, John P., ed. 1997. *Islam, Democracy, and the State in North Africa.* Bloomington: Indiana University Press.

Escribano, Gonzalo, and Alejandro V. Lorca. 2008. "Economic Reform in the Maghreb: From Stabilization to Modernization." In *North Africa: Politics, Region, and the Limits of Transformation,* edited by Yahia H. Zoubir and Haizam Amirah-Fernández, 135–158. New York: Routledge.

Esposito, John. 2005. *Islam: The Straight Path.* Revised 3d ed. New York: Oxford University Press.

Evans, Martin, and John Phillips. 2007. *Algeria: Anger of the Dispossessed.* New Haven: Yale University Press.

Fahmy, Khaled. 1998. "The Era of Muhammad 'Ali Pasha, 1805–1848." In *The Cambridge History of Egypt: Modern Egypt, from 1517 to the End of the Twentieth Century,* vol. 2, edited by M. W. Daly, 139–179. Cambridge: Cambridge University Press.

Fanon, Frantz. 1967. *Black Skin, White Masks.* Translated by Charles Lam Markmann. New York: Grove Press.

———. 1968. *The Wretched of the Earth.* Translated by Constance Farrington. New York: Grove Press.

al-Fasi, Alal (Allal). 1954. *The Independence Movements in Arab North Africa.* Translated by Hazem Zaki Nuseibeh. Washington, D.C.: American Council of Learned Societies.

Fayad, Mona. 2000. "Cartographies of Identity: Writing Maghribi Women as Postcolonial Subjects." In *Beyond Colonialism and Nationalism in the Maghrib,* edited by Ali Abdullatif Ahmida, 85–108. New York: Palgrave.

Fenner, Louise. 2007. "Kantara's Message of Peace Blends Tunisian and American Music." 1 June. http://usinfo.state.gov/xarchives/display.html?p=washfile-english&y=2007&m=June&x=20070601132636xlrennefo.1257135.

Ferrié, Jean-Noël. 2002. "Succession monarchique et désenchantement de l'alternance partisane." *Annuaire de l'Afrique du Nord,* 40 (1999). Paris: CNRS, 215–231.

Finch, Charles S. 1991. "The Kamitic Genesis of Christianity." In *African Origins of the Major World Religions,* edited by Amon Saba Saakana, 33–58. 2d ed. London: Karnak House.

Folorunso, Caleb A. 2003. "Views of Ancient Egypt from a West African Perspective." In *Ancient Egypt in Africa,* edited by David O'Connor and Andrew Reid, 77–92. London: UCL Press, Institute of Archaeology.

Franzen, Cola, ed. 1989. *Poems of Arab Andalusia.* Translated from Spanish versions of Emilio García Gómez. San Francisco: City Lights Books.

Frend, W. H. C. 2004. "From Donatist Opposition to Byzantine Loyalism: The Cult of Martyrs in North Africa 350–650." In *Vandals, Romans and Berbers,* edited by A. H. Merrills, 259–270. Aldershot, England: Ashgate.

Fuller, Mia. 2000. "Preservation and Self-Absorption: Italian Colonisation and the Walled City of Tripoli, Libya." *Journal of North African Studies* 5, no. 4 (Winter): 121–154.

Gellner, Ernest. 1969. *Saints of the Atlas.* Chicago: University of Chicago Press.

Gellner, Ernest, and Charles Micaud, eds. 1972. *Arabs and Berbers: From Tribe to Nation in North Africa.* Lexington, Mass.: D. C. Heath and Company.

Gelvin, James L. 2003. "Napoleon in Egypt as History and Polemic." In *Napoleon in Egypt,* edited by Irene A. Bierman, 139–160. Reading, UK: Ithaca Press.

George, Judith W. 2004. "Vandal Poets in Their Context." In *Vandals, Romans and Berbers: New Perspectives on Late Antique North Africa,* edited by A. H. Merrills, 133–144. Aldershot; Burlington, Vt.: Ashgate.

German, Richard, and Elizabeth Taylor. 2007. "Economy." In "Egypt," *The Middle East and North Africa 2008,* 54th ed., 359–377. London: Routledge.

Gershovich, Moshe. 2000. *French Military Rule in Morocco: Colonialism and Its Consequences.* London: Frank Cass.

Geyer, Georgie Anne. 2003. *Tunisia: A Journey through a Country That Works.* London: Stacey International.

Gladiss, Almut von. 2004. "History." In *Islam: Art and Architecture,* edited by Markus Hattstein and Peter Delius, 166–171. Cambridge, UK: Könemann.

Goddard, John. 2007. "If Mick Jagger Spoke Tamashek: Tinariwen Bring Their Nomadic Desert Music, and Their Rebel Aesthetic, to Town." *Toronto Star,* 15 November, E03.

Gold, Peter. 2000. *Europe or Africa? A Contemporary Study of the Spanish North African Enclaves of Ceuta and Melilla.* Liverpool: Liverpool University Press.

Gomaa, Tayseer. 2002. "Who Is Behind the Camera? (Post-Colonial Visual Anthropology, Orientalism, and Latter-Day Egyptomania)." Translated by R. Kevin Lacey. *Journal of Middle Eastern and North African Intellectual and Cultural Studies* 1, no. 1: 67–106.

Goodman, Jane E. 2005. *Berber Culture on the World Stage: From Village to Video.* Bloomington: Indiana University Press.

Gordon, David C. 1962. *North Africa's French Legacy, 1954–1962.* Cambridge, Mass.: Harvard University Press.

———. 1966. *The Passing of French Algeria.* London: Oxford University Press.

Gordon, Lady Duff. 1969. *Letters from Egypt (1862–1869).* Re-edited with additional letters by Gordon Waterfield. New York: Frederick A. Praeger.

Green, Peter. 1990. *Alexander to Actium: The Historical Evolution of the Hellenistic Age.* Berkeley: University of California Press.

Gsell, Stéphane. 1920–1928. *Histoire ancienne de l'Afrique du Nord.* 8 vols. 4th ed. Paris: Librairie Hachette.

Hahn, Lorna. 1960. *North Africa: Nationalism to Nationhood.* Washington, D.C.: Public Affairs.

Haikal, Fayza. 2003. "Egypt's Past Regenerated by Its Own People." In *Napoleon in Egypt,* edited by Irene A. Bierman, 161–180. Reading, UK: Ithaca Press.

al-Hakam, Ibn abd. 2004. *Futuh misr wa-l-maghrib.* Cairo: Maktabat al-Thaqafat al-Diniyyat.

Halm, Heinz. 1997. *The Fatimids and Their Traditions of Learning.* London: I. B. Tauris/ Institute of Ismaili Studies.

Hamdani, Abbas. 1962. *The Fatimids.* Pakistan Chowk, Karachi: Pakistan Publishing House.

Hanna, Nelly. 1998. "Culture in Ottoman Egypt." In *The Cambridge History of Egypt: Modern Egypt, from 1517 to the End of the Twentieth Century,* vol. 2, edited by M. W. Daly, 87–112. Cambridge: Cambridge University Press.

———. 2003. "Introduction." In *Napoleon in Egypt,* edited by Irene A. Bierman, 5–12. Reading, UK: Ithaca Press.

Harlow, Barbara. 1986. "Introduction." In *The Colonial Harem* by Malek Alloula, translated by Barbara Harlow, ix–xii. Minneapolis: University of Minnesota Press.

Harten, Stuart. 2003. "Rediscovering Ancient Egypt: Bonaparte's Expedition and the

Colonial Ideology of the French Revolution." In *Napoleon in Egypt,* edited by Irene A. Bierman, 33–46. Reading, UK: Ithaca Press.

Hattstein, Markus, and Peter Delius, eds. 2004. *Islam: Art and Architecture.* Translated by George Ansell and others. Cambridge, UK: Könemann.

Hazard, Harry W., comp. 1954. *Atlas of the Islamic History.* 3d ed. Princeton: Princeton University Press.

Heers, Jacques. 2003. *The Barbary Corsairs: Warfare in the Mediterranean, 1480–1580.* Translated by Jonathan North. London: Greenhill Books.

Heggoy, Alf Andrew (with Robert R. Crout). 1981. *Historical Dictionary of Algeria.* Metuchen, N.J.: Scarecrow Press.

Henry, Clement M. 2008. "Reverberations in the Central Maghreb of the 'Global War on Terror.'" In *North Africa: Politics, Region, and the Limits of Transformation,* edited by Yahia H. Zoubir and Haizam Amirah-Fernández, 294–310. London: Routledge.

Herodotus. 1978. *The Histories.* Translated by Aubrey de Sélincourt. New York: Penguin Books.

Hess, Andrew C. 1978. *The Forgotten Frontier: A History of the Sixteenth-Century Ibero-African Frontier.* Chicago: University of Chicago Press.

Hill, Derek, Lucien Golvin, and Robert Hillenbrand. 1976. *Islamic Architecture in North Africa.* Hamden, Conn.: Archon Books.

Hillenbrand, Robert. 1976. "Introduction." In *Islamic Architecture in North Africa* by Derek Hill, Lucien Golvin, and Robert Hillenbrand. Hamden, Conn.: Archon Books.

Hitti, Philip K. 1970. *History of the Arabs: From the Earliest Times to the Present.* 10th ed. London: Macmillan.

Hodges, Tony. 1983. *Western Sahara: The Roots of a Desert War.* Westport, Conn.: Lawrence Hill & Company.

Hodgson, Marshall G. S. 1974. *The Venture of Islam.* 3 vols. Chicago: University of Chicago Press.

———. 2000. "Hemispheric Interregional History as an Approach to World History." In *The New World History: A Teacher's Companion,* edited by Ross E. Dunn, 113–123. Boston: Bedford/St. Martin's.

Hoisington, William A., Jr. 1984. *The Casablanca Connection: French Colonial Policy, 1936–1943.* Chapel Hill: University of North Carolina Press.

———. 1995. *Lyautey and the French Conquest of Morocco.* New York: St. Martin's Press.

Holland, Tom. 2005. *Rubicon: The Last Years of the Roman Republic.* New York: Anchor Books.

Homer. 1996. *The Odyssey.* Translated by Robert Fagles. New York: Penguin Books.

Horne, Alistair. 1987. *A Savage War of Peace, Algeria, 1954–1962.* Rev. ed. New York: Penguin.

Hornung, Erik, and Betsy M. Bryan, eds. 2002. *The Quest for Immortality: Treasures of Ancient Egypt.* Washington, D.C.: National Gallery of Art.

Hourani, Albert. 1991a. *A History of the Arab Peoples.* Cambridge, Mass.: Harvard University Press.

———. 1991b. *Islam in European Thought.* Cambridge: Cambridge University Press.

Howe, Marvine. 2005. *Morocco: The Islamist Awakening and Other Challenges.* New York: Oxford University Press.

Humbert, Jean-Marcel. 2003. "How to Stage Aida." Translated by Daniel Antoine and Lawrence Stewart Owens. In *Consuming Ancient Egypt,* edited by Sally MacDonald and Michael Rice, 47–62. London: UCL Press.

Hutt, Antony. 1977. *North Africa: Islamic Architecture.* London: Scorpion Publications.

Ibn Battuta. 1929. *Travels in Asia and Africa, 1325–1354.* Translated and edited by H. A. R. Gibb. London: George Routledge & Sons.

Ibn Idhari (al-Marrakushi), and Abu'l Abbas. 1948–1951. *Histoire de l'Afrique du Nord et de l'Espagne musulmane, intitulée Kitab al-Bayan al-mughrib [fi akhbar al-Andalus wa-l-Maghrib].* 2 vols. Leiden: E. J. Brill.

Ibn Khaldun. 1967. *The Muqaddimah: An Introduction to History.* 2 vols. Translated by Franz Rosenthal. Princeton, N.J.: Princeton University Press.

———. 1968–1969. *Histoire des Berbères et des dynasties musulmanes de l'Afrique septentrionale.* 4 vols. Translated by Le baron de Slane. Paris: Librairie Orientaliste.

Ibrahim, Hassan Ahmed. 1998. "The Egyptian Empire, 1805–1885." In *The Cambridge History of Egypt: Modern Egypt, from 1517 to the End of the Twentieth Century,* vol. 2, edited by M. W. Daly, 198–216. Cambridge: Cambridge University Press.

Ikram, Khalid. 2006. *The Egyptian Economy, 1952–2000: Performance, Policies, and Issues.* London: Routledge.

Imber, Colin. 2002. *The Ottoman Empire, 1300–1650: The Structure of Power.* New York: Palgrave Macmillan.

International Monetary Fund (IMF). 2004a. *Tunisia: Selected Issues.* IMF Country Report No. 04/360. November.

———. 2004b. *Morocco: Selected Issues.* IMF Country Report No. 04/164. June.

———. 2005a. *Arab Republic of Egypt: Selected Issues.* IMF Country Report No. 05/179. June.

———. 2005b. *The Socialist People's Libyan Arab Jamahiriya 2004 Article IV Consultation—Staff Report; Staff Statement; and Public Information Notice on the Executive Board Discussion.* IMF Country Report No. 05/83. March.

———. 2005c. *The Socialist People's Libyan Arab Jamahiriya: Statistical Appendix.* IMF Country Report No. 05/78. March.

———. 2005d. *Algeria: Statistical Appendix.* IMF Country Report No. 05/51. February.

————. 2007a. *Arab Republic of Egypt: Selected Issues.* IMF Country Report No. 07/381. December.

————. 2007b. IMF Working Paper. "Buoyant Capital Spending and Worries over Real Appreciation: Cold Facts from Algeria." 21 pages. December.

————. 2007c. *Tunisia: Selected Issues.* IMF Country Report No. 07/319. September.

————. 2007d. *The Socialist People's Libyan Arab Jamahiriya: Statistical Appendix.* IMF Country Report No./07/148. May.

————. 2007e. *Algeria: Statistical Appendix.* IMF Country Report No. 07/95. March.

————. 2007f. *Algeria: Selected Issues.* IMF Country Report No. 07/61. February.

al-Jabarti, Abd al-Rahman. 1970. *Tarikh Aja'ib al-Athar fi-l-Tarajim wa-l-Athar.* 3 vols. Beirut: Dar al-Faris.

————. 1975. *Al-Jabarti's Chronicle of the First Seven Months of the French Occupation of Egypt,* 15 June–December 1798. *Tarikh muddat al-faransis bi-misr, muharram-rajab 1213.* Edited and translated by Shmuel Moreh. Leiden: E. J. Brill.

————. 1993. *Napoleon in Egypt: Al-Jabarti's Chronicle of the French Occupation, 1798.* Translated by Shmuel Moreh. Princeton: Markus Wiener Publishers.

————. 1994. *'Abd al-Rahman al-Jabarti's History of Egypt (Aja'ib al-Athar fi'l-Tarajim wa'l-Akhbar).* 4 vols. Edited by Thomas Philipp and Moshe Perlmann. Translated by D. Crecilius and others. Stuttgart: Franz Steiner Verlag.

Jabri, Mohammed 'Abel al-. 1999. *Arab-Islamic Philosophy: A Contemporary Critique.* Translated by Aziz Abbassi. Austin: Center for Middle Eastern Studies, University of Texas.

Jackson, Robert B. 2002. *At Empire's Edge: Exploring Rome's Egyptian Frontier.* New Haven, Conn.: Yale University Press.

Jankowski, James. 2000. *Egypt: A Short History.* Oxford: Oneworld Publications.

Jasanoff, Maya. 2005. *The Edge of Empire: Lives, Culture, and Conquest in the East, 1750–1850.* New York: Vintage Books.

Jensen, Erik. 2005. *Western Sahara: Anatomy of a Stalemate.* Boulder, Colo.: Lynne Rienner Publishers.

Joffé, George, ed. 1993. *North Africa: Nation, State, and Region.* London: Routledge.

John, Bishop of Nikiu. 1916. *The Chronicle of John, Bishop of Nikiu.* Translated by R. H. Charles. London: Williams & Norgate.

Julien, Charles-André. 1970. *History of North Africa: Tunisia, Algeria, Morocco: From the Arab Conquest to 1830.* Edited and revised by Roger Le Tourneau. Translated by John Petrie. London: Routledge & Kegan Paul.

Kably, Mohamed. 1999. "Legitimacy of State Power and Socioreligious Variations in Medieval Morocco." Translated by Seth Graebner and Susan Gilson Miller. In *In the Shadow of the Sultan: Culture, Power, and Politics in Morocco,* edited by Rahma

Bourquia and Susan Gilson Miller, 17–29. Cambridge, Mass.: Center for Middle Eastern Studies, Harvard University Press.

Kaddache, Mahfoud. 2003. *L'Algérie des Algériens: de la préhistoire à 1954.* Paris: Editions Paris-Méditerranée; Algiers: EDIF, 2000, 2003.

Kaegi, Walter E. 1998. "Egypt on the Eve of the Muslim Conquest." In *The Cambridge History of Egypt: Islamic Egypt, 640–1517,* vol. 1, edited by Carl F. Petry, 34–61. Cambridge: Cambridge University Press.

Karabell, Zachary. 2004. *Parting the Desert: The Creation of the Suez Canal.* New York: Vintage Books.

Karsh, Efraim. 2007. *Islamic Imperialism: A History.* New Haven: Yale University Press.

Keaton, Trica Danielle. 2006. *Muslim Girls and the Other France: Race, Identity Politics, and Social Exclusion.* Bloomington: Indiana University Press.

Keddie, Nikki R. 1968. *An Islamic Response to Imperialism: Political and Religious Writings of Sayyid Jamal ad-Din "al-Afghani."* Berkeley: University of California Press.

Kennedy, Hugh. 1996. *Muslim Spain and Portugal: A Political History of al-Andalus.* London: Longman.

———. 2007. *The Great Arab Conquests: How the Spread of Islam Changed the World We Live In.* London: Weidenfeld & Nicolson.

Keys, David. 2004. "Kingdom of the Sands." *Archaeology* 57 (no. 2) (March/April). http://www.archaeology.org/0403/abstracts/sands.html.

Khadduri, Majid. 1963. *Modern Libya: A Study in Political Development.* Baltimore: Johns Hopkins University Press.

Khatibi, Abdelke(é)bir. 1983. *Maghrib pluriel.* Paris: Denoël.

———. 1985. "Double Criticism: The Decolonization of Arab Sociology." In *Contemporary North Africa: Issues of Development and Integration,* edited by Halim Barakat, 9–19. Washington, D.C.: Georgetown Center for Contemporary Arab Studies.

Khiari, Sadri. 2005. "Les balbutiements du mouvement altermondialiste au Maghreb." *Annuaire de l'Afrique du Nord* 41 (2005). Paris: CNRS, 113–125.

Killian, Caitlin. 2006. *North African Women in France: Gender, Culture, and Identity.* Stanford, Calif.: Stanford University Press.

Kish, George, ed. 1978. *A Source Book in Geography.* Cambridge: Harvard University Press.

Knapp, Wilfrid. 1977. *North West Africa: A Political and Economic Survey.* 3d ed. Oxford: Oxford University Press.

Lacoste, Yves. 1969. *Ibn Khaldoun: naissance de l'histoire passé du tiers-monde.* 2d ed. Paris: François Maspero.

Larguèche, Abdelhamid. 2001. "The City and the Sea: Evolving Forms of Mediterranean Cosmopolitanism in Tunis, 1700–1881." In *North Africa, Islam, and the Medi-*

terranean World: From the Almoravids to the Algerian War, edited by Julia Clancy-Smith, 117–128. London: Frank Cass.

Laroui, Abdallah. 1977. *The History of the Maghrib: An Interpretive Essay*. Translated by Ralph Manheim. Princeton, N.J.: Princeton University Press.

Lawless, Richard I. 2007. "History." In "Libya," *The Middle East and North Africa 2008*, 54th ed., 768–794. London: Routledge.

Lawless, Richard, and Laila Monahan, eds. 1987. *War and Refugees: The Western Sahara Conflict*. London: Pinter Publishers.

Lawrence, William. 2003. "Representing Algerian Youth: The Discourses of Cultural Confrontation and Experimentation with Democracy and Political Islam since the Riots of 1998." Ph.D. dissertation, Fletcher School, Tufts University, Medford, Massachusetts.

Lawson, Fred H. 1992. *The Social Origins of Egyptian Expansion during the Muhammad 'Ali Period*. New York: Columbia University Press.

Layachi, Azzedine. 1996. "The Domestic and International Constraints of Economic Adjustment in Algeria." In *North Africa: Development and Reform in a Changing Global Economy*, edited by Dirk Vandewalle, 129–152. New York: St. Martin's Press.

———. 1998. "Conclusion: The Maghreb in Transition." In *Economic Crisis and Political Change in North Africa*, edited by Azzedine Layachi, 165–172. Westport, Conn.: Praeger.

———. 2005. "Political Liberalisation and the Islamist Movement in Algeria." In *Islam, Democracy, and the State in Algeria: Lessons for the Western Mediterranean and Beyond*, edited by Michael Bonner et al., 46–67. London: Routledge.

Layachi, Azzedine, ed. 1998. *Economic Crisis and Political Change in North Africa*. Westport, Conn.: Praeger.

Lazreg, Marnia. 2000. "Islamism and the Recolonization of Algeria." In *Beyond Colonialism and Nationalism in the Maghrib: History, Culture, and Politics*, edited by Ali Abullatif Ahmida, 147–164. New York: Palgrave.

Le Gall, Michel, and Kenneth Perkins, eds. 1997. *The Maghrib in Question: Essays in History and Historiography*. Austin: University of Texas Press.

Leo Africanus. 1970. *The History and Description of Africa and of the Notable Things Therein Contained*. Translated by John Pory. 3 vols. New York: Burt Franklin (reprint of the Hakluyt Society 1896 edition).

Le Sueur, James. 2001. *Uncivil War: Intellectuals and Identity Politics during the Decolonization of Algeria*. Philadelphia: University of Pennsylvania Press.

Le Tourneau, Roger. 1961. *Fez in the Age of the Marinides*. Translated by B. A. Clement. Norman: University of Oklahoma Press.

———. 1962. *Evolution politique de l'Afrique du Nord musulmane, 1920–1961*. Paris: A. Colin.

———. 1970. "North Africa to the Sixteenth Century." In *The Cambridge History of Islam,* vol. 2, edited by P. M. Holt and others, 211–237. Cambridge: Cambridge University Press.

Levinson, Charles. 2004. "$50 Billion Later, Taking Stock of US Aid to Egypt." *Christian Science Monitor,* 12 April, www.csmonitor.com/2004/0412/p07s01-wome.html.

Lewis, Bernard. 1974. *Islam from the Prophet Muhammad to the Capture of Constantinople.* Volume 1: *Politics and War.* Volume 2: *Religion and Society.* New York: Harper & Row.

———. 1982. *The Muslim Discovery of Europe.* New York: W. W. Norton & Company.

———. 2002. *What Went Wrong? The Clash between Islam and Modernity in the Middle East.* New York: HarperCollins.

Liauzu, Claude. 2005. "At War with France's Past." Translated by Donald Hounam. *Le Monde Diplomatique* (June). http://mondediplo.com/2005/06/19colonisation.

Livy (Titus Livius). 2006. *Hannibal's War: Books Twenty-One to Thirty.* Translated by J. C. Yardley. New York: Oxford University Press.

Lloyd, Alan B. 2000. "The Ptolemaic Period (332–330 BC)." In *The Oxford History of Ancient Egypt,* edited by Ian Shaw, 395–421. Oxford: Oxford University Press.

Lorcin, Patricia M. E., 1995. *Imperial Identities: Stereotyping, Prejudice and Race in Colonial Algeria.* London: I. B. Tauris.

Lorcin, Patricia M. E., ed. 2006. *Algeria and France, 1800–2000: Identity, Memory, Nostalgia.* Syracuse, N.Y.: Syracuse University Press.

Louis, William Roger. 2006. *Ends of British Imperialism: The Scramble for Empire, Suez and Decolonization.* London: I. B. Tauris.

Lyautey, Hubert. 1900. "Du rôle colonial de l'armée." *Revue des Deux Mondes,* 156 (15 January): 308–329.

MacDonald, Kevin C. 2003. "Cheikh Anta Diop and Ancient Egypt in Africa." In *Ancient Egypt in Africa,* edited by David O'Connor and Andrew Reid, 93–106. London: UCL Press, Institute of Archaeology.

MacDonald, Sally, and Michael Rice, eds. 2003. *Consuming Ancient Egypt.* London: UCL Press.

al-Madani, Ahmed Tewfiq (Ahmad Tawfiq). 1968. *Al-Harb al-thalathamia'at bayna al-Jaza'ir wa Isbanya, 1792–1492.* Algiers: SNED.

———. 1984 (1931). *Kitab al-Jaza'ir.* Algiers: al-Mu'assasa al-wataniyya.

Maddy-Weitzman, Bruce, and Daniel Zisenwine, eds. 2007. *The Maghrib in the New Century: Identity, Religion, and Politics.* Gainesville: University Press of Florida.

Maghraoui, Driss. 2004. "The 'Grande Guerre Sainte': Moroccan Colonial Troops and Workers in the First World War." *Journal of North African Studies* 9, no. 1 (Spring): 1–21.

Mahdi, Muhsin. 1964. *Ibn Khaldun's Philosophy of History: A Study in the Philosophic Foundation of the Science of Culture.* Chicago: University of Chicago Press.

al-Makkari, Ahmed ibn Mohammed (Ahmad bn Muhammad al-Maqqari). 2002. *The History of the Mohammedan Dynasties in Spain.* 2 vols. Translated by Pascual de Gayangos. London: RoutledgeCurzon (previously published in 1840 and 1843 by the Royal Asiatic Society).

Manley, Deborah, and Sahar Abdel-Hakim. 2004. *Traveling through Egypt: From 540 B.C. to the Twentieth Century.* Cairo: American University Press in Cairo.

Mantran, Robert. 1970. "North Africa in the Sixteenth and Seventeenth Centuries." In *The Cambridge History of Islam,* vol. 2, edited by P. M. Holt and others, 238–265. Cambridge: Cambridge University Press.

Marsot, Afaf Lutfi al-Sayyid. 2007. *A History of Egypt: From the Arab Conquest to the Present.* 2d ed. Cambridge: Cambridge University Press.

Martinez, Luis. 2000. *The Algerian Civil War, 1990–1998.* Translated by Jonathan Derrick. New York: Columbia University Press.

———. 2005. "Why the Violence in Algeria?" In *Islam, Democracy, and the State in Algeria: Lessons for the Western Mediterranean and Beyond,* edited by Michael Bonner et al., 14–27. London: Routledge.

Mattar, Philip, ed. 2004. *Encyclopedia of the Modern Middle East and North Africa.* Vols. 1–4. Detroit: Thompson Gale.

Mazot, Sibylle. 2004. "Decorative Arts." In *Islam: Art and Architecture,* edited by Markus Hattstein and Peter Delius, 154–157. Cambridge, UK: Könemann.

McDougall, James. 2006. *History and the Culture of Nationalism in Algeria.* Cambridge: Cambridge University Press.

McDougall, James, ed. 2003. *Nation, Society and Culture in North Africa.* Special Issue. *Journal of North African Studies* 8, no. 1 (Spring).

McNeill, William H., and Marilyn Robinson Waldman, eds. 1983. *The Islamic World.* Chicago: University of Chicago Press.

Mercer, John. 1976. *Spanish Sahara.* London: George Allen & Unwin Ltd.

Merrills, A. H., ed. 2004. *Vandals, Romans and Berbers: New Perspectives on Late Antique North Africa.* Aldershot, England: Ashgate.

Messier, Ronald A. 2001. "Re-Thinking the Almoravids, Re-Thinking Ibn Khaldun." In *North Africa, Islam, and the Mediterranean World: From the Almoravids to the Algerian War,* edited by Julia Clancy-Smith, 59–80. London: Frank Cass.

Messier, Ronald A., ed. 2008. "The Worlds of Ibn Khaldun." Journal of North African Studies 13 (Special Issue), no. 3.

al-Mili. Mubarak bn Muhammad. 1963–1964. *Tarikh al-Jaza'ir fi-l-qadim wa-l-hadith.* 3 vols. 2d ed. Algiers: Maktabat al-nahda-l-jaza'iriyya.

Military Journal of General Buonaparte; Being a Concise Narrative of His Expedition from Egypt into Syria, in Asia Minor: Giving a Succinct Account of the Various Marches, Battles, Skirmishes, and Sieges, including That of St. John D'Acre, from the Time He Left Cairo, until His Return There. Together with an Account of the Memorable Battle of Aboukir, and Recapture of the Fortress. 1800. Baltimore: Warner & Hanna.

Miranda, Ambroxio Huici. 1970. "The Iberian Peninsula and Sicily." In *The Cambridge History of Islam,* vol. 2, edited by P. M. Holt and others, 406–440. Cambridge: Cambridge University Press.

Mitchell, Timothy. 1992. "Orientalism and the Exhibitionary Order." In *Colonialism and Culture,* edited by Nicholas B. Dirks, 289–317. Ann Arbor: University of Michigan Press.

Moaddel, Mansoor, and Kamran Talattof, eds. 2000. *Contemporary Debates in Islam: An Anthology of Modernist and Fundamentalist Thought.* New York: St. Martin's Press.

Mohrmann, Christine. 1961. *Etudes sur le Latin des Chrétiens.* Vol. 1: *Le Latin des Chrétiens.* 2d ed. Rome: Edizioni di Storia e Letteratura.

Momigliano, Arnaldo. 1975. *Alien Wisdom: The Limits of Hellenization.* Cambridge: Cambridge University Press.

Montagne, Robert. 1973. *The Berbers: Their Social and Political Organisation.* Translated by David Seddon. London: Frank Cass.

Moore, Clement Henry. 1970. *Politics in North Africa: Algeria, Morocco, and Tunisia.* Boston: Little, Brown and Company.

Moreh, Shmuel. 2003. "Napoleon and the French Impact on Egyptian Society in the Eyes of Al-Jabarti." In *Napoleon in Egypt,* edited by Irene A. Bierman, 77–98. Reading, UK: Ithaca Press.

Moore, Clement Henry. 1984. "The Maghrib." In Vol. 8: *The Cambridge History of Africa: Africa from c. 1940 to c. 1975,* edited by Michael Crowder, 564–610. Cambridge: Cambridge University Press.

"Morocco and Polisario Agree to Talk." *Al-Jazeera,* 1 May 2007. http://english.aljazeera .net/NR/exeres/7EB6326C-8585-4A7C-A1BA-15D84D984907.htm.

Morsy, Magali. 1984. *North Africa 1800–1900: A Survey from the Nile Valley to the Atlantic.* London: Longman.

Mortimer, Robert A. 2006. "State and Army in Algeria: The 'Bouteflika Effect.'" *Journal of North African Studies* 11, no. 2 (June): 155–171.

———. 2007. "Algerian Identity and Memory." In *The Maghrib in the New Century: Identity, Religion, and Politics,* edited by Bruce Maddy-Weitzman and Daniel Zisenwine, 36–49. Gainesville: University Press of Florida.

———. 2008. "Boualem Sansal: Novelist, Polemicist, Eulogist." *Journal of North African Studies* 13, no. 1 (March): 119–125.

Mundy, Jacob. 2006. "Neutrality or Complicity? The United States and the 1975 Moroccan Takeover of the Spanish Sahara." *Journal of North African Studies* 11, no. 3 (September): 275–306.

Munson, Henry, Jr. 1999. "The Elections of 1993 and Democratization in Morocco." In *In the Shadow of the Sultan: Culture, Power, and Politics in Morocco*, edited by Rahma Bourquia and Susan Gilson Miller, 259–281. Cambridge, Mass.: Center for Middle Eastern Studies, Harvard University Press.

al-Muqaddasi. 2001. *The Best Divisions for Knowledge of the Regions*. Translated by Basil Collins. Reading, UK: Garnet Publishing.

Nasr, Seyyed Hossein. 2003. *Islam: Religion, History, and Civilization*. New York: HarperSanFrancisco.

Nassar, Hala Khamis, and Marco Boggero. 2008. "Omar al-Mukhtar: The Formation of Cultural Memory and the Case of the Militant Group That Bears His Name." *Journal of North African Studies* 13, no. 2 (June): 201–217.

Naylor, Phillip C. 1990. "Maghrib Unity: Illusive or Elusive?" *Africana Journal* 15: 305–315.

———. 1992. "Spain and France and the Western Sahara: A Historical Narrative and Study of National Transformation." In *International Dimensions of the Western Saharan Conflict*, edited by Yahia Zoubir and Daniel Volman, 17–51. Westport, Conn.: Praeger Press.

———. 2000a. *France and Algeria: A History of Decolonization and Transformation*. Gainesville: University Press of Florida.

———. 2000b. *The Wider West: A Survey in Trans-Cultural Context*. 4th ed. Vol. 1: *From Antiquity to the European Age of Exploration*. Boston: Pearson Custom Publishing.

———. 2001. *The Wider West: A Survey in Trans-Cultural Context*. 4th ed. Vol. 2: *From the European Age of Exploration to the New Millennium*. Boston: Pearson Custom Publishing.

———. 2006a. "The Formative Influence of French Colonialism on the Life and Thought of Malek Bennabi (Malik bn Nabi)." *French Colonial History* 5: 129–142.

———. 2006b. *Historical Dictionary of Algeria*. 3d ed. Lanham, Md.: Scarecrow Press.

Nickerson, Jane Soames. 1968. *A Short History of North Africa: From Pre-Roman Times to the Present*. New York: Biblo and Tannen.

Norris, H. T. 1986. *The Arab Conquest of the Western Sahara*. Harlow, Essex, and Beirut: Longman and Libraire de Liban.

"North Africa, History of." *Encyclopædia Britannica*. 2005. Encyclopædia Britannica Online. http://search.eb.com/eb/article?tocId=9110707.

Northrup, Linda S. 1998. "The Bahri Mamluk Sultanate, 1250–1390." In *The Cambridge History of Egypt: Islamic Egypt, 640–1517*, vol. 1, edited by Carl F. Petry, 242–289. Cambridge: Cambridge University Press.

Nouschi, André. 1970. "North Africa in the Period of Colonization." In *The Cambridge*

History of Islam, vol. 2, edited by P. M. Holt and others, 299–326. Cambridge: Cambridge University Press.

O'Connor, David, and Andrew Reid. 2003. *Ancient Egypt in Africa.* London: UCL Press, Institute of Archaeology.

Ouali, Aomar. 2007. "Algeria's Dominant Party Keeps Power." Associated Press. http:// www.washingtonpost.com/wp-dyn/content/article/2007/05/18/AR2007051800341 .html.

Ouannes, Moncef. 1999. "Libye: Chronique intérieure." *Annuaire de l'Afrique du Nord* 36 (1997). Paris: Centre National de la Recherche Scientifique.

Owen, Roger. 1993. "Egypt and Europe: From French Expedition to British Occupation." In *The Modern Middle East: A Reader,* edited by Albert Hourani, Philip S. Khoury, and Mary C. Wilson, 111–124. Berkeley: University of California Press.

Pargeter, Alison. 2000. "Anglo-Libyan Relations and the Suez Crisis." *Journal of North African Studies* 5, no. 2 (Summer): 41–58.

Parker, Richard B. 1981. *A Practical Guide to Islamic Monuments in Morocco.* Charlottesville, Va.: Baraka Press.

———. 1985. "Appointment in Oujda." *Foreign Affairs* 63 (Summer): 1095–1110.

———. 1987. *North Africa: Regional Tensions and Strategic Concerns.* Revised and updated edition. New York: Praeger.

———. 2004. *Uncle Sam in Barbary: A Diplomatic History.* Gainesville: University Press of Florida.

Pazzanita, Anthony G., and Tony Hodges. 1994. *Historical Dictionary of Western Sahara.* 2d ed. Metuchen, N.J.: Scarecrow Press.

Pennell, C. R. 2000. *Morocco since 1830: A History.* London: Hurst & Company.

———. 2003. *Morocco: From Empire to Independence.* Oxford, England: Oneworld.

Pérennès, Jean-Jacques. 2000. *Pierre Claverie: Un Algérien par alliance.* Paris: Cerf.

Perkins, Kenneth J. 1997. *Historical Dictionary of Tunisia.* 2d ed. Lanham, Maryland: Scarecrow Press.

———. 2004. *A History of Modern Tunisia.* Cambridge: Cambridge University Press.

Peters, F. E. 1972. "Islam as a Western Civilization." *Arabic World* 18, no. 3 (May–June): 13–19.

Petry, Carl F., ed. 1998. *The Cambridge History of Egypt.* Vol. 1, *Islamic Egypt, 640–1517.* Cambridge: Cambridge University Press.

Peyrouton, Marcel. 1966. *Histoire générale du Maghreb.* Paris: Albin Michel.

Pitock, Todd. 2005. "Open Desert: Libya, Africa's Newly Reformed Rogue State, Rolls Out the Magic Carpet." *Forbes FYI,* October, 100–106.

"Plant at the Crossroads." 2006. *Rolling Stone,* 14 December, 18.

Pliny. 1942. *Natural History.* Vol. 2 (Books II–VII). Translated by H. Rackham. Cambridge: Harvard University Press.

Plutarch. 1986. *Plutarch's Lives.* Vol. 7. Cambridge, Mass.: Harvard University Press.

———. 1988. *Plutarch's Lives.* Vol. 9. Cambridge, Mass.: Harvard University Press.

The Poem of the Cid: A New Critical Edition of the Spanish Text. 1975. Introduction by Ian Michael. Translated by Rita Hamilton and Janet Perry. Manchester, UK: Manchester University Press.

Pohl, Walter. 2004. "The Vandals: Fragments of a Narrative." In *Vandals, Romans and Berbers,* edited by A. H. Merrills, 31–48. Aldershot, England: Ashgate.

Polo, Marco. 1958. *The Travels of Marco Polo.* Translated by Ronald Latham. New York: Penguin.

Porch, Douglas. 1984. *The Conquest of the Sahara.* New York: Knopf.

Polybius. 1962. *The Histories of Polybius.* 2 vols. Translated by Evelyn S. Shuckburgh. Bloomington: Indiana University Press.

Price, David Lynn. 1979. *63: Western Sahara.* Georgetown Center for Strategic and International Studies. Beverly Hills, Calif.: Sage Publications.

Pritchard, James B., ed. 1958. *The Ancient Near East: An Anthology of Texts and Pictures.* Princeton, N.J.: Princeton University Press.

Prochaska, David. 1990. *Making Algeria: Colonialism in Bône, 1870–1920.* Oxford: Oxford University Press.

Procopius. 1953. *History of the Wars.* Volume 2. Cambridge, Mass.: Harvard University Press.

Quataert, Donald. 2005. *The Ottoman Empire, 1700–1922.* 2d ed. New York: Cambridge University Press.

Qutb, Seyyid (Sayyid). n.d. *Milestones.* Damascus, Syria: Dar al-Ilm.

Rabinow, Paul. 1989. *French Modern: Norms and Forms of the Social Environment.* Cambridge, Mass.: MIT Press.

Raven, Susan. 1993. *Rome in Africa.* 3d ed. London: Routledge.

Raymond, André. 1970. "North Africa in the Pre-Colonial Period." In *The Cambridge History of Islam,* vol. 2, edited by P. M. Holt and others, 266–298. Cambridge: Cambridge University Press.

Reebs, Stéphane. 2006. "Long Dig." *Natural History* (May): 14.

Reid, Donald Malcolm. 1998. "The 'Urabi Revolution and the British Conquest, 1879–1882." In *The Cambridge History of Egypt: Modern Egypt, from 1517 to the End of the Twentieth Century,* vol. 2, edited by M. W. Daly, 217–238. Cambridge: Cambridge University Press.

———. 2002. *Whose Pharaohs? Archaeology, Museums, and Egyptian National Identity from Napoleon to World War I.* Berkeley: University of California Press.

Ritner, Robert K. 1998. "Egypt under Roman Rule: The Legacy of Ancient Egypt." In *The Cambridge History of Egypt: Islamic Egypt, 640–1517,* vol. 1, edited by Carl F. Petry, 1–33. Cambridge: Cambridge University Press.

Rivet, Daniel. 2002. *Le Maghreb à l'épreuve de la colonisation.* Paris: Hachette Litteratures.

Roberts, Hugh. 1993. "The FLN: French Conceptions, Algerian Realities." In *North Africa: Nation, State, and Region,* edited by George Joffé, 111–141. London: Routledge.

———. 2003. *The Battlefield Algeria, 1988–2002.* London: Verso.

Robinson, Ronald, and John Gallagher. 1961. *Africa and the Victorians: The Official Mind of Imperialism.* London: Macmillan.

Rogerson, Barnaby. 2001. *A Traveller's History of North Africa,* 2d ed. New York: Interlink.

Roller, Duane W. 2003. *The World of Juba II and Kleopatra Selene: Royal Scholarship on Rome's African Frontier.* New York: Routledge.

Rollman, Wilfrid J. 1997. "Introduction." In *The Maghrib in Question: Essays in History and Historiography,* edited by Michel Le Gall and Kenneth Perkins, xi–xxv. Austin: University of Texas Press.

Rosello, Mireille. 2005. *France and the Maghreb: Performative Encounters.* Gainesville: University Press of Florida.

Rosenthal, Erwin I. J. 1979. "Ibn Khaldun as a Political Thinker." *Maghreb Review* 4, no. 1 (January–February): 1–5.

Roussillon, Alain. 1998. "Republican Egypt Interpreted: Revolution and Beyond." In *The Cambridge History of Egypt: Modern Egypt, from 1517 to the End of the Twentieth Century,* vol. 2, edited by M. W. Daly, 198–216. Cambridge: Cambridge University Press.

Rubin, Barry, and Judith Culp Rubin, eds. 2002. *Anti-American Terrorism and the Middle East.* New York: Oxford University Press.

Ruedy, John. 2005. *Modern Algeria: The Origins and Development of a Nation.* 2d ed. Bloomington: Indiana University Press.

Ruedy, John, ed. 1994. *Islamism and Secularism in North Africa.* New York: St. Martin's Press.

Ruf, Werner. 2004. "Sahara Occidental: un conflit sans solution?" *Annuaire de l'Afrique du Nord* 40 (2002). Paris: CNRS.

Russell, Terence M., ed. 2001. *The Napoleonic Survey of Egypt (Description de l'Egypte): The Monuments and Customs of Egypt.* 2 vols. Aldershot, England: Ashgate.

Russman, Edna R., and others. 2001. *Eternal Egypt: Masterworks of Ancient Art from the British Museum.* Berkeley: University of California Press.

Russo, John Paul. 2005. *The Future without a Past: The Humanities in a Technological Society.* Columbia: University of Missouri Press.

Saakana, Amon Saba, ed. 1991. *African Origins of the Major World Religions.* 2d ed. London: Karnak House.

as(al)-Saffar, Muhammad. 1992. *Disorienting Encounters: Travels of a Moroccan Scholar in France in 1845–1846 (The Voyage of Muhammad as-Saffar)*. Translated by Susan Gilson Miller. Berkeley: University of California Press.

"Sahara." *Encyclopædia Britannica*. 2005. Encyclopædia Britannica Online. http://search.eb.com/eb/article?tocId=9108296.

Said, Edward W. 1979. *Orientalism*. New York: Vintage.

St. John, Ronald Bruce. 1998. *Historical Dictionary of Libya*. 3d ed. Lanham, Maryland: Scarecrow Press.

———. 2008. "Libya: Reforming the Economy, Not the Polity." In *North Africa: Politics, Region, and the Limits of Transformation*, edited by Yahia H. Zoubir and Haizam Amirah-Fernández, 53–70. New York: Routledge.

Sallust. 1967. *The Jugurthine War. The Conspiracy of Catiline*. Translated by S. A. Handford. Baltimore: Penguin.

Sanders, Paula A. 1998. "The Fatimid State, 969–1171." In *The Cambridge History of Egypt: Islamic Egypt, 640–1517*, vol. 1, edited by Carl F. Petry, 151–174. Cambridge: Cambridge University Press.

Sansal, Boualem. 2007. *Petit éloge de la mémoire: Quatre mille et une années de nostalgie*. Paris: Gallimard.

Savage, Elizabeth. 1997. *A Gateway to Hell, A Gateway to Paradise: The North African Response to the Arab Conquest*. Princeton, N.J.: Darwin Press.

Schade-Poulsen, Marc. 1999. *Men and Popular Music in Algeria*. Austin: University of Texas Press.

Schroeter, Daniel J. 1999. "Royal Power and the Economy in Precolonial Morocco: Jews and the Legitimation of Foreign Trade." In *In the Shadow of the Sultan: Culture, Power, and Politics in Morocco*, edited by Rahma Bourquia and Susan Gilson Miller, 74–102. Cambridge, Mass.: Center for Middle Eastern Studies, Harvard University Press.

Segrè, Claudio G. 1974. *Fourth Shore: The Italian Colonization of Libya*. Chicago: University of Chicago Press.

Shaw, Ian. 2000a. "Egypt and the Outside World." In *The Oxford History of Ancient Egypt*, edited by Ian Shaw, 314–329. Oxford: Oxford University Press.

Shaw, Ian, ed. 2000b. *The Oxford History of Ancient Egypt*. Oxford: Oxford University Press.

Shelley, Toby. 2004. *Endgame in the Western Sahara: What Future for Africa's Last Colony?* New York: Zed Books.

Silverstein, Paul A. 2003. "Martyrs and Patriots: Ethnic, National and Transnational Dimensions of Kabyle Politics." *Journal of North African Studies* 8, no. 1 (Spring): 87–111.

———. 2004. *Algeria in France: Transpolitics, Race, and Nation*. Bloomington: Indiana University Press.

Slackman, Michael. 2007. "A Quiet Revolution in Algeria: Gains by Women." *New York Times,* 26 May, A1, A6.

Smith, Richard L. 2006. *Ahmad al-Mansur: Islamic Visionary.* New York: Pearson Longman.

Sonbol, Amira. 2003. "The French and Egypt's Medical Profession." In *Napoleon in Egypt,* edited by Irene A. Bierman, 115–138. Reading, UK: Ithaca Press.

Sorkin, Michael. 2001. *Some Assembly Required.* Minneapolis: University of Minnesota Press.

Starr, Chester G. 1991. *A History of the Ancient World.* 4th ed. New York: Oxford University Press.

Stillman, Norman A. 1998. "The Non-Muslim Communities: The Jewish Community." In *The Cambridge History of Egypt: Islamic Egypt, 640–1517,* vol. 1, edited by Carl F. Petry, 198–210. Cambridge: Cambridge University Press.

Stora, Benjamin. 1991. *La Gangrène et l'oubli: La Mémoire des années algériennes.* Paris: La Découverte.

———. 2001. *Algeria, 1830–2000: A Short History.* Translated by Jane Marie Todd. Ithaca, N.Y.: Cornell University Press.

———. 2003. "Algeria/Morocco: The Passions of the Past, Representations of the Nation that Unite and Divide." *Journal of North African Studies* 8, no. 1 (Spring): 14–34.

———. 2007. "The Maghrib at the Dawn of the Twenty-first Century." In *The Maghrib in the New Century: Identity, Religion, and Politics,* edited by Bruce Maddy-Weitzman and Daniel Zisenwine, 1–9. Gainesville: University Press of Florida.

Strabo. 1949. *The Geography of Strabo.* Vol. 8. Translated by Horace Leonard Jones. Cambridge: Harvard University Press.

Symcox, Geoffrey. 2003. "The Geopolitics of the Egyptian Expedition, 1797–1798." In *Napoleon in Egypt,* edited by Irene A. Bierman, 13–32. Reading, UK: Ithaca Press.

Taha, Abdulwahid Dhanun. 1989. *The Muslim Conquest and Settlement of North Africa and Spain.* London: Routledge.

al-Tahtawi, Rifa'a Rafi'. 2004. *An Imam in Paris: Account of a Stay in France by an Egyptian Cleric (1826–1831).* Translated by Daniel L. Newman. London: Saqi.

Taleb (Ibrahimi), Ahmed. 1966. *Lettres de prison, 1957–1961.* Algiers: SNED.

Tessler, Mark. 2003. "The Influence of Islam on Attitudes toward Democracy in Morocco and Algeria." In *Democratization in the Middle East: Experiences, Struggles, Challenges,* edited by Amin Saikal and Albrecht Schnabel, 103–126. New York: United Nations University Press.

Thompson, Ann. 1987. *Barbary and Enlightenment: European Attitudes towards the Maghreb in the 18th Century.* Leiden: E. J. Brill.

Tlemçani, Rachid. 2008. "Algeria under Bouteflika: Civil Strife and National Reconciliation." Carnegie Paper. Carnegie Endowment for International Peace. http:

//www.carnegieendowment.org/publications/index.cfm?fa=view&id=19976&prog
=zgp&proj=zme.

Toledano, Ehud R. 1998. "Social and Economic Change in the 'Long Nineteenth Cen-
tury.'" In *The Cambridge History of Egypt: Modern Egypt, from 1517 to the End of the
Twentieth Century,* vol. 2, edited by M. W. Daly, 252–284. Cambridge: Cambridge
University Press.

Tyldesley, Joyce A. 1996. *Hatchepsut: The Female Pharaoh.* New York: Viking.

"UN Calls for Talks on Western Sahara." *Al-Jazeera,* 30 April 2007. http://english
.aljazeera.net/NR/exeres/BAF5B976-0D1A-42B6-A70D-77491213A403.htm.

Valensi, Lucette. 1977. *On the Eve of Colonialism: North Africa before the French Conquest, 1790–1830.* Translated by Kenneth J. Perkins. New York: Africana Publishing
Company.

Vandewalle, Dirk. 1996. "Qadhafi's Failed Economic Reforms: Markets, Institutions,
and Development in a Rentier State." In *North Africa: Development and Reform in a
Changing Global Economy,* edited by Dirk Vandewalle, 203–225. New York: St. Martin's Press.

———. 1998. *Libya since Independence: Oil and State-Building.* Ithaca, N.Y.: Cornell University Press.

———. 2006. *A History of Modern Libya.* Cambridge: Cambridge University Press.

Vandewalle, Dirk, ed. 1996. *North Africa: Development and Reform in a Changing Global
Economy.* New York: St. Martin's Press.

Vansina, Jan. 1984. *Art History in Africa: An Introduction to Method.* London: Longman.

Voll, John O. 1997. "Sultans, Saints, and Presidents: The Islamic Community and the
State in North Africa." In *Islam, Democracy, and the State in North Africa,* edited by
John P. Entelis, 1–16. Bloomington: Indiana University Press.

Walker, Paul E. 2002. *Exploring an Islamic Empire: Fatimid History and Its Sources.* London: I. B. Tauris.

Wallerstein, Immanuel M. 1974. *The Modern World-System.* 3 vols. New York: Academic
Press.

Waltz, Susan E. 1999. "Interpreting Political Reform in Morocco." In *In the Shadow of
the Sultan: Culture, Power, and Politics in Morocco,* edited by Rahma Bourquia and
Susan Gilson Miller, 282–305. Cambridge, Mass.: Center for Middle Eastern Studies, Harvard University Press.

Warmington, B. H. 1954. *The North African Provinces from Diocletian to the Vandal Conquest.* Cambridge: Cambridge University Press.

———. 1969. *Carthage.* Rev. ed. New York: Praeger.

Waterbury, John. 1970. *The Commander of the Faithful: The Moroccan Political Elite: A
Study in Segmented Politics.* New York: Columbia University Press.

———. 1997. "From Social Contracts to Extraction Contracts: The Political Economy of Authoritarianism and Democracy." In *Islam, Democracy, and the State in North Africa,* edited by John P. Entelis, 141–176. Bloomington: Indiana University Press.

Watt, W. M. 1972. *The Influence of Islam on Medieval Europe.* Edinburgh: Edinburgh University Press.

Welch, Galbraith. 1972. *North Africa Prelude: The First Seven Thousand Years.* Westport, Conn.: Greenwood Publishers.

Wellard, James. 1964. *The Great Sahara.* London: Hutchinson.

———. 1967. *Lost Worlds of Africa.* New York: E. F. Dutton.

Wheatcroft, Andrew. 1995. *The Ottomans: Dissolving Images.* New York: Penguin.

White, Gregory W. 2008. "The 'End of the Era of Leniency' in Morocco." In *North Africa: Politics, Region, and the Limits of Transformation,* edited by Yahia H. Zoubir and Haizam Amirah-Fernández, 90–108. New York: Routledge.

Whitlock, Craig. 2007. "Algeria's Voters Uninspired as Limited Democracy Slowly Evolves." *Washington Post,* 16 May, A09.

Wilbour, Charles Edwin. 1936. *Travels in Egypt (December 1880 to May 1891): Letters of Charles Edwin Wilbour.* Edited by Jean Capart. Brooklyn, N.Y.: Brooklyn Museum.

Wilfong, Terry G. 1998. "The Non-Muslim Communities: Christian Communities." In *The Cambridge History of Egypt: Islamic Egypt, 640–1517,* vol. 1, edited by Carl F. Petry, 175–197. Cambridge: Cambridge University Press.

Williams, Caroline. 1993. *Islamic Monuments in Cairo: A Practical Guide.* 4th ed. Cairo: American University in Cairo Press.

Willis, Michael J. 2008. "The Politics of Berber (Amazigh) Identity: Algeria and Morocco Compared." In *North Africa: Politics, Region, and the Limits of Transformation,* edited by Yahia H. Zoubir and Haizam Amirah-Fernández, 227–242. New York: Routledge.

Wilson, John A., trans. 1958. "The Hymn to the Aton." In *The Ancient Near East: An Anthology of Texts and Pictures,* edited by James B. Pritchard, 226–230. Princeton: Princeton University Press.

Winter, Michael. 1998. "Ottoman Egypt, 1525–1609." In *The Cambridge History of Egypt: Modern Egypt, from 1517 to the End of the Twentieth Century,* vol. 2, edited by M. W. Daly, 1–33. Cambridge: Cambridge University Press.

———. 1998. "The Ottoman Occupation." In *The Cambridge History of Egypt: Islamic Egypt, 640–1517,* vol. 1, edited by Carl F. Petry, 490–516. Cambridge: Cambridge University Press.

Wolf, John B. 1972. *The Barbary Coast: Algeria under the Turks.* New York: W. W. Norton & Company.

Wright, Gwendolyn. 1991. *The Politics of Design in French Colonial Urbanism.* Chicago: University of Chicago Press.

Zartman, I. William, ed. 1973. *Man, State, and Society in the Contemporary Maghrib.* New York: Praeger Publishers.

Zartman, I. William, Mark A. Tessler, and others. 1982. *Political Elites in Arab North Africa: Morocco, Algeria, Tunisia, Libya, and Egypt.* New York: Longman.

Zeghal, Malika. 2008. *Islamism in Morocco: Religion, Authoritarianism, and Electoral Politics.* Translated by George Holoch. Princeton, N.J.: Markus Weiner Publishers.

Zisenwine, Daniel. 2007. "From Hasan II to Muhammad VI: Plus Ça Change?" In *The Maghrib in the New Century: Identity, Religion, and Politics,* edited by Bruce Maddy-Weitzman and Daniel Zisenwine, 132–150. Gainesville: University Press of Florida.

Zoubir, Yahia H. 2000. "Algerian-Moroccan Relations and Their Impact on Maghribi Integration." *Journal of North African Studies* 5, no. 3 (Autumn): 43–74.

———. 2004a. "The Resurgence of Algeria's Foreign Policy in the Twenty-First Century." *Journal of North African Studies* 9, no. 2 (Summer): 169–183.

Zoubir, Yahia H., and Haizam Amirah-Fernández, eds. 2008. *North Africa: Politics, Region, and the Limits of Transformation.* New York: Routledge.

Zoubir, Yahia H., and Karima Benabdallah-Gambier. 2004. "Morocco, Western Sahara and the Future of the Maghrib." *Journal of North African Studies* 9, no. 1 (Spring): 49–74.

Zoubir, Yahia, and Daniel Volman, eds. 1992. *International Dimensions of the Western Sahara Conflict.* Westport, Conn.: Praeger.

INDEX

Abbas, Ferhat, 186–187, 189–190, 217–218
Abbasid Caliphate (Abbasids), 58, 66–70, 73, 75–76, 79–80, 84, 87, 93, 97, 111, 115, 266n18, 267n31, 268n34, 268n39, 268n41, 269n46, 269n48, 271n70
Abd al-Karim (Abdel Krim), 181, 289–290n30
Abd al-Mu'min, 93–94, 101, 273n16
Abd al-Qadir, 154–155, 160, 186, 282n13, 282–283n22
Abd al-Rahman (bn Mu'awiya), 66, 72, 75
Abd al-Rahman II, 75–76, 78
Abd al-Rahman III, 76, 78–79, 268–269nn41–42, 269n47
Abd al-Wadids. See Zayyanids
Abduh, Muhammad, 151–152, 167, 182, 186, 280n46, 289n28
Abu Madyan, 95, 99, 102, 105, 274n25
Abu Ya'qub Yusuf, 94–95
Abu Yazid, 73–74
Afghani, Jamal al-Din al-, 151, 167
African Union (AU), 205, 242. See also Organization of African Unity (OAU)
Agathocles, 27, 35, 258n21, 258n23
Aghlabids, 7, 68, 70–72, 87, 97, 267n28, 267n31, 268n33
Ahmadiyya (Mahdist movement), 150
Ait Ahmed, Hocine, 218, 223
Akhenaten, 21–23, 257n7
Akrama Agreement, 176–177
Alawis, 7, 109, 129–131, 140, 157, 160, 162, 182, 278n35
Alexander III (the Great), 29, 31, 51, 259n35

Alexandria, 250; Christianity in, 50–51; founding of, 31; Museum and Library of, 31–32, 43, 260n37, 261n11, 270n59; and Ptolemies, 29, 31–34, 44
Algeria (Algerians), 2–4, 7–8; and Alawi incursions, 130; Almohads in, 93–94; Almoravids in, 90–91; Arab invasion of, 64–65; Berber tribes in, 26; Byzantine, 54–55; Christianity in, 52–53; colonialism in, 155–157, 182, 283nn25–26, 283n28, 286–287n55; and French, colonial resistance to, 154–155, 283n24; French conquest of, 152–155, 282nn20–21; Hammadids in, 84–85; and Mauretania, 40, 41, 44–45; nationalism in, 185–187, 290nn39–40; and Numidia, 38, 40–43; prehistoric, 5–6; regency in, 117, 119–121; Roman, 46–48, 262n23, 262n25; Rustamids settle in, 69; and Sa'di incursion, 125; Shi'ism in, 72; and Umayyads, revolt against, 66; Vandals in, 53; and War of Liberation, 175, 187–191, 217, 226, 249; and World War II, 173, 184; Zayyanids in, 96–99
Algeria (post-colonial): civil strife (*fitna*) in, 215, 222–228, 296nn13–16, 302n4; economy and society of, 215, 217, 219–224, 227–228, 244–245, 295nn2–5, 296n11, 296n20, 297n21, 300nn51–53, 301n55–56; and Kabyle conflicts, 217–218, 222, 226, 296n9, 296nn18–19; and October riots, 215, 223, 228, 296n10; political affairs of, 193, 213, 217–228,

Bardo, Treaty of, 159

Barghawata, 90, 272n2

Barrage Vert, 245

Baybars I, 111–113

Belisarius, 9, 54

Ben Ali, Zine el-Abidine, 211, 213, 295n41

Ben Badis, Abd al-Hamid, 186

Ben Barka, Mehdi, 229

Ben Bella, Ahmed, 190–191, 217–219, 221, 223, 296n8

Benhadj, Ali, 223

Benjedid, Chadli, 221–223, 234, 296n8, 296n17

Ben Jelloun, Tahar, 249, 297n28

Ben Khedda, Youssef, 190

Ben Mami, Laila, 249

Bennabi, Malik, 8, 13, 33, 56, 60, 62, 87, 89, 104–105, 167, 191–192, 246–248, 250–251, 256n28, 280n46, 287n2, 291n46, 292n3, 295n6, 295n39, 301n59, 302n6, 302–303n7; and colonizability, 11, 167, 192, 255n20; and post-Almohadean period, 11, 13; principal ideas of, 11–12, 255n22

Bennouna, Mohammed, 181–182

Ben Salah, Ahmad, 211–212

Ben Salih, Muhammad al-Hadi, 249

Ben Shaprut, Hasdai, 78

Ben Yusuf, Salah, 211

Berber Decree (*zahir/dahir*; 1930), 182–183, 290n31

"Berber Myth," 166, 182

Berbers: and Amazighism, 217, 246, 253n7, 301n60; Arabization of, 75, 85, 222, 265n15; and Arabs, resistance to, 7, 64–66, 70; Byzantine enlistment of, 264n41; and Byzantines, resistance to, 55; and Carthaginians, 26–28, 34, 37–38; empires and successor states of, 89–108, 124–125; etymology of, 4; and Fatimids, resistance to, 73–74; and French, resistance to, 155; geographic location and origins of, 3–4; and insurgency, Moroccan, 229; and Kharijism, 68–69;

kingdoms of, 6–7, 40–45; language of, 4, 253n7, 254n11, 260n6; and Lyautey, 163–164; repel O'Reilly, 121; and Romans, resistance to, 45–46, 49, 52; and slavery, 266n17; transcultural experience of, 4–5, 34, 57, 257n17; under Roman rule, 46–48; and Vandals, 53. *See also* Barghawata; Kabylia; Kutama; Lamtuna; Masmuda; Rifs; Sanhaja; Tuaregs; Wattasids; Zanata

Berlin, Congress of, 159

Bernal, Martin, 23, 257n12

Berque, Jacques, 8, 17, 60, 103, 105, 124, 140, 149–150, 165, 167, 171, 173, 191–192, 246, 248, 250–251, 255nn24–26, 256nn27–28, 267n26, 274n27, 286n52, 287n2, 290n36, 302n2; principal ideas of, 12–13

Bin Ladin, Usama, 200, 294n32

Black Africans, 75, 80, 90, 123, 127, 253n6, 278n34

Black Death, 102, 104, 111, 114

"Black Saturday," 174

"Black September," 197

"Black Thursday," 212

Blum-Viollette legislation, 186

Bonaparte, Napoleon, 8, 123, 131–135, 138–139, 140, 143, 153, 157, 203, 256n3, 278n36, 279n38, 279n41, 280n44, 282n21, 288n21

Bornu, 122, 127, 276n18

Boudiaf, Mohamed, 223–224

Boumedienne, Houari, 190–191, 217, 219–221, 225, 230–231, 295n6

Bourguiba, Habib, 180–190, 208, 211–213, 253n3, 295n38

Bouteflika, Abdelaziz, 215, 219, 225–227, 231, 233, 243, 297n29

Braudel, Fernand, 13, 75, 102; and Ibn Khaldun, 255–256n27; on Islam, 104; and Ottoman Greeks, 275n8; on Ottoman-Habsburg empires, 138–139, 156, 251

CPSIA information can be obtained at www.ICGtesting.com
Printed in the USA
LVOW092128301111

257283LV00002B/3/P